THE DETROIT TIGERS:
CLUB AND COMMUNITY, 194_ ____

This study of the Detroit Tigers over a half-century demonstrates how baseball has reflected the fortunes of America's postwar urban society. Patrick Harrigan shows that the declining fortunes of this franchise have been inextricably linked with those of its city and surrounding community. Attention is paid to major on-field exploits, but the focus is on the development of the ball club as a corporate enterprise and its symbiotic relationship with metropolitan Detroit.

Established as a baseball club in the nineteenth century, the Detroit Tigers have been an integral part of the community in and around Detroit. At one time, Detroit was even regarded as the best town for baseball in the country. The club has interacted with the city's various communities, but it has also neglected or clashed with some – most notably with the African-American community.

The relationship of club and community in Detroit has distinctive features, but it also has much in common with baseball in other metropolises. Harrigan examines the development of baseball's modern institutional and economic structure; the role of major-league teams in large urban centres; the influence of radio and television on the popularity of the game; racial integration; unionization and free agency; and stadium renovation or rebuilding, and the financing of such projects. A declining city population base, the riot of 1967, and alienation between the city, its surburbs, and the state have highlighted the Tigers' own troubled history. The controversy surrounding the building of a new stadium – viewed as the key to revitalizing the downtown core, as well as the team's fortunes – demonstrates that baseball is still a major community concern in Detroit.

The Detroit Tigers is the most complete view of the finances of any sports organization yet published. It also illustrates baseball's human dimension. Harrigan has conducted more than a hundred interviews with former players, their wives, team executives, media personalities, sports writers, and politicians and uncovered many previously unused sources to give us a vivid portrayal of a sport and its far-reaching influence.

PATRICK J. HARRIGAN is a professor in the Department of History at the University of Waterloo, Waterloo, Ontario.

PATRICK J. HARRIGAN

The Detroit Tigers:
Club and Community,
1945–1995

UNIVERSITY OF TORONTO PRESS
Toronto Buffalo London

© University of Toronto Press Incorporated 1997
Toronto Buffalo London
Printed in Canada

Reprinted 1997

ISBN 0-8020-0934-4 (cloth)
ISBN 0-8020-7903-2 (paper)

Printed on acid-free paper

Canadian Cataloguing in Publication Data

Harrigan, Patrick J. (Patrick Joseph), 1941–
   The Detroit Tigers : club and community, 1945–1995

   Includes bibliographical references and index.
   ISBN 0-8020-0934-4 (bound)   ISBN 0-8020-7903-2 (pbk.)

   1. Detroit Tigers (Baseball team) – History.
   2. Baseball – History.   I. Title.

   GV875.D4H37 1997   796.357'64'0977434   C96-931762-X

This book has been published with the help of a grant from the Humanities
and Social Sciences Federation of Canada, using funds provided by the Social
Sciences and Humanities Research Council of Canada.

University of Toronto Press acknowledges the financial assistance to its publishing program of the Canada Council and the Ontario Arts Council.

Contents

LIST OF TABLES   vii

LIST OF APPENDICES   viii

ACKNOWLEDGMENTS ix

Introduction 3

1 Baseball in Postwar American Society   9

2 The Briggs Era of Detroit Baseball   40

3 Transitions and Adaptation of the Detroit Baseball Club
   in the 1950s   66

4 Community Problems and a World Championship   92

5 The Players   125

6 The Era of Personalities, 1969–1977   155

7 Free Agency and Big Money for Baseball, 1977–1983   182

8 The Golden Age of Detroit Baseball   203

9 A Franchise in Decline   225

10 The Stadium as Symbol   254

Epilogue: The 1994 Strike and Its Aftermath   278

TABLES   285

APPENDICES   311

NOTES   333

BIBLIOGRAPHY   395

INDEX   407

Tables

1 Major-league paid regular-season attendance, 1930–60 287
2 Minor-league total attendance, 1930–95 288
3 Salaries/bonuses as percentage of total expenditures, 1929–93 289
4 Baseball's total broadcasting revenues, 1933–90 289
5 Detroit Tigers' attendance figures, 1945–96 290
6 Detroit Tigers' profits, 1938–51 291
7 Detroit Tigers' profits, income, and expenses, 1952–6 292
8 Detroit Tigers' payroll and players' salaries, 1929–57 293
9 Detroit Tigers' won-lost records, 1945–96 294
10 Demographic statistics, Detroit area 295
11 Major-league paid regular-season attendance, 1948–96 296
12 Detroit Tigers' broadcasting revenues, 1952–91 297
13 Average baseball ticket prices, 1920–96 298
14 Place of birth of Detroit Tigers and all major-league players 299
15 Baseball career patterns of Tiger alumni, 1940–90 300
16 Major-league players' salaries: Minimum and mean, 1950–96 307
17 Post-baseball occupations of major-league players and Detroit
    Tigers, 1950–90 302
18 Performance of black players 304
19 Detroit Tigers' mean salaries, 1978–96 305
20 Budgets of Jim Campbell, 1980s 306
21 Detroit Baseball Club income statement, 1987–91 307
22 Detroit Tigers' local broadcast ratings, 1980–90 308
23 Detroit Tigers' and league revenue and expenses, 1993 309

Appendices

1 Major League Steering Committee Report (1946, excerpt) 313
2 First Dates That a Black Player Played for Each Major-League
   Team 316
3 Detroit Tigers' Owners and Presidents, 1901–1996 317
4 Detroit Tigers' Broadcasters and Stations, 1943–1996 319
5 Jim Campbell's Scouting Book (c. 1961, excerpts) 320
6 Detroit Baseball Club Prospectus (1992, excerpts) 326
7 Chronology of Stadium Controversy, 1956–1996 330

Acknowledgments

Many individuals have helped in the preparation of this manuscript. I thank all of those who gave of their time and knowledge in the hundred interviews that were conducted for the book (they are all mentioned in the appropriate endnotes). I am especially indebted to the late Jim Campbell, who served the Detroit club for more than forty years. He not only provided a wealth of information but also introduced me to many others whom I interviewed. Similarly, Robert Buchta, as a historian of Detroit, provided many perceptive ideas about the history of the city. As a photographer, he helped in the selection of photographs for the book. He also introduced me to others who agreed to interviews. Reno Bertoia, then president of the Detroit Tiger alumni organization, supported my efforts and introduced me to other former Tigers. Basil 'Mickey' Briggs was candid about the Briggs era. Among Detroit sports writers, Jerry Green, Bill McGraw, and Charlie Vincent were especially generous. So too were former Tiger broadcasters Paul Carey, Ernie Harwell, and Bob Rathbun.

Robert Giles, publisher of the *Detroit News*, and Neal Shine, publisher of the *Detroit Free Press*, allowed me access to their papers' clipping, computer, and photographic files. Pat Zacharias, Linda Culpepper, Rose Ann McKean, Chris Kucharski, and Bernardine Aubert guided me through those materials. The Detroit Baseball Club supplied media guides and press releases. Both Michael Ilitch and Tom Monaghan declined interviews. Cheryl Reilly, former archivist for Canada's Sports Hall of Fame, made available to me its collection of *The Sporting News* since 1945. The Social Sciences and Humanities Research Council of Canada supported research costs.

A joyful and integral part of this profession is its collegiality and amicability. This book owes as much to the inspiration and support of friends and family as it does to my toil. My wife, Mary Helen, first suggested the project despite her lack of interest in the game of baseball itself. She and my adult children tolerated my ill humor and grumbling when things hit their inevitable snags.

Colleagues Donald Baker, John English, Carol Cooper, and David Wright read the entire manuscript, offered moral support, and graced the study with their sage insights. Dr Cooper also researched published materials and badgered me to keep on schedule. Dr Peter Dembski lent me materials from his vast collection of clippings and Tiger yearbooks. He and John New also read portions of the manuscript, offering both encouragement and admonition. Professors Heather MacDougall and Wendy Mitchinson encouraged me in this new venture. Troy Visser assisted with bibliographic research. Gail Heideman typed the many drafts of the manuscript with her usual good humor and patience; Christine Burke assisted. Robert Ferguson and John St James were splendid editors. My sincerest appreciation to all of them.

Detroit, Michigan
May 1996

Hal Newhouser in 1944 or 1945, with the wartime emblem on his sleeve. (Courtesy of the Burton Historical Collection, Detroit Public Library)

Walter O. Briggs Sr surveys game preparation in 'his' stadium. (Courtesy of the Burton Historical Collection, Detroit Public Library)

Norm Cash barbecuing in the backyard of his suburban Detroit home in 1961. (Courtesy of the Burton Historical Collection, Detroit Public Library)

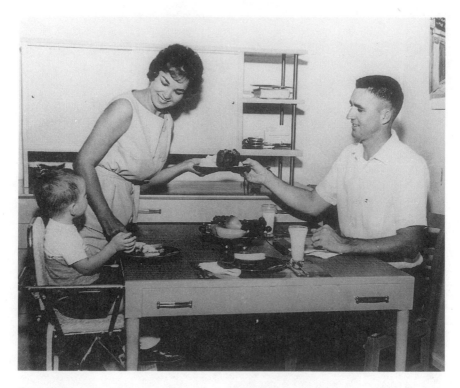

Dick Brown and family enjoying a meal at home in 1961. Note the modest setting. (Courtesy of the Burton Historical Collection, Detroit Public Library)

Al Kaline and family playing bumper pool in the rec room. (Detroit *Free Press*)

Eighteen-year-old Willie Horton with Tiger scout Louis D'Annuzio, who first scouted Horton at age nine. They are pictured at Horton's signing with Detroit, 7 August 1961. (Detroit *Free Press*)

Julie Nixon and David Eisenhower, taking a breather from the 1968 presidential campaign, meet Denny McLain at Tiger Stadium, 14 September 1968. (Reprinted with permission of *The Detroit News*, a Gannett newspaper, copyright 1993)

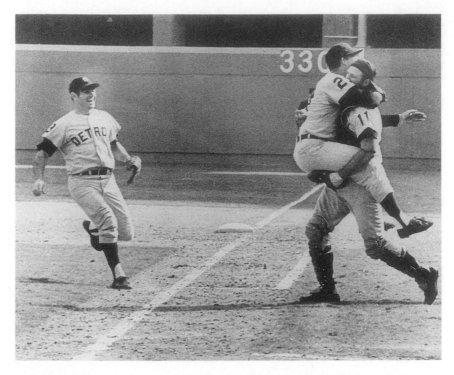

Mickey Lolich leaps into Bill Freehan's arms to celebrate the Tigers' seventh-game victory in the 1968 World Series, 10 October 1968. Lolich pitched three winning games in the series. (Reprinted with permission of *The Detroit News*, a Gannett newspaper, copyright 1993)

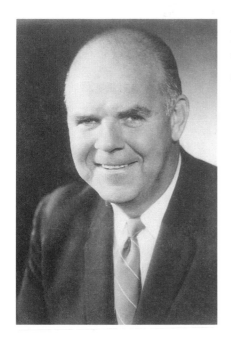

Jim Campbell in 1968 when he won the Major League's Executive of the Year Award. (Courtesy of Jim Campbell)

Mickey Lolich, 12 April 1973. (Courtesy of the Burton Historical Collection, Detroit Public Library)

Manager Billy Martin berates umpire George Maloney, 28 April 1973.
(Reprinted with permission of *The Detroit News*, a Gannett newspaper,
copyright 1993)

Mark 'The Bird' Fidrych addressing the ball. (Detroit *Free Press*)

Fidrych celebrates another strikeout. (Reprinted with permission of *The Detroit News*, a Gannett newspaper, copyright 1993)

Tiger fans couldn't get enough of 'The Bird' in 1976. (Detroit *Free Press*)

Lou Whitaker (left) and Alan Trammell in 1982. (Detroit *Free Press*)

Kirk Gibson and Dave Rozema off the field in 1983. (Detroit *Free Press*)

Kirk Gibson celebrates his three-run home run in the eighth inning of the final game of the 1984 World Series. (Detroit *Free Press*)

Post-game revellers celebrating the Tigers' 1984 World Series victory were peaceful at first, but then turned nasty. Rioters overturned and set fire to this police car. (Detroit *Free Press*)

Kirk Gibson rounding second in 1987; Seattle's Harold Reynolds is in the background. (Detroit *Free Press*)

George 'Sparky' Anderson relaxing in the clubhouse. (Detroit *Free Press*)

Panoramic view of Tiger Stadium, April 1989. (Detroit *Free Press*)

Cecil Fielder watches one of his 51 home runs in 1990. (Detroit *Free Press*)

Michael Ilitch announcing his purchase of the Tigers at a press conference,
August 1992. (Detroit *Free Press*)

Aerial view of Tiger Stadium. (Detroit *Free Press*)

Club and community: Tiger Stadium, in its deserted neighborhood. (Detroit *Free Press*)

THE DETROIT TIGERS

Introduction

Baseball is a boys' game played by men and run by promoters for profit.[1]
Baseball is also about community – local and regional community as well
as the community of players – and about American society. Indeed,
sports often inspire national pride. At the national level World Cup soccer, where entire countries support their teams, provides perhaps the
best example. Baseball has its place as well, encouraging a sense of pride
in the American people for a sport that was their invention and that
continues to have its finest expression in their country. When Clark
Griffith suggested to Baseball Commissioner Kenesaw Mountain Landis in 1944 that 'Americanism could be promoted by fostering amateur
athletics, especially baseball,'[2] he was simply giving expression to what
many Americans already held to be self-evident.

In the local community baseball provides cohesive value, as the
Brooklyn Dodgers did for their polyglot neighborhoods earlier in this
century. Baseball can also be a source of community pride, an important
consideration, especially when the community is attempting to deal with
a bad reputation, as Detroit was after the riot of 1967. Many believed
that the Tigers' championship reunited the city. Joe Falls, senior sports
writer in Detroit at the time, wrote: 'It was a year when an entire community, an entire city, was caught up in a wild, wonderful frenzy.'[3] The
euphoria was short-lived, for Detroit continued to experience deep racial
divisions and economic problems. Yet the myth of unity is important,
illustrating the importance many Detroiters give to baseball as a bonding
element.

Baseball is a thing of myth. The philosopher Jacques Barzun once said that to know the heart and mind of America one must know baseball. Sociologists have called it a microcosm of America.[4] Others have related it to the American dream, personified in the success of Joe DiMaggio, a boy from an immigrant family who became a national hero.[5] Baseball also recalls a sense of youth, of strength, of encountering and surmounting challenges – notions that have informed so many of Americans' historical images of themselves and their country. Pastoral images, dreams of a romantic past and of summer games played on grassy fields during sunny afternoons, have been important elements in the myth of baseball as well, particularly as America urbanized and citizens of its developing cities sought links with their past. Those images are resilient despite the changes the nation has experienced, for the game continues to connect 'America now with an earlier America that we remember (falsely in so many ways) as democratic and sweet and robust and green and essentially innocent.'[6]

These myths have a ring of truth, but let us not claim too much for baseball. It is a single, albeit important, aspect of American popular culture. It can be a cohesive element for a community, but it certainly does not obliterate divisions within it. Baseball clubs often deliberately tried to isolate themselves from tensions in American or local society, but found that they were not the self-inclusive institutions they thought they were or wanted to be. As the late A. Bartlett Giamatti, president of Yale University and then commissioner of baseball, stated, 'Baseball reflects issues of social justice, affirmative action, the role of minorities, issues of substance abuse, financial issues, municipal issues. These are all American issues.'[7] Eventually baseball has had to face all of them.

What follows is a study of the trials, tribulations, and successes of one baseball club in one American city. It is a history of a corporation, specifically the Detroit Baseball Club, rather than of the team, considering the operations of a professional sports organization within its socioeconomic matrix. The Detroit franchise has always had a symbiotic relationship with metropolitan Detroit. One of the most successful franchises after the Second World War, the club, like the city, has suffered declining fortunes in recent years because of its own policies, because of economic troubles in Detroit, and because of alienation between residents of the city and those of the suburbs.

Baseball has had a long and rich history in Detroit. By the 1930s

Detroit was regarded as the best baseball town in the country. Briggs Stadium, so named in 1938 after a three-year expansion of Navin Field, had a reputation as the finest ballpark in the country and was the most recognized building in the state. When night baseball came to Detroit in 1948, people dressed up for games as they would for a concert or a night on the town. Opening day has been a major social event. To this day, the city seems 'most alive' then.[8] WJR's morning show, conducted for a quarter-century by the late J.P. McCarthy, may be unique nationally in its attention to local sports and sports personalities. The way the city mourned McCarthy after his death, on 16 August 1995, reflected the status of media/sports personalities in Detroit. In recent years Tiger Baseball has been one of the few things capable of bringing the suburbs and the city together. It has provided memories of better times as well as continuity over generations. Recent promotions have invited children 'to run the same basepaths that Cobb and Kaline did.' Past championships remind Detroiters not only of success on the field but of an age when downtown Detroit was a vibrant place, the center of social and economic activity in the city and even the state.

Ownership provided continuity. The Briggs family and then John Fetzer were the two principal owners for half a century. Jim Campbell oversaw day-to-day operations for thirty years. Two sports writers dominated the media for a century – H.G. Salsinger in the first half, Joe Falls in the second. Two voices – Ernie Harwell on radio and George Kell on television – reported Tiger games for three decades. The game has been played on the same site for a century. Continuity has been one of the charms of baseball in Detroit, but it has also created problems. Walter O. Briggs was both a sportsman and a racist. That legacy left the African American community of Detroit alienated. Campbell wanted to run the club in 1990 as he had in 1960. Many of the press had too cosy a relationship with management.

The changing environment of metropolitan Detroit presented challenges. Always subject to the volatility of the auto industry, the city itself became poorer, depopulated, and more separated economically and politically from the outlying metropolitan area. Between 1950 and 1990 the population of Detroit proper declined from nearly two million to one million, while the adjacent suburbs grew from one to nearly three million. The team's fans had been the working class of Detroit. Increasingly, they became affluent white suburbanites, divorced physically and psychologically from the city proper. John Fetzer resisted enticements to move the team to the suburbs, as first the Lions and then the Pistons did. When he promised 'a joint venture between city and club to combat decay in the inner city with which the team has cast its lot,'[9] the media deified him. When his successor, Tom Monaghan, trashed the city as crime-infested and a bad baseball town, politicians, the media, and fans made him a pariah. The isolation between club and community was never greater than in Monaghan's last years. Nor was the separation of the suburbs from Detroit.

The 1967 riot and the reputation of Detroit as 'Murder City, U.S.A.' in the 1970s inhibited ventures downtown, close to the stadium. Still, attendance really suffered only when fear coincided with poor performance by the team. Detroit set attendance records during the 1980s. A much wider audience watched games on television both in the city and in the suburbs. WDIV-TV had the largest audiences for baseball of any local television channel in the country, and made lots of money from Tiger Baseball. The club itself made a profit every year from 1935, when Walter O. Briggs acquired it, to 1994, the year of the strike. Detroit baseball has been popular and prosperous.

The controversy surrounding the proposed building of a new stadium – a controversy that raged for a decade – shows that baseball is still a major community concern in Detroit. By the 1980s, a new or renovated stadium had come to be touted as the key to the revitalization, or even the salvation, of downtown Detroit and the preservation of baseball there. The club, the mayor's office, and many community leaders argued that a new stadium was necessary. A grass-roots civic-action group demanded renovation of a historic landmark – Tiger Stadium – and opposed the use of a struggling city's dollars to subsidize private ownership. Whether for or against, everybody claimed that they had the 'community's interest' at heart. Did the ball club belong to its fans, the community of Detroit, and a wider community throughout the state, or was it just another business, owned by two different pizza entrepreneurs?

Two unique sources inform this book. The first is rich financial detail. Data prepared for the 1956 and 1992 sales of the club together with information from the Celler House Committee's inquiry into baseball during the 1950s and Jim Campbell's private records for the interim period allow us the most complete view of the finances of any professional sports organization over a lengthy period. These are compared with information for baseball generally from the Celler Commission, the Major League Baseball Players' Association, and Andrew Zimbalist's pioneering study, *Baseball and Billions*. The second source is the testimony culled from more than one hundred interviews, about half of them with former players. I and, ultimately, readers of this book have been most fortunate that so many gave of their time to discuss their experiences as players, or their role in the operations of the franchise, or, in the case of sports writers, their perceptions of and relations to the club.

Players talked about managers and management, about race relations, unionization, and the city. Those insights are scattered throughout the book. They talked especially about their careers, hopes, traumas, and successes. Chapter 5 offers a prosopography of them and a unique sense of what it meant to be one of the fortunate 400, eventually 500, who were on major-league rosters annually in the years before free agency. Perhaps because I was able to meet players on their own turf, at alumni outings, and spend the better part of two days with many of them, they were more forthcoming than they might have been in response to a letter or a telephone call. Players were once deemed both heroes and models. A popular baseball book in 1951 proclaimed: '[there is] no finer, friendlier, cleaner cut group of citizens than the men playing our national pasttime.'[10] That was never true, but neither were players until recently hired guns on short-term contracts. Mostly they were struggling human beings with one exceptional talent.

Club executives and two sons of 'Spike' Briggs have spoken frankly about club operations. Newspaper reporters and media personalities have also been forthcoming about their profession and its relation to the club. Although the Detroit branch of the Baseball Writers Association of America represents part of the baseball establishment, its members often disagreed among themselves about their role and proper relation to the club. Jim Campbell was particularly generous in granting me many hours during many days spread over two years and in introducing me to others associated with the Detroit Baseball Club and encouraging them to meet with me. During his final illness, Mr Campbell told me that he expected a gold-embossed, autographed copy of this book. I am sorry that he did not live to receive one, but he was able to read lengthy sections of the manuscript shortly before his death. He never asked me to change a word and stood by all his interviews. He told me that he 'would not interfere, just wanted to be sure that I got it right.'

To scholars who interview people in their research – what is called 'oral history' – I offer no magic tricks. I tried to conduct interviews in person whenever possible. I tried to treat each person respectfully, remembering that they were doing me a favor by giving of their time and knowledge. In our first meeting, Campbell told me that I had 'done [my] homework well.' I prepared carefully for each interview. Most of all, I listened. I offered to use a tape recorder for each interview; no one asked me to. I took notes and then sent a typed, edited transcript to each person for verification.

Baseball has had a different and more important role in Detroit than it has in New York or in many other American cities. Yet in spite of this distinctiveness, there are many commonalities with respect to baseball that Detroit shares with other metropolises. In the years immediately following the Second World War, the modern institutional structure (as opposed to the game) of baseball was established. The first chapter of this book introduces themes that recur later – the popularity of baseball, the role of television, racial integration, the unionization of players, congressional investigations and court decisions, and relations between the major and minor leagues. The history of the Detroit Baseball Club proper begins with chapter 2, which itself begins with a sketch of the club and the city of Detroit before 1945.

This book was finished in Spring 1996. Developments concerning the stadium during the summer of 1996 and final, unofficial statistical information for the 1996 season were added to final proofs in October 1996.

1

Baseball in Postwar American Society

Baseball embarked on a new era after the Second World War. It was a period of recovery and prosperity that brought with it new issues emanating more from postwar American society than from within baseball itself. This period witnessed the spread of major-league baseball across the nation and the rising popularity of professional and amateur baseball, followed quickly by declines in attendance at both the major- and minor-league levels. New technology – more powerful lights for night baseball, airplanes for travel, and television – transformed the game's audience. Integration, the organization then unionization of players, and corporate ownership destroyed the cosy relationships of old. Power baseball, platoon players, and relief specialists modified the game within the constant dimensions of the diamond. Baseball's owners adapted more easily to changes on the field than they did to those that arose out of the particular circumstances of postwar American culture and society, of which baseball was an integral part. Baseball's response to new forces in these first years after the war was crucial because that response ordained its direction for decades and determined the parameters of its ability to accommodate itself to future challenges. First it had to weather wartime.

WARTIME BASEBALL

The Second World War was the most devastating war in human history, costing the lives of 20 million soldiers, 20 million civilians, and perhaps another 15 to 20 million lives from starvation, infection, or injuries.[1] Millions of young Americans were drafted, 322,000 American soldiers died, another 800,000 were wounded, and the entire country was mobilized. No one foresaw in 1941 the full fury of the war, but everyone expected a long and bloody struggle. Professional baseball was only a game. Not surprisingly, there was some question whether it should continue amidst such carnage. England had suspended professional soccer matches for the duration of the war.

Clark Griffith, owner of the Washington Senators and 'a long-time acquaintance of the President if not actually a close friend,' contacted President Franklin D. Roosevelt to win approval for the 1942 season. Roosevelt, in turn, on 15 January 1942 wrote Commissioner of Baseball Judge Kenesaw Mountain Landis a letter now known as the 'green-light letter': 'People need recreation. I believe it best for the community to keep baseball going.'[2] Such bitter enemies as J. Edgar Hoover, director of the Federal Bureau of Investigation (FBI), and the Communist *Daily Worker* agreed that baseball should be played during wartime because of the 'morale value of the game.'[3] Baseball continued on familiar diamonds with the same rules as before, but the game was not what it had been.

Many players were drafted. About 300 former major leaguers were in the service in 1944, about 1000 over the course of the war, and about 5400 of the 5800 playing professional baseball in 1941 served sometime during the war; about forty of them died during it.[4] Clark Griffith combed Latin America for substitutes, but no one apparently thought of signing players from the Negro leagues. Travel restrictions meant that spring training and exhibition games had to be held in cold northern towns. There were shortages of cabs, hotels, and meals en route.[5] Tiger General Manager Jack Zeller suggested facetiously that the team might walk 112 miles to Terre Haute, Indiana, where the White Sox trained. Manager Steve O'Neill responded: 'I can't walk that far.'

The war really hit home for baseball on 7 May 1942, when Hank Greenberg was called up.[6] The first baseman–outfielder of the Tigers, who had received the Most Valuable Player Award for the American League in 1940, was the first star drafted. The Tigers lost Pat Mullin and Fred Hutchinson in the same year and, later, Barney McCoskey, 'Hoot' Evers, 'Birdie' Tebbetts, Al Benton, Charlie Gehringer, Dick Wakefield, Jimmy Bloodworth, Virgil Trucks, Tommy Bridges, and Hal White. Most of their replacements in 1944 and 1945 would have been in the minors in better times. A plucky Pete Gray managed to play 77 games in the outfield for the St Louis Browns despite having only one arm. The youngest player in major-league history, fifteen-year-old Joe Nuxhall, debuted on 10 June 1944. The St Louis Cardinals advertised in *The Sporting News* for players. Bill James has described wartime baseball as marked by poor hitting and an 'unusual number of bases stolen by anyone aged 37.'[7] The first name-player to enter service, Hank Greenberg was the first to return after Germany's surrender on 8 May 1945. His return was headline news.[8] Thirty-four years old, Greenberg had not played since 1941, but he led the Tigers to the 1945 pennant. Playing half a season, he led the Tigers in batting at .311, hit 13 home runs, and drove in 60 runs.

Appropriately for wartime baseball, the Tigers won the pennant with what was then the lowest winning percentage (.575) for any pennant winner in history. Eddie Mayo led the regulars with a .285 batting average; no player hit 20 home runs or drove in 100 runs.[9] Two pitchers, Hal Newhouser, who was exempted from service because of a heart condition, and 'Dizzy' Trout, accounted for 56 of the 88 Tiger victories. On 21 July the Tigers and A's played a record 24-inning game, with neither team being able to win. Darkness mercifully called an end to a 1–1 tie after 4 hours and 48 minutes. George 'Snuffy' Stirnweiss led the American League with a .309 average – the lowest for any batting champion in history to that point. Among American Leaguers, only Vern Stephens hit more than 20 home runs (24) and only Nick Etten drove in more than 100 runs (111). Wartime travel restrictions precluded an All-Star Game in 1945, but there were few stars that year anyway.

The Tigers led the league from 12 June onward, but stumbled in late September. They journeyed to Sportsman's Park in St Louis needing only to split a doubleheader to win the pennant.[10] Second-place Washington had ended its season a week earlier because its owner Clark Griffith had contracted to rent his stadium to the football Washington Redskins, believing that his team had no chance at the pennant. They had finished last the previous year. Such were the vagaries of wartime baseball that the Senators remained in the thick of a slow race on the final weekend. After rainouts, the Tigers' season came down to a doubleheader on 30 September. Trailing by a run in the ninth, the Tigers loaded the bases for Hank Greenberg, who hit a grand-slam home run into the left-field seats. The Browns loaded the bases in their half of the ninth, but Tiger ace Hal Newhouser, pitching in relief, retired the final batter, 'saving' both the game and the pennant.

The World Series opened inauspiciously for the Tigers against the Chicago Cubs on 3 October at Briggs Stadium. The Cubs bombed Hal Newhouser, who had won the Most Valuable Player Award (25-9, 1.81 ERA) but also suffered a wrenched back in the final month, for four runs in the first and three more in the third en route to a 9–0 shutout by Hank Borowy. In the second game, Hank Greenberg's three-run home run into the left-field seats in a four-run Tiger fifth inning gave the Tigers all the runs they needed in a 4–1 win for Virgil Trucks, who had been discharged from the Navy only a week before.[11] The next day, still in Detroit, the Cubs regained the Series lead on Claude Passeau's one-hit shutout (3–0). The Tigers rebounded to win Games 4 (4–1) and 5 (8–4) at Wrigley Field.

The sixth game is infamous in baseball lore and typical of wartime baseball. Frank Graham, a New York sports writer, called it 'the worst game ever played in a World Series. It was the fat men against the skinny men at the office picnic.'[12] The Tigers trailed 5–1 going into the seventh inning. Chuck Hostetler, pinch-hitting for 'Skeeter' Webb, reached first on an error. He advanced to second on a ground-out and was racing to score on a single to left by 'Doc' Cramer when he stumbled rounding third, fell, and was tagged out. The Tigers still scored two runs, but the Cubs answered with two of their own in their seventh. The Tigers rallied once again to tie the game with four in the eighth, climaxed by Greenberg's second home run of the Series (the only ones the Tigers hit). They lost in the twelfth when what appeared to be a routine single to left by Stan Hack took an unexpected bounce past Greenberg to the wall, scoring Bill Schuster from first.[13]

The Tigers finally won the Series in the seventh game, 9–3, on 10 October, to the likely surprise of Warren Brown of the *Chicago American*, who had observed that 'this is one series that neither team can win.'[14] Cubs manager Charlie Grimm brought back as his starter Hank Borowy, who had started and lost Game 5 and won Game 6 with four innings of shutout relief. After a five-run first climaxed by a bases-clearing double by Paul Richards off reliever Paul Derringer, the Tigers were never challenged. Thousands of exuberant fans met the victors at Union Station upon their return. Thus ended wartime baseball – happily for the Tigers.

THE POPULARITY OF BASEBALL

Baseball experienced a renaissance after the Second World War at both the major- and minor-league levels. Major-league attendance increased by 71 per cent in a single year from 1945 to 1946 and by 94 per cent from 1945 to a peak of nearly 21 million in 1948 (table 1). *The Sporting News* heralded its review of 1948 with the headline 'Gate Marks Smashed.'[15] Minor-league attendance burst from 10 million in 1945 to more than 40 million in each of the years 1947 to 1949 (table 2). Such books as David Halberstam's *The Summer of 1949* and Roger Kahn's *The Era 1947–1957* have mythologized this period as baseball's greatest time. Yet, baseball attendance had always had its ups and downs.

More than ten million fans paid to attend regular-season major-league baseball games for the first time in 1930. Four million fewer fans were attending in 1933 – the depth of the Depression – the fewest since 1918, the last year of the First World War. Attendance then recovered gradually during the rest of the 1930s, to decline again with the entry of the United States into the Second World War. After the war ended in Europe in May 1945 and players gradually rejoined their teams, the teams set a new season attendance record despite some continuing wartime restrictions. Detroit's attendance of 1,280,341 led the league and was only 9081 under the New York record established in 1920. Presaging the postwar revival, the 1945 World Series broke a nineteen-year attendance record. Baseball had prospered immediately after the Civil War and the First World War as well. Postwar attendance represented a true renaissance – a rebirth of attendance, which had been artificially held down by the Depression and the war. Baseball had averaged, after all, more than nine million fans annually during the 1920s and the late 1930s.

Attendance in the late 1940s marked more than just a rebirth, however. It climbed to new heights. Averaging nine million people for the first six years of the decade, major-league teams drew just under twenty million for the decade's final four years (table 1). The gate more than doubled from the first to the second half of the decade. No such increase occurred before or since. Attendance soon declined again, marking those four years as unique. They were unique not only for the major leagues but for professional baseball generally, as figures for the minor leagues show (table 2).

Minor-league gates suffered a similar pattern of decline during the Depression (35 per cent). They made a rapid recovery during the late 1930s (110 per cent), but declined dramatically during the war. Wartime restrictions struck hardest at the minor leagues[16] because the military draft created a shortage of talent. Within two years after the war minor-league teams spread throughout America, and crowds filled their seats. Combined major- and minor-league attendance averaged 60 million fans during the last three years of the decade of the 1940s, peaking at 62.8 million in 1948. The minor leagues are a separate topic needing more study, but their short-lived attendance surge in the late 1940s, which was even greater than that of the majors, reflects baseball's unique appeal in postwar America.

Baseball provided an important recreational release throughout the nation after arduous times. People had discretionary income too. Consumer spending increased 50 per cent in the five years following the Second World War. Spending on both movies and spectator sports doubled between 1940 and 1950.[17] Organized baseball offered cheap entertainment, with ticket prices averaging $1.40 in 1946 and $1.60 in 1950, and general admission or unreserved seats costing only $1.25 in 1954, when a bleacher bench remained only 60¢.[18] It was often the only game in town, with other professional team sports being in their infancy. Amateur baseball boomed as well. 3000 Little League, 9000 high-school, 650 college, 16,000 American Legion, and 8000 semi-pro teams operated in 1950.[19] Other forms of summer recreation – golf, tennis, boating, even excursions by auto and annual summer vacations – were still beyond the means of most urban families. Baseball was well placed to take advantage of this recreational demand. It had planted new seeds in the 1930s that would blossom in the postwar period. These were night baseball and radio broadcasts of games.

The minor leagues were the first to introduce night baseball. By 1934 fifteen of the nineteen minor leagues had at least one lighted park. The first major-league night game was played at Crosley Field in Cincinnati on 24 May 1935 before 20,442 fans. President Roosevelt threw the switch, and Ford Frick, president of the National League, threw out the first ball in a 2–1 Reds victory over the Brooklyn Dodgers. The Philadelphia Athletics were the first American League team to play at night, in 1939. Ten ballparks had lights in 1940.[20] With the installation of lights at Briggs Stadium in 1948, night baseball was being played throughout the majors except, of course, at Wrigley Field, which lacked lighting for another four decades.

Night baseball did two things. Its very novelty attracted fans, even though Detroit fans had opposed night baseball in a 1939 survey,[21] as did Tiger owners. The brilliant lighting of playing fields amazed observers at a time when street and house lighting was much dimmer than today, with 25- and 40-watt bulbs still commonplace. Lyall Smith, sports editor of the *Detroit Free Press*, reported that the 'action looks a lot faster under the lights.'[22] The *Detroit News* printed a picture of a groundskeeper reading a newspaper on the field at the first night game.[23] Electricity was still one of the technological marvels of the twentieth century.

The second thing that night baseball did was make the game more available to working men on day shifts. That was why Walter O. Briggs finally introduced night baseball in Detroit.[24] When the novelty wore off, attendance at night games declined by 1.1 million along with both minor- and major-league attendance generally in 1950. Detroit limited the number of night games to fourteen and enjoyed an increase of 41,000 fans at night in their pennant chase that year, but attendance fell at night by 190,000 the next year.[25] Analyzing statistics for the period 1946 to 1976, Leonard Koppett concluded that the first night games, but not the later expansion of them, promoted attendance.[26]

A more permanent factor in increasing baseball's audience may have been radio. The first baseball game was broadcast from Pittsburgh on 5 August 1921. Later that year the World Series was aired on the East Coast. The following year, 5,000,000 fans reportedly listened to one or more games of the World Series on radio.[27] Despite the fears of many that radio would hurt attendance (they would later fear television), all teams broadcast their games in 1939 when 80 per cent of American households had radios. In 1946 Gillette signed a ten-year contract for exclusive radio rights to the World Series, paying about $150,000 annually. Liberty Broadcasting and Mutual Broadcasting carried 400 games on 500 to 600 stations during the early 1950s.[28] Even more important were local broadcasts with local announcers – as many as 11,000 stations nationally. There were 45 million radios in the United States in 1950; there were fewer than 4 million televisions.[29] Rather than damaging attendance, radio broadcasts promoted discussion of baseball and widened its following, especially among women who reported on day games to their returning husbands. Although debates remain about the make-up of crowds in different eras, there is general agreement that baseball was played before families and less exclusively before males after the war.[30]

The apparently prosaic matter of baseball attendance reveals the place of baseball in American popular culture. No single factor explains the appeal of baseball at a given time. The evidence suggests some answers, however, concerning the late 1940s. First, the increase of attendance after the war was a resurrection from an artificially dormant stage engendered by economic depression and war. Second, the unique circumstances of postwar America created a desire for both recreation and more leisure time. Third, baseball was uniquely situated to take advantage of consumer demand, for which few alternatives were yet available. Baseball was still unchallenged as the national pastime among sports fans. It was still the only nationally based professional spectator sport, and participant sports had not yet captured the interest of most Americans. Finally, night baseball and local radio networks were firmly in place before the war. Their fruits were ready for harvest after the war.

Attendance patterns in the first decade after the end of the Second World War do not seem to have been contingent on exciting pennant races, as many have claimed they were. There were playoffs in the National League in 1946 and in the American League in 1948. Boston in 1946 and New York in 1947 won AL pennants by 12 games, and the 1947 and 1948 NL pennant chases were not close, but attendance rose. It declined slightly in 1949 when both the AL and NL races were decided by a single game. There was a three-team race in the American League into mid-September in 1950, and the Phillies and Dodgers went to the last weekend to decide the NL pennant that year. Attendance fell by 16 per cent from 1948 to 1950.

Perhaps the game had simply become dull. Bill James, who transformed the statistical compilation of baseball data to statistical analysis, believes that the baseball of the 1950s 'was perhaps the most one-dimensional, uniform, predictable version of the game that has ever been offered for sale.'[31] Yet attendance rose in the second half of the decade. What transpired off the field was more important than the game itself in determining major-league gates, although individual team performances affected differentials among teams. Cleveland had the largest stadium –

the first municipal stadium in the country – regularly challenged for the pennant, and drew the largest crowds. The St Louis Browns and Phila- delphia Athletics suffered both on the field and at the turnstiles.

Attendance peaked at nearly 21 million fans in 1948. It declined by 700,000 in 1949, by 2.75 million more the following year, and then by another 3 million over the next three years. The total decline was 6.5 million or 30 per cent in five years (table 1).[32] Attendance steadily rose thereafter until the 1994 strike (table 11). Like the boom of the late 1940s, the decline of the early 1950s was a temporary one, although it did not seem so to contemporary observers. National magazines were full of articles anticipating the imminent demise of baseball. As late as 1961, Arthur Daley of the *New York Times* wrote in *Esquire*: 'Statistics would only prove that more people watched major-league baseball last season than ever before in history, and that therefore it is more popular than ever. I for one do not think that this is the case. I don't think anybody cares about baseball at all any more.'[33]

Most pundits blamed television. Lee MacPhail, president of the New York Yankees, opposed televising the 1947 World Series for fear of hurting the gate. Clark Griffith and Branch Rickey attributed baseball's attendance problems in the early 1950s to the televising of games.[34] Writing in the 'Bible of Baseball,' *The Sporting News*, Tom Meany was not fooled. Television would not keep fans out of the park any more than radio had, despite the fears of 'the reactionaries, of whom there are more to the square foot in baseball than in any other industry.' Another writer anticipated correctly that television would bring new wealth that would pay for increasing salaries and increasing costs of travel.[35] In the long run, television widened baseball's audience and provided unforeseen riches.

Television may have contributed to the temporary decline in atten- dance during the early 1950s when it became an integral part of Ameri- can homes. Ninety per cent of those who watched the first televised World Series in 1947 watched the games in taverns.[36] Architecture then changed to accommodate both television sets and the baby boom in new 'family rooms' in suburban homes. A mere 3.8 million sets in 1950 (one- eighth of American households, but many sets were in bars) quickly became 27.7 million in 1954, 34.9 (three-quarters of households) in 1956, and 45.8 in 1960.[37] Broader changes in American society were inhibiting attendance as well. As James Miller astutely wrote: 'Baseball's conservativism ... led a number of owners to suspect the new technology of creating problems that, in fact, had deeper roots. TV in its early days needed sports during summer reruns. Baseball needed TV for revenue and marketing.'[38] Benjamin Rader has warned too that 'determining the precise impact of television at big-league games is fraught with difficulties.'[39] Statistical analysis of the 1960s shows no correlation between the number of games televised and gate attendance.[40]

Television was just one of many alternative forms of entertainment and recreation becoming available during the prosperity of the 1950s. Boating, golf, the auto, camping, summer vacations, and other professional sports provided entertainment as well. Americans spent twice as much on golf equipment in 1959 as on baseball equipment, although they bought ten million baseballs.[41] Leisure was becoming privatized. In the suburbs, there were lawns to mow and children in Little League baseball. Minor-league attendance was suffering more than the majors' (table 2). It began to decline before repeal of the blackout rule, which applied originally to radio and forbade broadcasts of major-league games in the immediate vicinity of minor-league clubs. Television was being piped into their towns only once, then twice, a week, and small-town America lagged behind urban centers in acquiring television. The Celler Commission attributed the problems of teams in Jersey City and Newark more to easier access to New York than to television.[42]

Urban decay in the areas surrounding ballparks troubled potential patrons in major-league cities. Ballparks were old too. Only three had been built after 1926. Shortages of parking space inhibited those who wanted to drive to games rather than use public transportation.[43] Attendance for the three New York teams declined from 5.5 to 3.2 million fans between 1947 and 1957, despite the fact that those teams won seventeen of twenty-two pennants in both leagues over that eleven-year period.[44] The attendance decline in New York City represented more than 40 per cent of the decline for all of major-league baseball. All New York games were played free on television by '1950 or so,'[45] but New York had urban problems and decaying ballparks. *The Sporting News* editorialized in 1955 that Ebbets Field was 'no longer suited for profitable operation.'[46] Worries about the neighborhoods surrounding ballparks were by no means new. A half-century earlier Barney Dreyfuss, owner of the Pittsburgh Pirates, had complained that his park was 'located in a poor neighborhood where many of the better class of citizens were ... loath to go.'[47] Nationally, there was a recession and the Korean War was under way. Fluctuating gates reflected a number of changing and complex circumstances. The unique atmosphere of the late 1940s had ended. Baseball would have to adjust to changing times.

THE WESTWARD MOVEMENT

The first reaction was not a courageous one. Teams fled from problems both figuratively and literally. The first franchise shifts came from two-team cities where the population base was not great enough to support both teams.[48] St Louis had the lowest population base of any major-league city and Boston's exceeded only Cincinnati's. Philadelphia ranked sixth (or eighth if one counts the New York teams separately), but it had to support two teams. If one divides its population in half to allow for two teams, its metropolitan base was less than two-thirds of other major-league cities.[49] All of these teams had aging parks in declining areas as well. No franchise had moved in fifty years, but the demography of the country had shifted out of the north-east quadrant, where two-thirds of the population had lived in 1900. Americans were on the move and acquiring tangible symbols of postwar prosperity. So was baseball.

The owners modified their rules in 1952 so that the approval of only six teams in one league was required to allow a franchise move. The Boston Braves dashed to Milwaukee the next year. The troubled St Louis Browns finally moved to Baltimore in 1954 after Bill Veeck sold the club. They had hoped to leave St Louis for the 1942 season, but Pearl Harbor was bombed two days before baseball's winter meetings. Branch Rickey predicted an imminent departure by the Browns in 1945, and *The Sporting News* ran a cover story in 1948 predicting their relocation to the West Coast. Owners of other clubs blocked every attempt by the Browns to move. They were not about to do any favors for maverick Bill Veeck, who had had the audacity to suggest revenue sharing. He also horrified traditionalists when he sent a 'midget,' Eddie Gaedel, to bat against Bob Cain of the Tigers on 19 August 1951.[50]

The Philadelphia A's went to Kansas City in 1955. These two teams promptly finished seventh and eighth, 57 and 60 games respectively behind the Cleveland Indians, who won a record 111 games. Nevertheless, they drew record crowds as the New York Mets would eighteen years later when the Mets broke these teams' records for futility, ineptitude, and confusion. These new franchises shifted baseball's geographical center westward and played in publicly funded stadiums, which would soon become the norm. The next moves, however, permanently changed the geography of major-league baseball.

A century after the California gold rush, major-league baseball went west. Walter O'Malley, owner of the Brooklyn Dodgers, convinced Horace Stoneham, owner of the New York Giants, to accompany him in 1958 to sunny, booming California, accessible because of commercial airplanes. The Dodgers were not losing money. Roger Kahn reports that in 1953 the Dodgers' income was $5,150,000, expenses $3,743,000, profit $1,407,000, plus $750,000 in radio and television income. In their last ten years in Brooklyn, they compiled 44 per cent of the total profits of teams in the National League.[51] These were the first 'healthy' franchises to pick up and move, although they would not be the last. Teams changed cities in the next decade not because of attendance woes but because of the promised lode of television money: 'and that's exactly why you had so much franchise-hopping in the sixties. Milwaukee moved. Kansas City moved. They saw the Yankees and Dodgers getting rich and they felt trapped – they hadn't the same local radio/TV money available to them.'[52] Baseball had extended its reach across the nation, but another reach was even more important.

INTEGRATION ON THE FIELD

'A revolution of no. 1 importance in baseball has gone virtually unnoticed ... not as a freak or attendance-stimulant, but as a talent factor which could bring a levelling off ... and a consequent prosperity.'[53] That revolution was the admission of blacks to major-league baseball – a step that opened the community of players to all Americans for the first time. On 23 October 1945, Branch Rickey signed Jackie Robinson, a college star in four sports, an All-American halfback at UCLA and the leading basketball scorer in the Pacific Coast Conference,[54] to a minor-league baseball contract with the Montreal Royals of the International League. Robinson played his first professional game in Jersey City on 18 April

1946. The following year he joined the Dodgers.[55] Rickey also signed future stars Don Newcombe and Roy Campanella, as well as John Wright and Roy Partlow, from the Negro leagues in 1946. This was ten years before the bus boycott in Montgomery, Alabama, that made segregation a national issue and nearly twenty years before Lyndon Johnson's civil rights legislation. Military units had been integrated during the war, but only overseas.

The integration of baseball was the issue most widely commented upon in American race relations of the time.[56] Whatever motivated Rickey, it was a courageous decision that changed the place of baseball in American society forever. For the first time it could rightly claim to be a national sport.[57] The success of black players belied racist claims of their natural inferiority, and the public bringing together of two races to the common goal of winning at least mitigated racism where teams performed.

Integration did not come easily, although players from the Negro leagues had competed with white major-league players in exhibition games and in Latin America, where Jorge Pascuel, financial backer of President Aleman of Mexico, recruited both black and white stars. Latin America was where integration first occurred. It took place without incident among the players. The talent of black players was 'known to those who looked by the end of the war.'[58] Wendell Smith of the African American *Pittsburgh Courier*, campaigned for integration throughout the 1930s, supported by Westbook Pegler, Shirley Povich, the *New York Daily News*'s Dan Parker, and the Communist *Daily Worker*.[59] Wendell Smith was a native Detroiter who attended Southeastern High School in the early 1930s and had enough talent but not the right color to play major-league ball. A scout told him: 'Wish I could sign you, kid, but I can't.'[60] Smith later worked for the *Chicago American and Sun Times* and for WGN. The first African American member of the Baseball Writers Association of America (BBWAA), he was inducted into the writers' wing of Cooperstown's Hall of Fame in 1994.

Baseball had always claimed that racial discrimination was not a factor in the absence of blacks in major-league baseball. John Heydler, president of the National League, declared in 1933: 'I do not recall one instance when baseball would allow either race, creed, or color to enter into the question of the selection of its players.' Commissioner of Baseball Kenesaw Mountain Landis insisted: 'Negroes are not barred from organized baseball, and never have been during the 21 years I've served as commissioner.'[61] Established in 1886 and based in St Louis, which was regarded still as a 'southern city,' *The Sporting News* consistently presented the views of the baseball establishment. It also received a subsidy from the Commissioner's Office in the form of payment for subscriptions of *TSN* to the armed forces overseas and purchase of *TSN*'s statistical guides for free distribution to members of the BBWAA.[62] An editorial of 6 August 1942 favored continued separation between the Negro and the established white major leagues. 'Clear minded men of tolerance of both races' recognized the 'tragic possibilities' of racial intermixture on the field. Another editorial of 1 November 1945 worried that Jackie Robinson would have difficulty competing with 'younger, more skilled and more experienced players.' It did chide those players of southern descent 'who gave out interviews blasting the hiring of a Negro and would have done a lot better by themselves and baseball if they had refused to comment.' Club owners had to 'work out difficult and perplexing problems.'[63] *The Sporting News* implied that the lack of talent of the Negro players would impede integration and that silence on the whole issue was the best tack. Clark Griffith, owner of the Washington Senators, conceived a different reason for excluding blacks from white baseball. He denounced those who stole players from Negro Leagues and 'act[ed] like outlaws.' 'In no walk of life can one person take another's property unless he pays for it.' The *St Louis Globe Democrat* thought Griffith hypocritical: 'Certainly Clark Griffith, of the Senators, should have little to say about that. He's been raiding Cuban, Mexican and even South American leagues for playing talent for years and up to now we've heard little about his buying the players' contracts.'[64]

The Sporting News remained unabashed. Following Robinson's debut, it stated that it 'has not changed its views' from its 1942 editorial, but now 'having taken the step of introducing a colored player to the rank the situation calls for tolerance and fair play on the part of players and fans.' Two months later it defined 'fair play': 'The vast percentage of white players in the league' were opposed to Negroes entering the major leagues. A white 'big-leaguer' 'felt threatened by those who didn't spend time in the Minors ... Let us not discriminate against a white player because he is white.'[65]

Unfortunately for those who claimed they wanted equality for all, Branch Rickey let the cat out of the bag. He revealed, in a speech in 1948 at Wilberforce University, a Negro school in Ohio, that the major leagues had confirmed a tacit policy of barring 'Negroes' in 1946. Lee MacPhail denied any such policy on 20 February in an interview in the *New York Daily Mirror*. Perhaps knowing a bit more about the 1946 meeting than J.G. Taylor Spink, editor of *The Sporting News*, was prepared to reveal, a *TSN* editorial condemned Rickey merely for bringing up an unpleasant past.[66] That past was indeed unpleasant. MacPhail and representatives of other clubs felt free to deny that such a policy ever existed because they had carefully destroyed what they thought were all copies of the 1946 report in the room after their meeting. Happy Chandler, the new commissioner of baseball, however, had kept a single copy of the Major League Steering Committee report of 1946, which he released in 1972 (appendix 1).[67]

A few influential leaders within baseball supported integration. One was Chandler, a Kentuckian. In 1946 he made a special trip to Daytona Beach, where Montreal trained, and asserted: 'I think he [Robinson] deserves a chance to make good. I think every boy in America who wants to play professional baseball should have a chance regardless of race, creed or color. I've always said that – and I repeat it now – that Negro players are welcome in baseball.'[68] Another was Bill Veeck, who was the first to bring a black player, Larry Doby, to the American League in 1947. He also broke segregation in the Pacific Coast League in 1948 when the San Diego Padres signed catcher John Ritchey.[69] Five years earlier, Veeck had wanted to buy the Philadelphia Phillies, but owners squashed his bid after he made it known that he wanted to put black players on the squad. In his book on Shibe Park, Bruce Kuklick describes the Phillies: 'Carpenter opposed a black presence in the Majors and certainly at Shibe Park. Both the Phillies and the A's were racist on principle. They willingly hurt the quality of their teams.' Connie Mack was also a racist, turning down Larry Doby, Minnie Minoso, and Hank Aaron.[70]

Philadelphia clubs were not the only ones in which racist attitudes persisted well after Robinson entered the majors. Six years after Robinson played his first game, only six teams had integrated (appendix 2). There were only nine blacks in the majors in 1950 and eighteen in 1957 out of four hundred, ten years after Robinson's debut.[71] Detroit did not have a black player until 1958. It was 1962 when the first black coach was hired by the Cubs, 1966 when Emmett Ashford became a major-league umpire (after having been in the minor leagues since 1952), and 1966 when CBS hired an African American announcer.[72] As *The Sporting News* admitted in 1949: 'the expected wholesale migration of Negro players failed to materialize.'[73] It came a decade later. In 1961, 59 more blacks were playing in the majors than in 1957. That influx prompted another *TSN* editorial, titled 'Games Shining Record on Racial Issue.' It warned that the major leagues should not be a crusader in Florida against segregation and that they should 'not be stampeded by private agencies or individuals who are trying to exploit baseball for their own personal gain.'[74] Justice and the American Constitution went unmentioned.

We will address the policies of the Detroit Tigers in chapters 2 and 3. Let us say a few words here about the policies of the New York Yankees, the dominant team in baseball. Elston Howard was the first black player to play for the Yankees, beginning his major-league career on 14 April 1955 – eight years after Brooklyn had put Jackie Robinson on the diamond and six after Hank Thompson had joined the New York Giants. There was no paucity of black players available for New York teams.

David Halberstam recounts how the Yankees had instructed Tom Greenwade, who had scouted both Jackie Robinson and Mickey Mantle, not to sign 'niggers' in the late 1940s. The Yankee travelling secretary in 1953 reportedly said about black players: 'I wouldn't want any of them on a club I was with.' Roger Kahn describes the Yankees management as bigoted. However, its bigotry cost the team a chance to sign Willie Mays. As he put it, 'Bigotry is not simply wicked. It is also pretty damn dumb.'[75] On 'Youth Wants to Know' on WNBC in New York, on 30 November 1952, Jackie Robinson charged: 'I think the Yankee management is prejudiced.' George Weiss of the Yankees responded: 'When a Negro comes along and plays good enough we will be glad to have him – we are not going to bow to pressure groups.'[76] Sports writer Dan Daniel explained, when Howard was signed, that the Yankees had waited for 'the right man to come along.' And Howard did not have a room-mate because he preferred to room alone.[77] Those became the usual explanations for many teams – either that there was not a player good enough to sign, or that teams wanted 'the right type of Negro' (whatever that meant), and that they certainly would not bow to pressure groups.[78] Had it not been for pressure groups and a few innovators, one wonders how long it would have taken major-league baseball to integrate.

Organized baseball did not fly in the face of American opinion by integrating its teams. Despite obstructionism by certain major-league owners and the reactionary attitude of *The Sporting News*, the national press reaction to integration of the majors was favorable. *Time Magazine* remarked that 'most baseball men, after an initial blush, realize that it could and perhaps would work (it had worked pretty well in college sports).'[79] A letter of 30 October 1945 to the editor of the *Detroit News* argued: 'Colored artists and performers in all other fields have proved that the absence of a colored player in the major leagues of baseball is nothing more than the absence of the true American spirit in the greatest of American sports.'[80] The Second World War, claimed the press, rendered arguments based on racial inequality un-American. The war demonstrated that baseball segregation derived from southern exceptionalism and was a violation of American democracy: 'The liberal consensus evident in press commentary on the signing of Robinson closely resembles the mid-1940s American Creed [of] ... "liberty, equality, justice and fair opportunity for everybody" ... Unlike militants of the late 1960s social critics of the mid-1940s reflected an ideological consensus; injustice, they believed, deviated from, rather than expressed, American values. Thus, "the right type" of black could redeem Organized Baseball from Southern practices and allow the game to once again truly embody American values.'[81]

Liberals hoped that baseball would become a motor of change in American society. Integration in America's national sport forced an awareness of discrimination and racism in American society. Even within *The Sporting News*, some writers were condemning racist attitudes by the end of the 1940s. After an exhibition game in Atlanta in which Roy Campanella and Jackie Robinson played provoked a protest by the Ku Klux Klan, Jimmy Cannon, a New York columnist, interviewed Klan leader Dr Sam Green. Cannon concluded: 'I hung up, took a bath, I stayed in the tub a long time.' *The Sporting News* published the interview and editorialized: 'Baseball in the south, no less than the north – should recognize no limitations of race, creed or color.' A street poll, by the *Atlanta Constitution*, showed 80 per cent of Atlanta's citizens in favor of integrated teams there. While Dan Daniel was excusing the Yankees for awaiting the 'right' Negro, Warren Brown of the *Chicago American* was noting how much better the game had become with Negro players.[82]

Whatever the press thought, the first black players had to face teammates and opponents every day. The initial reaction was resistance. Dixie Walker, supported by Hugh Casey and Bobby Bragan, all of whom were southerners, immediately circulated a petition against Robinson's joining the Brooklyn Dodgers. Apparently 'Cookie' Lavagetto, Carl Furillo, and Eddie Stanky, who were not southerners, supported them. Billy Herman, whose child had been treated by an African American doctor, told them to go away, and Robinson recalled that Peewee Reese, who was from Kentucky, 'put his arm around me.' Pete Reiser apparently also opposed the petition. Leo Durocher, in a clubhouse speech, told the team: 'Play or else!'[83]

Attempts by opponents to drive Robinson out of the league met with no better success. Ben Chapman, manager of the Philadelphia Phillies, steadily rode Robinson, referring to his 'gorilla-like' physical characteristics. Stanley Woodward of the *New York Tribune* reported that the St Louis Cardinals considered striking rather than playing against Robinson in May 1947, and there may have been a near strike by the Pittsburgh Pirates in June.[84] Other published comments included those of Rogers Hornsby: 'it would be tough for a Negro player to become part of a close knit group such as organized baseball'; and W.G. Bramham, commissioner of minor-league baseball: 'it is those of the carpet baggers' stripe ... who retard the race ... if the Negro is left alone – he will work out his own salvation.'[85] Herb Pennock, general manager of the Phillies, called Rickey, saying: 'We're not ready for Robinson and might have a riot. We won't take the field.' Rickey replied: 'Okay, we'll take the forfeit.'[86]

Despite problems in the first two years on the field and in the clubhouse, players adjusted quickly to integration. An editorial in Detroit's African American newspaper, the *Michigan Chronicle*, predicted: 'It is our guess, like that of the Dodger management, that the southern white boys who may be shocked will recover in due time. A good stiff democratic shock in the right place might do them a lot of good.'[87]

Belying the predictions of opponents of integration, 'the addition of blacks did not precipitate resentment from the fans or create significant problems on any major league club. Blacks generally found their team-mates supportive.[88] Common goals and day-to-day contact reduced prejudices. Black players complained, not about team-mates, but about problems in housing, baiting by fans in the still segregated South, the need for special behavior on the field, and the unwillingness of manage-ment to confront problems in the South and to treat black players equally.[89] Few black players, for example, received bonuses.

Discrimination occurred off the field much more than it did on the field or in the clubhouse, although many ballplayers were southerners and most were not highly educated.[90] Charles Fountain cautions us to be careful in judging the past, but concludes that most sports writers, including Grantland Rice, were 'bigots.' Dick Young wrote that Larry Doby had a 'persecution complex.' *The Sporting News* described Robin-son as 'that dusky Montreal's second basemen,' and criticized him for umpire baiting.[91] Many sports writers applauded the entry of blacks into baseball and their contribution, but most writers were no more enlight-ened than the players. Few then had formal schooling beyond high school and their social sphere was among those they wrote about.

Baseball did, however, slowly integrate. And it integrated without leg-islation. The American Army was integrated in the United States after the Second World War by presidential fiat. The Supreme Court ordered schools desegregated in 1954 in *Brown v. Board of Education of Topeka*. Congress legislated integration with the Civil Rights Act of 1964. In Jackie Robinson's words, 'Yes, baseball had done it.' As it had admitted immigrants earlier in the century while they were discriminated against in society at large, baseball admitted blacks before they were integrated into the mainstream of American culture. This happened because of the vision of a few courageous men, notably Branch Rickey, Happy Chan-dler, and Bill Veeck. By the beginning of the national civil rights move-ment, every major-league team had a minimum of four black players. Baseball did not obliterate racism within the sport, but it was better than many American institutions.

The first black players had to excel or their mission would have failed. They outperformed their white peers in the first decade after their admission to the majors. Jackie Robinson won *The Sporting News*'s com-bined Rookie of the Year selection in 1947. Beginning in 1949 when

American and National League awards were split, black players won six of ten and eight of twelve Rookie of the Year Awards in the National League, but only one in the American League. The National League had integrated much more quickly than the American League. In 1959, more than twice as many blacks played in the National circuit as in the American. Not coincidentally, National League teams won 10 out of 16 World Series between 1954 and 1969 and 28 of 35 All-Star games after 1950.[92] Non-white players won the following percentages of awards and championships between 1947 and 1980: Most Valuable Player, 64% NL, 25% AL; Rookie of the Year, 42% NL, 29% AL; batting average, 58% NL, 38% AL; home runs, 48% NL, 31% AL; runs batted in, 55% NL, 28% AL; Cy Young Award, 21%.

Black athletes consistently outperformed their white peers in major batting and pitching performances as late as the 1980s. In the early years black players did not sit on the bench; they either became starters or were sent to the minors. There was no overt salary discrimination against black players who made it, however. Once admitted to baseball, they were paid for their performances.[93]

PLAYERS ORGANIZE

Integration was a question not just for baseball, but for America as a whole in the postwar period. Labor problems too arose both in baseball and society at large. Two separate but related matters became issues between the owners and the players in the early years after the war. The first was the organization of the ill-fated American Baseball Guild in 1946 – the first serious attempt to organize baseball players since the Brotherhood of Professional Baseball Players in 1885. The second was a series of court challenges to the reserve clause, which had been instituted in 1879.[94] Both attempted to improve the bargaining power of players and set the stage for later labor problems in the sport.

The United States did not slide into another depression after the war, in part because of accumulated savings of $126 billion and pent-up consumer demand during the war. There were economic problems, however. Inflation ran at rates of 14 or 15 per cent a year. In this atmosphere major strikes occurred in the automobile, electrical, and steel industries. A major strike in April 1946 by the United Mine Workers under John

L. Lewis paralyzed transportation and led President Truman to seize the mines. A total of 4.6 million workers were on strike in 1946, a half-million more than in 1919 but a somewhat lower percentage of the labor force.[95] The beginning of the Cold War coincided with labor unrest and brought anti-communist and anti-union sentiment. A conservative reaction prompted passage in 1947 of the Taft-Hartley Act, technically known as the Labor-Management Relations Act, which passed Congress overwhelmingly by votes of 320 to 79 and 57 to 17, overriding a presidential veto.

The year before, Robert Murphy announced in Boston the formation of the American Baseball Guild. His press release promised: 'The days of baseball serfdom will soon be over.'[96] Murphy had favored affiliation with the National Labor Organization, but admitted that players were opposed to that. The Guild called for a minimum salary of $6500, a pension, impartial arbitration of salary disputes, and for the player to receive half of the price if he were sold to another ballclub.[97] It claimed support from 90 per cent of the Pittsburgh Pirates (although a small majority seems to be a more accurate figure) and demanded a meeting in a telegram of 15 May to William Benswanger, owner of the Pirates. The reaction of H.G. Salsinger, the senior Detroit sports writer then, reflected the general conservatism of the sports press and of the country at the time. He wrote: 'Baseball is a profession, not a trade ... The reserve clause is the backbone of baseball. Remove it and the game will be ruined.'[98] Salsinger thus linked the whole issue of player demands with their permanent bondage to ball clubs through the reserve clause. They were separate but related issues.

The major-league owners' steering committee met in the summer of that year. Despite later claims that the owners acted out of altruism and concern for the players, their confidential report, which was not released at the time, shows that fear of the players' organization prompted action:

Professional baseball, however, is more than a game. It is BIG BUSINESS, a $100,000,000 industry ... In the well-considered opinion of counsel for both Major Leagues, the present reserve clause could not be enforced in an equity court for specific performance, nor as the basis for a restraining order to prevent a player from playing elsewhere, or to prevent outsiders from inducing a player to breach his contract ... If the players' representatives agree that the reserve clause is necessary for the protection of the industry and benefits the players, your counsel and your Committee believe the courts will be inclined to recognize this fact and uphold the validity of the option clause.[99]

The result of the Major League Steering Committee's offers to players resulted in a joint player-owner contributory pension plan, a $5500 minimum salary (reduced to $5000 in July after Pittsburgh players voted against the union), a maximum salary cut of 25 per cent, $25 a week for spring-training expenses, and thirty days instead of ten days severance pay.

On 17 August 1946 the American Baseball Guild collapsed. Eight days earlier *Newsweek* had observed that the player-owner pension agreement left Murphy out: 'It was cooked up to get rid of the Guild.' The day after the Guild died, in an issue prepared before the formal demise of the union, *The Sporting News* declared that unionism in baseball was dead: 'The American Baseball Guild will be a strange memory.'[100] The Guild failed, but other players' organizations would follow.

Seven years later, in December 1953, players founded a new 'association.' That was prompted by a court decision in November 1953 upholding baseball's antitrust exemption and, implicitly, the owners' monopoly on players' services. This major-league baseball players' organization, led by Bob Feller and Bob Friend, was to be an 'advisory, fraternal, social organization.' It negotiated a raise of the minimum salary to $6000 and a continued 60 per cent of the All-Star and World Series TV revenue for the pension plan, but it was not a major force over the next decade. Its legal counsel was Judge Robert Cannon, who aspired to be baseball's next commissioner and saw himself as representing the interests of baseball as a whole. He told Congress in 1964: 'We have it so good we don't know what to ask for next.'[101] Only when Marvin Miller became its counsel in 1966 did the organization become aggressive (chapter 7).

A players' organization was necessary primarily because baseball's reserve clause effectively bound a player to one club for the duration of his career. The automatic renewal provision in each player's contract meant that he had to sit out an entire baseball season in order to negotiate with a different team. Within the cosy atmosphere of major-league baseball no American or National League team was about to challenge this provision by attempting to sign a player from another team.

The first legal challenge to the reserve clause occurred after the Federal League was inaugurated in 1914 and its teams tried to sign players from the established teams. A series of court cases culminated in *Federal Baseball Club of Baltimore, Inc. v. National League of Professional Baseball Clubs*, decided by the Supreme Court in 1922. The challenge was based on the Sherman Anti-Trust Act of 1890, which forbade every 'contract, combination ... or conspiracy in restraint of trade or commerce.' Justice Oliver Wendell Holmes wrote the unanimous opinion that baseball was exempt from antitrust legislation because it was locally based and not engaged in interstate commerce and also that baseball did not involve production and therefore did not constitute commerce.[102] That became a precedent that still stands today.

The next challenge to organized baseball's monopoly of players came as a result of the Mexican League's raids on the majors. Eighteen major leaguers went to Mexico in 1946, including Murray Franklin, who had played for Detroit in 1941 and 1942. The major leagues responded in draconian fashion by declaring any player who had played in Mexico ineligible to return to the major leagues for five years. After Commissioner Chandler refused to reinstate such players in 1947, blacklisted outfielder Danny Gardella filed an antitrust suit in New York. Fearing an adverse decision concerning the antitrust exemption, Commissioner Chandler reinstated Gardella, Fred Martin, Max Lanier, and Luke Klein in 1949 so as to 'temper justice with mercy.' Gardella dropped his suit in June after receiving a cash settlement of $60,000. Richard Irwin, in the *Marquette Sports Law Journal*, concluded that the Gardella case could have 'overturned the anti-trust exemption if Gardella had not been in a hurry.'[103] After the settlement, baseball asked Congress to confirm its exemption. The result was the establishment of Congressman Emanuel Celler's Subcommittee on the Study of Monopoly Power in 1951, the first of more than two dozen congressional inquiries into the place of sport in American society.

One more court case had to be decided. Much to the surprise of Celler, the press,[104] and to organized baseball itself, the Supreme Court affirmed baseball's reserve clause in *Toolson v. New York Yankees*, citing the precedent of the 1922 Federal Court decision. The *New York Times* gave the court decision page 1 headlines: 'Baseball a Sport, and not Business, High Court Rules.'[105] This mythology about the basis for the ruling has affected writing about the decision since: that baseball was exempt because it was a game, or a sport, and not a business. As late as 1993 the *Detroit News* repeated that baseball was exempt because it was a sport not a trade.[106] Legal experts, like Irwin, insist that is simply not true. Baseball was exempted in 1922 because it was found not to be interstate commerce, and later courts chose not to modify that decision. An arbitrator would overturn the reserve clause, but not the antitrust exemption, two decades later (chapter 7).

The first Celler Commission began its hearings in the charged atmosphere of those court cases. Celler, a congressman from Brooklyn, was a fan of the Brooklyn Dodgers and was expected to be sympathetic to baseball's establishment. His original memo to the committee anticipated that the courts would rule that baseball was interstate commerce.[107] An adverse court decision concerning baseball's antitrust exemption would have affected not only the reserve clause but also the monopoly that major-league baseball had over the location of franchises.

At the hearings Ford Frick, president of the National League, testified: 'There are those who are fearful this is the beginning of an action to tear away the very foundations of the game; to disrupt a typically American institution which is growing strong and venerable along with the nation itself.' As handwritten notes in the Celler papers show, Celler became more critical of baseball's monopoly as he collected data. He asked Frick, 'Was there not an agreement among Clubs, as well as between player and club, which would constitute a cartel?' Frick's response was: 'I'm not a lawyer.' Charles Wrigley, president of the Chicago Cubs, testified that there was 'no general demand for alteration of the reserve clause by fans, players or management.' That was correct. Fred Hutchinson, player representative for the American League and Detroit Tigers pitcher, believed that 'the reserve clause is a necessary and reasonable provision for the preservation of organized baseball.' J.G. Taylor Spink described the reserve clause as 'the very core of the competitive spirit that marks the game.' Only a few contrary voices were heard. Ned Garver, St Louis Browns pitcher, proposed in a letter a form of limited free agency, although 'I do not think baseball could exist, as we know it, without [the reserve clause].'[108]

The public, the press, and even leaders of the players' organization saw no alternative to the continuation of a reserve clause. Celler himself was not so sure. Privately, he wrote that 'owners of baseball clubs in the Big Leagues are like those riding in railroad cars backwards. They only see things after they have passed them by. Only after public outrage and condemnation, do they act.' Regarding the reserve clause, he wrote Spink, on 2 November 1953, that the owners were sitting on a keg of dynamite. An adverse court decision could render a 'severe, if not fatal, blow to organized baseball.' If 'the panjandrums of baseball are indifferent ... I suggest that you, Mr. Spink, take the helm.'[109] Four years later, on 19 May 1957, he called the reserve clause 'barbarous' in a television interview on *Face the Nation*. On the *Today* show he described it as 'obnoxious, illegal.'[110] His remained a minority opinion in the 1950s.

The second Celler Commission of 1956 was sparked by the Radovich (football) case. In it, the court refused to extend baseball's antitrust exemption to other sports, explaining that it would not grant baseball an exemption either, if reviewing it for the first time.[111] The press again speculated whether the baseball exemption could withstand another court case.[112] Celler proposed a bill to modify the exemption. It passed committee by a 17–15 vote but died in Congress. Baseball in the 1950s was too venerable an institution for either the courts or Congress to challenge it. They played political football with the antitrust issue, each hoping the other would reach some sort of decision. The result was that no decision was reached. Baseball remained constitutionally in the position it had occupied since 1922. The players' organization was a weak one, willing to accept what the owners gave. As baseball generally got richer, salaries rose, the pension plan became well vested, and players thought correctly that they had never had it so good. What they did not realize for another decade was that things could get much better.

FINANCES

Mystery surrounds the financial state of baseball after the war because club records have been kept private. We have some indications of their economic situation in the 1950s from data the Celler Commission collected and from Andrew Zimbalist's calculations in his fine study of baseball economics, *Baseball and Billions*. Zimbalist shows that baseball teams made steady profits over three decades up to 1950.[113] Other information from the Celler papers suggests that some major-league teams made higher profits than Zimbalist estimated, although he has been considered a critic of baseball management. Confidential club records reported in various sources paint an even brighter picture. According to them, the Brooklyn Dodgers, Cleveland Indians, Detroit Tigers, St Louis Browns, and St Louis Cardinals showed a combined total profit for the years 1946–7 of $4,000,000.[114] The Cleveland Indians alone showed a profit of $460,000 in 1950 and of $232,000 in 1957 because of depreciation, although they claimed a loss of $400,000 in 1957. Roger Kahn has reported Dodger profits in 1953 as $1,407,000 plus $750,000 from radio and television income. Records produced at the time of the sale of the Detroit Tigers in 1956 show that they had been a profitable operation every year since 1938 (tables 6 and 7).[115] Depreciation of player contracts over a five-year period meant that owners received considerable tax write-offs against income from their other businesses even if the baseball team had no operating profit.[116] Then as now, 'baseball's financial statements reflect accounting conventions that, while acceptable for legal purposes, are not accurate indications of the profitability of baseball teams.'[117]

The median player salary was only $12,000 through the middle 1950s, probably below $10,000 in the 1940s.[118] The minimum salary was only $5000 to $6000 until 1968. Players' salaries made up a steadily decreasing proportion of team expenses (table 3). Zimbalist estimates that players' salaries constituted only 22 per cent of expenditures in 1950 and decreased to 18 per cent in 1974.

Nearly every year *The Sporting News* warned of baseball's imminent impoverishment under the pressure of rising salaries. A headline in 1947 read: 'Soaring Costs Menace Less Wealthy Magnates.' In 1958 another headline read: 'Player Payrolls Rock to Outerspace.'[119] Yet the Celler Commission revealed that salaries were not so high as generally believed. Warren Giles, National League president, also admitted that published estimates were too high.[120] Furthermore, minor-league salaries were abysmal. Players spent about five years as apprentices in the minors.[121] Baseball was a part-time occupation for all but its stars. After careers ended, players had to move into other employment without any specific training or education.

The perception of baseball being mired in constant financial problems, of salaries rising beyond the ability of owners to pay, and of an economic crisis that might destroy baseball affected the press, the reaction of fans, and support for players' organizations.[122] The public and the press generally believed management's claims. The very popularity of baseball and the fear that something would adversely affect 'the game' led to an unwillingness to criticize ownership. American society was conservative and searched for consensus until the mid-1960s. Even today nostalgia about baseball's past conjures up an unsullied age of pristine happiness. Paradoxically, unwillingness to criticize aspects of the game in that era perhaps led to greater criticisms by future generations attentive to the civil rights movement, the aggressiveness of investigative reporting, and the increasingly publicized riches of baseball clubs. Sports publisher Allan P. Barron observed: 'Probably because people believe the myth that baseball is the national pastime, baseball is constantly raked over the coals for its mistakes.'[123] Baseball was indeed healthy in the 1950s. The introduction of television would both make it financially much healthier and expand its community of followers.

NEW SOURCES OF REVENUE

In 1946 broadcast revenue, then entirely from radio, was a tiny proportion of the total revenue of organized baseball. It grew quickly, however. In that year the Yankees sold their television rights for $75,000; the following year the World Series was shown in New York, Washington, Philadelphia, and Schenectady.[124] NBC put together the first 'network' along the East Coast for the 1949 World Series. Radio revenues exceeded television revenues for the World Series until 1950, when a new pact with Gillette brought $800,000 in TV money. Two years before Commissioner Chandler had been criticized for turning down a ten-year pact for $200,000 annually. New York sports writer Dan Daniel opined: 'It will never happen again.'[125] But it did. The next year a six-year $6 million television contract was sealed, even though it was another year before the World Series could be carried to the West Coast. Radio rights remained at $150,000 annually. Showing these spectaculars whetted interest in baseball throughout America, convinced baseball and television that they could serve each other's interests, and laid the foundation for local television contracts that enriched teams.

In 1953 ABC began televising a 'Game of the Week,' which was blacked out in major-league cities. The irrepressible Dizzy Dean, with malapropisms, songs, and anecdotes, put on a show that sometimes had only a tenuous relation to the game being played that day. Either he or the games attracted viewers. CBS took over the games in 1955 and added Sunday games in 1958. After NBC also established a regular-season baseball network, 96 games were being televised in 1959, along with another 687 games on local stations in major-league cities (411 in the American League, led by the Yankees' 123).[126] Thirty-two million Americans watched the 1959 World Series. Total broadcast income increased slowly but steadily, doubling from 1952 to 1957, doubling again by 1964, and then again by 1971. Local television and its resultant broadcast rights exceeded the income from national rights, bringing in three times as much in 1957, eight times in 1964. (See table 4 for broadcast revenues at five-year intervals.) Building upon their experience with radio, almost all teams were televising their own games by 1955. The Dodgers alone had a radio network of 117 stations.[127]

National but not local television income was shared. Visiting teams in the American League received 21 per cent of the gate and, in the National League, 14 per cent during the early 1950s. At the beginning of the century visitors had received 40 per cent.[128] Bill Veeck and Fred Saigh, of the St Louis Browns and Cardinals respectively, asked for a sharing of television revenue – a proposal that Walter O'Malley of the Dodgers condemned as 'socialistic.' Saigh threatened to ban visiting teams from bringing cameras into the Cards' park. Veeck actually did ban other teams from showing home games against the Browns in 1953 because, he claimed, television hurt attendance and the Browns' visitors' share of the gate.[129] Visiting teams received a proportion of attendance receipts, and no game could be played without two teams. Why should visiting teams not receive a proportion of television income? Through a combination of selfishness and conservatism, baseball missed an opportunity to use this new revenue to provide greater stability and equity within the game.

THE SUPREMACY OF THE MAJOR LEAGUES

Major-league owners were no more generous to the minors than they were to their peers. The televising of major-league games had an adverse effect on minor-league attendance.[130] Television alone did not ruin the minors, however. A 1946 rule forbidding the broadcasting of any game beyond fifty miles of the ballpark and intended then to restrict radio rather than television, limited broadcasts into minor-league cities until 1952. The number of leagues, clubs, and attendance had begun to decline two years earlier (table 2).

A second factor contributing to the crisis of the minors was cutbacks in the farm systems, which were no longer deemed sound financially or necessary to provide players, of which there was a positive glut with returning war veterans.[131] There were 11,000 players in the minors in 1950 and 8000 in 1952 against only 400 in the majors – a ratio of between 20 and 27.5 to one. More than one-third of the players in the minors in the early and mid-1950s had been there for five years or more.[132] Pittsburgh announced in July 1948 that it was cutting back its farm system from nineteen to twelve teams.[133] Five clubs – the Dodgers (26), the Yankees (24), the Cardinals (22), the Indians (20), and the Browns (20) – had twenty or more farm teams in 1948. A total of 112 minor-league teams depended on these five major-league franchises, which reduced their farm teams to 63 by 1952. Outright ownership of minor-league teams by the majors declined by two-thirds between 1948 and 1955 and had become mainly a memory by 1960.[134] The number of independent clubs actually increased during cutbacks in the late 1940s as towns attempted to keep their teams alive. Financial insolvency eventually doomed them as they faced the twin problems of withdrawal of funds by the majors and the establishment of national television networks for major-league baseball. The *Atlanta Journal* asked a pointed question: since the majors still controlled 80 per cent of the players in the minors, just whose fault was it that the minors were dying?[135] Neil Sullivan concludes in his pioneering study of the minors that providing the game to small-town America became less important than providing major-league baseball players.[136] The collapse of the minors owed more to the greed of the majors than to new technology. They rebounded in the mid-1970s when television was a much bigger force, but by then they were firmly under major-league control.[137]

Baseball after the Second World War would have looked much the same to someone who had taken a leap forward from the era of the First World War. Despite modifications the basic rules were unchanged.

Games were slower, from a constant of about one hour, 50 minutes to 2:26 in 1952, 2:32 in 1955, and 2:41 in 1963.[138] Batting averages were higher, more runs were being scored, there were more walks and strike-outs, and there were many more home runs. Speed was less important, as reflected in the decline of triples and the rarity of the stolen base.

	Runs	Batting avg.	HR	3B	SB	BB	SO
1914	9,408	.249	414	1,141	3,092	7,520	9,766
1954	10,827	.261	1,937	789	695	9,033	10,215

Many changes were temporary. Runs per team per game in the American League declined from 4.88 in 1950 to a low of 3.41 in 1968, and then returned to 4.9 in 1987. Maury Wills – whom the Tigers had in spring training in 1958 but let slip away[139] – made the stolen base a weapon again. As a Dodger, he broke Ty Cobb's stolen-base record in 1962, stealing 104 bases. The home run and longer games would become a permanent part of the game, but these statistical changes were minor compared to others that surrounded the game.

The most important social change was the breaking of the color line, which belied racist claims of white superiority, provided a focal point for black pride, and asserted the American claim of 'justice and equality' for all within a national institution. People saw blacks and whites together in pursuit of a common goal, even if the goal was only to win a ball game. This change also improved the quality of play.

Television brought major-league baseball into millions of homes and created a much wider community of followers for baseball. It provided the medium through which the number of people who could tune into a single World Series game would surpass the 60,000,000 who attended all the professional baseball games throughout the United States in base-ball's biggest drawing years of the late 1940s. Television also brought millions, then billions, of dollars into the coffers of clubs. It provided a reservoir of inexpensive entertainment for television stations.[140] Players began to demand at first merely a share, and then a greater proportionate share of that income. The first players' organizations had modest goals, but they provided a base for the labour-management battles that have afflicted baseball for the last two decades. Players became less thankful for the privilege of being in the major leagues and more demanding of the sort of recompense that movie and, later, rock stars received.

Major-league baseball spread its tentacles across the continent, making it for the first time a truly American sport. In its spread it smothered the minor leagues, which were transformed from institutions within small-town America into appendages of the majors. Major-league baseball had power beyond its dreams and beyond its recognition at the time. One of its most successful franchises was in the city of Detroit.

2

The Briggs Era of Detroit Baseball

CLUB AND COMMUNITY BEFORE 1945

Professional baseball in Detroit began with a franchise in the National League from 1881 through 1888.[1] Games were at Recreation Park, off Brush Street, and the club operated out of the mayor's office because Mayor W.G. Thompson was also president of the team.[2] Frank Bancroft, who ran a downtown cigar store at Woodward and Jefferson, was the manager. Twelve hundred and eighty-five fans attended the home opener on 21 May 1881. The 'Detroits,' as they were known, won the pennant in 1887 and in a fifteen-game 'World Series' beat the St Louis Browns. Despite that success, finances forced Detroit out of the National League. Following a fifth-place finish in 1888, the franchise moved to Cleveland.

A new team was formed in the International Association, winning a pennant in 1889 and finishing second in 1890. Then the city was out of baseball from 1891 until 1894, when Ban Johnson awarded it a spot in the Western League, which he was reorganizing. In 1900 Johnson changed the name to the 'American League' and the following season gained major-league recognition for the circuit.

During its sojourn in the Western League, Detroit played first at a park on the eastern city limits at Helen and Lafayette (then Champlain). It then moved to its present site at the intersection of Michigan and Trumbull on 28 April 1896. The park was christened 'Bennett Park' after Charley Bennett, a Tiger catcher of the 1880s whose career tragically ended when he lost a foot and a leg under a train. The wooden stands held barely 8500 people, not including those in 'wildcat' bleachers across the field. A Michigan blue law, strictly enforced in Detroit, prevented Sunday games within the city limits. Those contests were at Burns Park on Dix Road, which was then in Springwell Township west of Detroit. The team was also acquiring its present nickname of 'Tigers,' which the *Detroit Free Press* used in a headline on 16 April 1895. The Gothic 'D' (popularly called the 'English D') was first displayed on Tiger uniforms about the same time.

Detroit's first game in the new American Major League on 25 April 1901 included the greatest ninth-inning comeback in major-league history.[3] Trailing 13–4 before the remnants of a crowd estimated at 10,000, the Tigers scored ten runs in the ninth. First baseman Frank Dillon doubled home the tying and winning runs to give the Tigers their first victory in the American League, 14–13 over Milwaukee. The Tigers finished third their first year for owner and county sheriff James D. Burns, despite committing 425 errors, a club record that may never be broken. Tyrus Raymond Cobb, then eighteen years old, joined the Tigers on 30 August 1905. William Yawkey, uncle and foster father of Tom Yawkey, who later owned the Boston Red Sox, paid Augusta of the Sally League $750 for Cobb's contract. Hugh 'Ee-yah' Jennings became manager in 1907. He and Cobb led the Tigers to three straight pennants and three straight World Series losses.

A home attendance total of merely 297,079 fans in 1907 led Yawkey to sell to his bookkeeper Frank Navin a half-interest in the team for $40,000. Navin became president and held that post until his death on 13 November 1935. Between 1911 and 1912, Bennett Park and some nearby houses were razed and Navin Field built on the expanded site. The diamond was turned around, with home plate moved from what is now right field. A single-deck concrete grandstand seating 23,000 replaced wooden structures that were taxed when 14,000 showed up. Navin Field became double-decked from first to third in 1924 – the same year that future Hall of Famer Charlie Gehringer joined the team. The lower deck remains part of today's edifice.

Many other teams replaced their wooden parks with larger concrete and steel stadiums. Crowds had become much larger (50 million, 1900–10), fire was a real danger in wooden parks (the old Polo Grounds were levelled in a dramatic fire in April 1911), and technological innovations of reinforced concrete in heavy construction permitted new architecture. Within five years, clubs built a dozen highly individualistic new parks.[4] Accessibility, surrounding neighborhoods, and room for expansion were among the criteria for sites.

Detroit's new park was dedicated on 20 April 1912. George Mullin pitched the Tigers' first no-hitter on 4 July that year and Cobb batted .410 for the season. Detroit players also struck for one day after Ban Johnson suspended Cobb for punching a fan in New York. A pick-up aggregation of sandlotters in Tiger uniforms ('replacement players') absorbed the worst beating in the club's history, 24–2, at Philadelphia on 16 May. The next day the regular Tigers returned and the 'strike' fizzled.

In 1920 Walter O. Briggs (known as W.O. to his contemporaries) bought a share in the Tigers and by 1927 was an equal partner with Navin, although he deferred to the latter. From 1912 to 1933, despite twelve batting championships, the Tigers finished above fourth only five times, the last time in 1924. Then, in 1934, Walter Briggs loaned the Detroit Baseball Club $100,000 to purchase Mickey Cochrane from Connie Mack's A's; the loan stipulated that the money could be used only to purchase Cochrane.[5]

With Cochrane as catcher-manager, the Tigers won a team-record 101 games and captured the 1934 pennant with a seven-game margin over New York. Schoolboy Rowe set a record with 16 straight mound victories, while Gehringer hit .356 and Hank Greenberg .339. In the World Series, the Tigers lost to the 'Gas House Gang' of the St Louis Cardinals in seven games. Its finale produced the 'garbage shower' aimed at the Cardinals' Joe Medwick. With the Tigers trailing 9–0, Medwick had a confrontation with Tiger third baseman Mickey Owen after sliding into third. When Medwick returned to left field, fruits and vegetables pelted down from the bleacher section added for the Series. Play was suspended, and Commissioner Landis ordered Medwick off the field. The Tigers lost 11–0, and Detroit carried a stigma of fan violence thereafter.

The following year, the Tigers finally won their first world championship and drew more than a million fans at home for the first time. After a 93-58 season, they defeated the Cubs in a six-game World Series, with Cochrane scoring the winning run in the ninth inning of the last game on a single by Goose Goslin. A massive celebration followed, marking perhaps not just the world championship but a respite from the Depression as well.

Upon Frank Navin's death in 1935, the club passed exclusively into the hands of the Briggs family for the next two decades. On hearing of Navin's death, Briggs sent Harry Sisson, his business manager, with a cheque for the exact amount of book value plus $100,000 to Navin's family at the hospital. 'I've wanted all my life to own the Tigers. If he's not dead, they won't take the cheque.' Sisson later said: 'Maybe he wanted to help out with the funeral expenses.'[6] For the 1938 season the Tigers' home became Briggs Stadium, with a seating capacity of more than 53,000 and a total capacity of 58,000. It was to be recognized for decades as one of baseball's finest parks. In 1940 the Tigers won the last pre-war pennant (90-64), nosing out Cleveland by one game. They lost the World Series in seven games to the Cincinnati Reds, however, losing 2–1 in the final game.

Although the Tigers had won only one World Series, the individual exploits of Cobb, Harry Heilmann, Tommy Bridges, Gehringer, Cochrane, Rowe, and Billy Rogell became a part of the hagiography of Detroit baseball. A plaque outside the stadium commemorated Cobb, who won twelve batting titles in thirteen years (1907–19). Interviewers and biographers glorified him. Only recently has his violence become well known.[7] Fan ballots to the *Detroit News* chose an all-time Tiger team in 1969: Greenberg, Gehringer, Rogell, Kell, Heilmann, Cobb, Kaline, and Cochrane in the field, McLain and Newhouser on the mound. They selected Cobb as the greatest player, 9193 votes to 3928 for Kaline. Sixteen years later Rick Ferrell, Ernie Harwell, and Eli Zaret from Channel 4 and former sports editors of the three major Detroit newspapers, Edgar Hayes, Lyall Smith, and Joe Falls, named a nearly identical team, with Alan Trammell replacing Rogell at shortstop, and John Hiller added as relief pitcher.[8]

Player exploits lived on, in part, because of continuity off the field. Briggs rewarded Bridges and Rowe before the days of baseball pensions by naming them coaches after the war. Rogell became a city councilman and served for three decades. Gehringer became general manager in 1951. Heilmann broadcast Tiger baseball on radio from 1934 until his death in 1950. (For a list of Tiger broadcasters and stations, see appendix 4.) Ty Tyson, who had broadcast the games from 1927 to 1942, then returned for a year. Heilmann regaled his listeners with anecdotes from his playing days of the 1920s. H.G. Salsinger, who was born in 1885 and began covering the Tigers in 1909, was still reminding readers of his favorite player, Ty Cobb, and the glories of the past in his column 'The Umpire' in the 1950s. Salsinger never ventured into the clubhouse and, in his last years, was living in the past. He disliked radio (television wasn't enough of a factor to concern him), but described the game with authority and was the first regional sports writer to win the J.G. Taylor Spink Award from the Baseball Writers Association of America, post-humously in 1968.[9]

In the year that Detroit entered the National League, it was a provincial trading center of 116,000 people,[10] reliant on Great Lakes shipping and related manufacturing. The community more than doubled to 286,000 in 1890 and nearly doubled again to 466,000 in 1910, with most of its residents being foreign born. The automobile industry that drove Detroit's economy also came to town in that period and helped make Detroit 'the greatest ball town in the country.'[11] Forty per cent of Detroit's industrial workers and half of its industrial product were based in the auto industry in 1914, as against 3 per cent a decade earlier. The first significant black migration occurred to this 'city of promise' during the First World War. After the war, the city quadrupled its area, incorporating the areas north of Grand Boulevard to extend to its present Eight Mile Road limits. It became the fourth largest city in the United States in 1920. The assessed value of 'dynamic Detroit' soared from $244 million in 1900 to $3.1 billion in 1926. Olympia Stadium, the Institute of Arts, City Airport, and the Livernois-McNichols Campus of the University of Detroit opened in 1927 – the year that Babe Ruth hit sixty home runs and American Legion baseball began in Detroit. Within a year the Fisher and Penobscot buildings opened their doors. The national media was spellbound by Detroit's vitality.[12]

Amidst prosperity and expansion, some sour notes sounded. An economic downturn led to lay-offs in the auto plants in 1927, which then had more than one-quarter of a million employees in Michigan. The city struggled to adjust its institutions, sanitation facilities, and transportation for all the newcomers. Social dislocation and poverty led to increasing crime, social unrest, and general concern. The eighty-nine murders in 1917 approximated the average for the 1950s. A 'boom or bust' economy with dependence on the automobile industry, tensions between established citizens and immigrants, fears of crime, increasing unionization, and beleaguered social services troubled Detroit then as they would in later generations.

The Depression struck hard. Unemployment throughout Michigan reached 40 per cent in 1931. Employment in Detroit's auto industry had fallen to less than 40 per cent of the 1923–5 average by Roosevelt's inauguration. Unemployment and lowered wages led to attempts to organize labor. Violence and strikes, in turn, brought condemnation of 'communist ringleaders of riots,'[13] and national scrutiny of the least unionized industrial city in the country. These problems became a major concern of a Tiger owner when one of the most bitter and violent confrontations occurred at Briggs Manufacturing.

Briggs Manufacturing was founded in 1909 in a small two-storey building on Clay Avenue and grew into the world's largest independent producer of automobile bodies. For the first ten years it 'finished' bodies. In 1919 it made its first complete bodies. Between 1914 and 1921 it expanded to Hamtramck and Cleveland; it added the Mack Avenue plant, its largest, in 1923.[14]

In January 1933 workers were being paid at the Briggs plant only when the production line was running – sometimes only two or three hours a day – and management had reduced their wages at least twice. That month 9000 workers walked out, putting an additional 60,000 out of work. Briggs refused to negotiate and hired strike-breakers, who performed their service violently but effectively. The production line was running again the next month, and wages increased to 25 cents per hour, but half of those who had struck lost their jobs. To his death, Briggs never understood the strike and believed he had done the workers a favor by keeping the plant open despite declining sales. He also paid his workers partly in scrip so they could not waste money and deprive their families.[15] This paternalistic attitude, which was typical of nineteenth-century manufacturing, carried over to Briggs's perspective and policies towards 'his' baseball team.

The Second World War brought an artificial boost to Detroit's economy and new immigration. About 300,000 whites – mainly from the South – and about 50,000 blacks sought work at war plants in the first eighteen months after U.S. entry. The Willow Run plant, twenty-seven miles from downtown, employed 20,000 workers. Detroit became known as the 'Arsenal of Democracy.' Because Washtenaw County did not want its pristine environment disturbed by housing for these workers, Detroit's first major expressway (now I-94) was begun in 1942, although it was not completed until 1945. Its task was to take people from Wayne to Washtenaw County.[16] Detroit constructed a network of expressways after the war, but these transported suburbanites to jobs in Detroit. The automobile brought prosperity to Detroit, but it eventually provided the means for an urban exodus.

Migration also increased racial tension. In August 1942 *Life* warned that 'Detroit is dynamite,' and secret federal reports predicted trouble in northern cities where black and white immigrants were in competition for jobs. Southern whites were used to segregated facilities and privilege by race. Although housing and neighborhoods were effectively segregated in Detroit, washrooms, transportation, and public institutions were not. Nevertheless, blacks remained in menial jobs despite the establishment of the Fair Employment Practices Commission. On 11 April 1943, 10,000 people attended an 'equal opportunity' rally at Cadillac Square. Shortly afterward, at least 25,000[17] white workers walked out at the Packard plant after three blacks insisted that they receive promotions due them to positions previously reserved for whites. Racial tensions finally exploded on 20 June 1943 at Belle Isle, and federal troops arrived to quell disturbances. Nine whites and twenty-five blacks died. On 15 July, Attorney-General Francis Biddle's report to the president recommended that 'careful consideration be given to limiting, and in some instances putting an end to, Negro migration into communities which cannot absorb them ... It would seem pretty clear that no more Negroes should move to Detroit.'[18] In the same year Mayor Jeffries forbade the Housing Commission to allow blacks into white neighborhoods. 'Race-mixing' was to be prevented. Exclusion or isolation of blacks, rather than equal opportunity, became official policy.

Rather than returning to the segregated South as many southern whites did, immigrant blacks remained in Detroit after the war. Thirty-four per cent of them versus 10 per cent of whites lived below the poverty line in Detroit during the 1950s. They would not have been better off in the South, however. Of the 225,000 new citizens that Detroit gained in the 1940s, 150,000 were black. From about 9 per cent of the population in 1940, blacks composed 16 per cent in 1950 and 29 per cent in 1960. Both the absolute number of whites and the total population of Detroit declined during the 1950s for the first time.

THE CITY AFTER THE WAR

Although prosperity soon returned after the war, Detroit suffered immediate postwar adjustments. Price increases exceeded wage increases during the war. The value of Detroit's assessed property in 1945 was almost $1 billion less than it had been in 1930. A $730 million capital improvement program seemed enormous, but it included no funds for public transportation. The last streetcar ran in 1955. Eight thousand new houses were built annually, but that number was less than the pre-war average and many more were being built in the suburbs. 'Slums' were 'cleared,' first near Hastings, then in Corktown around the ballpark, but little adequate new housing was built despite discount sales of property to developers.[19] 'Urban blight' became part of local parlance.

On 11 November 1945 a strike by 200,000 workers shut down 96 General Motors plants nationally for 113 days. Strike-breakers beat union leaders outside the Briggs plant the same year. Nationally, 4.6 million workers went on strike in 1946. Chrysler and Ford experienced shutdowns in 1948 and 1949 respectively. Detroit was the most unionized city in the United States and benefited from new wage contracts that increased wages three times as fast as consumer prices from 1949 to 1961, but jobs were disappearing with the increase of car imports by the late 1950s (imports rose from 57,000 to 445,000, 1955–60). Even during good times increased automation meant that rising car production was not creating new jobs. Especially threatened were low- or unskilled jobs, which decreased by 13 per cent in the 1950s. Closings of Packard and Hudson cost the east side alone 71,000 jobs by the early 1960s. Skilled workers received good wages, but there were wide disparities within Detroit. Median white family income rose to $7219 in 1960, but it was only $4385 for black families and $2640 in the ghettos. The Detroit economy reacted to every fluctuation in the auto industry.

Forty million cars were registered nationally in 1950 and 62 million in 1962, as against 25 million in 1945. The increased number of autos, creation of the new Edsel Ford and John Lodge Expressways (in 1950) to serve them, higher wages in the industry, and government housing loans permitted Detroiters to seek out the suburbs. Twenty-five per cent of white Detroiters – nearly a half million of them – moved during the 1950s to suburbs, notably Dearborn and Warren where exclusionary housing policies maintained. Twenty new auto plants opened in the suburbs from 1947 to 1955. Symbolically, Northland, opened in 1953, became the first suburban shopping center in the United States. Within the city, freeways shattered neighborhoods and reduced the tax base.

Two Detroits were developing by the late 1940s – a thriving metropolitan area surrounding a poor central city.[20] Suburbanization, decentralization of the automobile industry, regional shopping centres, a shift of capital, great wealth juxtaposed to abject poverty, racial tensions, and a tender economy were not only changing the nature of the city and its environs but also impinging on major-league baseball, which was very much a part of the community of Detroit. Detroit was 'less a big city than a federation of ethnic villages bound together by auto plants ... with more bowling alleys than any other metropolis in the country. The only hint of sophistication was downtown ... Detroiters held an awe and affection for their downtown that was unmatched in other cities. The touchstone was Hudson's Department Store.'[21]

Another touchstone was Briggs Stadium. Baseball often gave the community hope and brought disparate groups together. After the World Series victory of 1945 a *Detroit News* editorial reflected: 'The fact remains that there is a strange, almost mystical, connection between Detroit's fortunes in the world of sport and the state of the local mind and morale.' It also quoted the *Washington Post*, which had written: 'It is precisely because it makes no great difference to the future of civilization ... that these contests are so valuable. They offer us a sort of catharsis for the tensions of our prejudices and our fears.'[22]

PRIDE AND PATERNALISM

The Tigers had a unique relationship with the city of Detroit. Amidst all the change within and around their city, Detroiters took pride in Detroit's reputation as one of the great baseball towns in the country. Roger Angell, columnist for the *New Yorker* and the finest literary stylist about the game, wrote: 'Detroit in the 1930s had few visible economic virtues, but it may just have been the best baseball town in the country.' Similarly, in 1949 J.G. Taylor Spink observed: 'Detroit is the best baseball city in the country,' and two years later remarked on the enthusiasm there.[23]

The *New York Times* was no less enthusiastic about Detroit in the 1950s. Arthur Daley thought that the Detroit Tigers were 'a franchise most diamond men considered the best in baseball.'[24] John Drebinger described Detroit as 'one of the finest and soundest franchises in the major leagues, peaked in tradition, rich in worldly goods.'[25] The *Times* could be snobbish in its praise, however: 'this is easily one of the top baseball towns in the nation, if not actually the best,' because industrial workers there enjoyed good wages and had rather simple tastes.[26] The *Times*'s portrayal implied that Detroiters loved baseball because the city had little else to offer; the fans were beer-drinking factory workers for whom sports were a distraction from their dreary existence. This myth of allegiance to baseball in Detroit deriving from the working-class composition of the city has persisted to this day.

But the popularity of baseball cut across class lines as did the popularity of other sports. (Both University of Michigan football and Detroit Lions professional football drew large crowds and captured attention in the sports pages.) Opening Day was a major social event, and people dressed up for night baseball in the 1950s.[27] When the Tigers won the World Series in 1968 and had the highest advance season-ticket sales the following year, *Sports Illustrated* reminded its readers that 'few cities in the country have cared so much throughout the years as Detroit.'[28] WDIV-TV picked opening day for its biggest party in 1984, at the Roostertail, with top hats required.[29] A decade later Mitch Albom observed that the city was 'most alive' on opening day.[30] Whoever you were, Tiger baseball mattered in Detroit.

Attendance at Navin Field and Briggs Stadium justified these accolades. In 1935, 1,034,929 Detroiters bought tickets at Navin Field; they represented 27 per cent of total attendees for the American League that year. In 1945, the Tigers accounted for 23 per cent of American League attendance, and, in 1950, 22 per cent when the Tigers again made a run at the pennant. Between 1934 and 1962, only once, in 1953, did the Tigers draw fewer than 1,000,000 fans and only in 1952 less than the league average (table 5 lists attendance, 1945–95).[31] There was even talk of bringing a second major-league team into Detroit in 1958 because of its metropolitan population base, which was the largest among single-team cities in the 1950 census, and because of the popularity of baseball in Detroit.[32] Detroit newspapers printed Tiger scores on page one. They regularly covered Federation Baseball and high-school teams even during the Tiger pennant race of 1950. Detroiters took pride in 'their' team. So did the owner in 'his' team. Both regarded the team as a personal possession. Years later, owners and the city would clash about 'ownership' rights, but there was little conflict during the Walter Briggs era.

Briggs and the city shared a common interest in the team. As a young man, Walter O. Briggs had been unable to get tickets to the Tigers' first World Series in 1907; he never forgot that. H.G. Salsinger, who was a close friend of W.O., reported that on the day Briggs became sole owner he said: 'I am not in baseball to make money. My one purpose is to give Detroit the best team in the finest park in the country. I am just a fan.' Arthur Daley described him as 'baseball's number one fan.'[33] Briggs achieved what most fans could only dream about. He owned a ball club and could do with it pretty much as he pleased.

He pleased to make his operation a showcase. 'Briggs Stadium was the best maintained baseball plant in the country'[34] in the late 1940s and the early 1950s, with an underground sprinkler, the first nylon tarp, and annual paint jobs. Tiger offices were 'palatial and the swankiest in the business.'[35] The Tigers paid stadium personnel $200,000 annually in the 1950s to keep it that way.[36] Briggs did not like the idea of football 'tearing up his field,' but followed his son Spike's advice to rent the park to the Lions because of a notion of civic solidarity. As he sat in his box by the dugout, he timed the groundskeepers during rain delays. He 'ran things to his death and tolerated no shenanigans.'[37]

Briggs also received recognition as the owner of the Tigers that he would not have had as simply owner of Briggs Manufacturing. A police motorcycle escort accompanied him everywhere from at least 1940. He chaired the Community Chest campaign in 1948. He built St Hugo's School, where his family attended, in Bloomfield Hills and sent announcer Harry Heilmann and baseball stars to its athletic awards night. He decreed that clergy were to be admitted without charge to the ballpark. Special days rewarded safety-patrol boys, boy scouts, and even altar boys. Although his wife or his son Spike initiated much of the charity work,[38] Walter O. Briggs was a very visible part of the Detroit community. His death was headline news in the local newspapers. The national press ran obituaries, and national figures attended his funeral. Auxiliary Bishop Babcock, who was visiting him in Florida at his death, gave him the last rites of the Catholic church. Briggs had converted to Catholicism at age sixty and was both a 33rd Degree Mason and a Knight of Malta. He might have agreed with the observation that George Steinbrenner made years later: 'When you're a shipbuilder no one pays attention to you, but when you own the New York Yankees, they do and I love it.'[39]

Briggs was rich enough that the Detroit Baseball Club did not have to make money, but he was enough of a businessman that it did. The team showed a profit every single year during Briggs's ownership (table 6). Between 1945 and 1951 the team showed a return of as much as 25 per cent of gross revenues.[40] About 80 per cent of the club's income derived from gate receipts in 1947; that reduced to 65 per cent in 1956. The remainder came from broadcasting income and concessions (table 7).

The team was well paid. In the late 1940s the Tigers' payroll was second to the Yankees', and it may have exceeded the Yankees' payroll one year. Including players and managers, the Detroit payroll exceeded $500,000 from 1946 to 1951 (table 8). Tigers' players' salaries, excluding coaches and managers, totaled $477,000 in 1947.[41] Mickey Briggs observed: 'If my grandfather had the highest paid team he thought he had the best team.' W.O. raised Bobo Newsom's salary to $32,500 after 1940 to top Bob Feller's salary. Later he raised Hal Newhouser's salary to $60,000, again to top Feller's. He cut both those salaries after bad seasons.[42] Performance bonuses were common too. He gave Hank Greenberg suits and a $10,000 bonus in 1940; he gave another $10,000 bonus to Ted Gray after a stellar weekend performance. Such largesse applied only to stars. The average player was fortunate to receive $10,000; only stars made $15,000. As Virgil Trucks put it: 'There were no real negotiations for salaries. There was an abundance of ball players and they flat out told you and that was it. Writers never asked players what the salaries were and printed what management told them.'[43] It was a highly personal and paternalistic ownership. Players were like sons who might be rewarded, punished, or ignored.

The treatment of three players is illustrative of this personal style of ownership and the power that owners had over players. Rufus Gentry was a promising journeyman. He pitched 204 innings for the Tigers in 1944 and held out for a $1000 raise. When the Tigers refused the raise, he declined to sign a contract. The reserve clause prevented him from seeking out another team. The result was that he sat out the entire 1945 season, missing both his salary and a World Series share that year. He returned in 1946, but pitched only ten innings for the remainder of his career.[44]

At the other extreme was Dick Wakefield, the first of the bonus boys, who signed a Tigers contract for a reported $52,000 bonus. He hit .316 for the Tigers in 1943 and then in an abbreviated season, when he was drafted into the armed forces in 1944, hit .355. He never hit .300 again and was a part-time player for the Tigers until his trade to the New York Yankees in 1950. He remained a favorite of Mrs Briggs, whom he called 'Ma.' She occasionally picked him up with her chauffeur on the way to the ballpark. He was the only ballplayer that Mickey Briggs could remember who talked about money, asking regularly, 'How are the Briggs's dividends?'[45] He flaunted money in the clubhouse and had kids deliver pennies to pay a couple of hundred dollars' fine. Threatened with a fine of $25 per step for walking in the locker room on his spiked shoes, he peeled off the money for the fine while still walking. Contemporary players said: 'Wakefield had all the talent but didn't care.' When told that if he didn't hustle he'd be out of baseball, he reportedly replied: 'Yes, but I'll be driving a limousine.'[46] Clearly out of the control of managers, disliked by his fellow players, and criticized in the press,[47] he was an untouchable for many years because of his relations with the Briggs family.

Despite some fan prejudice against his Jewish heritage, Hank Greenberg had been a Briggs favorite and fan favorite until a picture of Greenberg in a New York Yankee uniform appeared in newspapers in 1946. The picture had been taken in August of 1943 when Greenberg was in the service, but Dan Daniel used it in 1946, reporting that Greenberg wanted to finish his career with the Yankees. Detroit sold Greenberg's contract to the Pittsburgh Pirates within weeks. Mickey Briggs leaves no doubt that it was because W.O. was offended by the publicity. It was 'a snap decision that he should later have apologized for but never did. Greenberg was sent to the National League so he couldn't hurt us.'[48] Ira Berkow recounts the event:

Walter Briggs 'hinted that the sale ... might have been influenced by national publicity of a week ago suggesting that Greenberg might like to finish his major league career ... with the Yankees.' In a statement to the press Briggs said: 'In light of recent happenings, it was felt that a change of scenery might prove highly beneficial to player Henry Greenberg and the Detroit club ...'

Billy Evans, the *Detroit Times* reported, 'declared' that 'all seven American League clubs were interested in his contract at that figure, making it possible for us to send him to the National League.

'Several years ago Jack Zeller, the general manager of the Tigers, attempted to sell Greenberg to the Yankees, but the Yanks were reluctant to assume his high salary contract at that time ...'

On the following day, January 19, Larry MacPhail, president of the Yankees, refuted Evans's contentions: 'We did not claim Greenberg because Detroit would not let us have him on waivers. All we would have accomplished by claiming him was to keep Greenberg on the Detroit club or some other American League club other than New York ...

'We approached Detroit last fall, [and twice more] regarding Greenberg. The Detroit club had no intention of letting Greenberg come to New York, except in a player deal which would help them and hurt us.

'When we made up our minds that we couldn't get Greenberg we decided not to claim him and backed a National League deal. We would rather leave Greenberg at Pittsburgh than at Detroit.'[49]

Greenberg recalled his treatment: 'I thought he [Briggs] had a lot of Detroit newspaper people in his hip pocket and they started to write derogatory columns about me. He got very annoyed with this unappreciative slave who had worked for him and whom he had treated so grandly.'[50]

Thus, one journeyman who chose to challenge the authority of ownership was effectively banished from baseball. Another player who caused problems in the clubhouse and never lived up to his reputation remained because of his relations with the family. A third star and former favorite was punished for his 'disloyalty.'

The Tigers received nothing in return for Greenberg, but they did make two major trades in the late 1940s – one of the best of the decade and one of the worst. Briggs had a hand in both. In the favorable trade he yielded to better advice; in the second he did not. In May 1946 the

Tigers traded Barney McCosky, a local boy and a favorite of Walter, to the Philadelphia Athletics for George Kell, who had hit .396 in the minors. Kell played with the Tigers for seven years, won the batting championship in 1949, and later became a Hall of Famer and a Tiger broadcaster. Connie Mack apparently suggested the trade; Spike Briggs supported it, as did Wish Egan, Detroit's premier scout. Egan later said: 'I was a little ashamed of myself for taking advantage of the old man.'[51]

On 10 November 1948 the Detroit Tigers and Chicago White Sox made a trade that has been described as 'the worst trade the Tigers ever made,' and 'the most lopsided of the decade' – that of pitcher Billy Pierce to the Chicago White Sox for catcher Aaron Robinson.[52] Briggs felt the Tigers needed a catcher to challenge for the pennant. The year before the Tigers had traded Birdie Tebbetts to Boston for Hal Wagner. Tebbetts played four years for Boston, never hitting below .270, but Wagner was a disappointment. Briggs remembered the Cochrane trade that had brought the Tigers two pennants and a world championship. He wanted immediate help because the farm system was in disarray and because he thought each year he was going to die;[53] by then he was in a wheelchair. The Tigers could have sent either Art Houtteman or Ted Gray instead of Pierce, but both Gray and Houtteman were native Detroiters.[54] Robinson hit .269, .226, and .207 in two and one half years with the Tigers; Gray's career record was 59-74; Pierce won 211 games in his career. Robinson was also guilty of a crucial blunder of not tagging Bob Lemon, sliding in from third base, in a critical 2–1 loss to Cleveland in the last week of the 1950 pennant race. The Tigers did not win another pennant in W.O.'s lifetime.

Other Briggs favorites included Kell, Hoot Evers, and Newhouser. None as traded until Walter's death despite press concerns that the Detroit Tigers were getting too old and that a country-club atmosphere had developed on the Tigers.[55] Charlie Gehringer criticized Walter O. Briggs's 'meddling' after his death. 'He wasn't good for the team.'[56]

TROUBLE ON THE FARM

In the era before teams signed 'bonus boys' or recruited from colleges, almost all future major leaguers passed through the minor leagues. Branch Rickey built his great St Louis Cardinals teams of the 1930s and

Brooklyn Dodgers teams of the 1940s on an elaborate farm system that fed his major-league teams. The Tigers tried to follow his path.

The Detroit Tigers had eleven farm clubs, second only to the Yankees' twelve and the Dodgers' fourteen in 1941.[57] Then they got caught 'covering up' minor-league players by having their minor-league affiliates hold players' contracts for them. Secret agreements permitted control of two clubs in the Texas League (Beaumont and Fort Worth) and two in the Evangeline League (Alexandria and Lake Charles). 'Detroit practically controlled Toledo player acquisitions and transfers ...; Toledo acting mainly as a "covering-up" agent for Detroit.'[58] Detroit had to pay $47,250 to fourteen players in lieu of free agency and ninety-one players were given free agency. The *Free Press* concluded that Jack Zeller, general manager of the Tigers 'did more of the forbidden thing than other general managers,' but 'no player was hurt by this action.'[59] One player who was originally freed and then returned to the Tigers was 'Dizzy' Trout, who asked, 'How can they take nine months to decide that I am not a free agent and fifteen minutes to decide that I am?' Salsinger later reported that Trout was covered up by Frank Navin himself and that Judge Landis had protected Navin by not releasing Trout. Salsinger went on to comment: 'Detroit is not the only club that has covered up talent, it has long been a common practice.'[60] That was true enough, for years later there were continued complaints, even by general managers, of hoarding and of 'judicious juggling of players.'[61] That did not excuse Detroit's violation of baseball's rules.

Under George Trautman, who replaced Jack Zeller in 1947 and later became commissioner of the minor leagues, and then under Billy Evans, the Tigers attempted to rebuild the farm system. Once again they were caught in an illegal arrangement – this time with the Dallas ball club of the Texas League, which had a working agreement with the Tigers, beginning in September 1945 and signed by Zeller. The commissioner's office's official judgment stated: 'There is not the slightest doubt that the rights to the contracts of these players were asserted by the Detroit clubs and that the movements of these players have been entirely directed by the officials of the Detroit Baseball Company contrary to the laws of baseball.'[62] Evans, who had been in baseball forty-two years and was a former umpire, was officially exonerated for a 'mistake' that he had inherited.[63]

Evans may have inherited that 'mistake,' but he violated baseball law on other occasions. George Lerchen was dispatched to a Detroit farm affiliate on 21 March 1949 after having been in spring training only twelve days. Major-league rules required his being there twenty days before he could be sent to the minors. The league office called Lerchen and asked him if he wanted free agency because the Tigers had violated contractual obligations. Lerchen went to Evans, who said to him, 'Here is an extra fifty dollars. Sign these papers which are dated April 1st.' Four players later received a release from the Flint team for similar violations.[64] Despite these machinations and spending $274,000 on player development in 1949, the Tiger farm system was dry in the early 1950s. Mickey Briggs says that the farm system was never a priority for W.O., who worried that he might die before young players reached the majors. The Tigers decreased spending to $205,000 on player development in 1950 – $98,000 of which went to base salaries in the minor leagues.[65] Jim Campbell, who had joined the Tigers in December 1949 after graduation from Ohio State University and worked at Tiger farm clubs in Thomasville, Georgia, Toledo, and Buffalo, was appointed farm director of the Tigers on 22 December 1951. He would rebuild the Tigers' farm system in the 1950s, but it would take years for it to produce major-league talent (chapter 3).

The dollars spent on farm clubs was small change within the Tigers' total income of $2,000,000. It was also a small amount compared to the bonuses laid out to two individual players before the bonus era of the 1950s and 1960s. Wakefield's $52–55,000 was the largest bonus of its time. Lou Kretlow, who was described as the best service prospect by the National Baseball Congress, reportedly received between $25,000 and $30,000 from the Tigers in 1946.[66] Kretlow won six games for the Tigers. In 1950 the Tigers set another record, giving catcher Frank House $50,000 and two cars; House never hit above .259 in five and one-half years with the Tigers. Other players resented him because he could have a car, which they could not afford, and because of his manicured nails.[67] The Tigers spent freely but perhaps not too wisely in an attempt at a quick fix to win one last pennant for Walter O. Briggs. They violated rules, but in the cosy atmosphere of major-league baseball of the time, no one seemed to mind. The establishment Detroit press, represented by H.G. Salsinger, and even the league office protected first Navin and then Evans.

DRAWING CROWDS

Little of that mattered to the fans. Baseball was booming in Detroit. Federation baseball was popular too. Five players from the Michigan Trumbull championship team and eleven players from Joe Gentile's teams eventually played in the majors. Three thousand teams played sandlot baseball, and eight or nine scouts regularly visited Northwestern Field to search out future major leaguers. The Tigers supported amateur baseball by annual benefit exhibition games and enlisted Councilman and former Tiger Billy Rogell to establish clinics at Detroit schools 'to develop ballplayers ... and reduce juvenile delinquency.'[68]

The Tigers led the league in average attendance between 1945 and 1950, with nearly 1.6 million fans annually. *The Sporting News* applauded the Tigers after their last place finish in 1953 for having one of the best advance sales in the league without organized fanfare.[69] With baseball generally so popular, the Tigers had only to 'open the gates and let them come.' They spent, on average, less than $50,000 annually (2 per cent of total expenses) between 1952 and 1956 on advertising and public relations.[70] Doc Fenkell remembered inheriting an empty file cabinet from his predecessor as public relations director, who told Fenkell his main job would be to keep Briggs's name out of the newspapers.[71] They did not have to market the team then, but the Tigers became over-confident in their appeal. The policy of 'open the gates and let them come' would serve them badly when they had to compete with other sports and other forms of entertainment for the loyalty of the next generation of fans and when the demographics of the city changed.

According to Mickey Briggs, it was Spike Briggs who convinced Walter to play some games at night because some workers could not attend any day games. The Tigers were the last team in the American League to play at night. When they did it was a great success. In the first three years of night baseball between 1948 and 1950, the Tigers drew just more than 1.8 million fans to its fourteen annual night games – one-third of their total attendance for those years. The first night game on 15 June 1948 was attended by 54,480 fans. It did not begin until 9:30 p.m. because management feared that the lights would not take effect before total darkness had set in. A 4–1 victory over the Philadelphia Athletics behind Newhouser sent the fans home happy.

Baseball was inexpensive entertainment, appropriate for a blue-collar city. In 1950 a box seat could still be had for $2.50, a reserve seat for $1.75, general admission was $1.20, and a bleacher seat 60¢. The Tigers kept back for every game 20,000 of the cheaper general admission and bleacher seats to accommodate the last-minute fan and to make the game available to the working man. The Tigers were also reluctant to spend money to process mail orders.[72] Games still started at 3 p.m., reflecting the old ten-hour working day and shift work; the Tigers changed to a 2:30 start only in 1951. The *Detroit News* applauded that move because it would alleviate rush hour traffic in Detroit.[73]

Except for a few night games, baseball in Detroit was much like it had been twenty years before. But a new arrival would force change. WWJ-TV televised its first Tiger game in 1947. The game was miniaturized on a screen five and a half by eight inches in black and white and viewed mainly in bars. The *Detroit News* observed that 'it had flaws but was OK' and would be accepted like the automobile and the first radio broadcast.[74] The next year twenty-seven games were televised, while church groups protested brewery sponsorship. In 1949 forty-five games appeared on a total of 30,000 sets in the city watched by 100,000 people, mostly in bars. Detroit was the first to place a television camera behind home plate, sparking criticism of umpires' ball and strike calls.[75] There was no televising of Sunday, holiday, or night games and no long-term television contracts. *The Sporting News* observed that the Tigers turned down 'a lot of money for unlimited TV' because of the conservatism or 'traditionalism' of Briggs.[76]

THE COLOR LINE

Such conservatism or traditionalism reflected American society and the city of Detroit in the 1950s. But there was one area of change to which the Tigers were stubbornly resistant. That concerned the club's policy towards integration on the field. It is generally well known that the Tigers were the second-last team (Boston was the last) to place a black player on its major-league roster. Less well known is that the Tigers were the last team to sign a black player to any contract. That was Claude Agee, whose signing received only small notices in the *Detroit News* and

Detroit Free Press on 27 August 1953, eighteen months after the death of Walter O. Briggs. The delay was not accidental.

George Lerchen, who played with the Tigers and in their farm system in the late 1940s and early 1950s, said: 'It was well known that any scout who signed a colored player would be fired.'[77] Richard Bak quotes Edgar Hayes, sports editor of the *Detroit Times* from that period: 'The saying around the clubhouse was no jiggs with Briggs ... He was dead set against having any blacks play for him. The club did not even recruit minor leaguers until after Briggs died in 1952 and the club was sold.'[78] Michael Betzold wrote:

In Detroit's large and growing black community in the 1950s, the Briggs name was synonymous with racism. Though no definitive Briggs quote on the subject ever saw the light of print, many black Detroiters believed Walter Briggs had vowed never to have black players on the roster so long as he was in charge of the club.

Walter Briggs III vehemently denies the allegation. He said his father and grandfather were waiting for the right time and player and were afraid of fans' reactions to integration.

'They were just absolutely terrified that it would not work,' he says.[79]

Regarding the Briggs policy to exclude blacks from the Tiger roster, Jim Campbell would comment only that he himself was not based in Detroit until after Briggs's death. Ralph Snyder, who was in Detroit then, stated that if there was such a policy 'naturally it would not have been a written one.' In an interview in 1994, Walter Briggs III did not deny the allegation of exclusion as he is quoted as doing by Betzold. He said only that his grandfather's racial attitudes were 'typical of the time, like those of Henry Ford.' 'Segregation as a term was never used, the fear was: What if we bring in a Negro and he's not right? Grandfather did make the final decisions.'[80] Mickey Briggs simply described his grandfather's and Evans's attitude to black players as 'wrong.'[81]

Whether any policy was formally established, the Tigers did not sign any black player to any contract, even a minor-league one, until after W.O.'s death. Despite a policy of picking home-grown talent, the Tigers passed on two of Detroit's sandlot stars – Sammy Gee in 1947, who was signed by the Dodgers, and Roosevelt Evans.[82] Until 1945 Negro teams in Detroit had to play in Mack Park rather than in Briggs Stadium. General Manager Billy Evans, in an interview with the Detroit African American newspaper the *Michigan Chronicle*, set out Tiger policy rather clearly in 1951:

I know the Tigers are lagging but as I told the Chronicle two years ago, the question of hiring Negro ballplayers has never bothered us. I think it would be unreasonable to say that the Tigers would be better if they had Negro players. The Tigers got along many years without Negro players ... In fact, all the teams in the major leagues got along without colored players. [Attendance in Detroit remains 'tremendous' and sustains his 1949 prediction that Negroes would support the Tigers.] Where are there any good Negro players now available? [He denied Briggs issued a direction to hire only whites.] I'm not going to answer any third-degree questions. There are no plans at present that involve hiring of colored players.[83]

The white press never challenged Tiger policy. H.G. Salsinger contemplated the possibility of Negroes playing in the white major leagues. If they did, '[the Negro] would have to subdue his natural bent and inclination, Satchel Page couldn't have the rules. He ... does what he pleases, goes where he pleases ... Negro baseball is as distinctive as Duke Ellington music. To merge Negroes with whites would destroy the individual style that is their main asset.'[84] The *News* attacked Cleveland's signing of Larry Doby as a move to boost attendance; Bill Veeck had hired a 'snake charmer' as well. 'If Negroes are to have a place in organized baseball, they must prove themselves as capable as white players.'[85] In 1953 the *Free Press* published a series of four articles: 'Is there a Negro in Detroit Tigers' future?' by Lyall Smith, its sports editor. In the first article he wrote: 'Communist-front organizations, ever alert for methods of sowing discordant seeds have directed much of the frontal attack ... to the extreme dislike and embarrassment of prominent Negro groups and leaders.'[86] Two days later, he described the old Negro leagues as being 'full of laughs as well as being serious.' With regard to 'communist-front organizations,' Coleman Young is unfortunately correct in pointing out: 'The communists historically had been out in front in the struggle for civil rights. It seemed like the government [*Ed.:* one might say Detroit baseball as well] was unable to make any distinction between civil rights and subversion ... The paradoxical and alarmingly unconstitutional notion that the struggle for equality was inherently un-American.'[87]

African Americans in Detroit were interested in baseball. They sat in the right-centrefield bleachers in Briggs Stadium. But they searched elsewhere for a symbol to support. More than three hundred booked a train and travelled to Montreal in 1945 to see Jackie Robinson play. The *Michigan Chronicle* heralded Robinson's debut in the minors. Judge Damon Keith remembers travelling to Cleveland to see Larry Doby play and following National League teams, where the black stars were. Coleman Young remembers listening to Ty Tyson on radio: 'Jackie Robinson ... heightened our interest and expectations. The signing of Larry Doby focused attention on the Tigers.' Pickets outside of Briggs Stadium in 1946 demanded the signing of a black.[88]

Players of the time could accept blacks as their team-mates as we saw in chapter 1. Steve Gromek, a future Tiger, was pictured hugging Doby after his home run had won the fourth game of the World Series in Cleveland in 1948. People in his home town of Hamtramck asked, 'Why did you hug that guy? Why did you not kiss him?' He replied, 'Well he won a game for me.'[89] Among the Detroit players of the time, Jerry Davie, Bill Hoeft, Don Lund, and George Lerchen recalled their shock at how black players were baited, especially in the South and in the minors. What the Tigers meant by waiting for the right Negro to come along will always remain a bit of a mystery. But the policy left a legacy that would haunt the Tigers over the years, especially as the population of the city of Detroit became more multiracial.

In 1980 Gates Brown observed: 'Briggs ... The name doesn't set well in the black community. Say that name some places and you might get jumped on.'[90] Dr Edward Turner, long-time Detroiter and activist in the African American community, attributes suspicion of African Americans today towards the Detroit Baseball Club to the Briggs legacy. Both Reverend Jim Holley and Gates Brown believed that Doby had not been allowed to play in Detroit when he was a member of the Cleveland Indians.[91] Doby did, of course, play when Cleveland came to town, and neither Brown nor Holley was in Detroit at the time, but they had heard such a story. In his work on the subject, James Grier stressed the importance of abuses and insults of the past in shaping contemporary black consciousness.[92] The club would have had to make positive efforts to counter the myths – both founded and exaggerated – that derived from the Briggs era.

ON THE FIELD

On the field the Tigers enjoyed modest success but won no more pennants for Briggs. They played over .500 each year through 1950, finishing second in 1946, second in 1947, fifth in 1948, fourth in 1949, and second in 1950 before dropping below .500 to finish fifth in 1951 and then falling to last place for the first time in Tiger history in 1952 (table 9 lists the Tigers' won-lost records, 1945–95). The Tigers actually won more games in 1946 (92) than they had in 1945 (88). That year Newhouser finished 29-9 (1.94 ERA), belying taunts that his 1944 and 1945 achievements were due to the league's depleted talent during the war. Greenberg hit 44 home runs and drove in 127 runs in 1946 (23 of them to win games), but he was sold to Pittsburgh the following year because of Briggs's pique.

In 1947 an 18-8 May put the Tigers in the lead, but the Yanks took over on 16 June then won nineteen in a row in July, effectively ending the pennant race. Detroit ended this record streak on 18 July, 8–0 behind a two-hitter by Fred Hutchinson. The largest crowd in Tiger history (58,369) attended a Sunday doubleheader against the Yanks two days later. The Tigers soon abandoned doubleheaders, except as make-ups for rainouts, however, because they found that they could draw more fans in two games than in a single booking. In an 11–10 victory over St Louis on 5 September, a then record thirty-seven players were used and the eleven pitchers in the game – a modest number by today's standards – tied a major-league record.

The Tigers were around .500 during all of 1948. They suffered the ignominy of the first no-hitter pitched against them, by Bob Feller, on June 30. Although the Tigers were out of the pennant race, 57,788 fans attended a duel between Feller and Newhouser on 26 September.[93] A week later, in a second match-up, Newhouser beat Feller 7–1 in Cleveland to force the Indians into a playoff with the Boston Red Sox, which the Indians won for the pennant. Between 1946 and 1950 the Tigers drew eighteen crowds of more than 55,000 fans. After they eliminated standing room and seating in the third deck and seats near the right-field foul line (Kaline's Corner), they could draw only one more crowd of more than 55,000 – that on 27 June 1961, a twilight doubleheader against Chicago that brought 57,271.

The Tigers fell behind in the race early in 1949 and even an 18-2 streak in August could not raise them above fourth. That was the year Kell won the batting title on the last day over Ted Williams, .3429 to .3427. Boston's game had ended and Kell was assured the title if he did not bat in the ninth inning. The fourth scheduled hitter in the ninth, he was in the on-deck circle with one on and one out when Eddie Lake grounded into a double play, ending the Tiger season but giving Kell the batting title.

The Tigers made a valiant run at the pennant in 1950. They were in first place for 119 days, 82 days in succession; their maximum lead was four and a half games. On 26 July they were 51-26 and the *Free Press* was anticipating that they might surpass their 1934 record of 101 wins. Early in June they dropped two out of three in New York, 5–4 and then 11–4 when the Yankees scored seven in the ninth, but in the finale the Tigers scored eight runs in the sixth inning for a 13–7 win. The team returned to Briggs Stadium for a crucial four-game weekend series 23–25 June. Lyall Smith called the first game 'the greatest slugfest ever witnessed.' The teams hit eleven home runs, which accounted for all nineteen runs scored that night.[94] The Tigers hit four in the fourth inning – by Jerry Priddy, Vic Wertz, whose homer bounced off the right-field roof, and Hoot Evers and a grand slam by pitcher Dizzy Trout. Tommy Henrich put the Yanks ahead with a pinch-hit home run in the ninth, but Evers then hit an inside-the-park homer in the bottom of the ninth for a 10–9 Tiger victory. The Tigers won again the next day 4–1. The Sunday doubleheader drew 55,628 fans, who saw the Tigers lose the first game 8–2 but win the nightcap 6–3 on a three-run home run by Evers off Vic Raschi after another pinch-hit home run by Henrich had tied the game. There was a lot of scoring that year. Earlier in the month Boston had run up the following scores over a nine-game period: 11–5, 11–9, 17–7, 12–0, 4–8, 20–4, 29–4, 7–12, and 8–18, the last in a loss to Detroit.

Early in August the Tigers swept the Yankees, but then lost two of three in New York later that month, culminating a 4-8 eastern road swing that left the Yankees in first place. The Tigers had managed to lose nine of eleven games in one stretch by a single run. Then the teams met again in Detroit on 15 September. Johnny Mize hit three home runs, but the Tigers won 9–7 to take the lead. The next day, before 56,548 patrons, Whitey Ford beat the Tigers 8–1, putting the Yanks back in first. After a sweep against the A's the Tigers went to Cleveland where they lost three straight, 4–3, 10–2, and 2–1; at the same time the Yankees swept two in Boston. The Tigers were eliminated a week later on 30 September by Cleveland. The Tiger pennant race was front-page news in the Detroit newspapers through the heat of the summer.[95]

Ray Herbert and Houtteman were called into service because of the Korean War, Newhouser suffered an injury, and Evers was in a season-long slump in 1951. The Tigers spent 131 of the season's 167 days in fifth place. There were a couple of scoring binges. They defeated Cleveland on 7 July 13–3, getting twenty hits, but that came after eleven straight losses during which they only scored thirteen runs on fifty hits. Tiger run production dropped dramatically that year. They gave up only 28 more runs than they had in 1950 (741 vs. 713), but scored only 685 runs as against 837 the year before. The following year the offence completely collapsed, dropping .022 in average, finishing seventh in batting, and scoring only 557 runs while giving up 738. They finished last. The reasons most often given for the Tigers' failure in 1950 were a weak bench and the lack of relief pitching. Both of those problems would plague the Tigers throughout the 1950s.

Walter Briggs died in January 1952, so he did not have to suffer the basement finish. His great friend and another institution of Tiger baseball, Hall of Fame player and then announcer Harry Heilmann, had died the previous year, on 9 July. He was quoted as saying to Lyall Smith: 'I'm a sick man, Lyle [sic], but I'm an awfully happy one; I never knew anyone that had so many friends.'[96] He began broadcasting for the Tigers in 1934 on WXYZ as the number-two man behind Ty Tyson. In an era when 'hysterics and fabricated situations' were the rule, he just informed his listeners and told interesting stories. He introduced a whole generation of Detroiters to Tiger baseball and taught the game to people who had never been to the stadium. Some years later Thomas Monaghan remarked that he wished he could have a tape of Harry Heilmann to listen to; Ernie Harwell acquired one for him in return for a substantial donation to Harwell's son's church.[97]

The deaths of Briggs and Heilmann were symbolic of the passing of an era based in pre-war attitudes. Continuity and memories combined with postwar prosperity to produce a feeling of security within management and a sense among Detroiters that Detroit baseball was one of the constancies of life. But the city was changing, television would expand the followers of baseball beyond a core of ardent fans, and the team needed rebuilding. New people would have to make decisions about how Detroit baseball would respond.

3

Transitions and Adaptation of the Detroit Baseball Club in the 1950s

The Detroit Tigers Baseball Club conjures up images of conservatism and dependability.[1] Those epithets describe the Navin-Briggs era and the later Campbell-Fetzer era. Although the Tigers remained mired in the middle of the American League during the 1950s, the decade was one of critical transition and importance off the field. The ownership of the team was in limbo after the death of Walter Briggs. Payrolls and expenses were rising. Television was expanding baseball's audience and providing new sources of revenues. Detroit's metropolitan base continued to expand, but the population of the city itself – and noticeably its white population – was declining for the first time in history. The farm system had to be restored if the Tigers were to compete successfully on the field. And the Tigers could not neglect forever the growing pool of black athletes who had added so much to other teams.

Management had an erratic, even zany, quality during the 1950s. Between 1951 and 1960 the Tigers had seven managers – Red Rolfe, Fred Hutchinson, Bucky Harris, Jack Tighe, Bill Norman, Jimmy Dykes, and Joe Gordon. They had six general managers – Billy Evans, Charlie Gehringer, John McHale, Rick Ferrell, Jim Campbell, and Bill DeWitt, who was his own general manager while president. A plethora of owners – Walter O. Briggs, his estate with his son Spike as president, and then eleven owners simultaneously – came and went. The Tigers traded players with a fury unknown before or since. They spent money on a variety of bonus boys – some future Hall of Famers, some who had brief careers in the majors. The result of all this frenetic activity was mediocrity on the field. The Tigers never finished closer than fifteen games behind the pennant winner or higher than fourth between 1951 and 1960. In 1952 they stumbled to the basement and finished with the worst winning percentage in Tiger history, .325 (50-104). The next year they spent 96 days in last place and were 20-49 (.290) on 1 July. They climbed out of the basement on 27 July 1953 and managed to play about .500 ball for the next eight and a half years.

There were some highlights. Virgil Trucks pitched two no-hitters in 1952, winning 1–0 on 15 May after a ninth-inning home run by Vic Wertz off Bob Porterfield of Washington, and 1–0 over New York on 26 August. Trucks won only three other games that year: a two-hitter on 21 May, a seven-hitter on 24 June, and a one-hitter marred by a lead-off single by Eddie Yost of Washington on 22 July. Art Houtteman also pitched a one-hitter on 26 April, spoiled by a two-out ninth-inning single by Harry 'Suitcase' Simpson of Cleveland at Detroit. Lore has it that Trucks borrowed Houtteman's spikes for his first no-hitter.[2] Over two days during the same year, newly acquired Walt Dropo got twelve consecutive hits, tying Pinky Higgins's league record; no walks interrupted Dropo's streak.

The next year Harvey Kuenn hit .308 with 209 hits in a Tiger record 679 at bats and was named rookie of the year with 194 votes out of 217.[3] Ray Boone hit four grand slams for the Tigers and had 20 per cent of the Tiger runs batted in after joining the team from Cleveland. He led the team in game-winning RBIs from 1953 to 1955.[4]

The Tigers started 1954 in first place and remained there until 11 May, mainly because rain-outs allowed them to pitch the best of a very thin staff. On 11 June they hit six home runs, including two grand slams and a home run by pitcher Ray Herbert, while defeating Philadelphia 16–5. They lost the second game 2–1 before '4,753 disinterested fans.'[5]

Nineteen fifty-five and 1956 brought some heroic hitting. On 17 April 1955 twenty-year-old Al Kaline hit two home runs in one inning and three in the game. He went on to become the youngest player in history to win the batting championship (one day younger than Ty Cobb) at .340. He also hit 27 home runs and drove in 102 runs. Ray Boone drove in 116 runs to tie for the league lead after driving in 114 in 1953. The Tigers led the league in batting in 1956 at .279; Kuenn hit .332, Maxwell .326, Kaline .314, and Boone .308. Maxwell hit 28 home runs and Kaline another 27, with 128 RBIs. Bill Hoeft and Frank Lary won

20 and 21 games respectively and Paul Foytack 15, but no other Tiger pitcher won more than six. After finishing each of the previous four months below .500, the Tigers climaxed the season with a 17-12 August and 20-5 September, ending the year 82-72.

Jim Bunning won twenty games (20-8) in 1957 after a 5-1 rookie year. Kaline, dubbed the new Dimaggio,[6] hit eleven home runs in twenty-three games. In 1958 Frank Lary became the first pitcher since Al Cicotte in 1916 to beat the New York Yankees seven times, finishing 7-1 against them (then a career 16-5). Kuenn and Kaline finished 1-2 in the batting race at .353 and .327 in 1959; Maxwell hit 31 home runs and Kaline 27, despite suffering a broken jaw on 18 June. On 3 May Maxwell welcomed Jimmy Dykes's managerial debut with four straight home runs in a doubleheader sweep of the Yankees at Briggs Stadium. That began a 32-14 run that brought the Tigers to within a half game of first place on 20 June. 'Paw Paw' (Maxwell) had a flair for the dramatic, hitting an inordinate number of home runs on Sunday and in extra innings (a league record five in extra innings in 1960) and became a crowd favorite.

There were embarrassments too. Despite his no-hitter, Trucks lost 19 games in 1952 and sat out the last two weeks to avoid the ignominy of 20 defeats.[7] The team posted its highest (until 1955) ERA of 5.25 in 1953; the whole staff had only 16 saves versus New York's 39.[8] On 19 June the Tigers lost 23–3 to Boston, which scored a record 17 runs in the seventh inning. In 1955 the Tigers lost ten of thirteen games in August as a change of pace from their usual dreadful beginning and furious finish. In 1958, when Lary defeated the Yankees seven times, he was 9-14 against the rest of the league. The Yankees got a kind of revenge by scoring 39 runs and getting 51 hits in one series sweep against the Tigers. The Tigers began the 1959 season 2-15 under Bill Norman. After a 15–3 loss to Washington, the Tigers' owners walked out en masse and ordered the firing of Norman.[9] The team left 1160 men on base, 200 more than any other club. They stole a mere 34 bases, and their ace reliever, Ray Narleski, finished 4-12 with a 5.80 ERA. On 7 September the Tigers lost a doubleheader to Cleveland that typified the decade. Nineteen pitchers were used; the Tigers scored 19 runs but lost each game by one run as Cleveland twice scored two runs in the bottom of the ninth. In 1960 the Tigers lost 31 games by one run. Lack of depth, unreliable relief pitching, lack of speed, and a poor infield defence troubled the Tigers throughout the decade despite a few star performances.[10] They were 111-157 in one-run games 1955–60 and were outhomered in Briggs Stadium every year 1956–61.[11]

The Tigers did not stand pat. Five deals in 1952 involving 33 players (four trades with St Louis, which had finished seventh, one with Boston) dismantled Walter Briggs's team. The Tigers eventually made trades involving forty-three players over two years and another fifty players over another two-year period.[12] The team had become old (an average of 29.6 years in the spring of 1952) and complacent, and got off to terrible starts in 1952 and 1953. Mickey Briggs recalls that the age of the team and the bad starts were the reasons for the trades. They were not intended to save money,[13] although they had the effect of reducing the Tiger payroll. Favorites of Walter Briggs and of the fans departed: George Kell, Johnny Lipon, Hoot Evers, Dizzie Trout, Johnny Groth (who had been called 'one of the greatest prospects to hit the majors in years ... another Dimaggio'[14]) Virgil Trucks, and Hal Newhouser. By the summer of 1953 only five players from the Tigers' roster of the spring of 1952 remained.

Although the trades were attributed to general manager Charlie Gehringer, the hand of Spike Briggs was in many of them. Too long under his father's shadow, Spike may have wanted to put his stamp on the team. Gehringer had tried unsuccessfully to keep him away from Bill Veeck at the winter meetings, where Spike was drinking heavily.[15] The flurry of trades in 1952 and 1953 exchanged journeyman players between two very bad ball clubs. Some players stayed only long enough to unpack their bags before being traded to another team. Fans everywhere like to think that their team gets the better of each deal, but the fact that the Tigers floundered was the best evidence that the trades were not successful.

The key players in two trades in the summer of 1952 were Kell for Dropo with Boston and Wertz for Garver with St Louis. Kell hit .297 for the remaining five and a half years of his career and became a Hall of Famer. Dropo played with the Tigers two and a half years and hit .279, .248, and .281. Despite a bout with polio, Wertz hit 88 home runs for the Indians between 1954 and 1957 after he was moved to first base and no longer had to lumber after balls in the outfield;[16] Garver went 38-40 with the Tigers.

The best trade in this early flurry was the one with Cleveland on 15 June 1953 in which the Tigers obtained Steve Gromek, who won 18 games in 1954, Ray Boone, who hit 105 home runs and drove in 460 runs during five seasons with the Tigers, and Al Aber, who was a workmanlike reliever. The principal loss to the Tigers was Art Houtteman, who went 34-22 for Cleveland.

Neglect of the minors had left the Tigers with little talent there. Despite 250 players in the minors, there seemed no immediate help. Of the fourteen players mentioned as leading prospects, only Hoeft, Foytack, and Bill Tuttle had any impact on Tiger teams.[17] Trades seemed the only solution. In 1957 the Tigers made their biggest swap, this time with Kansas City, bringing an aging Billy Martin to the Tigers. Martin, whom the *Saturday Evening Post* had tabbed 'the most unhappy young man in the major leagues,' was expected to fire up the Tigers. Billy called the Tigers 'spoiled babies' – a comment that Al Kaline resented.[18] He departed after a year, but would return in 1971 as manager to fire up 'an aging and complacent team.' The Tigers traded him to Cleveland for Don Mossi, who would win fifteen games in the pennant run of 1961.

Within five days in April 1960 the Tigers made two more trades with Cleveland (12 and 17 April) that brought power to the Tigers' line-up and prepared them for the pennant run of 1961. Probably the best deal in Tiger history was the acquisition of Norm Cash for Steve Demeter, who played only fifteen more big-league games. Cash hit 373 home runs, including four that cleared the roof of Tiger Stadium, over a fifteen-year career with the Tigers and became a fan favorite despite problems with alcohol and amphetamines.[19] The second was the trade of American League batting champion Harvey Kuenn for home-run champion Rocky Colavito. The deal had been discussed during the winter when Kuenn and Colavito were holdouts, although it was not finalized until two days before opening day. Rick Ferrell engineered both trades, although Bill DeWitt was credited with being the 'bold trader.'[20] Kuenn later described the trade as 'the most shocking thing that ever happened to me in baseball. In those days trades were made like that, we never had anything to say about it.'[21] There were lynch parties in Cleveland against Frank Lane for trading the popular teenage idol from Cleveland. For more than thirty years, it was said, Cleveland was a doormat in the

American League because of 'the curse of Rocky Colavito.' Colavito had an inauspicious beginning in Detroit, striking out four times and hitting into a double play in the opening game. Recovering, he hit three home runs in the first week and 35 for the season – his average over his four years with the Tigers. He also led the team with 55 game-winning RBIs during those years. Lane's first trade had been the theft of Billy Pierce, but Detroit wreaked its vengeance twelve years later in getting Cash and Colavito.

One final cog needed to be put in place for the pennant challenge of 1961. That was the acquisition of Billy Bruton, with Dick Brown, Terry Fox, and Chuck Cottier, for Frank Bolling. Campbell made the deal with Milwaukee, whose general manager was former Tiger general manager John McHale. Campbell describes John McHale as one of his friends and said the trade helped both teams, but Brown, Bruton, and Fox played important roles in 1961 for the Tigers. The advantage was to Detroit.

DeWitt and Lane had one more trade to make. They traded managers in August 1960 – with Jimmy Dykes going to Cleveland and Joe Gordon to Detroit. Foytack 'could not believe the trade.' Dykes called it 'weird and crazy.' The two appointments were announced separately because, if the managers knew that they had been traded, neither would have reported. After the season and a few drinks, Gordon went to Campbell's apartment at 1300 Lafayette Avenue at 1:00 a.m. and told Campbell he was going to quit because of DeWitt's interference. DeWitt called Campbell while Gordon was there and said, 'I intend to fire Gordon.' Campbell kept them apart 'lest there be blood.'[22] Gordon had resigned as coach of the Tigers in 1956 because of front-office interference. At his resignation as manager he sighed, 'I knew the Tigers were a bad team but I didn't think they were this bad.'[23] He might have had similar thoughts about management. Gordon's decision meant that an eighth Tiger manager in a decade would begin the 1961 season. Bob Scheffing inherited the fruits of the Tiger trades of the previous year.

Who were these managers who attempted to direct the Tigers during the 1950s? New York sportswriter Dan Daniel described Rolfe as 'the Yankees' Yankee' in 1948. Newhouser thought that 'he could have been an excellent manager ... The problem was he could not get the college out of his system, realize that he had professional ball players playing underneath him ... The players resented it and just folded.' Kell called him his favorite manager. Many respected him, but Evers 'could not tolerate him'; he was 'too much a Yankee.'[24] He was an improvement on Steve O'Neill, who had a booze problem. O'Neill was 'slightly tipsy one opening day,' so much so that he could hardly walk back to the dugout.[25] Hearing from a newsman about a wire-service report of his dismissal while he was in Cleveland Heights, he complained that the club did not notify him personally. Hank Greenberg commented: 'O'Neill is lucky to have heard at all.'[26]

Hutchinson broke lights in the clubhouse when the Tigers lost, but maintained players' respect[27] and successfully managed the St Louis Cardinals and Cincinnati Reds until cancer struck in 1964. Despite reports that the Tigers fired him, Spike Briggs admitted, 'Hutch quit, he wasn't fired,' because the Tigers would not grant him a two-year contract.[28]

Next was Bucky Harris, who had begun his managing career thirty-one years earlier as the boy-wonder manager of the Washington Senators in 1924 and had managed the Tigers from 1929 to 1933. By 1955 his hands were shaking from a nervous disorder. Then came Jack Tighe and Bill Norman from the farm system: they had been good minor-league managers, but were over their heads in the majors. Joe Falls and Jerry Green, long-time sports writers in Detroit, asked each other who was the nuttiest manager: 'Name one who wasn't nutty, Dykes maybe.'[29]

Asked to name a baseball mind among the managers and coaches, Reno Bertoia replied: 'I never met a baseball mind.' Players agreed that coaches then were 'cronies of managers.' Bill Denehy, a farmhand with both the Tigers and Mets, found 'about five people who know something and can convey it; ... too many [coaches] in the majors hit fungoes and shout "way to go, babe."'[30] Jerry Davie recounts how Willis Hudlin called him over to say: '"You're not getting the curve ball over," which 30,000 people could see; there was no real coaching.'[31] In an interview in 1979 Mickey Lolich said: 'They [coaches] don't do much ... They are mostly full of baloney.'[32] Exceptions were pitching coaches Roger Craig (1984) and John Sain (1968), a common thread in two championships; both were teachers and psychologists.

On the day Jack Tighe was dismissed, Sam Greene said, 'Congratulations.' Bill Norman liked to talk baseball but also liked to drink. After he was fired he was reportedly talking to himself while drunk in the club-house. Kaline told reporters, 'Leave him alone.' Kell called Dykes a 'hard-line manager of the old school,' but most newspaper stories dwelled on his preferences among cigars. Like the others, he was expected to shake the 1950s Tigers out of their complacency.[33] Foytack and Gromek say the team lacked talent rather than suffering complacency. Hoeft, how-ever, describes the teams as being 'very relaxed' and having 'played up to the competition.' Foytack summed up the teams' performances well: 'We got a lot of guys fired.'[34]

BASEBALL FOR SALE

When Walter O. Briggs died on 17 January 1952, the Briggs Commer-cial and Development Co., which was a holding company that included both the automobile section (sold to Chrysler in 1953) and the Detroit Baseball Club, passed into trust. The trustees were his son Spike Briggs, Harry Sisson, secretary-treasurer of the club since the 1930s, and Flo-rence McCredie, Walter's secretary. The executors of the estate were Spike Briggs and the Detroit Bank and Trust Company – not the National Bank of Detroit, which financed the syndicates that bid for the Tigers in 1956 and whose president was Charles Fisher, husband of Elizabeth Briggs Fisher, daughter of Walter.

The original trust was established in 1932 under state laws that restricted investments that savings banks could make. Thus, the trustees were unsure whether banking laws would allow continuing investment in a baseball operation. In September 1955 Judge Thomas Maher ruled that because the relevant banking laws had been repealed in 1937, what applied was simply the 'prudent man rule,' – that banks had to make investments that a prudent man would. Unfamiliar with the finances of baseball, the bank still encouraged sale of the team by the estate. The bank had a legitimate concern that it could be sued if investments did poorly. In fact, the team did not have to be sold because Walter had $17 million in 2 per cent government bonds from which to pay estate taxes. The two younger sisters at first were willing to keep the team, confident that their husbands could control Spike. John McHale, a graduate of Catholic Central High who had played with the Tigers and married a

Briggs niece, could run the team if necessary. Beneficiaries of the estate were Briggs's twenty-four grandchildren, 'remainder men' in legal parlance. Spike Briggs and his four sisters – Mrs Dean (Grace) Robinson, Mrs Charles (Elizabeth) Fisher, Mrs Phillip (Jane Cameron) Hart, and Mrs Averell (Susan Ann) Fisher (two Briggs sisters had married two Fisher brothers) – merely had rights of income.

Within months following his father's death, Spike Briggs had attempted to put together a syndicate to purchase the Tigers from the estate. He quickly enlisted the financial support of Henry Ford II, but Ford withdrew on the advice of his colleagues in the Ford Motor Company. Ernie Kanzler, in particular, worried about the image of the Ford Motor Company should there be problems with the club. Both Henry Ford and Spike Briggs were heavy drinkers who shared too many liquid hours. The unexpected loss of Ford's money doomed Spike's first efforts.

Spike could not put together a syndicate until September 1955. That was seven months after the death of Mrs Walter Briggs on 13 February 1955, but the timing was coincidental. The death of Mrs Briggs affected negotiations only in one way.[35] According to grandsons Mickey and Walter Briggs, Mrs Briggs exercised a strong influence over the family. Had she lived she might have influenced her daughters to sell the team to Spike, who dearly wanted it. In the final syndicate Spike Briggs held a 46 per cent share. Other participants were Ozzie Olson, Donald Mitchell of Mitchell-Bentley Corporation, and Tiger executives Harry Sisson and Charlie Gehringer.[36] The first offer, for $2.5 million, was raised to $3.5 million, which was the average price of franchises sold in the 1950s. Mickey Briggs (nicknamed after Mickey Cochrane from his birth in March 1936, although he was named Basil after his maternal grandfather Basil Manly) describes his father's reaction to the outcome: 'My father fully expected his sisters to sell to him. His voice was choking when he told me. He pretended that the two younger sisters supported him but he was drinking heavily then and his sisters thought it would be bad for him, for baseball, and for the family image. Elizabeth was a devout Catholic, who probably had a moral problem as well as a public relations problem with his drinking. The sisters might have considered selling if Ford had been in the syndicate, although Ozzie Olsen, Ray White, and Henry Ford were all drinking cronies.'[37]

When that bid failed, courts gave the estate a 'reasonable time' to sell the team. Meanwhile, the Cleveland Indians sold for almost $4 million, boosting the value of the Tigers.[38] Reportedly, twenty-eight syndicates had enquired about buying the team. One of those was the Detroit Lions, but on 23 June Commissioner of Football Bert Bell forbade the Lions to be involved in baseball. Mayor Cobo considered having the city buy the stadium and lease it to the club. The Council split 4–4 and that came to naught. Twenty years later a different mayor and owner would reach such an agreement. A board of assessors valued the stadium for tax purposes at $2,031,640,[39] and that assessment would prove useful to a syndicate attempting to show collateral. There were eight to ten bidders, but the main contenders were Bill Veeck and the Knorr/Brown/Fetzer group. Tiger broadcaster Van Patrick played a role. Patrick and Spike Briggs both had small shares in Knorr Broadcasting and were friends. Briggs tipped off Knorr to the impending sale. The attraction to Knorr, who owned station WKMH, was the rights to Tiger broadcasting. Baseball and broadcasting would become partners. At a bar in Grand Rapids Fred Knorr and Carl Lee discussed the importance of broadcast rights and proposed putting together a syndicate of Michigan broadcasters to purchase the Tigers. They lacked sufficient funds, however. Enter John Fetzer.

Carl Lee introduced Fetzer and Knorr at Willow Run Airport. Out of this meeting developed the successful syndicate. Knorr, Harry Hansen, and McCoy, each of whom owned one-third of Knorr Broadcasting, were to put up one-third of the bid; Fetzer, Lee, and a Washington lawyer, Paul O'Brien, put up another one-third; Ken Brown, George Coleman, Joe Thomas, and Fred Woolworth were the main participants in a third group. These also had a silent backer in the person of Lou Jacobs, who had held the rights to concessions at Tiger Stadium since 1936. He had offered to finance the club for Spike in return for a lifetime contract for concessions, but Spike refused because 'that would be immoral.'[40] Ancillary benefits from baseball again entered the picture.

The other principal bidder was Veeck, who had recently lost the St Louis Browns franchise. That caused consternation in Detroit, although he was popular among African Americans for having promoted integration on the field. In April Spike promised: 'We won't sell to just anybody.' When asked in July about Veeck, he demurred: 'Let's not bring personalities into it just now.'[41] Walter Briggs III believed that 'Veeck never had a chance; father was a purist and hated showmanship.'[42] H.G. Salsinger, dean of Detroit sports writers, who had been injured by a foul ball on opening day in 1954 and never returned to the ballpark,[43] wrote a vicious attack on Veeck in his column, 'The Umpire.' Veeck was 'a man with the heart of a carnival barker and the soul of a medicine show pitchman.' He was an exhibitionist who wore open-throat sports shirts and had an aversion to neckties and hats. He had served breakfast for war workers, shot off fireworks, and had the fans manage the game. He had dismissed Roger Hornsby for being 'too strict.'[44] Salsinger did not mention that Hornsby was a racist. Salsinger's tirade, which had no effect on the negotiations, presented an extreme expression of the conservative mood surrounding Detroit baseball.

The problem was that Veeck's group made the highest initial bid. Fetzer later explained how the group, conceived by Knorr but increasingly dominated by Fetzer, got the franchise:

Our bids had to be sealed and submitted, and our group was going to bid something like $4.5 million for the franchise. Then Bill Veeck called a press conference and announced he had just been extended a line of credit from the National Bank of Detroit for $2.5 million.

By this time I was sitting on the boards of several banks and I said to myself, if they've extended him a $2.5 million line of credit, in order to secure that loan he must have at least $2.5 million in equity capital. So that means his bid must be around $5 million.

As I said, our bid was going to be $4.5 million, ... So I called our group together and explained that we weren't even in the ball park. Then we revised our bid, upped it to $5.2 million, and when the sealed bids were opened, we were the highest.[45]

Later Fetzer acknowledged that he increased his bid because he feared that he would lose broadcast rights and that the final figure was $5.5 million.[46]

Charges flew that the deal was fixed from the beginning. Knorr denied any collusion in a published interview.[47] The National Bank of Detroit financed both bids, so it is possible that the amount of the Veeck bid leaked through Charles Fisher to Briggs to Knorr, but there is no way of knowing that for certain. The bank took a $2 million mortgage on the recently appraised stadium, and the Briggs family took a note, payable over a five-year period, for $900,000. Its granting of what amounted to a loan to one group violated the spirit perhaps even the letter, of the provision requiring cash bids only. Spike personally called Knorr at his hotel suite to inform him of his success. In his excitement, Knorr pulled the knob off the door between rooms but asked the newspapers not to print that incident and they did not. Veeck sent a messenger to Spike Briggs in Washington the day *after* the bids had been opened, attempting to raise his bid with a similar note or 'time bid.' The grandchildren thought about blocking the sale to keep ownership within the family, but most were teenagers or younger and did nothing.[48] The result was that the Tigers had communal ownership. The sale became final on 1 October 1956 and Fred Knorr became president, succeeded by Harvey Hansen on 19 April 1957. The groups had been heavily financed with loans and mortgages. Both Fenkell and Mickey Briggs remember that the entire group put forth only about $1 million from their own funds.

Spike announced that he would continue to run the ball club 'his way,' but he soon ran into trouble from his impetuosity, probably accentuated by his drinking, and from the difficulty of appeasing eleven different owners. After he publicly criticized the manager and coaches, Gordon resigned as coach on 28 June 1956. At the Adcraft Club in January 1957 he berated Al Kaline for wanting a salary like Mickey Mantle's.[49] Knorr, who had bitter disputes with Fetzer and other owners, was forced out on 19 April. A week later Spike followed after days of speculation in the newspapers.[50] Knorr had apparently promised Spike, 'You will be here a long time,' and Spike thought that he would be. Upon his resignation he called Bill Veeck and said, 'Well, Bill, you were right.'[51] By now Fetzer, who was becoming the spokesperson for the owners, explained Briggs's departure: 'This is the best thing for all parties.' The owners claimed that he resigned; Briggs at first insisted that he had been fired. Later he said: 'I wanted them to fire me, but they wouldn't ... so I got out.'[52] This mercurial and troubled but decent man died at age fifty-eight. He had never fully recovered from a cerebral edema that struck ten years earlier. Red Smith described Spike Briggs as a 'sportsman,' uninterested in money or personal publicity. A 'bad thing happened to baseball' when the syndicate bought the Tigers.[53] He had been accustomed to running things and could not work for eleven different owners. Probably no one could have.

After the death of Knorr, scalded in a bathtub in Florida, Fetzer bought up the Hansen/McCoy shares; their interest had been in association with Knorr. He then bought the Kenyon Brown shares and other little pieces, assuming full control and becoming president on 11 October 1961. With Knorr's death and Fetzer's control, DeWitt was doomed.[54] Fetzer appointed thirty-eight-year-old James Campbell, vice-president since 1957, as general manager. Thereafter, the Campbell-Fetzer team directed the Tigers for almost a quarter-century, until the sale to Thomas Monaghan on 1 December 1983. Campbell ran the baseball operations. By his own testimony, he had 'full authority.' That management team produced the world championships of 1968 and 1984.

FINANCIAL MATTERS

During the 1950s the Detroit Tigers remained a profitable enterprise despite press concerns about finances (table 7).[55] Harry Sisson provided continuity as chief financial officer from 1936 through the Fetzer era. Attendance, which remained the major source of revenue, topped one million every year except 1953, following the Tigers' basement finish (table 5). The team's most profitable year was 1955 under Spike, in which both home and road attendance topped one million fans. Both Fenkell and Campbell point out that the press concentrated on attendance figures in judging profitability, but that the team could and did adjust expenses when income dropped. Pleading poverty served the owners well, both in negotiations with players and in getting fans' support against players' organizations. Reports of the time indicated that Fetzer purchased the remaining shares of the team for about the amount paid in 1956, but Carl Lee remembers that all participants made at least a little profit. The club adopted new accounting measures for player depreciation in 1959 that produced $586,000 in tax savings that could be applied to other business ventures.[56] Amidst ups and downs, both income and non-salary expenses increased by about 10 per cent between 1952 and 1956.

There may have been some penny pinching. Mickey Briggs recounts how president Harvey Hansen worried about the cost of broken lights from foul balls. The players' payroll decreased during the 1950s. As a percentage of the team's income, players' salaries declined from about 28 per cent in 1951 to about 14 per cent in 1956 (tables 7–8). That 14 per cent was similar to the American League average of 17 per cent in 1958, as reported by J. Norman Lewis, lawyer for the players' association. According to his figures, players' salaries had been 44 per cent of total revenues in 1933 and fell thereafter.[57] Andrew Zimbalist calculates players' salary shares as a per cent of expenditures rather than revenues. His tables also reveal a steadily decreasing proportion of players' salaries relative to total expenditures until after 1974 (table 3). The second-highest salaried team during the Walter Briggs era, Detroit fell below the league mean in the early 1950s, but the team also finished no higher than fourth in the standings. The median of players' salaries both for the Tigers and for the league generally was always below the mean because of the high salaries a few stars received. The press, which emphasized the salaries of the stars, seldom mentioned low salaries. Salsinger began criticising high player salaries in the 1930s and continued to do so until his death.[58]

As we saw in chapter 1, the players' organization concentrated primarily on pensions and improved minimum salaries during the 1950s. It helped the lot of the journeyman ball player, who usually left baseball with little savings, few skills, and no pension equity. Many players attempted to stay on as coaches, minor-league managers, or scouts. Their vulnerability encouraged them to accept what management offered. Robert Murphy, who unsuccessfully tried to organize players in 1946, said that he did not even approach the Tigers, the Yankees, or the Red Sox because 'they are the best paid and have the least gripes.'[59] Both Kuenn and Bunning were leaders in the players' association in the late 1950s. As Jerry Davie points out, most players were sympathetic but not at all knowledgeable about such affairs. Spike Briggs, who had often dealt with union representatives of stadium employees, had no sympathy for a players' union. When J. Norman Lewis proposed that a share of World Series receipts go to the players' pension fund, Briggs demanded: 'Let's see whether he's in favor of the United States or some other country.'[60]

No Tiger salary during the 1950s reached the heights of those of

Greenberg and Newhouser during the 1940s, but the club spent richly for 'bonus babies.' In 1958 *The Sporting News* estimated that the Tigers spent $250,000 on bonus players in a single season.[61] Some players who received bonuses had only brief careers, including Jim Brady, Jim Small, and Bob Miller, the last of whom received a reputed $60,000. Bertoia, who signed the same year as Kaline, roomed with him, and was deemed to have as much potential,[62] had a respectable career, as did George Thomas, but neither achieved renown. Bertoia was leading the league in hitting (.398) on 17 May 1957, but suffered an injury to a rotator cuff and never reached that plateau again. Kuenn and Kaline became big stars. Ed Katalinas, who signed Kaline, reported that he was excellent to outstanding in arm, speed, and body control: 'He was a natural out-fielder, the best kid player I ever scouted.' Later manager Bob Scheffing told Ernie Harwell: 'Al Kaline is the best defensive right fielder I have ever seen. He instinctively plays the ball the correct way, he has the speed to range far and wide, and his throwing arm commands respect ... He instinctively makes the right play every time.'[63]

Kaline enjoyed a brilliant twenty-two-year career with the Tigers, sur-passing Katalinas's prediction of a twenty-year career, and entered the Hall of Fame in 1980. Despite his success, Kaline suffered many criti-cisms early in his career.[64] He had the misfortune of winning the batting championship in 1955 at age twenty, driving in his career high of 128 RBIs the following year, and in both of those years hitting 27 home runs, just two below his career high. Kaline himself bemoaned his early success: 'After winning the batting championship everyone expected too much of me, it set me back in my career.' Al Kaline Day was held in August 1970 and his uniform number was retired in 1980. To the end he remained Campbell's favorite player.[65] He was named *TSN*'s outstand-ing player in 1955, played in eighteen All-Star Games, and won eleven Gold Gloves.

ATTRACTING FANS

To pay the bills, one needs fans. They may come to games or listen to radio and television broadcasts, the rights for which sponsors pay. Tiger baseball remained a bargain at the gate in the 1950s. At the beginning of the decade ticket prices were $2.50 for box seats, $1.75 for reserved seats,

$1.20 for general admission, and 60¢ for bleachers. At the end of the decade they were still only $3.00, $2.00, $1.25 and 75¢ respectively; the small increase was well below the rate of inflation. Afternoon games started earlier so that people could avoid rush hour (2:30 in 1951, 1:30 in 1958), as the automobile rather than the streetcar brought most people to the games. The team increased its night offerings to twenty-one in 1957 and started them at 8:15. Increasing the number of night games did not diminish their attraction in this working-class city. The nineteen night games had outdrawn the forty-seven day games through August 1959 as more attractive teams like New York were scheduled at night.[66] The average for twenty-one yearly night games, 1957–9, was approximately 27,000 fans versus the 30,000 fans for fourteen games, 1950–6, almost double the league average for night games. In 1960 DeWitt increased the number of night games to twenty-four and dropped all Sunday doubleheaders and Monday day games.

After a survey of other teams, the Tigers attempted to modernize a 'somewhat archaic ticket policy' in 1956. Two years later the Tigers allowed fans to order by mail or at the counter any game two weeks beforehand.'[67] But the team did not embark on any major new ventures to bring people to the ballpark. Baseball itself remained the attraction.

The Tigers made a modest effort to draw women to the games by reinaugurating Ladies' Day in 1959 – the first in Detroit in sixteen years. This feature had ceased after 1943 because of complaints from male fans. Ladies' Day apparently goes back to 1889, when the Cincinnati Reds proclaimed a Ladies' Day on those days that their handsome pitcher Tony Mullane started. Detroit newspaper accounts of the first Ladies' Day, which allowed women to be admitted for 50¢, are embarrassing today. Russell Harris in the *Detroit News* noted the 'shrill, shrieking, screech.' 'Some men cowered among the ladies,' but 'New Ladies' Day [was] a screaming success.' The *Free Press* noted that 'the eerie massed shriek of 3,460 female voices was a fearsome thing.' Four years later J.L. Hudson Co. sponsored a Ladies' Day to 'enlighten the weaker sex.' The question-and-answer period proved the women very knowledgeable about baseball.[68] In 1976, 'Ladies' Days' became 'Tiger Days,' which allowed reduced admissions for women, retirees, youth groups, and children under the age of fourteen.

More women listened to Tiger baseball or watched it on television than attended games, and radio and television rights were steadily rising (tables 7 and 12). In the early 1950s the Tigers received $300–350,000 annually. A new five-year contract with Strohs Beer in 1959 brought $600,000 annually. Strohs replaced Goebel Beer, Speedway (later Marathon) Oil, and Phillips (R.G. Dunn) Cigars as principal advertiser. Reportedly, Strohs paid the Tigers $1.8 million up front to help defray mortgage and interest payments.[69] The Tigers had a thirty-seven station radio network in 1957 and a seven-city television network in 1959, showing forty games. The outstate Michigan network of both radio and television was strong because of the Knorr-Fetzer interests. The network whetted the interest of Michiganders in Detroit's team and prompted them to drive to Detroit for games. In 1960, when the Tigers televised twenty-four Saturday day games among the forty-two televised games (all day games), Saturdays' ratings audience at 81 per cent was the highest in the nation, well surpassing the 65 per cent in Chicago and 35 per cent in New York.[70] However, Strohs's contract for both radio and television had a series of implications.

In January 1960 Strohs filed suit against Knorr broadcasting (WKMH) to broaden coverage of Tiger games; WKMH had a weak signal that became garbled at night, even within the city. The advertiser sued the owner of the club. Strohs withdrew its suit on 18 February after an agreement that WKMH and WWJ would cover day games and WKMH and the more powerful WJR would carry night games. Strohs soon became a national brewer, while Goebel, which had sponsored the Tigers for two decades, disappeared. Van Patrick was dismissed as Tiger announcer, perhaps because of his identification with Goebel beer. The Tigers paid his salary, and it may also be that 'Tiger officials were just fed up with his loudness.'[71] The result of the dismissal of Van Patrick and the death of Tiger broadcaster Mel Ott in an automobile accident of 14 November 1958, was the hiring of George Kell in 1959. In turn, partly through Kell's efforts, Ernie Harwell was hired as an announcer.[72] At first they alternated, one reporting four and one half innings on radio, then switching booths to do a television portion. Ultimately Kell took responsibility for television and Harwell for radio. Harwell would broadcast Tiger games for the next thirty-one years and Kell for thirty-five (and still counting). Kell and Harwell marked a return to the low-key style of Harry Heilmann. Van Patrick had suffered in comparison. The harsh judgment by an ardent Tiger supporter, shared by many others in the 1950s, was that Van Patrick's 'principal qualification was self-esteem.' He was 'simultaneously boring and maddening.'[73] Harwell commented on the difficulty of succeeding Heilmann: 'Because listeners grew up on this style, woe to the broadcaster later on in these towns who departed from those guidelines.'[74] It was a prescient comment about the problems his successors would encounter.

INTEGRATION ON THE FIELD

The Tigers did little to attract support from the African American community of Detroit. The Tigers signed their first black ballplayer in 1953, signed two pitchers from the Negro American League to minor-league contracts in 1955, and had seventeen black players out of 250 in the farms in 1958.[75] Two African American activists of the time, Willie Baxter and Joe Williams, said that Cleveland's acquisition of Larry Doby and the All-Star Game played in Detroit in 1951 spurred desires within Detroit's African American community for the Tigers to sign a black player. After the 1951 interview with Billy Evans (chapter 2), however, there was little public agitation for integration, even by the *Michigan Chronicle*, Detroit's African American newspaper. The memories of Baxter and Williams probably reflect private as opposed to public concern. Coleman Young remembers that he wrote Spike Briggs about the lack of Negro ball players when he was secretary for MANTU, the Michigan Association of Negro Trade Unions, whose prime objective was getting jobs for blacks in the community by the force of boycott. He does not recall whether that was before or after the sale in 1956.[76] Although Spike Briggs was a popular visitor to night clubs in Paradise Valley, the African American district in Detroit then, he took no initiatives to put a black player on Detroit's roster during his tenure.

A few African American leaders organized a committee in 1958 to demand that the Tigers bring a black player to the majors and threatened to boycott Briggs Stadium if they did not. Among those involved was the Reverend Charles Hill, long-time pastor of Hartford Avenue Baptist Church, 'an old time hell-fire preacher,' president of the Michigan branch of the National Negro Congress, and Coleman Young's 'mentor and role model.'[77] Representatives of that body and of MANTU, including some white union representatives like James Pita, joined the Briggs Stadium boycott committee. The leader was another Reverend Hill – George Hill, dean of United Theological Seminary at 1308 Broadway. He threatened a boycott of Briggs Stadium if the Tigers did not bring up a black player by 7 May. The boycott was later set for 1 June. John McHale responded that the Tigers were 'willing' but 'would not be pressured into it' and that the Tigers had spent $75,000 on the development of 'colored players' since 1954.[78] Harvey Hansen, president of the club, told the *Detroit News* that the team would have a Negro 'whenever we can get a good one.' The twelve in the farm system were 'not window dressing'; he sought the best team 'regardless of race or creed.' He would not make a definite commitment: 'They insisted we make such a commitment whether we had a qualified major league ball player or not. We will not use Negroes as a gate attraction.'[79] He told the *Michigan Chronicle*: 'We would like very much to have a colored player. We have seventeen in our farm system now. But we are not going to bring up a colored player because he is colored.' Reverend Hill responded: 'You could clear it up right now.'[80] A week earlier, William C. Matney in an editorial in the *Chronicle*, 'Tiger Policy Unrealistic,' had written: 'Management has not been able to specify what it means by the right type of Negro player; unfortunately the color complexion of parent club has remained lily white. We consider it a shame and a travesty that the city of Detroit must be bracketed with Boston for the dubious distinction of being the only American league cities to have not fielded a player of color. A directive from President Harvey Hansen and his board of directors can change the present Jim Crow policy of Briggs' Stadium.'[81]

Two months earlier the Tigers had acquired Ozzie Virgil, with Gail Harris, for Jim Finnegan and cash. McHale described Virgil as 'a native of the Dominican Republic,' who did not fit into 'plans for the present.' The article made no mention of his skin color.[82] Virgil reportedly said in the Detroit Tiger dugout, 'I'm not Negro; I'm Dominican; I'm Spanish.' To this day Gates Brown says that 'he was not black,' but Coleman Young insists, 'He was black; he lived on Hastings Street; too much is made of skin shades.'[83] When the Tigers brought him up, he was recognized in Detroit as the team's 'first Negro' player.

The Briggs Stadium boycott committee held a meeting on 7 May at Central Congregational Church, 7625 Lynwood. The FBI was there too. Although the worst of McCarthyism had passed, Hoover and the FBI still seemed to equate the civil rights movement with communist agitation.[84]

Although these protests involved only a couple of hundred people, although the Detroit white newspapers gave little attention to them, and although the meeting with Harvey Hansen in April had come to naught, on 6 July 1958 the Tigers brought up Virgil from Charleston. The *New York Times* noted both Virgil's debut and that the Tigers were the fifteenth team to put a Negro on its roster. Lyall Smith wrote: 'If the Detroit Tigers ever drew a so-called "color line" they ended it Thursday.' The *Detroit News* quoted Hank Aguirre, who had been born in Mexico, as saying there would be no problems among players who were 'a great bunch of guys who embraced anyone who could play. I never thought that [racism] existed in the world until I came to Detroit.' In his first starting assignment Ozzie Virgil went 5-5 before 29,794 fans, twice the normal crowd for a game against the Washington Senators. Watson Spoelstra attributed the large crowd to other factors, including 'a winning streak and a warm night.'[85] In an editorial in the *Michigan Chronicle*, Charles J. Wartmen summed up the silence of the Detroit press well: 'Up to the time this article was written no metropolitan newspaper had published an editorial saying this was good for Detroit ... they stood in the wings and seldom if ever ventured into the controversial waters of Tiger policy on race.'[86]

Although the front office denied that it had yielded to pressure, the coincidence of agitation and Virgil's promotion on 6 June strongly suggests that this small group had an influence. Campbell later admitted: 'They were after my ass to bring up a black man but there was no one available that we liked.' The following year the Tigers traded Tito Francona to Cleveland for an aging Doby. Campbell attributes that trade to 'p.r. reasons; Doby had been popular with Negro Detroiters while he was with Cleveland.'[87] Two years later Billy Bruton, Bubba Morton, and Jake Wood were filling important roles for the Tigers. In the decade after they broke the color line, the Tigers had as high a proportion of black players as the American League average – 18 per cent – but below the National League average of 25 per cent.[88] At the same time, black addresses did not get prime seats because management was afraid of alienating white fans.[89]

Lenny Green, who played with the Tigers in 1967 and 1968, said that the Tigers' organization was not racist in the 1960s, but 'in retrospect it was racist in 1958.'[90] That judgment seems a fair one. Individuals in the management may not have been racist in their personal dealings with blacks, but the organization followed racially discriminatory practices.

The club also ignored segregation in cities that housed its minor-league affiliates and training facilities. The Birmingham, Alabama Club in the southern Association was affiliated with the Tigers from 1957 to 1961, when the Southern Association and the Birmingham franchise folded.[91] Birmingham became notorious in May 1961 when President John F. Kennedy sent U.S. marshalls to both Birmingham and Montgomery, Alabama after freedom riders were beaten. Birmingham became infamous in May 1963 when Bull Connor turned fire hoses on peaceful black demonstrators. Recorded by national television, his actions horrified the nation and aided the civil rights movement, but there was more to come. On 15 September 1963 a bomb at Birmingham's 16th Street Baptist Church killed four young African American girls.

Problems in Birmingham were long standing and well known. An article by Red Smith of the *New York Times* attacking the Birmingham ban on Negroes and whites competing in the same athletic event and calling for the New York Yankees to boycott the city had been reprinted in the *Detroit News* in 1954. Pittsburg and Kansas City had cancelled an exhibition game in 1958 because of Birmingham's city ordinance against 'racially mixed' sporting events. Cincinnati had broken its working agreement with clubs in the Southern League because of their racial policies. Birmingham city officials made it clear that they were going to enforce the ordinance against racially mixed sporting events although it had been ruled unconstitutional.[92] After Nashville replaced Birmingham as the Tigers' AA farm, the *Free Press* noted simply that Birmingham had 'dropped out of baseball recently because of integration problems.' When I asked Campbell about the Tigers remaining in Birmingham, he merely said: 'I did not perceive a big problem in Birmingham. Those fans didn't harm our colored players. I never thought about pulling the club from Birmingham because of that incident [police turning dogs on people] or because of the fans.'[93]

The same Jim Campbell let Maury Wills stay with him in Campbell's own apartment in Lakeland, Florida, because of the difficulty of finding decent accommodation for blacks then. On a personal basis Tiger executives could be generous, but institutionally they preferred to accommodate themselves to the practices that surrounded them. The Tigers trained in Lakeland, which was one of the most segregated towns in Florida. They were proud that they had trained there continuously since 1934 except during the war years. They also had the longest-standing working agreement of any major-league team with any minor-league affiliate – that with Durham (which later gained national notoriety with the movie *Bull Durham*). They returned time and time again to Toledo as a AAA farm. The Tigers preferred familiarity. Moreover, the South was generally segregated and the Tigers had few black players in the high minors. Ernie Harwell, who began his career in Atlanta, concluded that 'baseball couldn't fight segregation in the South too much.'[94]

THE FARM SYSTEM

Following his appointment as director of farms and player development in 1952, Campbell reinvigorated a neglected farm system. He established Tigertown, which brought major- and minor-league players together for spring training in 1953. Once an airport, it had quarters for 350 players and instructors. By 1957 it was serving as a 'try-out camp' for eighteen to twenty-four year olds, with a fancy brochure produced mainly for the benefit of parents. Campbell was dubbed its 'mayor.'

The base of Tiger recruitment in the early 1950s remained in Michigan. In 1953, 33 of the 150 minor leaguers had been born in Michigan. The 1958 Tiger roster included three born in Detroit, five in the suburbs, and five from outstate Michigan.[95] Fourteen per cent of those who played with the Tigers a year or more and whose careers began between 1940 and 1969 had been born in Michigan (chapter 5). The Tigers also gave baseball scholarship funds to Michigan colleges and conducted outstate try-out camps for 2500 players in 1959.[96]

Progress was slow at first. The only players of note who emerged from the Tiger farms in the 1950s were Foytack in 1953, who was touted as a potential thirty-game winner but suffered from wildness,[97] Bolling and Lary in 1954, and Bunning in 1955. Then there was a dry spell until Steve Boros and Jake Wood came up in 1961. The Tigers had seven to ten farm teams until 1961, then five or six during the 1960s.[98] According to the Celler Commission the Tigers spent $600,000 annually on their minor-league operations (nearly twice what they were spending on major-league salaries) from 1952 to 1956. They lost $370,000 annually on minor-league operations. Harry Sisson claimed that they were spending $1.3 million in 1953 and 1955 and nearly $1.6 million in 1958. The latter figures may have included spring training, bonus payments, and the purchase of players. Campbell says: 'He must have been counting something else.'[99]

A comparison of the performance of Tiger farm teams between the early 1950s and the late 1950s suggests significant improvement. Only Jamestown in Class D won a pennant in 1953; three of the eight minor-league teams finished in the second division. Only one farm club won a pennant in 1955; half the clubs finished in the second division. Four teams won pennants and all made the playoffs in 1958. Four years later the Tigers' farm clubs had the best combined records in baseball.[100] They laid the foundation of the team that won the World Series in 1968. Bill Freehan recalls that twelve players from his rookie camp with the Tigers played ten years or more in the majors.[101] Among the notable products of the farms, with the year of their first appearance in a Tiger uniform, were the following: Steve Boros (1961), Jake Wood (1961), Dick McAuliffe (1961), Gates Brown (1963), Bill Freehan (1961), Willie Horton (1963), Mickey Lolich (1963), Jim Northrup (1964), Ray Oyler (1965), Mickey Stanley (1966), Pat Dobson (1967), John Hiller (1967), Fred Lasher (1967), Tom Matchick (1967), and Daryl Patterson (1968). Ironically, the Detroit press was criticizing the inadequacy of the Detroit farm system then.[102]

In 1959 Jim Campbell began to move towards area scouting arrangements with a hierarchy of scouts. The 'Jim Campbell Scouting Book' is a rare insight into such scouting arrangements (excerpts in appendix 5). One discerns in it the personal touch and attention to individuals in which the ball club had taken justifiable pride since the Briggs era. It also reflects a concern with the character of players, pride in the Stadium, and the promotion of Detroit as a good sports town. Players could settle and expect good jobs afterward in Detroit – which many players did. The handbook also reveals a frugality. Jim Campbell laughs about how George Moriarty, Tiger infielder (1909–15), later an umpire, and then scout of the Tigers, labelled him 'the clamp' because of Campbell's clamping down on expense accounts. Frugality anticipated the club's attitudes towards free agency.

The handbook stresses the Tiger organization as a community, even a family. That sense of belonging and loyalty was both a strength and a weakness of the Tigers. Don Lund, Campbell's successor as farm director, emphasized that Campbell was always very loyal to long-time employees. Campbell himself said that perhaps sometimes he was 'too loyal to people.' The warnings to scouts about talking to others suggests a mistrust of outsiders. Even after the Tigers joined a common scouting bureau with Pittsburg, Cleveland, and Milwaukee in 1965, Lund worried whether the scouts from other teams would turn in honest reports.[103] Schoolboy Rowe and Tommy Bridges became Tiger coaches because of their contributions to the pennant-winning teams of 1934 and 1935 although Rowe was a racial baiter and no teacher. Moriarty was an old man by the 1950s. Katalinas, who had personally wooed Kaline and drove both Al and his father to the Tigers' hotel in Philadelphia, took charge of scouting at the very time that cooperative scouting and the draft made the personal touch less important than evaluation of talent throughout the country. The Tiger farm system was revivified in the late 1950s and was successful for a decade, but it had new adjustments to make by the 1960s.

The scouting and signing of players was always something of a crap shoot. The sports pages listed each year promising prospects. Some names, like those of Boros, Horton, and Northrup, are familiar. Most are not because most never made the major leagues. In 1958 the Tigers conducted a review of scouting results since 1950. Between 20 and 25 full-time Tiger scouts, paid $7000 a year, and 175 'part-time sleuths' had looked at 5000 players, recommended 300, and signed 50 yearly. About 25 per cent of the 200 minor leaguers in the system were new each year, 64 of 210 in 1958. Between 1950 and 1957 the Tigers signed 632 young men, sixteen of whom were in the majors and seventeen regarded as still possible prospects in 1958. The study produced a 'rule of thumb' that 3 per cent of players signed should reach the majors and that the minors should send up four players annually. During that period, 2.5 per cent of those signed by the Tigers reached the majors. The Tigers had 44 full time scouts over that period, 24 of whom were still with them. The 20 who were not had signed 220 players, none of whom had yet reached the majors.[104] An analysis of the major leagues as a whole found that 30 per cent of major-league players left baseball or returned to the minors each year between 1968 and 1977. Of those in the rookie leagues, 27 per cent played no longer than one year. A player in AAA had a fifty-fifty chance of ultimately reaching the majors, but 45 per cent of those would stay in the majors for one year or less; another 25 per cent lasted two years.[105] The odds were long and the pay was low. In 1955 monthly salaries ranged from AAA to D as follows: $920, $635, $500, $370, $300, $245.[106] Even in 1994 a minor leaguer observed that 'in Triple A you're one step away from being the best in the world, and you have to be a fry cook in the off-season.'[107] Eighteen players on the AAA Indianapolis roster that year had been in the majors once before returning to the minors.

Campbell deserves credit for resurrecting the troubled farm system and building the successful teams of the late 1960s and early 1970s. By the mid-1960s, the farms were again struggling as the Tigers were slow to adjust to changing conditions. They did not send any scouts to Latin America or the Caribbean until 1960. Campbell said that they tried to get players, but people there spoke Spanish and Pittsburg and the Giants had 'the in.' It is difficult to imagine the older scouts whom the Tigers had on their payroll making much headway there. The Tigers did have a friend in Babel Perez, who owned the Havana Sugar Kings in the days before Castro, but they never capitalized on this friendship. When Perez tried to sell Mike Cuellar and others to the Tigers, Ralph Snyder, assistant farm director, called Frank Carswell, manager at Charleston, where Cuellar was pitching. Carswell recommended against Cuellar, who had many fine seasons with Baltimore.[108]

When Campbell became general manager, his former duties were split between Lund, who took over the farm system, and Katalinas, who became responsible for scouting and ultimately the player draft, which began in 1965. Each major-league team drafted youngsters in January and June, retaining exclusive rights for six months. Before 1965, teams could sign anyone who had graduated from high school or college or who had reached his twenty-first birthday. Campbell attributes the fall-off in the Tiger recruitment by the late 1960s to the team's high finishes and low draft choices, but other teams maintained successful recruitment patterns. Snyder's comments are more suggestive. He criticized the separation of direction of the farm systems from scouting. Each group blamed the other for their collective failure; there was no real accountability. Furthermore, the Tigers continued to rely too heavily on Michigan. They never trusted the cooperative scouting bureau and were one of the last to use the computer to evaluate talent. Lund acknowledged that the Tigers never really changed their scouting patterns when the draft was introduced.[109] The Tigers' system and the Campbell scouting book were innovative in the 1950s and early 1960s. Following a prospect for two to three years and getting to know his parents yielded few rewards with the new draft system. In 1966, Bill Tuttle, who had played with Detroit from 1952 to 1957, was leading the Tigers' AAA farm team in hitting, and the *Free Press* worried that the Tigers were the only team without rookies.[110] The first rookie position player to win a starting berth after Stanley was Tom Veryzer in 1975. A statistical analysis of later careers of draft choices puts Detroit's drafts eighteenth (of twenty) from 1965 to 1969.[111] The Tigers suffered more from their failure to recruit in Latin America and to adjust to the new draft than they did from high finishes.

Although the Tigers were mediocre on the field between 1951 and 1960, they made important adjustments off the field. The club was successful financially, the turnstiles were busy, the color line had finally disappeared, the farm system was prospering, the radio-television contract was the biggest in history to that point, new popular announcers broadcast Tiger games to a wide audience, and young players were bringing hope for the future. Major-league baseball in Detroit was an important part of the community, and Briggs Stadium (renamed Tiger Stadium effective 1 January 1961) was a downtown focal point. It was both a symbol and a gathering place in the city for former Detroiters who had moved to the suburbs. It provided a continuing sense of identity for people who lived in the suburbs but still wanted to identify themselves as being 'from Detroit.' The renaming of the stadium symbolized the passage of the Briggs era but the continuity of Detroit's team. John Fetzer stressed that the team belonged to the community. He was only its 'custodian' or 'caretaker.' The Campbell-Fetzer era began with promise.

4

Community Problems and
a World Championship

The Campbell-Fetzer regime won a world championship in its first decade and cemented the club's financial base. League expansion, rising attendance, and television provided increased sources of revenue, while the reserve clause kept payrolls constant. Breaking of the color line allowed the club a wider base for recruitment and attracted more African American fans, but its black players still faced segregation during spring training. The city of Detroit was becoming more multiracial, with resultant tensions that culminated in the 1967 riot. Civil rights movements and protests against the Vietnam War challenged America's ability to adapt. Baseball was not immune to the society around it.

AN EXPANDING COMMUNITY OF FANS

In 1961 the American League expanded to ten teams. This completed expansion to the West Coast, bringing the American League to Los Angeles in a new franchise and permitting Clark Griffith to move his franchise from Washington, DC, to Minneapolis–St Paul. Washington received the second expansion franchise. Congress insisted that the nation's capital have a major-league franchise. The idea of expanding the majors, either by increasing the number of teams or by creating a third league, had been muted since the late 1940s, but baseball moved slowly as usual.[1] Expansion both reflected and encouraged wider media attention and television markets. Expansion also infused money. Each new franchise paid an entry fee of $2.1 million in 1961. (That was only the beginning. No one foresaw that Colorado and Florida would pay $95 million thirty years later.)[2] The monopoly of franchises held by major-league baseball allowed owners to charge increasing fees to those cities and owners that wanted a major-league team. These became an important source of revenue for ball clubs. About a quarter of the Detroit Baseball Club's total profitability between 1961 and 1981 was due to expansion fees in the draft of players to man these teams.[3]

Expansion also diluted talent, especially second-line pitching, for a short time. Ineffective pitching, an additional eight games in the season, and the bandbox ballpark in Los Angeles led to an increase in average team home runs from 136 to 153 and in runs from 677 to 734 from 1960 to 1961 in the American League. Two hundred forty-eight home runs were hit in Los Angeles; Tiger Stadium was next with 185. The New York Yankees hit a then major-league record 240 home runs, breaking their own AL record of 193, set in 1960, and the major-league mark of 221, held jointly by the 1947 Giants and the 1956 Reds. Roger Maris broke Babe Ruth's home run record, although Commissioner Ford Frick insisted that an asterisk accompany the record because it was achieved in a 162-game season.

This first increase of major-league teams in sixty years elicited fears that baseball would never be the same. In a poll of baseball scribes by *The Sporting News*, thirty foresaw expansion as doomed, eighteen adopted a 'wait and see' attitude, and twenty-three thought it would be successful. Among Detroit writers, E.A. Bachelor, who held the first card issued by the BBWAA in 1908, described it as a 'travesty.' Lyall Smith predicted a decline in attendance for established clubs. Sam Greene and Joe Falls were also among those listed as opposed.[4] Writers also warned about dilution of talent. They forgot, however, that the population of the United States had doubled since the turn of the century. The influx of new talent from the Caribbean and from African Americans provided more than enough talent to sustain the quality of baseball.[5] Rather than declining, attendance in the major leagues increased by 36 per cent during the 1960s as compared to the 1950s; with allowance made for the greater number of teams, the increase was about 10 per cent (tables 1, 11). National prosperity brought increased spending on spectator sports, which doubled during the 1950s and tripled during the 1960s.[6] Although other sports, particularly football, were attracting more fans, baseball still accounted for 61 per cent of total attendance at all major-league professional games in 1964.[7] Despite some inflation, baseball ticket prices remained the least expensive among professional sports (table 13).[8]

Detroit experienced even greater success at the gate. More than 12,825,000 fans passed through the turnstiles during the 1960s, against 11,902,000 during the 1950s. Detroit's 8 per cent increase in the decade was like that of major-league teams as a whole, but attendance in the American League lagged behind that of the National League. Detroit's attendance was 2.9 million over the American League club average for the decade – almost 16,000 per game versus the league's 14,000; it had been 1.8 million above the American League average during the 1950s. Attendance in 1961 was the biggest since 1950. The Tigers drew over two million fans at home for the first time in 1968 (table 5). That success carried over to the early 1970s as Detroit led the American League in average attendance between 1969 and 1974.[9]

Attendance very much reflected Tiger fortunes on the field. Annual attendance showed a strong, direct mathematical relationship to victories during each year.[10] Attendance did fall below one million fans and the league average in 1963 and 1964, creating worries that the Tigers were losing money,[11] but the Tigers were prosperous through the period. Jim Campbell's records show that the Tigers made money every year during the Fetzer era. Income from the Detroit Lions' rental of Tiger Stadium put them in the black in 1963 and 1964. Detroit profits from baseball operations averaged $1 million annually during the 1960s and 1970s. They received an additional $8 million in rental from the Detroit Lions plus money from expansion and from the World Series of 1968. Fetzer Enterprises had an average annual profit of about $2 million from the baseball club between 1961 and 1981.[12] Ticket prices in 1961 were $3.00 for box seats, $2.00 for reserved, $1.25 for general admission, and 75¢ for bleachers. In 1969 they were $3.50, $2.75, $1.50, and $1.00 respectively. In 1967 a scorebook cost 25¢, the yearbook 50¢, a beer 45¢, Coca-cola 15¢ and 25¢, red-hots 30¢, and ice cream 20¢. There were about five Ladies' Days annually, with a maximum of 13,000 women admitted at discount. The Tigers reached out to the young with twenty-one dates for little leaguers and boy scouts.[13]

Detroit's first big promotion was Bat Day, attended by 46,642 fans at its inaugural in 1964, a dozen years after Bill Veeck had distributed free bats in Sportsman's Park. On 29 May 1967 the *Detroit News* carried a picture of Gordie Howe, Red Wing hockey star, with his son in a bat day crowd of 52,357 the day before. A less successful promotion was Cap Day. The Tigers had 24,000 caps available for give-away in 1966, but the total attendance was only 24,056. Opening day remained a major event, and Detroit was always among the teams with the highest attendance. In 1958 450 vendor and counter personnel served the crowd $400,000 dollars' worth of concessions. By 1970 there were five family nights, six ladies' days, six special events, and seventeen events at which fans received novelties and souvenirs.[14] The Tigers did some work with some group sales to organizations and at bars,[15] but the era of special promotions would come later.

Fans at home were becoming as important as fans at the gates. For major-league baseball as a whole, income from the sale of local broadcasting rights doubled during the 1960s, income from the national rights tripled, and income on a per club basis increased by two-thirds (table 4). Within a year, 1964 to 1965, two events combined to demonstrate the increasing importance of television for baseball. CBS purchased the New York Yankees in August 1964. Baseball and television had had a symbiotic relationship since the inception of television. This sale of the then pre-eminent team in baseball to the leading television network of the time dramatized that relationship. It also engendered concern about whether baseball could retain its independence. Arthur Daley editorialized in the *New York Times*: 'This strange union brings on feelings of disquietude. It means that the world of electronics has established its strongest bridgehead on the world of sports and this is an industry with a history of expanding every foothold without so much as a step backward.' He went on to say: 'TV enriches and destroys, it demolished boxing and killed minor leagues with its "scorched-earth" policy; only football survived well.'[16] *Sports Illustrated* also condemned both the arrangement and other owners for approving it.[17] CBS would continue to show Yankee games on its network, but the following year ABC agreed to a national pact with the other teams for a 'Game of the Week.'

A new era of national broadcasting began in 1965. The primary mover in the arrangement was John Fetzer. Fetzer convinced his fellow owners to establish a committee to seek a new national television contract after baseball saw its national television income cut almost in half over the previous five years. Separate NFL and AFL contracts brought football a combined $21 million – twelve times baseball's previous contract. Fetzer actually proposed a Monday Night prime-time baseball game (the idea that would serve football so well from 1970). ABC rejected it then – perhaps because it was still too early for prime-time sports, perhaps because Roone Arledge believed that television was a better medium for football than it was for baseball: 'Baseball was a game that was designed to be played on a summer afternoon at Wrigley Field in the 1920's, not on a 21 inch screen. It is a game of sporadic action interspersed with long lulls. Last year we tried running plays in slow motion. It was redundant. Television has to cover sectors of the diamond; instead of being able to watch a player, you see him only in the middle of a play.'[18]

Television soon introduced replays and slow-motion images of baseball games, but baseball never captured the television audiences that football did.[19] The number of games shown nationally decreased dramatically from 123 to 28 in the new contract. Nevertheless, this pact tripled the national television income for organized baseball and tripled (to $300,000) the income of every team that participated. The Yankees had a separate arrangement with CBS, for which they received $500,000. Advertising spots, which ABC sold for $28,500, were directed to males. (Gillette never advertised its Toni permanent.) Busch (Budweiser) allocated 70 per cent of its advertising budget to sports; Gillette spent 90 per cent of its budget on sports; Chrysler, Phillips Cigars, and R.J. Reynolds Tobacco were other major sponsors.[20] Market areas and advertising demographics became the new watchwords.

Fetzer's role at the time received little attention from the national media – perhaps because of his quiet demeanor, perhaps because the national media doubted that such innovation could originate from Detroit. Carl Lee, Fetzer's right-hand man, said that the big-city teams opposed the game of the week and sharing revenues. Fetzer had to lobby for a national television contract against the resistance of owners who did not appreciate the possibilities of television. He had connections with CBS and Frank Stanton, but CBS demurred, perhaps because of its ownership of the Yankees. Peter Kitzer, then of WWJ-TV in Detroit, also emphasized Fetzer's role: 'Fetzer desired not just the money, which he had enough of, but also to bring America's pastime to every nook and cranny in the country; at the same time he wanted to protect local television rights.'[21]

Baseball's national television ratings reached a peak of 5.31 (Nielsen) in 1967, which meant that 9.5 million fans watched the game of the week. Local broadcasting expanded as well. Teams showed an average of 43 games at the beginning of the decade, but 57 at the end; the Tigers stayed with 40 to 43. Despite this increase in games shown, stadium attendance steadily rose.[22] Ironically, by pushing the owners into a national television agreement, Fetzer created the very monster he feared. Television brought in unprecedented amounts of money that permitted baseball magnates to compete for free agents with big dollars. Fetzer hated free agency, but he brought the dollars to the game that allowed free agency to run amok.

More important to the Tigers than the national contract were local radio and television rights. In 1965 they sold exclusive radio rights to WJR for $900,000 over three years; WWJ had broadcast day games and WJR at night until then. Radio was still important. That annual $300,000 equalled what the Tigers received from national television rights and was about half what they had been receiving from local television rights under the 1959–64 contract with Strohs.[23] WJR was 'in charge of managing and running the network' of fifty-two stations and negotiating with the sponsors, who would have 'a say' about announcers. Simulcasts ended that year, with Ernie Harwell and Gene Osborne assigned to radio and George Kell and Ray Lane to television. A major change in the marketing of broadcast rights also occurred in 1965. WJR took over radio rights from the sponsors and sold spots at the same time that Capital Cities Broadcasting bought WJR. The radio station and the Detroit Tigers split the pay of announcers. WJR took responsibility for air-time, but the Tigers used announcers for off-season promotions.

The approach to local television rights similarly changed in 1965. Instead of selling television rights directly to major sponsors as they had with Goebel or Strohs, the Tigers took over television production and advertising sales. The reason that they did so remains unclear. Perhaps they thought they could make more money that way, or perhaps the sponsorship was becoming too expensive for a single sponsor.[24] In any event the Tigers were not well prepared for the new venture. 'Doc' Fenkell took over production but, as he himself said, he 'knew nothing about television, except how to turn it on.' As a result, the early efforts of the Tigers were amateurish. Fenkell sold only eight spots for twenty minutes in the first few months and had to use the remainder for promotion of the Tigers. The breakthrough was a contract with Sunoco that included special inducements: if the sponsor bought two minutes per game the first year and three the next, it would receive an extra three minutes in the first year. Major advertisers received additional opening and closing credits. Tiger income from local rights apparently doubled as a result of their new marketing, but in the first two years the Tigers incurred extra expenses and did not sell all the spots. Not until 1967–8 were the full benefits of the new venture realized, by which time the package was 'selling itself' as the Tigers challenged for the pennant.[25]

This new concept of 'multiple sponsorship' and brief spots rather than a single sponsor marked a break in Tiger tradition that the press bemoaned.[26] The experiment would become practice as sports advertising became more expensive. A variety of new sponsors also showed that baseball was a form of family entertainment at home. Major sponsors on WJR in 1969 with thirty-one other stations were B.F. Goodrich, Buick, National Bank, Pure Oil, and Strohs. On WJBK-TV (in its seventeenth year) they were AC Spark Plugs, Allstate, Faygo, General Cigars, Hygrade, RJ Reynolds, Sun Oil, Oldsmobile, and United Airlines.[27] Television also became a way of advertising the team. Fetzer realized that 'there would be no way to keep our name on the front door without tv.'[28] His outstate network profited from the sale of sponsorship of Tiger games. The *Free Press* correctly noted that the relationship between the New York Yankees and CBS and between the Fetzer network and the Detroit Tigers meant that money was simply being transferred from one part of a corporation to another.[29] Tiger games played not just in the city of Detroit but to fans in the tri-county base, which included more than four million people by 1970. Eight million people, with the highest metropolitan individual income in the nation, lived within ninety miles of Tiger Stadium.[30] Through the outstate network – which consisted of seven stations in Michigan and one in Toledo and, for a time, one in Fort Wayne, Indiana – the entire state could watch Tiger games. Fans who might be disinclined to venture often to downtown watched games on television. The Detroit area provided a wide base and attractive demographics. Television ratings for Tiger baseball were among the highest in the country and local television rights about one-third over the league average in the period (tables 4, 12).[31]

A CHANGING COMMUNITY

While the ball club prospered on and off the field, radio and television expanded the community of fans. During the pennant drive in 1961, the *Detroit News* claimed Detroit was 'the greatest baseball town' in America and that the success of the team carried over to the social life and business in the city.[32] The *Detroit Free Press* and the Detroit Tigers jointly sponsored clinics in five Michigan cities for 'junior baseball players and coaches' that drew about 5000 boys. An exhibition game on 8 May 1962 between the Tigers and Astros infused $50,000 into sandlot baseball throughout Michigan.[33] Tradition was upheld with the restoration of the Gothic D on Tigers home uniforms after DeWitt soiled them by slapping 'Tigers' on them.[34] To his credit, DeWitt allowed fans to upgrade their tickets on game day at the stadium and removed the 10¢ coin slots from women's toilets in 1960. He did nothing about the urine troughs in the men's restrooms – perhaps because of a legend that the aroma that emanated from them made restrooms easy to locate. The team made a goodwill trip to Japan, the Phillipines, Hawaii, and Korea in 1962. That same year the Detroit Round Table of Catholics, Jews, and Protestants sponsored Baseball Brotherhood night on 23 August. The theme was 'various backgrounds of race, religious faith, and national origins are one in the devotion to their country and to their American way of life.'[35] *Look* magazine dubbed Detroit in 1962 'the city on the go,' a place for poor people to fulfill the American dream. Mayor Jerome Cavanagh, who reminded people of John F. Kennedy, was elected in 1963. Martin Luther King visited the city that same year. The city regarded itself as 'an avant-garde of American liberalism.' Macomb County was then the most solidly Democratic suburban county in the United States.[36] The community was vibrant, and the baseball team was a unifying force.

Still, the city was becoming poorer and more separated from the white suburbs surrounding it (table 10). Between 1949 and 1971, 27 separate renewal projects used $116 million in federal funds and $174 million of the city's money, but only 758 low-income units were built in the city between 1956 and 1965.[37] Sit-ins at the First Federal Savings and Loan Association in 1963 and picketing of the GM building in 1964 protested segregation. The Civil Rights Commission investigation into the police and fire department showed that only 7 and 3 per cent respectively of their members were African Americans and that there was only one non-white at high levels.[38] Dearborn Mayor Orville Hubbard announced in 1967 that he did not believe in integration: 'When that happens, along comes socializing with the whites, intermarriage, and then mongreliza-tion.' A point system for buying property in the Grosse Pointes rated color, accent, religion, and the 'American way of life.' African, Hispanic, and Asian Americans automatically failed. Only fifteen African Ameri-cans resided in six major suburbs in 1970 (for instance, Dearborn, one; Warren, five; Grosse Pointe, two).[39]

Expressways were chopping up the city and producing poor enclaves. Access to Tiger Stadium by expressways was easy, but the population was shifting to the suburbs, especially to the north-west. Near the ball-park there were only 6000 licensed parking spaces, with another forty-five to fifty unlicensed operators.[40] John Fetzer saw a role for the Detroit Tigers preserving the city's downtown: 'My purpose is to lend a con-structive influence to the operation of a gigantic and important institu-tion in the city of Detroit.'[41]

The problems were beyond the power of a baseball club to mediate, however. A routine raid on a well-known blind pig precipitated the Detroit riot of 1967. Twelve officers raided the United Community League for Civic Action on Twelfth Street just north of Clairmount at 3:45 a.m. on Sunday 23 July 1967. At 6:15 a.m., Inspector Charles Gen-try ordered mobilization of the day patrol to a staging area at Twelfth Street and the John Lodge Expressway, later moved to Herman Keifer Hospital. Leaders of the African American community – including Rev-erend Robert Potts, director of Grace Episcopal Church, John Conyers, and the Tigers' Willie Horton – attempted to moderate the crowd with-out success. Willie Horton said: 'I could not believe the riot, I went out on my own to Livernois and the freeway in my uniform.'[42] By the after-noon of 24 July all vital installations in the city were guarded because civic leaders incorrectly suspected a plot. State police and national guardsmen were on the street by evening. The Tigers were playing a doubleheader against the Yankees that day, and the crowds on their way home viewed the beginnings of violence and fires. By midnight there had been incidents in eleven of Detroit's thirteen precincts; 600 police officers, 352 troopers, and 900 guardsman were on the street, but so were 10,000 civilians. The trouble began in an area of high crime but also in the area of highest unemployment. While unemployment in Detroit was 6 per cent, it was 15 to 20 per cent in the inner city, and probably twice as high among male inner-city youth, whose numbers had risen dramatically. At 3:00 a.m. on 24 July, Mayor Cavanagh and Governor George Romney requested federal troops, which arrived twenty-two hours later at 1:00 a.m., 25 July. When the state police were withdrawn two days later, 1671 people were in custody. By 30 July the riot was over.

Detroit had been occupied by 4700 troops of the 82nd and 101st Airborne Divisions, its third occupation (1863, 1943, 1967) by federal troops. Forty-three people had died, thirty-three of them African American. Thousands were arrested, 1000 businesses were burned, and another 2700 ransacked.[43] Detroiters were shocked. So was the nation. Newspapers like the *Washington Post* and the *New York Times* wondered how such a devastating riot could occur in Detroit. 'In the attempt to cope with the problems that lie behind the present convulsion in American cities, Detroit may well have been number one,' the *Times* wrote on 27 July 1967.[44]

Detroit was not alone in suffering such violence. There had been disturbances three years earlier, notably in New York's Harlem. The first major riot occurred in 1965 in the Watts section of Los Angeles and resulted in thirty-four deaths. There were forty-three additional outbreaks in 1966, the most serious in Chicago and Cleveland. Following the assassination of Martin Luther King in 1968, major riots broke out in sixty American cities. But in that year only forty-three people died,[45] the number that died in Detroit in a single week. The *New York Times* made the Detroit riot its lead story: 'It looks like a city that has been bombed ... Looters roamed freely.'[46] John Hershey's novel *The Algiers Motel Incident* popularized one deadly occurrence.

'Nothing affected Detroit like the 1967 riot.'[47] Nor did anything affect Detroit's image in the nation as much. Although Coleman Young describes the week as 'rebellion but not a race riot,' he concludes that 'the riot put Detroit on the fast track to economic desolation.' Seventy thousand people left Detroit in the final months of 1967, a further 80,000 in 1968, and another 46,000 in 1969; businesses left as well.[48] The number of registered guns tripled in Detroit from 1966 to 1968 (they quadrupled in Los Angeles after the Watts riot).[49] In retrospect, Joe Falls described the city after the riot as an 'armed camp.'[50] Despite efforts to 'change the image of downtown, ... arrest 10 years of disinvestment, and provide a catalyst for the renewal of the central city,' the movement of middle-class Detroiters to the suburbs accelerated while African Americans continued to immigrate from the South.[51] Auguring ill for the future, committees to revitalize the downtown, like the New Detroit Committee, which included Henry Ford II, Joseph L. Hudson Jr and John Richie of General Motors, were unable to secure funds from an increasingly antagonistic state legislature.

Crime and race became a preoccupation in the tri-county area. After a white policeman was killed and his partner wounded by an African American, police raided New Bethel Baptist Church and arrested 143 churchgoers. Judge George Crockett released those arrested. Both the *Free Press* and the *News* condemned his actions. The *Free Press* later apologized in an editorial, admitting that the arrests violated constitutional rights. The *News* continued its inflammatory tone, publishing a daily log of crime, with the race of the perpetrators. Its readership was increasingly composed of blue-collar groups in the suburbs.[52] Murders within Detroit increased sharply, reaching 1109 in 1971–2 versus a total of 988 for the entire 1950s. Detroit became known nationally as 'Murder City.' A record eighty-nine murders occurred in the single month of April 1974. Property crime and assaults increased with poverty, but their increase was exaggerated by Detroit's adoption in May 1966 of the FBI's uniform crime reporting method, established by Washington in 1958. With adoption of the statistics, minor crimes, especially black-on-black assaults that had been handled at the discretion of precinct commanders, entered the official records. Reported domestic assaults and larceny doubled even in white precincts. Local television shows made crime their lead story, day after day, night after night. One could easily conclude that everyone in Detroit was either a criminal or victim and that anyone venturing into the city from suburban havens did so at extreme risk. The demagogy of Donald Lobsinger, self-appointed spokesperson of 'Breakthrough,' an offshoot of the John Birch Society, and of Reverend Albert Cleague, a black militant, who called for a 'nation-wide rebellion,' accentuated tension.[53] Judge Stephen Roth's ordered school busing across city lines antagonized suburbanites. Roth received death threats to the end of his life.

DISTURBANCES AT THE STADIUM

Violence increased in the stands and around Tiger Stadium as well. Incidents do not seem to have been more numerous or more serious in Detroit than in other cities, but those in Detroit captured the attention of the press. Images are important. The image of Detroit was that of a violent city. Each episode seemed to confirm that image in the popular mind.

As we have seen, the saga of fan violence in Detroit as a public issue began with the 'garbage shower' of Joe Medwick during the 1934 World Series. Occasional outbursts from the stands and promises to bring an end to ungentlemanly behavior were long a part of baseball's history. In 1907 Ban Johnson, president of the American League, had promised to end rowdiness after an incident of bottle throwing.[54] An angry mob had laid seige to the Boston clubhouse in 1915 after an altercation between George Moriarity and Red Sox catcher-manager Bill Carrigan, but that event was long forgotten. Because the attack on Medwick occurred in the World Series, it lived on in the public mind in both Detroit and in the nation.

Booing was part of the game, although a few fans went beyond the bounds of decency. Both Horton and Kaline admitted being hurt by the boos. Cash allowed, however, that even his 'wife was booing' during a slump. McLain wrote: 'In Detroit the few bad ones [fans] are so rotten they sometimes make it difficult to remember the good.' Most cruelly, some fools yelled to Hiller, 'Have another heart attack.' Fan abuse contributed to his retirement.[55]

Security of the stadium in the 1950s consisted of little more than a police detail, mainly to handle traffic. Peerless Security personnel, both uniform and plain-clothes, were there as much to prevent turnstyle personnel from allowing ticketless fans through in return for 'tips' as they were to discourage rowdiness.[56] One game with the Red Sox was delayed nine minutes in 1955 because of a beer-can barrage, but the *Detroit News* concluded that it 'wasn't as bad as the Medwick incident.' Casey Stengel still thought that 'they run the park pretty well there.' *Sport* magazine that year described Detroit as the players' favorite town to visit because of the fans.[57]

Things got worse, however. A free-for-all in the bleachers in 1959 led to guards at the gate, the banning of liquor, and two private police put on the foul lines to prevent fans on the field. That June a fan threw a firecracker at Mickey Mantle. Eleven months later Jim Piersall was showered with firecrackers, and a seventeen-year-old youth was arrested and fined for his effrontery. In the eighth inning of the second game of a doubleheader on 17 July 42,956 fans 'threatened to wreck Briggs Stadium' after umpire Joe Paperella called Bill Skowron's drive to right field a home run. There was a thirty-minute delay after Roger Maris left his position in right field, carrying the back of a wooden chair that someone had thrown towards him. Shocked at increasing rowdiness, the press warned that Detroit would get a reputation as a 'city of hoodlums.'[58] Police Inspector Lesley Caldwell's official report described the incident as a 'normal crowd reaction to an unpopular decision by the umpire.'[59] On 25 August Common Council passed an ordinance against throwing anything at an athletic contest that could 'cause injury or damage': known as the 'DeWitt' law, it carried a $500 fine.[60] There were more attacks on Piersall in Detroit and other cities. After a pop bottle hit Maris in Detroit in 1962, the Tigers declared that they would prosecute fans in the future.

Following the Tigers' defeat in the second game of the doubleheader against the California Angels that cost them the pennant in 1967, the crowd turned mean. Police warned the Angels: 'The sooner you guys are out of here, the better.' After the California players marched en masse to their bus, fans threw rocks at it, their dugout was destroyed, 200 seats were smashed, and 500 were thrown on the field.[61] Beer drinking and rowdiness had increased as the game went on. Both this incident and the Skowron incident had occurred late in the second game of doubleheaders during which fans had consumed a lot of beer.[62] Joe Falls called the 1967 eruption 'the lowest point in the history of baseball in Detroit.'[63] During the pennant race of 1968 Campbell limited standing room to control behavior, and the club prosecuted fans for running on the field. Still, the pennant-clinching celebration resulted in sod being torn up and the left-field fence torn down.[64] After the World Series victory in 1968 there was a celebration but little violence.[65] Crowds tore up sod again after the Tigers won the division championship in 1972, and after they lost the play-offs to Oakland that year. The Detroit News complained that the victory celebration 'verged on crowd violence; the police [were] in riot gear.' Falls in the *Free Press* blasted the 'lunatics in the bleachers' who damaged Detroit's image on national television.[66]

Over the last thirty years, fan violence and rowdiness has often been a theme in Falls's columns. When asked about that, he commented: 'I write about fan misconduct because families should be able to go to games. Jerks impose themselves on others' sensibilities. That's why I write about it. Sometimes worse, sometimes not in Detroit [*Ed.:* as against other cities]. It's not okay to loot and murder because your team wins. There is more sensitivity among Detroit writers because of its national image.'[67]

There is no question that fan violence in Detroit and elsewhere increased in the 1960s and 1970s, as did violence in the United States as a whole. The *Saturday Evening Post* in 1961 noted new confrontations in an article 'Ball Players versus the Fans.' Yet, it did not single out Detroit as a particular problem. Cleveland's beer night in 1974 prompted an article, 'The Ugly Sports Fan,' in *Newsweek*: 'One of the ugliest incidents in the history of the game occurred in Cleveland on beer night.' When Cleveland sold beer for a nostalgic 10¢, fans felt the need to take advantage of the bargain and became a mob of obstreperous drunks. Although the article recounted a series of incidents throughout the nation, none had occurred in Detroit. David Voigt counted forty incidents in the 1970s, emphasizing the 1974 Cleveland beer riot, the 1979 Chicago disco-record smashing, and violent celebrations in 1969 and 1976 after New York Mets and Yankee championships. He did not cite Detroit as a problem. The Harwell collection in the Detroit Public Library is full of clippings regarding fan violence elsewhere in the league. Al Kaline described the crowd at Yankee Stadium throwing things at the Tigers in 1969 as 'scary.' Tiger outfielders donned protective helmets in Boston in 1970 after fruit and concrete rained on the field. Milwaukee customers doused Horton with beer in May 1974, and later threw bottles and fire-crackers when Mark Fidrych pitched.[68]

Detroit suffered in the national media then as it would again after the 1984 World Series. Jim Murray wrote in the *Los Angeles Times* in 1962 that Detroit was 'not a city, [but] a shrine to the internal combustion engine ... a tough town, a town in overalls, a great sports town ... The enemy outfield is a dart board.'[69] Although Detroit newspapers occasionally claimed that the Cub bleacherites or New Yorkers were the worst, they remained concerned about Detroit's national image.[70] This unfortunate image of Detroit as a violent city, and the notion of Tiger Stadium as an unsafe place to visit became part of the mythology surrounding Detroit. Not only the national media but suburbanites as well equated the city with violence and crime. From a symbol of success and hope, Detroit became a symbol of failure and despair. These attitudes affected attendance at Tiger Stadium and the fortunes of the baseball club.

PROBLEMS IN THE SOUTH

Racial problems were not unique to Detroit. Because the American South was still segregated, black players suffered enormous problems in the southern minor leagues and during spring training in Florida. After an usher told Bill Veeck to move when he was sitting in the 'colored' section of the stands in Florida and because of other incidents, Veeck moved the spring training camp of the Cleveland Indians to Arizona. Problems existed there too, however. Bill White could not buy a ticket to a movie in Phoenix. James Miller concludes that black concerns about the racism of the Baltimore club, which trained in Arizona, were 'understandable but exaggerated. Like most clubs, they were insensitive to racial segregation in cities that hosted their training facilities.'[71] Some were more insensitive than others.

When Clark Griffith received approval to move his Washington club to Minneapolis in 1960, he told an audience there that he decided to move when he 'found out that you only had 15,000 blacks out here ... Black people don't go to ballgames ... You've got good, hardworking white people here.'[72] Every major-league club had at least one black player by 1960. Yet spring-training facilities, buses and cabs, housing, public washrooms, drinking fountains, movie theaters, and the like remained segregated. Black players were subject to daily humiliation. In the simplest acts of travelling, drinking water, riding a bus, eating a meal, and using a toilet, black players were treated as subhumans. Many from the North were used to prejudice but had never experienced legally countenanced, public segregation.

Curt Flood recounts 'colored' drinking fountains at spring training, special seats in movies, special cabs, and racial epithets from the stands that included 'you black nigger.' There were separate cubicles for dressing in Georgia because Georgia law forbade interracial dressing. One Jim Crow lunchroom in a bus terminal was the 'smelliest, dirtiest, greasiest, grimiest restaurant in the world.' Willie Stargell could not eat at an airport in Jackson, Mississippi, in 1959; he was sent to the back where they chopped up meat. 'I used to cry myself to sleep.' John Roseboro remembered being unable to stay in downtown Vero Beach and believed in 1967 that Vero Beach would 'never change.'

Embarrassed white players tried to support their fellows. They marched out of a restaurant in Wichita because they could not eat with their black team-mates. Buddy Gilbert brought food onto the bus in Florida for black players; Dave Bristol was threatened with a shotgun while buying food for black players in Florida.[73] Bill Freehan remembers driving from Ann Arbor to Denver and stopping outside St Louis at a drive-in restaurant. The car hop said, 'I won't serve those niggers in back.' Freehan said: 'Okay, I want six hamburgers for myself. As a white American I was irate and embarrassed.' Henley Field in Lakeland had 'colored' drinking fountains even for children.[74]

Reno Bertoia recollected four exemplary incidents from his days with Washington and Detroit. While on a Washington team bus in Florida one player noted the absence of Lenny Green and inquired, 'Where's Lenny?' The bus had to go to the Negro section to pick him up. Some players asked, 'Why can't Lenny stay with us?' Billy Hitchcock, the coach, told them to 'shut the fuck up.' On another occasion, Bertoia was sitting with Green on the third-base side of the field before a Florida game when an usher came along and shouted, 'Hey nigger, you belong on the first base side.' Bertoia admonished the usher, 'He's playing today,' only to be told, 'I don't care, he goes to the first-base side – the colored section.' In Omaha, Nebraska, Bertoia once waited with Gates Brown and Jessie Queen for an hour, but received no service. Bertoia thought that a mixed group offended some rednecks more than blacks sitting together did. The final story he calls the 'white women's washroom story.' Because there were no washrooms on the team bus travelling at night between Florida cities, the bus occasionally stopped for a 'piss call.' There were thirty-five guys on the bus, so there were line-ups. Vic Power, 'not one to go along,' used the washroom restricted for white women. An attendant yelled at him, 'Hey nigger, stop!' The bus took off in a hurry. One and one-half hours later it came to a road block set up by two state police cars. Lou Boudreau, the manager, after long negotiations with the police, who wanted to arrest Power, told everyone to throw every cent they had in a bucket. They bribed the police.[75] What would have happened to a black man taken off the bus in rural Florida in the middle of the night?

These problems need to be recorded because newspapers of the time generally ignored them. When Elston Howard joined the Yankees, Dan Daniel reported that he *preferred* to room alone. Jim Murray in his autobiography, published in 1993, claimed: 'Neither the blacks or whites were happy with the arrangement [rooming together] ... I have never observed [interracial friendships].'[76] He was not very observant. A number of former Tigers players roomed or formed friendships across racial lines: Frank Howard and Horton, Pat Jarvis and Vern Holtgrave (though they had to use separate bathrooms while travelling through Birmingham in 1962), Pat Underwood ('It just seemed natural') and Lynn Jones. Milt Wilcox roomed with a black player while he was with Cincinnati. Reno Bertoia and Lenny Green never roomed together but are 'best friends.' Mike Heath called Duane Murphy his 'best friend.'[77] Green commented on the scene in Florida:

It was reported that black players were not interested in rooming with white players. Nobody asked. Sarasota and Lakeland were totally segregated; you couldn't room together if you wanted to. Tony Oliva couldn't even dress in the clubhouse because of racial laws. The man in the uniform is the law, not what's writ on some paper. There was always the sense: don't rock the ship or you won't go anywhere. Black fans had their own section. It was part of the era. Nobody made noise. I was dropped off at downtown Vero Beach and had to walk to Dodgerstown because no colored cabs were open at 3 a.m. There were constant racial epithets. We were never protected by those people who signed us. They hired black ballplayers who could handle it. Causing any problems, raising voices was taboo. In 1955 Johnny Gora got on a train with the team, was forced to separate into colored quarters on the way to Thomasville, Georgia. Southerners actually were more inclined to avoid racial slurs than northerners, but I can't remember any slurs in majors; the problem was in the minors and spring training. I refused to play one day after separate transportation meant 3:30 a.m. arrival. All black players had to know how to survive; thus a closeness developed among them. Simple matter of where do we eat? Things were terrible. [*Ed.:* I asked, 'Were they worse some places?'] There is no such thing as worse when they are that bad. Attitude of they won't beat me. I'm not the ignorant one, it's the politicians, owners, and dignitaries who are ignorant. Many ballplayers were good; Bertoia, Allison, Killebrew come to mind.[78]

Baseball inherited a social problem, but it was slow to confront it. By 1961 some major-league teams were beginning to address problems in Florida. Arthur Allyn of the Chicago White Sox purchased the Sarasota Terrace Hotel for a half-million dollars so that all players could reside there. Dan Topping of the Yankees had fought with the Hotel Soreno in the St Petersburg area. When they refused to admit black players, the Yankees first leased a motel wing and later moved from St Petersburg to Fort Lauderdale. Milwaukee and Cincinnati changed hotels.[79] Curt Flood asked general manager Bing Devine why teams did not move to southern California. Devine said it would have been too big an investment.[80] Jackie Robinson had pleaded in 1956 for organized baseball to put pressure on Florida towns.[81] *Ebony* summarized the situation in 1962:

Although Negro ballplayers are reaping a bonanza in 1962, money did not buy complete equality of treatment for them at all of the 14 spring training camps in Florida. The New York Yankees had booked a motel wing, private swimming pool and dining room. The New York Mets were privately housed in a wing of the new Colonial Motel on St Petersburg Beach. The Chicago White Sox bought a hotel of their own (Sarasota Terrace) and the Milwaukee Braves, St Louis Cardinals and Cincinnati Reds also made special arrangements to integrate their players.
But the Negro superstar with his $50,000 salary was not always accorded the same respect as the $7,500 white rookie. Minnie Minoso, for instance, was not welcome on the deck of the motel leased by the St Louis Cardinals. Negro players with the New York Mets 'understood' they were not to 'congregate' in the lobby of their team's motel, although white teammates were not similarly restricted. And if infielder Charles Neal wanted to stop into a bar for a beer, he had to travel into town, paying a round trip cab fare of about six dollars. The Philadelphia Phillies' Negro players lived with their teammates at a white motel but did not eat there.

While nine of the 14 clubs either weakened or wiped out training site segregation in Florida, four others, Pittsburgh, Minnesota, Washington and Kansas City tried sincerely to integrate their Negro players but encountered temporary obstacles they expected to solve by 1963. *The one club which showed least progress in any attempt to elevate its Negro players to a respectable status was the Detroit Tigers who now promise a 1963 change.*[82] [emphasis added]

Why did so many teams move in 1961? It may be simply that there were so many black players that the problem could not be ignored. It may be that when one team made a change, others had to follow. Agitation from black players and the NAACP may also have prompted change. A brief UPI notice, printed in the *Detroit News* of 3 February 1961 announced that the NAACP in Florida would ask major-league ball clubs to help break segregation in Florida.[83] Lenny Green remembers: 'About that time certain veteran black ball players were discussing the problems and even considered a boycott of spring training unless accommodations improved. The NAACP started pressure and the White Sox bought the Sarasota hotel property in 1961; some owners were discussing problems, they smelled things. Veterans like Minoso, Smith, Doby discussed problems. Pirates were given cars in 1963.'[84] Some members of the NAACP who were active in Florida then have a vague memory of discussions but could find no records of any planned action.[85] Both Willie Horton and Gates Brown say that veteran Bill Bruton pushed the Tigers to improve accommodations after he joined the team.[86]

Detroit was one of the last teams to integrate its Florida accommodations. It finally moved from the New Florida Hotel in the center of Lakeland to a Holiday Inn (Central) in 1963 after Jim Campbell had tried to get the new manager of the New Florida Inn to take black players.[87] He went to Henry Landswirth, manager and owner of a small piece of Holiday Inn. Landswirth had been in a Nazi concentration camp with his sister as a youngster. A Holocaust survivor, Landswirth readily admitted black players. By 1962 the press was addressing Detroit's situation, although perceptions varied. While *Ebony* singled out the Tigers for dragging their heels, the *Free Press* blamed racial attitudes in the town rather than Tiger policy. The *Detroit News* called Lakeland 'one of the most prejudiced areas of Florida,' but commended

Tiger management regarding equal treatment and eating facilities for Tigers.[88] That spring Henley Field integrated entrances that had formerly been marked white and colored.

Willie Horton described the problems when he joined the Tigers in 1963:

Florida was hard times. I went to the back of the bus only once in Tampa because it was full. A Yellow Cab would not move when I got in; I had to walk to Tiger Town. In 1969 after the World Series, I could not stay with my teammates. The Tigers had no one in charge of finding places; I pushed for that. We would plan trips to Florida so we did not have to stop in Georgia; now we can stop there. Bruton fought for his rights – integrated the Lakeland motel. Milwaukee [*Ed.:* where he had last played] already had integrated. When at the hotel, we could not eat in the public dining room; there was a special one for ballplayers. Bruton threatened to go back home after being refused service. That opened my eyes. Seven non-white ballplayers had to stay in one room; we had pillow fights because there was nowhere to go. Even in North Dakota in the minors, I couldn't go places. The Briggs heritage carried over. As a rookie, I didn't ask questions. Later I became involved in civil rights and Big Brothers in Lakeland. Bruton started the change.

Gates Brown also has vivid memories:

I told Campbell there should be indoctrination for northern blacks about Florida. Refused by cab, I didn't know why. A bus left me off 1½ miles from my house. At first, I was so happy to be there I didn't care but then I started looking around. Team never put any pressure on Lakeland, which they could have. Bruton pushed Tigers in 1962/63. I was no Bruton or Horton. Man got to know his limitations. I played with a grudge, a vengeance.

Judge Damon Keith, Horton's legal guardian, occasional dinner companion of Jim Campbell, and now U.S. Circuit Court judge, said:

Jim Campbell was fair but conservative. The Tigers were not an aggressive team in civil rights and integration. There were no attempts to deal with Florida problems. There was no affirmative search for African American ballplayers but they would not deny one a position on the team. It was an 'old boys' network,' with inbreeding and suspicion of everybody else. Jim Campbell genuinely liked Willie Horton, who was impulsive. Jim's whole life was dedicated to baseball; he was one of the best baseball minds, a fair man with high integrity but very conventional.[89]

Integrated housing for the team at the motel did not end the problems that black players had if they wished to bring their families to Florida. Living accommodations were an insult. After the heroics of the world championship season in 1968, Gates Brown and Willie Horton continued to encounter problems. 'The only houses they showed us down there, you wouldn't take a dog into.' The only house that the Hortons could find Connie Horton described as an 'unattractive little place, completely isolated except for a liquor store ... 25 miles from Lakeland, too far out from the schools.' She recalled sitting in a restaurant and not being waited on while whites were. Brown's wife said: 'I don't have to live that way, and I don't want my children to.'[90] In response, Campbell explained that the club tried to help all ballplayers find housing, 'although we are not obliged to. It's tough to get reservations this time of year. We have lots of white players who cannot find places to stay too.'[91] White players did have problems. Six Tiger wives and fourteen children stayed at the Acer Nook Motel, five miles from the ballpark; others lived in trailers and private homes. Dick McAuliffe's wife Joanne saw her husband only once in two months.[92] Players on the minor-league roster stayed in a converted army barracks with common toilets and showers. Blacks resided in a separate wing there. Conditions for black players were unique. Housing may have been scarce, expensive, and uncomfortable for white players and their families, but only black players had to deal with the humiliation of segregation.

Horton's walking off the field on 19 May 1969, to return on 23 May must be reconsidered in the light of this atmosphere. Born in the mining town of Arno, Virginia, one of nineteen children, he moved to Detroit at age eight. A host of scouts followed this promising teenager in the sandlots of Detroit. Playing for Northwestern High at age sixteen, he hit a home run into the upper deck of Tiger Stadium in the city championship game. His parents, to whose memory he remains very devoted to this day, were killed in an auto accident on 1 January 1965. His father had played for the Birmingham Black Barons but became a semi-invalid;

in Willie Horton's words, 'he was just burned out.' As Detroit's first homegrown black star, 'at first I had a real lot of pressure on me. Three or four years ago I tried to do too much.'[93] Two perceptive commentaries in May 1969 hinted that Horton's exit might have resulted from racial prejudice and experiences in Florida.[94] At the time he attributed it to 'a personal problem and I got it settled now ... Little bitty things just kept piling up, somehow they were never corrected.' He said then that he was sorry about the impact on the 'kids' and that it did not have to do with racial problems.[95] It did.

Horton walked off the field to prompt the Tigers to give young black ballplayers, specifically Ike Brown and Ron Woods, a chance. His memory about this is correct because Ron Woods had been brought up by the Tigers on 22 April and Ike Brown debuted on 17 June 1969. He claims that he met John Fetzer to discuss his feelings, but his memory may be faulty about that. Campbell insists that no such meeting took place. Perhaps Horton talked with Fetzer at another time.[96] The chronology of the housing problems in Florida and Horton's specific memories of black players being promoted make it nearly certain that his actions in May 1969 were a protest.

Brown, Horton, and Elliot Maddox were all fined $100 for missing the annual Capuchin benefit dinner in April 1970. Detroit newspapers gave no reasons for their absence.[97] Both Brown and Horton separately state now that the boycott was deliberate because 'there were no black kids in attendance.' The following year organizers of the benefit sent tickets to Judge Keith for distribution in the black community.[98] The Capuchin charity served blacks as well as whites, but the fundraising dinner itself was white. It serves as an example of people doing good who were insensitive to the dignity of the recipients of their charity. It was a different age.

PENNANT RACES AND A CHAMPIONSHIP

Things were better on the field. When Joe Gordon quit as manager of the Tigers after the 1960 season, Campbell attempted to get a 'name' manager: 'I tried to get Paul Richards or Casey Stengel; I needed something to jack the town up. Fetzer met me and Ferrell in Los Angeles. Casey had picked his coaches, but his doctor said no and Edna Stengel called me to tell me that. Baltimore would not release Richards. Then I tried for Al Lopez in Florida. We again agreed to who the coaches would be, but he was loyal to Veeck who was trying to buy the White Sox and wanted Lopez to manage. I came back to Scheffing who turned out to be American League Manager of the Year his first year.' The press mentioned Bill Rigney and Bobby Bragan as possibilities, but Campbell insists that Scheffing was his choice after Richards, Stengel, and Lopez declined. Scheffing was attracted by the new regime: 'The way the club was before I wouldn't have been interested – the rule of 11 owners, managers' turnover, and the reputation of fat cats.'[99]

The Tigers surprised everyone by making a great run for the pennant in 1961. They made the greatest improvement in Detroit's history (from 71 to 101 victories). *The Sporting News* had picked them for fifth, Falls for 'no higher than fourth.' Even when they were in first place in May, *Sports Illustrated* judged that the Tigers 'can't possibly win the pennant.'[100] After an opening day loss they won ten in a row and occupied first place for thirty-nine days between 21 April and 6 June, when Cleveland took the lead. After beating the Yankees 4–2 and 12–10, the Tigers took over first place from Cleveland on 17 June, but they lost the next day to Whitey Ford 9–0. During July they exchanged the lead with the Yankees eight times while Cleveland fell out of the pennant race. The Yanks pulled ahead in early August, but the Tigers won 11 of 14 in late August to bring them within 1½ games of the Yankees.

The teams met in New York for a crucial three-game series that began 1 September and was seen by a record 171,503 fans. The first game matched Mossi and Ford, the latter replaced after a muscle strain in the fifth inning by Bud Daley and then Luis Arroyo. The game was scoreless with two out in the bottom of the ninth when consecutive singles by Howard, Berra, and Skowron gave the Yanks a 1–0 victory. The second game in 95-degree heat was close until the eighth inning, when the Yanks scored four on a two-run single by Kubek and a two-run home run by Maris, who hit home runs 52 and 53 in the 7–2 Yanks victory. The Tigers led 5–4 Sunday in the ninth inning of the third game, but Mantle's fiftieth home run tied the game. Then Berra singled off Gerry Staley, Ron Kline relieved, Arroyo sacrificed, Skowron received an intentional walk, and Clete Boyer flied out, but Howard hit a 0-1 pitch for a three-run home run. Arroyo won games 1 and 3 and saved the second for Ralph Terry while the Detroit bullpen collapsed in games 2 and 3. Relief pitching was probably the greatest difference between the two teams as the Yankees had a reliable stopper in Arroyo; the Tigers had none. Their bullpen was by committee. They acquired Kline, Staley, and Hal Woodeshick in mid-season and used starters in relief, but the bullpen remained a problem. The Tigers lost eight in a row on their road trip while the Yankees won eight in a row, effectively ending the pennant race. About 8000 loyal fans nevertheless cheered the Tigers on their return.

The Tigers' main improvement was in run production, going from 44 runs below the league average in 1960 to 107 above in 1961.[101] There were some stellar individual performances. Cash had one of the greatest years in baseball history. He led the league in hits (193), average (.361), and on-base average (.488). He also led in more sophisticated measures of offence: production (1.15), total average (1.372), and total player rating (7.6). Cash ranked that year in the top all-time forty in production, adjusted production, batting runs, adjusted batting runs, and runs created.[102] The only players to better his statistics in any of those categories 1945–90 were Mantle, Stan Musial, and Ted Williams. Cash hit home runs over the right-field roof four times in 1961 and 1962, the first time on 11 June 1961. After his career ended, Cash admitted doctoring his bat in 1961, boring an 18-inch hole in it in which he glued cork and shavings. He said: 'I owe my success to expansion pitching and a short right field fence and my hollow bat.' In 1973 he carried a table leg to the plate in an attempt to hit Nolan Ryan during a no-hitter.[103]

Colavito hit career highs in home runs (45), RBIs (140), and total player rating (5.4). It was his second-best year in batting (.290) and slugging average (.580). Kaline had his second-highest total player rating (5.3) and would never again hit for a higher batting average (.324) than he did that year. Boros and Wood would never better their rookie seasons; Boros never hit .270 again and 1961 was the only year that Wood got more than 100 hits. Frank Lary led the league with 22 complete games and won a career-high 23 games; he would win eleven over the rest of his career and be back in the Sally League, riding buses, in 1963. Nineteen sixty-one was Mossi's best season (15-7, 2.96 ERA); he would win only 26 more games in the majors. Bunning (17-11, 3.19) would win 137 more games, but 106 of those would be in the National League after his trade from the Tigers following the 1963 season. When he retired, his 2855 career strikeouts were second only to Walter Johnson's 3509; he was inducted into the Hall of Fame in 1996. Bunning's success derived from a great slider and the brushback; he and Don Drysdale were called the 'meanest men in baseball.'[104] He managed for some years in the minors and eventually was elected a congressman from Kentucky.

Over the next five years the Tigers won an average of 85 games and finished in the first division each year, but never seriously challenged for the pennant. They hit a then Tiger record and league-leading 209 home runs (Cash, 39; Colavito, 37; Kaline, 29) in 1962. Kaline might have had his greatest season ever, but he broke his collarbone in New York on a summersault catch on 26 May and was out for sixty-one games, returning on 23 July. He had been leading the league in hits, average, and RBIs at the time of his injury. In the interim the Tigers played the longest game in their history and the longest game in American League history to that point, 22 innings against New York on 24 June, won by New York (9–7) on a Jack Reed home run off Phil Regan. It set records for total at-bats and for its time of seven hours; 35,638 fans ate 32,200 hot dogs and drank 41,000 beers and 34,500 soft drinks.[105] Hank Aguirre led the league with a 2.21 ERA, but the Tigers were below .500 on 1 August, and only 588 fans showed for a September game with Kansas City. Fan dissatisfaction would carry over to 1963–4, when the Tigers attracted barely 800,000 customers each year, the fewest since 1943.

With the Tigers in ninth place, attendance lagging, and resurrected complaints about player complacency,[106] the Tigers released Scheffing on 19 June 1963. He broadcast Tiger games the next year, but proved to be inarticulate, greeting fans one day with 'Hi everyone, this is Ernie Harwell along with Bob Scheffing.' Bruton liked him as an individual, but thought that he was an ineffective manager. Falls and Jerry Green thought that he was suited to be neither manager nor announcer. They also believed that his successor Charlie Dressen 'did one thing well in Detroit. He made great chili.'[107] Dressen was garrulous, old, and sick when hired by the Tigers and would die three years later – in the same year as his successor Bob Swift. Dressen reflected Detroit's penchant for an established, old-time manager. When Mayo Smith became manager in 1967, the move was generally criticized: 'Sportswriters covering the team at the time regarded Smith as a bland man without imagination.'[108]

He had been known as 'America's guest,' availing himself of free food and drinks in press rooms.[109] Bill Freehan described him as 'low-key, quiet, thoughtful, not easy to anger, doesn't second guess.'[110] His teams had three very good years.

Players brought up through the Tiger farm teams – Brown, Freehan, Lolich, McLain,[111] McAuliffe, Northrup, Sparma, Stanley, and Wert – were all at or near the peak of their careers from 1967 to 1969. Cash and Kaline were still productive players. Detroit added Earl Wilson from Boston on 14 June 1966. After the Tigers had four players in the top ten in slugging average in 1966 (Kaline, McAuliffe, Horton, and Cash), *Sports Illustrated* picked Detroit for first in 1967. They brought 4–1 odds in Las Vegas.[112]

Nineteen sixty-seven produced the closest pennant race in history. Four teams (Boston, Chicago, Detroit, and Minnesota) were within 1½ games of each other on Labour Day and again with a week to go in the season. Had it not been for two injuries, the Tigers might have won the pennant. On 27 June Al Kaline broke his finger, slamming his bat into the bat rack after a strikeout. He called it the 'dumbest thing I ever did.'[113] McLain injured his toes and foot on 18 September and did not win a game after 2 September. In his first memoir McLain said he hurt his ankle when his dog Pepsi heard a noise at the garbage cans, barked, and caused McLain to jump up and tear ligaments. In his second he admitted kicking a locker and hurting his toes, but still insisted that he strained ligaments in jumping from the couch. Once he blamed bears as the culprits, on another occasion, raccoons. Jim Campbell says that Jack Hand told him after the incident that McLain had kicked a locker and injured both his toes and foot, and Mickey Lolich reported the same. McLain 'made up stories'; '[his injury] cost us the pennant.'[114]

The Tigers lost crucial leads to Boston on 18 and 19 September, the first when Fred Lasher, who had had thirteen straight saves, grooved a pitch to Carl Yazstremski. They later lost a game to Washington with two out in the ninth. Relief pitching proved an Achilles heel and would remain a problem for the Tigers until the heyday of John Hiller in the 1970s.

It went down to the final weekend. Minnesota led both the Tigers and Red Sox by one game. The Red Sox hosted the Twins in single games Saturday and Sunday. Because of rainouts the Tigers had to play consecutive doubleheaders Saturday and Sunday at home against the California Angels. Boston won 6–4 Saturday on a three-run homer by Yazstremski in the seventh after Twins starter Jim Kaat injured his arm in the third inning. Lolich pitched a three-hit shutout in Saturday's first game, which the Tigers won 5–0. They led 6–2 after seven innings in the second game, but California scored six runs off four relievers in the eighth to win 8–6.

On Sunday 1 October Boston won again, eliminating Minnesota. Detroit won its first game 5–3. In the nightcap the Tigers took an early 3–1 lead on Northrup's homer into the right-center-field seats, but left-handed hitting Don Mincher hit a home run off Hiller, a left-hander, who relieved McLain, to put California ahead. The Angels scored three in the third and three in the fourth, and led 8–5 in the ninth. The ball-park came alive when Freehan opened the ninth with a double and Wert walked, but Jim Price, pinch-hitting, flied to left and McAuliffe grounded into his only double play of the season, 4–6–3.[115] The Tigers hit into 140 double plays that year, stole only 37 bases and left 1209 runners on base (versus opponents' 1042). Lack of relief pitching, speed, and clutch hitting, and injuries, cost Detroit the pennant.

Las Vegas picked Detroit for first in 1968, as did *Sports Illustrated*, but the latter warned 'they will find a way to lose it.' 'They have a bull pen of untested kids ... a team with little finesse ... [and] the aura of defeat.'[116] Opening day was postponed for a day because of the assassination of Martin Luther King on 4 April. Fearful of another riot, city officials imposed a curfew. Although the curfew had been raised only an hour before, 40,000 fans attended the opener. The season began inauspiciously with a 7–3 loss to Boston. The next day, however, Gates Brown's ninth-inning pinch-hit home run gave Detroit a 4–3 victory over Boston. That victory was typical of Brown's great pinch-hitting season and the Tigers' come-from-behind victories. On 10 May a 12–1 victory over Washington put the Tigers in first place for good. By 20 May they had won eleven games in their last at-bat. McLain won his fifteenth game on 7 July, three days ahead of the mid-point of the season. On 4 July the Tigers led by 8½ games – the largest Fourth of July lead in the decade; it was 9½ at the All-Star Game. After the Tigers lost four of five, 17–21 July, Baltimore closed to within 4½ games. McLain won his twentieth game on 20 July, and the Tigers were back in front by 7½ games. The lead was again down to four games on 27 August, but the Tigers won four of five, including two of three from Baltimore to re-establish a seven-game lead. On 14 September McLain won his thirtieth game on national television, 5–4 over Oakland, as the Tigers fittingly rallied for two runs in the ninth inning. The team won eleven straight from 9 to 21 September clinching the pennant on 17 September, 2–1 over New York. The Tigers had actually clinched the pennant minutes before their own victory because of a Boston victory over Baltimore, but fans at the park did not know that. Campbell asked Harwell to delay the announcement of the victory because he feared the fans would rush onto the field. Harwell recalled: 'I didn't totally agree with Jim – it was a form of censorship.' In the Tiger ninth, Kaline, pinch-hitting for Cash, walked, Freehan singled to left, Brown walked, and Wert singled, driving in the winning run. In his professional style, Harwell simply said, 'Let's listen to the bedlam here at Tiger Stadium.'[117] Their 103 victories were a Tiger record, subsequently broken by the 1984 team's 104.

The slogan in Detroit had been 'Year of the Tiger.' The 1968 season also might be called the 'Year of the Pitcher.' The 3.34 runs per team scored that year were the lowest in postwar history.[118] As a team the Tigers hit only .235, but they led the league in home runs with 185 and runs scored with 671. That year Northrup hit four grand-slam home runs, Horton hit 36 home runs, Cash had more than 20 home runs for the eighth straight season, and Kaline topped Greenberg's home run record of 306, ending the season with 314. Brown hit .462 as a pinch-hitter after hitting only .154 in that role in 1967.[119] McAuliffe did not hit into a double play all season after ending the 1967 season with one. Stanley did not make an error in the outfield and Freehan set an AL record for put-outs (971); both he and Stanley won Gold Glove awards. Freehan would win five Gold Gloves and retire with a then record .993 fielding average. Freehan and Northrup made *TSN*'s All-Star Team.

The big story was Denny McLain, AL Pitcher of the Year, unanimous choice for the Cy Young Award,[120] the first pitcher to win thirty games since Dizzy Dean in 1934. McLain was 31–6 with a league-leading 28 complete games in a league-leading 336 innings and a 1.96 ERA. Like the Tiger team as a whole, he was best in the clutch. As a team the Tigers won forty games from the seventh inning on and thirty in their last at-bat; because of low scoring, most games were close.[121] The team had an esprit de corps, perhaps because many had played in the minors together. They partied together[122] and many continued to live in Detroit. Both Campbell and the late J.P. McCarthy described it as their favorite Tiger team because it was 'home-grown.'[123]

Before the World Series began a crucial decision had to be made. Kaline had missed thirty-seven games after his arm was broken by a pitch from Lou Krausse. During the stretch run the Tigers' outfield consisted of Northrup, Stanley, and Horton, with Ray Oyler at shortstop. Would Kaline play? In a bold move, especially for the conservative Mayo Smith, Smith sent Kaline to right field, moved Northrup to center, and put Gold Glove center fielder Stanley at shortstop. Stanley recounts that he had always practised at shortstop because of nervous energy, wanting an extra workout. He thought that Cash had probably suggested the move and that Campbell ordered it. Learning about it six days before the World Series, he worried only about embarrassing the team. He was certain that Kaline was going to play; it was a question of whether he or Oyler would sit. Campbell says that the idea was Mayo Smith's; he only approved it.[124]

The first game on 2 October in St Louis was a classic confrontation between thirty-game winner McLain and Bob Gibson, who had compiled a still-standing NL record ERA of 1.12 – the best in baseball since Dutch Leonard's 1.00 in 1914. It was no contest. The Cards scored three runs in the fourth inning and Gibson struck out a record seventeen in a 4–0 victory in St Louis. The only good omen was that Stanley handled five chances without an error, including the first ball hit in the game, a one-hopper to him by Lou Brock. In the second game Kaline made two great catches, and Lolich, who had won ten of his last twelve regular-season decisions, hit his first professional home run. Cash and Horton also hit home runs. The Tigers won 8–1.

The teams returned to Detroit on 5 October for Game 3, won by the Cards 7–3 behind three-run home runs by Orlando Cepeda and Tim McCarver. Lou Brock stole three bases, giving him a total of six in three games. Game 4 was an embarrassment as the Cards clubbed McLain for six runs in three innings and went on to a 10–1 victory. Brock stole his seventh straight base, tying the record he had set the year before. The stalling tactics of Smith during the rain and the hurry-up tactics of the Cards, attempting to make the game official, accentuated a sense of fiasco. New York sports writer Jimmy Cannon complained: 'I never saw anyone play so bad in the World Series. They're stinking out the joint is what they're doing.' Falls called it 'the worst game we've played all year.' *Sports Illustrated* judged that Detroit 'had a right to be embarrassed in game 5.' Out-of-town sports writers left Detroit for dead.[125]

They seemed ready for burial in game 5 when St Louis scored three runs in the first inning off Lolich. It was 3–2 in the Tiger seventh with one out when Smith decided to let Lolich bat. He blooped a single to short right. After Joe Hoerner replaced Nelson Briles, McAuliffe singled to right, Stanley walked, loading the bases, and Kaline singled to right-center scoring two runs and putting the Tigers in the lead. Cash then singled, finishing the scoring in a 5–3 Tiger victory, again won by Lolich. The first chink in the Cardinals' running game occurred in this game. Brock was thrown out twice: attempting to steal second in the third inning and then at the plate by Willie Horton in the fifth while he was attempting to score from second on a Javier single to left. Inexplicably, he did not slide. Back in St Louis on 9 October the Tigers scored ten runs in the third inning, tying a Series record, highlighted by a grand-slam home run by Northrup into the right-field bullpen. They went on to a 13–1 victory for McLain.

The Tiger victory in Game 5 received front-page headlines in Detroit newspapers, but so did the pre-game singing of the national anthem. The *New York Times* put the anthem on its front page too. Harwell had been appointed 'designated pitcher, a non-paying job' of anthem singers. Margaret Whiting, whose songwriter father Richard was from Detroit, sang the anthem before Game 3 and Marvin Gaye, a Motown celebrity, did the honors before Game 4. For Game 5, Harwell had selected José Feliciano, who had a hit 'Light My Fire,' originally a Doors' tune. A friend had told Harwell that Feliciano had done a stirring rendition of the anthem at the Greek Theater in Hollywood. Blind, he appeared with his guide dog, dark glasses, a recorder and guitar. The *Times* described his version as between soul and folk singing. It brought some boos.

Symbols were important then. Young Americans had burned flags in protest against the brutal quagmire in Vietnam. Many equated opposition to the war with a lack of patriotism. This was the year of the Tet offensive, Lyndon Johnson's announcement that he would not seek re-election, Robert Kennedy's assassination, and the clubbing of demonstrators by Chicago police during the Democratic Convention. Some thought Feliciano was disgracing America. Fetzer sent Harwell a letter 'chastising him mildly,' but Harwell also received many letters of support. As he rightly says today: 'In retrospect, it was a watermark in anthem singing. It could be sung as felt afterward.'[126]

The Cards were heavily favored to win Game 7. Lolich had to return to face a more rested Bob Gibson, who had won seven straight World Series games in 1964, 1967, and 1968. Mayo Smith told the Tigers before the game that Gibson was no Superman, but Cash, ever the wit, asked, 'What was he doing in a telephone booth changing his clothes?'[127] The game was a classic pitchers' duel. In the third inning Gibson struck out Lolich, his thirty-second strikeout in the series, breaking his own record of thirty-one set in 1964. In the bottom of the sixth, Lolich picked Brock and then Flood off first. The game remained scoreless. With two out in the Tiger seventh Cash singled to right and Horton singled to left, bringing Northrup to bat. He hit a hard liner directly towards Flood in center, who took a step in, hesitated, tried to go back, and slipped. The ball went over his head for a two-run triple. Freehan then doubled Northrup home and the Tigers led 3–0. They scored another run in the ninth; Mike Shannon hit a meaningless home run for the Cards in the bottom of the ninth. At 4:06 p.m. Freehan caught a foul off the bat of McCarver to end the game.

At the time Flood said, 'I couldn't see the ball at all when it left Northrup's bat. I slipped on the wet grass and I couldn't get back there. What that all amounts to is I loused it up.' It has incorrectly entered baseball mythology as an 'error.'[128] It would have been a difficult catch. Regardless, Lolich had won his third straight complete game and the Tigers were world champions. Campbell said in 1994: 'of all the pitchers I have had, for one game give me Mickey.'[129] An estimated 35,000 fans went to Metropolitan Airport to greet the Tigers. The crowd made landing unsafe and Metro had to be closed. The Tigers landed at Willow Run, where there were 1500 fans. Another 150,000 congregated downtown. Office workers couldn't get home; bars were jammed and closed their doors. The victory was headline news on the front pages of both Detroit newspapers, a parade was held, and Tiger heads were painted on Michigan Avenue.[130]

Out of this celebratory feeling a myth developed that the 1968 championship brought the city together after the 1967 riot's scars. It almost certainly did not prevent another riot, for there were no riots for two consecutive years in any American city. In a column in the *The Sporting News*, excerpts of which have been reprinted, Falls expressed the euphoria some felt in October 1968:

My town, as you know, had the worst riot in our nation's history in the summer of 1967, and it left scars which may never fully heal ...

And so, as 1968 dawned and we all started thinking ahead to the hot summer nights in Detroit, the mood of our city was taut. It was apprehensive. It was fearful ...

But then something started happening in the middle of 1968. You could pull up to a light at the corner of Clairmount and 12th, which was the hub of last year's riot, and the guy in the next car would have his radio turned up: '... McLain looks in for the sign, he's set – here's the pitch ...'

This was a baseball team trying to win a pennant. Men playing a boy's game. Pretty silly when you stop to analyze it. Especially when you thought of the boys who were losing their lives in Vietnam.

But my city needed a release; it needed an outlet to release its pent-up emotions. It found it in a baseball team, men playing a boy's game.

Willie Horton is colored. It didn't matter. Did you see the one he hammered off Kaat last night? People who were prejudiced to the center of their souls found themselves rooting like mad for the Willie Hortons ... and the Gates Browns ... and the Al Kalines ... and the Mickey Stanleys ... and the Denny McLains ...

It made you think. Why were these people so happy? Because a ball team won a championship? That's part of it. But I can't believe it's all of it

I believe that they wanted to express their hope ... a belief that life is good, and can be good, under the proper circumstances ... I don't think any other sport could have turned my town on the way the Tigers did this summer.

It was a year when an entire community, an entire city, was caught up in a wild, wonderful frenzy.[131]

Pete Waldmeir wrote then: 'If Detroit has anything left it is pride in its athletic teams.'[132] Fetzer reportedly told Mayo Smith, 'You've not only won the pennant and the series. You may have saved the city.'[133] Eckhouse repeats the theme: 'While baseball in Detroit could not take credit as the cure for the troubles of the community, it did give many people a rallying point, a display of racial harmony in a champion period.'[134] A decade after the riot, the *Detroit News* recalled that the 1968 pennant 'seemed to reunite a city torn asunder by the 1967 Detroit riot.'[135] In a brochure written for the Tiger Stadium Fan Club in 1992, Michael Betzold reminded readers: 'The remarkable ability of the Tigers to unify a divided region was shown most vividly after the team won the pennant in 1968.'[136]

In hindsight the sense of bonding in the community seems somewhat exaggerated, especially in light of community divisions that followed over the next few years. Twenty years later Falls himself wrote: 'It would be foolish to say it cooled off the city in the spring of 1968, but they gave us something else to think about.' Harwell likens it to the 1935 world championship during the Depression, providing a 'distraction.' George Puscas, another columnist of the period, de-emphasizes its importance: 'It did not create bonding because blacks did not attend games.' The *Michigan Chronicle*, Detroit's African American newspaper, gave little attention to the pennant race. During the 1984 pennant chase, it was ambivalent about whether African Americans should support the team because of Tiger racial policies.[137]   Baseball should not be overemphasized, although it is an important aspect of community life. Many African Americans were fans, but the 1968 championship was most important to white Detroiters who followed the Tigers. Sports writers, who credited the 1968 pennant with reducing tension, were the ones most attached to team and downtown. The world championship gave a respite from economic and racial problems in Detroit; it did not solve them. But it was a justly proud time in the history of the Detroit Tigers.

5
The Players

Baseball is one aspect of American popular culture. Its history redounds on the history of television, race relations, and business. Recent books about baseball have focused especially on the economics of baseball, even as earlier histories were confident that the only things that mattered were those who played the game and how they played it. A typical title from a generation ago was *The History of Baseball: Its Great Players, Teams, and Managers* (by Allison Danzig and Joe Reichler, 1959). Such books belong to a simpler, more naive age, but they recognized that without the players, there would be nothing to write about. Today's players revel in their multimillion-dollar salaries, have agents, and carry cellular phones on which they talk to their investment brokers,[1] but we need to remember that it was not always so. The lifestyles of today's stars are closer to those of movie celebrities than to those of average players a few decades ago. Before considering the first modern players' strike, arbitration, celebrity status, and free agency – which inaugurated a new era in baseball – let us consider who played for the Detroit Tigers and what it meant to be a ballplayer from 1940 to 1970.

The Detroit Baseball Club recruited historically in Michigan and adjoining states as befitting a community-based and conservative organization. That pattern even continued for a decade after inauguration of the national player draft in 1964. Between one-third and 40 per cent of Tiger players whose careers began from 1945 to 1979 came from the Midwest (table 14). Recruitment was first from the high schools in and around Detroit (especially Catholic Central) and from American Legion teams (notably Trumbull Chevrolet).[2] In the 1960s and 1970s Michigan universities were a source of players. The University of Michigan and Michigan State University in combination produced more than one major-league player annually for the major leagues as a whole then. Only in the 1980s, after free agency, did Detroit's recruitment become national. Beginning in the 1970s and especially in the 1980s, California became a major recruiting ground for the Tigers as it did for major-league baseball as a whole, but the Tigers never attracted many from Latin America. As with other policies, the club felt more comfortable with the familiar. Recruiting patterns ensured that most players had rooted for the Tigers in their youth and would relish an opportunity to join the team.

Players were better educated than the average American male, and their schooling increased over time. In a sample of forty Tiger players from the 1940s, eight (20%) had post-secondary schooling. Among the fifty players listed in the 1957 Tiger yearbook, twelve had attended university, four of whom had graduated. Six had attended college, for a total of 36 per cent with post-secondary schooling. Of the forty-two players in the 1970 yearbook, nine had attended university, six others had graduated; six had attended college and one other had graduated from a college (52%). Samples of players for the 1970s and 1980s indicate that 57 per cent and 61 per cent respectively had pursued post-secondary schooling. Percentages for graduation are minima because some players attended college during the off-season.[3] Although we lack detailed information concerning the social background of those who were on Tigers' rosters, other studies reveal that players born in the United States were more likely to be middle class than was the population as a whole.[4] Median pay was better than median income in the United States. Better educated, better paid, from a higher social background, players might have been expected to organize and assert rights against management soon after the Second World War ended. They did not.

Several factors inhibited any aggressive behavior. One was early marriage. Until the 1980s players married within a year of beginning their major-league career and soon began families. Most players from the 1940s married while they were in the minors (table 15). Of the fifty players – major and minor leaguers – listed in the 1957 Tiger yearbook, only seven were still single, thirty-five married before or within a year of signing a professional baseball contract, and eight married during their career.[5] In 1954, the twenty-five players on the New York Yankees had a total of sixty-five children. The general population was marrying young then, too – and having children quickly. Family responsibility encouraged caution. Although many players had gone beyond high school, few had college diplomas or another career in train.

The dream also made them vulnerable. Playing in the majors fulfilled boyhood hopes. There were only four hundred men in the major leagues at any one time until expansion. The monopoly held by the sixteen teams meant that there was no other game around. Anyone who was tempted to stray needed only to remember the failures of the Federal and Mexican Leagues. The reserve clause meant that there was no other team available. Stars had some clout, although Mickey Mantle recounts how he was offered a cut of $5000 after hitting .365 in 1957 before settling for a $10,000 raise: 'I had no choice; it was that or stay home.'[6] The marginal player had little. The twenty-second player on a roster of twenty-five had little impact on a team's standing in the league. There was not much difference in talent between the player who sat on a major-league bench and the starters in AAA. Excluding players brought up for a brief late-season trial, exactly half the players (249 of 598) on the Tiger roster between 1945 and 1989 were with the Tigers a year or less. Eighty of them spent only one year in the majors (table 15). A revolving door operated at the tail end of the roster. Of the players who persisted more than one year, however, most put in the five years necessary to qualify for the pension plan. Nearly half of them had a decade-long career in the majors. The above prosopography allows a perspective for considering the situation of the real Detroit Tigers – the players. Their individual experiences tell us what their lives off-the-field were like before the era of free agency.[7]

SIGNINGS

Before the national draft, selection depended very much on the personal relationship between a scout, a teenager, and his parents. Although major-league baseball teams spent $63 million on bonuses between 1958 and 1969,[8] few players in the 1940s and 1950s had received a large bonus. Most signed minor-league contracts. They were delighted to be offered any professional baseball contract.

Virgil Trucks played sandlot and semi-pro ball for a company that provided a job and paid $25 weekly for baseball. He signed for a $100 bonus. Upon graduation from high school in 1937, Hal White also agreed to a $100 monthly minor-league contract. Joe Coleman Sr signed for $85 monthly, George Lerchen for $125. Signing fulfilled a childhood dream for Lerchen, who grew up eight blocks from Briggs Stadium. Joe Ginsberg was seventeen years old, a senior at Cooley High School, when he signed a Class D contract at Jamestown. Bob Cain too signed a Class D contract in 1943, although eight clubs had scouted him. Uniquely, Dick Kryhoski was offered a baseball scholarship at Yale University. From an immigrant family, he needed money and signed with the Yankees immediately after the war. Scouts told him that at age twenty-five, when he would have graduated from Yale, he would be too old to begin a professional baseball career.

Most players who signed in the 1950s had similar experiences. Jerry Davie signed from a federation league to Jamestown in 1952 at age seventeen for $150 a month for six months – a total salary of $900 for his first year. Ray Herbert signed upon graduation from Catholic Central High School. Turning down a $25,000 bonus on his father's advice because bonus rules required a player be put on the major-league roster, he signed a three-year contract with Toledo. John Hiller's father refused a $2000 bonus from Cy Williams for fear it would spoil Hiller, who was ecstatic with a $400 monthly minor-league contract.[9] Bunning did receive a bonus for $4000 while at Xavier, but only a $150 monthly minor-league salary; as a secretary, his wife earned more money.[10] Reno Bertoia's bonus was not $25,000 as reported at the time but $11,000, including $1000 for his mother to visit her family in Italy, plus tuition fees for him at Assumption College in Windsor. Kaline received a bonus contract the same year (1953) after Ed Katalinas had scouted him throughout high school. Bertoia and Kaline roomed together until Bertoia was traded to Washington after the 1958 season.

In the 1960s many players depended on try-out camps where the odds were long against being offered a contract. They felt fortunate to receive anything. After Vern Holtgrave pitched twelve no-hitters in high school, the *Chicago Tribune* predicted future stardom. He went to a Pittsburgh Pirates try-out camp in Illinois, where only three of 150 attendees were offered a contract. A Tiger scout finally signed him in the kitchen of his parents' home for a $5000 bonus plus $400 per month. Too late, Pittsburgh offered him $8000 plus $600 monthly. His father, a German immigrant, cried at the lost money. Tom Timmerman was working as a steeplejack when he missed the try-out camp from which Holtgrave signed. Later Mr Thomas, a 'bird dog' (a part-time scout, paid only for players signed), signed him for a $1000 bonus and a $400 monthly contract with Montgomery. Leo Marentette went to a Tiger try-out camp, where he struck out nine batters. He signed with Montgomery for $350 monthly with a $5000 bonus promised in 1960 if he made the big-league roster.

A few, touted as future stars, did not have to worry about try-out camps. Louis D'Annuzio kept a book on Willie Horton – which he later showed Horton – from the time Horton was nine years old. The Tigers tried to sign him during his freshman year in high school. He eventually signed for a $75,000–80,000 bonus and dropped out of high school in his sophomore year. Pat Underwood and his brother Tom were around ballparks from age three or four, playing with older kids because their father, a former minor leaguer, was president of the Little Leagues in Kokomo, Indiana. The Phils drafted Tom when Pat was a freshman in high school. Pat was chosen out of high school in 1976 as the number-one draft choice overall. He received less than $80,000 in bonus and salary. Some number-one draft choices have received more than $1 million in the 1990s.

By the late 1960s college campuses had become recruiting grounds. Jon Warden was not drafted when he finished high school. The University of Georgia (his pets' veterinarian had connections at the school of veterinary medicine there) gave him a 50/50 basketball/baseball scholarship, without which he could not have attended college because his family could not afford it. The Tigers then drafted him in the third round. In January 1966, he received a $15,000 bonus and $400 monthly to play at Daytona Beach in the Rookie League. Bill Zepp had been a superstar in high school but decided to go to college, where he lost his velocity and confidence. After graduation, he settled for a minor-league contract. Dave Bergman too decided to attend college, although he was drafted out of high school.[11] Jim Northrup gave up a chance to attend medical school after undergraduate years at Alma College for his 'childhood dream.' Bill Freehan, who played baseball and football at the University of Michigan, signed for a bonus midway through his studies. He promised his dad that he would finish his degree later and did; he now coaches baseball at Michigan. Fred Holdsworth turned down several baseball and football scholarships to colleges. Although he had been class valedictorian, he signed with the Tigers out of high school. He later completed a degree in accountancy. Kip Young came from a farm town of 450 people, a high school of 50. He was scouted as a hitter in high school but not signed. He pitched at Bowling Green (37-6), where he broke most school records. A twenty-third-round draft choice, he signed for $500.

Two unusual scouting ventures occurred at prisons. Chuck Harman, warden at the Ohio penitentiary where Gates Brown was serving time for armed robbery, contacted Wayne Blackburn, Detroit's chief scout, about Brown's potential. The Tigers signed him upon his release. Ron Leflore had played baseball in prison to get special privileges. Some former patrons of the A.C. Lindell Bar – then inmates – called bar owners the Butsicaris brothers collect about Leflore's talent. During a 'goodwill' tour of the prison, an inmate, Jimmy Karella, pushed Leflore out of a crowd of inmates towards a nervous Billy Martin and told him to 'give this guy a tryout.' Surrounded by inmates, Martin agreed. Weeks afterward, while on prison furlough, Leflore called Martin about the tryout. Martin asked, 'Who is Ron Leflore?' At the promised tryout Leflore's talent dazzled. He signed with the Tigers and was paroled to Bill Lajoie, then chief scout.[12]

Players took many different routes to professional baseball. Except for the Kalines, Freehans, Hortons, and Underwoods, the common denominator was that the path was uncertain. Finding it required a certain amount of luck, and it did not guarantee a major-league career. Entry to the majors demanded an arduous time in the minor leagues. Unlike basketball and football players, almost all baseball players spent time in the minors. Even players who had long careers with the Tigers spent an average of three years in the minors (table 15). Some never made it. Each step up was like facing a team of all-stars from the previous league. A slow start could lead to release, as could the alienation of a manager. Several players believe now that a single manager ruined their or a pal's career. A common threat was 'I can bury you here.' The front office depended on weekly reports from managers and less frequent ones from 'roving scouts.' Despite a near fist-fight with Jay Johnstone, Jim Bunning recommended Johnstone for promotion, but not all managers were so forgiving.[13] Three memoirs about the 1970s, by Frank Dolson, Pat Jordan, and Bob Ryan, give vivid accounts of the struggles of minor leaguers.

THE MINORS

Jim Bunning, who both played and managed in the minors, described them as 'an endurance contest.' Ryan describes bus rides of six, even sixteen, hours with frequent breakdowns, greasy spoons along the way, and 'lousy' hotels at the end. Daily meal allowance in the 1970s was $5 (A), $6 (AA), or $7 (AAA), even for the bigger towns. Players often slept late to save on breakfast. Their lot included bad lighting, dirty clubhouses, competition for jobs, difficulty in getting off-season work, and housing shortages – all while most players were newlyweds. Jordan described McCook, Nebraska (population, 7687), with a cemetery, a drive-in theater, an A&W, a Phillips gas station, and a diner. Its main street had one- or two-story brick buildings, a drugstore, a hardware store, a J.C. Penney, a cafe, a hotel, a movie theater, a YMCA, and a small hospital – hours from any commercial airport. There was 'dead time somehow to be filled' at pool halls, with drugstore coffees, beer, or sex.[14]

Ginsberg remembers a hotel in Rockport, New York, whose fire escape was a rope hanging from the third floor. Kryhoski's favorite was Wellsville, New York, which had grass up to one's knees, a chicken-wire fence, and pools of water to slosh through. He took home $250 per month, but others were making only $75. 'I nearly went crazy there. There was nothing to do, no movies even, $2.50 meal money, two-hour bus rides.' Lerchen garnered free dinners at private homes and free meals in a Jamestown restaurant because the meal allowance was 'totally inadequate.' One owner, Harry Bisquere, 'loaned' him $10 every other week and told him to 'forget it' after the season: 'We stayed in rooms, walked through the town or gawked at television in the lobby or sat with the potted plants – all free entertainment. There was a division among the washed up and hot-shots on the way up.'

Bus rides could be an adventure. Out of Troy, Alabama, a bus hit a tractor, costing $30,000 in repairs. On another ride the team bribed the bus driver to get beer. Lacking a toilet, they used douche bags that they threw out the window. Manager Red Rolfe, following in a car, thought he was in a rainstorm. A rickety bus in Williamsport, Pennsylvania, could not make a hill; everybody had to get out and push. One bus carrying Detroit prospects journeyed more than 1000 miles in 1985.[15] Not having collected meal money and missing his train connection, Holtgrave had to take a bus from Chicago to Duluth, where he was assigned at age eighteen. He borrowed money from a woman to have a meal and walked to the hotel because he had no money for a cab.

Even if one received an invitation to spring training with the big leaguers, accoutrements were grim. Tigertown was a converted army barracks on a former air-force base with common showers and toilet facilities, no shade, and intense heat. Polk County, which encompassed Lakeland, was dry. Entertainment was dinner, a movie, or the Elks Club bar in the next county. If families accompanied players, they had to scrounge for short-term, expensive housing miles from the camp.[16] The toughest time was when one's name was called at release time. Being returned to the minors was bad enough. Outright release meant the end of a dream, a sense that one's youth had ended, a feeling of failure, no income, and a life-crisis – often before the age of thirty. 'Cut-down is a time of married tears and tribulations.'[17] George Kell concluded: 'Baseball can be a very, very tough sport for a player who is on the fringe ... I know from actual experience the terrible agony that wives and children suffer when players are traded or sent down.[18]

A job could be won only by taking one from someone else. As George Lerchen commented, 'You always look at who is ahead and behind you. When you are in AAA, you look at the majors but you also look at AA.' Northrup won two batting championships in the minors but lay there for four years. Bruton, Colavito, and Kaline constituted the Tiger outfield when Brown, Horton, Northrup, and Stanley were in the minors. All the forementioned experienced success in the majors. Others, who were just as highly regarded when they were in the minors, never found a place.

George Lerchen lost three crucial years to military service when he was coming into his prime.[19] When he returned in 1946, Buffalo had 25 pitchers, 11 catchers, 17 infielders, and 12 outfielders on its roster for 20 places. On 17 July 1948 the *Flint Journal* called him the 'best outfielder in the league' (AAA); Pittsburgh offered the Tigers $75,000 for him. He never replaced Wertz, Evers, or Groth. As the *Toledo Blade* observed (15 January 1949): 'It will be rather difficult for a newcomer to break into the Detroit outfield.' Lerchen once called Wertz and said, 'Please get hurt.'[20] Jerry Davie compiled an 87-35 career minor-league record, 20-8 in winter ball, and 7-1 in spring training of 1956. He was 'the most important name in the farm system then,'[21] but could not break through. Ultimately, an injury ended his career.

Much could depend on a single outing or two. Kip Young recalls Hoot Evers telling him in the rookie league: 'It's between you and X. Whoever pitches best goes to Lakeland.' Hiller tells a similar story about Martin making him and Les Cain pitch against each other for a job.[22] Holdsworth got his chance by pitching two shutouts in the Florida Instructional League in the fall of 1971, while Martin, who 'formed opinions about players quickly,' was on a whirlwind tour. Holdsworth broke his cheekbone in his last outing during spring training, 1972, and missed the first month of the season.

Jordan recounts the tales of Bruce Brubaker, who remained in the minors for fourteen years, and a bonus-boy, Dennis Overby, who hurt his arm at age eighteen and could no longer pitch but struggled for four more years.[23] Among Tigers, Ed Mierkowicz labored fourteen years in the minors following the war ('that was better than carrying that lunch bucket').[24] Ike Brown spent thirteen years there during the 1960s and 1970s. Gary Ignasiak, whose younger brother debuted with Milwaukee in 1991, suffered nine years in the bushes. Why hang on so long? The answer lies in what happened to two with whom Ignasiak spent his last year on the farm. Like Ignasiak, they seemed finished and were giving it 'one last shot.' One was Milt Wilcox, who pitched ten more years in the majors, won 97 regular-season games and a play-off and World Series game in 1984 after having been relegated to the minors for the 1976 season. The other was Bruce Sutter, who won the NL Fireman of the Year award four times.

INJURIES

Injuries put a premature finish to many careers. We remember players who surmounted injuries to play vital roles – like Kaline in 1968, Hiller after his heart attack in 1971, or, earlier, Ernie Mayo, George Kell, Hoot Evers, and Art Houtteman.[25] We often forget players who played through injuries or never recovered from them. Bob Cain developed calcium on his wrist but never knew what it was and played because there was no injured reserve list. Hal White was struck by a line drive in 1954, removed from a game, and never pitched again, although his career was 'winding down.' He had played with injuries for years for 'fear of losing his job.' When Joe Coleman Sr suffered a rotator-cuff injury, no one knew what to do and he was released. Kryhoski injured his rotator cuff in 1947, an injury that scared him 'to death. It was always in the back of my mind afterward. I was afraid to sit out a game because I might never get back in. I would have been finished if I played any other position than first base; no one really knew what the injury was.' Horton played through four major surgeries and was told his career was over after only seven years, although he played ten more. He played only one full year without pain and suffers from those injuries today.

Rotator-cuff injuries were the most serious and pitchers were the most vulnerable. Here, five pitchers from four different decades recall a career-ending injury:

Jerry Davie: It began with a kink in the neck at Charleston in 1959, then gnawing pain in an arm tendon. It was treated by cortisone which relieved pain, but I was probably tearing it up. During recovery the next year, after throwing a curve ball, I felt like I had been shot in the elbow. I was only supposed to pitch to one more batter, but I had a one-hitter and pitched into the eighth inning at Denver. I pitched only nine innings in spring training after eleven straight wins in Charleston in 1958 under Bill Norman. But then I pitched one complete game and another two games into the ninth for Detroit. Then I lost strength in my arms. Two starts later I couldn't get anybody out. I was released in 1961 at age 26. You were like a racehorse, they didn't care.

Vern Holtgrave: Dressen and Campbell insisted on winter ball after my appendix broke in 1964 after an ERA of 1.91 the previous year. I pitched every Sunday and hurt my arm from overwork. The organization did not know how to take care of you. By 1966–67 everything hurt; I was tired of the aggravation and pain and could hardly raise my arm. After cortisone, 90 days in casts, hanging around soaking my arm, I quit.

Bill Zepp: I suffered a 'Tommy John' injury, tearing a tendon, and lost arm strength. I went to University of Michigan hospital and to Dr Korlan, team physician in Los Angeles. But there was no guarantee and a long and painful recovery to follow the operation. I decided not to risk further injury.

Jon Warden: A sudden shoulder injury effectively ended my career though I hung on for a while. I was drafted by KC after the 1968 season and went to Fort Dix for the National Guard. I may have done something in that cold weather. There were sixty guys in the big-league camp, including Warden at age 22, pushing it big. In an exhibition against the Twins in Orlando, I felt a pop in my shoulder – rotator cuff. There was no arthroscopic surgery then, just cortisone, darvon, etc. Perhaps a month off would have cured it, but I was expected back after three to four days. Charley Metro nearly killed me the next year throwing in the bullpen, telling me to throw harder. I was released by KC in '72; then went to Milwaukee, then Cards, then Little Rock in 1972, released in 1973. I was going back to school then. It was time to quit at age 27.

Pat Underwood: I tore a ligament in my elbow playing in the Dominican Republic in 1983, working on a fork ball for Roger Craig. I threw too many, had too much pain, was released. Later I suffered an elbow injury; there were no takers after surgery in 1985 at age 27.

Sports medicine was in its infancy, arms were fragile, and there was always that player in AAA awaiting his chance. As Kip Young put it, 'You work, work, all the time to get there and then the end ... and you're only 28.'

SALARIES

Baseball was seasonal work for most ballplayers. Until the 1970s, off-season work was necessary to supplement the salaries of most. Lacking schooling, most players worked blue-collar jobs during the 1940s and 1950s, although Tiger GM Charlie Gehringer attempted to restrict ventures that might 'interfere' with baseball.[26] Even Newhouser, who became a banker after his career, worked eleven years in a trade.[27] An oft-reprinted picture shows Richie Hebner digging graves.[28] As more players attended college, increasing numbers entered sales and made contacts that would serve them after the baseball career ended.[29] Baseball stars were celebrities in Detroit. Thus, many Tiger alumni would make the metropolitan area their permanent home (table 17). Bachelors could survive on their salaries, but families created both financial and psychological pressure.

The pay of big-league ballplayers was always above that of the average American wage-earner. According to the 1970 census, one-quarter of American families then had $6000 annual income or less, one-third $8000 or less, half $10,000 or less, and three-quarters $15,000 or less. The mean salary of major leaguers during the 1960s was always more than $15,000. Publicity given to salaries of the stars, however, gave a distorted picture of the circumstances of most players. The minimum salary, at which the vast majority began their careers, remained between $5000 and $6000 for two decades, until 1968. The median (typical salary) always remained substantially below the mean, which was inflated by a few big salaries. Half the major leaguers in the 1950s were making less than $11,000, and about half less than $15,000 during the 1960s (table 16).[30] Mean salaries increased significantly only in the 1970s. They doubled from 1967 to 1974 before free agency and tripled over the next six years. From the 1930s until free agency players' salaries constituted a steadily *decreasing* percentage of baseball revenues (table 3). Tiger salaries had been among the highest in the league under Walter O. Briggs, but declined during the mid-1950s. They were about average during the 1960s.

Not until after the world championship of 1968 did any Tiger surpass the salaries that Greenberg and Newhouser received in the 1940s. Kaline received the highest salary until his retirement. Despite reports that Colavito passed Kaline in 1962,[31] Campbell insists that Kaline was 'an institution' and that he refused to pay Colavito more. Colavito signed, but slammed the door and told Campbell that he was 'number one on the pole.' He reopened the still shaking door and shouted, 'I take that back. Frank Lane is still number one; you are number two.' They did not speak again until July. Campbell discussed with Lee MacPhail, his counterpart with Baltimore, Brooks Robinson's salary. Robinson and Kaline each received a $7500 raise.[32] Campbell thinks that he offered Kaline $100,000 after the 1970 season but that Kaline turned it down, taking $95,000 because neither he nor the team had a good year (Kaline hit .278 with 16 home runs and 71 RBIs; the team won only 79 games).[33] Kaline did draw $100,000 in 1972, but his salary acted as a cap on others. Horton says that he knew that he could never make more than Kaline. Marvin Miller, in a 1995 interview, complained that Kaline 'did a disservice to other players by limiting their salaries' and that the private conversations between Campbell and the Orioles were a practice that he worked to stop by making players' salaries public. Two decades later such discussions constituted 'collusion.'

Although the press regularly reported salary cuts after 'off years,' players recall that initial offers included cuts but final contracts seldom implemented them if the player remained on the major-league roster. Ginsberg was cut from $10,000 to $8000 because he hit only eight home runs ('we want 20') with a .260 average in 1951. Hoeft received a 25 per cent cut after winning only eleven games in 1957 after twenty the year before. These were rare occurrences.

The press more often erred by exaggerating salaries during holdouts and strikes, probably because their only source was management. Kryhoski remembers that Lyall Smith put his salary 25 per cent too high, Freehan that Joe Falls gave him a $20,000 raise during a brief holdout, and Timmerman was reported making $35,000 when he was making $24,000 during the brief 1972 strike. Some *maximum* salaries before free agency of players with respectable careers may surprise:

1940s/1950s		1960s/1970s	
D. Lund	$ 9,500	J. Warden	$15,000
R. Kryhoski	11,500	W. Zepp	17,500
E. Mayo	12,500	T. Timmerman	30,000
H. White	14,500	L. Green	30,000s
R. Bertoia	15,500	F. Holdsworth	40,000
J. Ginsberg	12,000 (Det.; later $17,500)	G. Brown	40,000 ($18,000 in 1968)
R. Wilson	15,000	M. Stanley	60,000 ($15,500 in 1968)
B. McConkey	17,500		
S. Gromek	20,000	W. Horton	80,000
P. Foytack	20,000	B. Freehan	80,000

Salaries were certainly respectable by historical standards and players were content at the time. A paternalistic management could and would give 'rewards.' Both Campbell and Horton recall Horton receiving an extra $5000 or $10,000 if he had 'the shorts.' Few alumni complain today about their former pay, although they often refer to what they 'were given' – a phrase they do not use with regard to their salaries from later occupations. What they complain about is how subject they were to management. Marginal players were especially vulnerable.

Phillips (Jack): 'Everyday players got whatever general managers wanted to give them after stars were paid.'

Ginsberg: 'The owners ran the whole show. Sign or you won't play with anybody else.'

Cain: 'Players had little say, they just accepted it. I'd like to be playing today.'

Wilson: 'Players had no bargaining power and no information about other salaries or profits.'

Hoeft: 'They played games with you. They gave players the least they could.'

Northrup: 'Take it or leave it. If you don't want it, quit. It was a one-way contract.'

Wertz told Lerchen: 'Always send back the first contract.' After sending back his second, he received a telegram: 'You won't get a third.' In 1951 he held out for a raise from $900 monthly to $1200 (the $6000 minimum annual salary). Gehringer told him: 'We can't give you more money but we will give you $2000 more if you make the team.' That was not in the contract. General manager John McHale advised Davie: 'You don't have a formal education, sign the contract' (for $4000). Pete Burnside, a graduate of Dartmouth, was shocked by McHale's arrogance.[34] After Herbert had sent back a contract, Kansas City's general manager suggested that he paste the contract on the wall of his new house because if he did not sign it, 'that's all it would be good for.' Herbert cut it up, sent it back, and wrote: 'You know what you can do with it.' A secretary called with the message: 'I've never seen him this mad.' Travel and maintenance of a second home meant that salaries were stretched.

FAMILIES

Spring training required at least one relocation annually. Trades or demotion meant more. Hal White remembers the 'problem of paying for two homes and the need for supplementary jobs.' His children and wife went to spring training but not on road trips.[35] 'Kids changing schools did not work out too well.' When Gromek's family went to Tucson for spring training, his wife drove back with her mother so she would not be alone. The car kept breaking down. There was an annual wives' caravan in old cars from Lakeland to Detroit for safety. Bertoia was married at twenty-four, had children early, and his career went down with the pressures of home life. 'We maintained two homes and had to pay for travel. In Minnesota, we had our baby in a motel room. I was getting up at 5 a.m. and trying to play a doubleheader. Stars' wives went to spring training; many others didn't, but mine did. While I was with the Tigers, I walked and took the tunnel bus from Windsor to Detroit.' Herbert's family could not afford to go to places where he played, having to stay in his home town where friends were: 'The family stayed in Detroit; we did not want to disrupt school and their friends. We could not rent anything for a month. Kids could not ride bikes, lacked friends, and did not want to live in a hotel room. I had less and less time with them when they got older. That was the toughest part. My wife did not work because of the children.'

Kaline emphasized that 'being a professional athlete involved the whole family.' His wife drove to spring training each year with their children: 'It was not easy pulling kids out of school. Now players ship cars back and fly families first-class.' He left baseball in part because his son was going to college and he wanted to spend one summer with him.[36] Wives and children made sacrifices. Birdie Tebbetts realized: 'Baseball life is tougher on the women than it is on the men. You know it's the old "see you later, take care of the kids." The price you pay by losing your kids is very high. You have to win your kids back later ... You're so deep into baseball that nothing in the world really makes any difference.'[37] Ginsberg married at twenty-three and soon divorced because 'one must love baseball above all else. I have been remarried for twenty-five years.' Stanley's wife went to spring training, but they had only an $81 weekly allowance. 'We lived in poverty but were young and didn't know it.'

Northrup regretted the toll baseball took when there were 'young kids.' He was home two weeks in summer, then around all winter: 'There was confusion about Jim Northrup the ballplayer and Northrup the person. Wives pretty much raised kids. There is a big change after the career when you are around all the time and try to define responsibilities. I spent more time with some team-mates than with family for eight months.' Lenny Green's wife would not go to Florida because of racial problems. He made special efforts to stay in touch with his child. 'I promised my mother that I would raise my daughter; I am more proud of my family than any baseball accomplishments.' Kip Young married in 1977, was called up the next day to Evansville, and went on a road trip. 'Welcome to baseball. It's not easy. Some just quit.' His wife took a year off from teaching and lost her salary.

Wives were helpmates and in charge of the family at home, as most American wives were during the 1950s and early 1960s. The press seldom emphasized this role, preferring to treat them as contestants in a beauty contest. A 1960 'Promo Flyer' for the Detroit Baseball Club noted that 'all the Detroit wives were knockouts' and pictured Mrs (Tom) Morgan in a swimsuit. A series on Tiger rookies took a similar tone.[38] There was something of the 'big man on campus' marrying a cheerleader, but wives offered more than pulchritude. Four wives from four different eras give a sense of their experience:

Ann Lerchen: We met again in 1945 after earlier attending the same high school. We had a child after eighteen months; I could not afford to go to spring training. At Williamsport we lived in a one-bedroom upper flat with a crib. Other wives lived below or nearby, whom I corresponded with for years afterwards. Half of our income went to rent; I guess we were poor. After moving to Flint, we had to make all new friends, had no car to go shopping, walked everywhere. Parents sent us $108 to buy a dining-room set. The glamour of the profession exaggerated the income. By the time George reached Toledo and Detroit, he made $1200 per month but only during the season. We were 'comfortable but not rich.' I quit travelling when he went to Tulsa because our child was challenged in school. For two years we went six months without seeing each other. He went from Tulsa to Cincinnati. I drove back to his mother's house in Garden City and lived there. That was hard, but she was a wonderful woman. At age 34, George said this is it [end of baseball]. Groupies were well-known even then, but we all trusted our husbands. I saw George with an arm around 'two young things' once. One woman who travelled with her husband would mention 'things.' A troublemaker. There were no marriage breakdowns that I know of. One cute woman mentioned as hanging around ballplayers turned out to be Ginsberg's fiancée. On a trip to Florida, the fuel pump kept breaking down in Alabama. It was difficult for a single woman to get a motel then. I ended up at the YWCA.

Dorothy Garver: Young, I didn't think life was difficult. It was quite a thrill, although I was in the background. I drove from Ney, Ohio, to San Antonio in a 1937 Ford with a two-year-old son in 1946. We rented Del Baker's house there, where expenses were much greater than in Ney. I told the kids it [fame] doesn't make him better, but just as good as other fathers. People looked up to him, but to the kids he was just another father. There was some jealousy in the community. A sign 'Home of Ned Garver,' at the outskirts of Ney was torn down, but I didn't want it there anyway. There was some jealousy when he was playing but [we have] many friends even now from fifty years ago here [in Ney]. Am I happy and proud – You bet!

Cheryl Zepp: Bill was fabulous in high school [1960s]. He decided to give it one more shot after the Tigers lost interest during his college years and signed with Minnesota to winter ball, then spring training. 'Follow your man' was the rule although I had a teaching job. Only one other wife had a degree. There was a big sacrifice in money. I worked at J.L. Hudson for $88 weekly. We used savings to pay for spring training because allowances were inadequate. Most wives went. We had a dumpy one-person apartment with ¾ bed and a door that wouldn't open but in a safe area. We took an apartment in Charlotte, storing furniture from our Detroit apartment with family. I met him on the road in New England with his parents. We lived in fourteen different places in two years. In Red Springs, I was afraid of break-ins while living alone, forced to be buddies with other wives. We drove in car caravans with little kids for protection. We had an apartment in Detroit. I commuted to Minneapolis. There were five different income taxes to pay, phone bills; I had to take care of all that. My friends remained, those I had before baseball, but [I] became buddies with wives. What was my career? Going shopping and to garage sales. I was a baseball bimbo after being a teacher. Back to the 19th century. Nobody watched you teach but they watched Bill pitch. Traditional game, traditional support role for husband. Some players were living with girlfriends during spring training. There was a team/family tension. I went on one road trip per year. There was concern about how cute the girls in stands are but I had no knowledge of 'groupies,' per se. Bill visited hospitals as part of a Christian athlete program.

Carol Warden: We met and married in 1970. My high school students 'fixed me up' with him. I had been an NCAA swimming star. We bought a house in 1974 in Grove City, Ohio, when Jon was with St Louis, moving our cats and dogs because hiding pets in an apartment was too much of a problem. I became more self-assertive, learning to fix things around the house. He ate at 1 a.m. after night games, slept until noon. I had a school teacher's schedule and went to the pool at 5 a.m. We delayed children, then I took two years off from teaching. We had to carry two houses. Some people did not want to rent to ballplayers. I commuted to see him on weekends, leaving our wedding presents in storage. We exchanged houses with Dick Drago but they had no furniture; we had a kitchen table, two chairs, a bed and television. We suffered a sudden drop in income after [Jon's] baseball career ended. Jon's souvenirs were on the mantelpiece, my ones from swimming were in the basement; but I went to gymnastics camp for two weeks without Jon and left him to settle in. You just made it work and made time for kids when he was home. Players took wives to some bars, girl friends to others. Wives knew what was going on. There was less playing around in Detroit than in KC. You don't want to know, hope it is not your husband. They bring tales home, 'stay away from this bar.' Lots of divorces from 1969 Royals, fewer from Tigers. But I let a 15-year-old stay in our house, to save him from a 'home for unwanted children.' Jon was told: your wife is having affair with Gregg. He's living with her. That talk was ridiculous. Gregg is a success in law, successful in Columbus. He named his first two children after me and Jon.[39]

Their words are far more eloquent than any of mine might be.

THE OTHER FAMILY

A common occupation, the financial circumstances of journeyman players, the time they spent together, and a goal of winning created both a physical and psychological sense of camaraderie among players. As Kryhoski put it: 'Players were forced to socialize on the road because they did not have anyone else.' White believes that the train created a 'sense of family' during the 1940s. Even with air travel two decades later, Northrup remembered more time with his team-mates during the season than with his wife or children.

Constant contact did not assure mutual respect or friendship. McLain's memoirs are derogatory in their portrayal of many team-mates, although the fault may lie more in his antics than in the qualities of his team-mates. Gehrig and Ruth did not like each other. Lolich and McLain fought publicly. Trammell and Whitaker complemented each other on the field for nineteen years without ever becoming personal friends. Not everyone liked everyone else, but they had to cooperate. Many lifetime friendships developed out of the years in baseball. Joe Coleman Sr, Ginsberg, Trucks, and White spend their retirement in Florida because other ballplayers are there. With little support from management, ex-players founded an alumni organization. Players from the 1980s described friendships as second only to competition as their greatest reward from their playing careers.[40] As Jon Warden points out, players were a 'cross-section of society, save for a special skill.' Some shared similar backgrounds and values; others differed greatly.

Two different perspectives emerge from talking with about forty Tiger alumni concerning the relations among team-mates. About half emphasize closeness, cooperation, and friendship. Freehan described about 18 or 20 out of 25 players on the 1968 team as 'close.' Red Wilson remembers 'groups' but not 'cliques' during the 1950s; Hoeft refers to 'great camaraderie and team loyalty.' Bertoia, however, observed a 'hierarchy' in the clubhouse, dominated by veterans, with stars rather distant. Jerry Davie and George Lerchen separately recall that the team bus dropped players off individually and that it was hard for a 'rook' to break in. Lenny Green believes that players at Minnesota were closer than in Detroit where there was a split between 'established players and newer ones.' Green's perspective fits with the memories of players generally – regulars emphasize unity; fringe players perceived division. Perhaps Ray Herbert offers the most balanced view:

In the 1950s one could live outside the team hotel in spring training only if the family was there and 90 per cent did not have their families there for the whole time. Twenty-five guys ate breakfast together. Players who played a long time together stuck together; many had played in the minors together. It took two or three years for new people to be accepted. A young guy might be taking a job from one of a veteran's friends. There was kidding but not real hazing. Rookies sat in the back of the bus and only sat with veterans if they were invited. There was lots of competition after the war, lasting until expansion.

Baseball players deported themselves within a male subculture. It involved hierarchy and passage. Rookies were assigned upper berths on trains and the clubhouse peg for dressing furthest from the training room. They were sent on false errands. It was a culture that emphasized action and physical prowess rather than contemplation. In his column 'Kell Tells' in 1951, Kell recounted how unusual Paul Calvert was – doing a crossword puzzle on the train. Kell allowed that it was understandable because Calvert was 'Canadian and a graduate of the University of Montreal.'[41] Freehan and Zepp (with an MA) were regarded as 'somewhat strange.' Martin, a throwback to a time when few players went beyond high school, denigrated formal schooling. 'Billy loathed college guys.'[42] On the other hand, Bertoia, among others, pursued university studies during his career and was teaching in high school by the end of his playing days. As more players attended college, players with the bare bones of literacy were rare, and they were the ones regarded as 'different.' Drinking and sexual escapades were more common.

FUN ON THE ROAD

Within an atmosphere of insecurity, masculinity, and loneliness, drink had long been a part of baseball. Ruth's prodigious capacity is now famous, or infamous, although reporters of the time concealed many of his excesses from an adoring public. During the 1950s and 1960s the adventures of Bo Belinsky, Ryne Duren, whom the *New York Times* observed had a 'low capacity for food consumption,' and Don Larsen, who wrapped his car around a lightpole at 3:00 a.m., appeared in newspapers. They were usually treated with a sense of tolerance and even humor. The *Washington Star* reported Larsen's escapade as an example of 'the Fun Worshippers.' *Esquire* titled an article 'Some Bad Boys Were Good for the Game,' Bill Veeck included a nostalgic chapter on past drinkers in his autobiography, and even in 1986 *Baseball Digest* waxed nostalgic about 'characters of the past.' Amidst hagiographic sports writing and the tolerant attitude of police forces, problem drinking was either not reported – Sam McDowell was stopped six times for drunk driving – or passed off as mere hijinks.[43] Jim Bouton's *Ball Four* focused attention on the sexual play and heavy drinking of athletes. It must be remembered, however, that Mickey Mantle and Billy Martin occupied center stage in his book. Both were abusers of alcohol, who paid a dear price for their substance abuse after their careers had ended. By the late 1960s, a few players smoked marijuana 'joints' privately, as did many young Americans, but marijuana was neither prevalent nor a part of the subculture of ballplayers. Trainers distributed 'greenies' or amphetamines in the clubhouse during the 1960s. We will discuss drugs in a later chapter, but let us be clear here – the first drugs were introduced in training rooms by baseball clubs who sought optimum performance from players.[44] Players did not bring them to the game.

The 1968 Tigers partied hard, many drank a lot, and there were some embarrassing incidents at the Hummer Bar that are private matters. Pat Dobson bragged that he 'received a $25,000 bonus and blew it all on cars and good living and enjoyed every second of it.'[45] During a rainstorm in Asheville, North Carolina, confident that the night game would be cancelled, Gary Ignasiak and two other players drank beer all afternoon only to have the skies clear. They were not at peak performance that evening. Brown admits that he fell asleep on the bench after 'a bad night,' but that he was not the only one to suffer from hangovers. He rightly complains that he alone was labelled a 'drunk' when the manager Billy Martin got drunk most nights. Kuenn and Cash were heavy drinkers during their playing days. They had long careers, but Ray Oyler, later in AA, had a brief one. Alcohol may have adversely affected his career.

Drink was an integral but not necessary part of the subculture. Despite the hijinks of a few, alcohol abuse was probably no greater among players than among U.S. males generally. As Reno Bertoia points out, 'booze and sex were exaggerated. We were part of the 1950s.' A non-drinker and non-smoker like Kip Young felt no pressure to drink, nor did Leo Marentette, who drank his first beer with team-mates at age twenty. There was a lot of scatological language and sexual innuendo that was not meant to be taken literally. Swearing was part of the vocabulary, but

John Feinstein's comment that using 'f---' a hundred times a day is 'part of the job description'[46] is typically hyperbolic. Dichotomous attitudes existed. Mickey Briggs remembers to this day being unsettled as a good Catholic teenager by fellow Catholic Jim Delsing's swearing. Attending Sunday Mass with Delsing, he was surprised when Delsing received Holy Communion in an age when Catholics were expected to purge their sins in the confessional before taking communion. He was positively shocked when, while others bowed in prayerful thanksgiving after communion, Delsing whispered, 'Let's get the fuck out of here.' Such language was inappropriate in church, but it was not different from what one would hear among any other group of young males in a factory, in the army, or at a fraternity house.

Despite Freud's theories, swearing was more instinctive and drink was more available than sex. Young men did think about sex, however, and sometimes acted out their fantasies when their wives were absent. We have seen from their own testimony that wives were conscious of and worried about their husbands' sexual temptations on the road. One threat came from 'Baseball Sadies,' as they were called in the 1950s. One came to prominent attention when she shot Eddie Waitkus, of the Phils, in his hotel room in 1948.[47] Hank Greenberg reported one sexual episode with a 'girl' he did not know. Jordan reports on visits to a brothel.[48] Hoeft remembers: 'Groupies were there in the 1950s near the buses. The opportunity was always there.' Bertoia agrees that even married players bragged about 'sexual conquests,' but emphasizes that he was from a strict Catholic upbringing and, like many others, did not participate. Nobody bothered him. Players taunted those regarded as too pure, however. Joe McIlvaine, who had studied to be a priest before briefly joining the Tigers, was greeted in the mornings with the question 'Did you get laid last night?'[49] Veterans sent a prostitute to the room of a rookie farmboy who had been reared by a strict bible-reading family. Sex was available. It was up to the player to make his own decision.

More aggressive 'groupies' replaced 'Sadies' with the sexual revolution of the late 1960s and 1970s. Fidrych recalled a girl jumping on his lap while he was on a date with another and others calling his room or besieging him in the halls. Marty Valvogyi, visiting clubhouse attendant in Detroit, delivered players' phone numbers to attractive young women in the stands and vetted 'groupies' outside the clubhouse for the players.

He also consoled one crying Tiger employee who had taken a job at the ballpark so she could marry a ballplayer and saw her dream vanishing.

Like Bouton, McLain tattled on some of his team-mates. A 'twenty-three-year-old goddess' delivered a lounging robe to one. Bill Faul tried to hypnotize a girl by flashing his car's directional signals. Leflore did not let marriage vows 'stop me from messing with the girls in Clinton. If a girl was willing to be with me or have sex with me that was all that mattered.' The only problem that Tiger management perceived about his behavior seems to have been his moving in with a white girl.[50] As Jim Brosnan pointed out three decades ago, players were 'human' rather than the heroes that fans, influenced by sports writers, romanticized them to be.[51]

Curt Flood described the pace as 'frantic, hours unmatched, strain enormous.'[52] Bertoia felt 'great pressure from newspaper criticism and the precarious job. I was my own worst enemy.' Jerry Davie's knees shook and his mouth went completely dry in his first start in Cleveland. Cleveland was a better place for Stanley, who played well there because crowds were small. His knees shook in his first start at Yankee Stadium: 'Please God,' he murmured, 'Don't let him [the pitcher] see my knees shaking.' He felt secure for only four or five years in his stellar fifteen-year career. Some players left the game because of the pressure, and some black players quit because they could not stand conditions in the South. For those who persisted it was a good life. They were fulfilling a child-hood dream. All of them had more than the fifteen minutes of fame that Andy Warhol allotted us. They were better paid than their peers and, if they were careful, they could save money and prepare for a second career.

SATISFACTION

Jim Bouton wrote in *Ball Four*: 'You spend a good piece of your life gripping a baseball and in the end it turns out that it was the other way around.' Members of the Tiger alumni speak with similar tones in praise of association with that ball:

Cain: 'My best memory is having played in the majors.'

Coleman Sr: 'It was a wonderful feeling to be major leaguer. Everybody would like to get there.'

Gromek: 'I have no complaints but wish I had won twenty.'

Phillips: 'It was just a thrill to walk into the ballpark. I played in a World Series; I was like a fan there.'

Wilson: 'It was still a privilege to be a major league ballplayer (despite the pay).'

White: 'I would do it all over again for nothing, just to be a big-league ball-player.'

Davie: 'My only regret is that I didn't get more of a chance when my arm was sound. It went just when my time had come. I would not have traded the experience for anything.'

Herbert: 'I enjoyed it very much, a pleasant experience; it set the tone for the rest of my life. It made me comfortable.'

Horton: 'I look back happily and feel the need to give something back.'

Timmerman: 'I played a kids' game for fifteen years professionally. I was happy, life was good to me. I might have made more money. I enjoyed every year I played. Those were the days. Baseball was good to me and I met a lot of good people.'

Ignasiak: 'Most wonderful experience in my life; fulfilled my first dream.'

Warden: 'I'm happy that I had the opportunity to play major league baseball that I dreamed about from age seven. God gives you a bit of talent. You think "what if" about injuries, but keep it in perspective. There aren't many World Series rings floating around – the greatest thrill of my life.'

Holdsworth: 'It's a great game. How much you miss it and the camaraderie. It's a part of you forever.'

Young: 'I still get a half-dozen cards a month and feel honored. Gates Brown said be glad somebody wants your autograph; some day you will be hoping someone will ask.'

Hiller: 'The greatest thing that ever happened.'[53]

NEW CAREERS

'Once you put a uniform on, it's pretty hard to get it out of the system.

It's like a disease.'[54] Whether players were stars, had a long career or took only the proverbial 'cup of coffee' in the majors, all had ultimately to face the need to begin a new career in their late twenties or thirties. The glory days had ended and a more mundane stage of life was to begin. Players usually suffered an immediate decline in income, a psychological adjustment to early 'aging,' and fear of change. Kryhoski judged: 'Nobody's prepared for it.' Ginsberg went through a 'life crisis' at age thirty-five. Marentette called it 'a big adjustment.' Wilcox thought: 'The hardest thing for a professional athlete to do is set his new life together. You think you're going to play forever.'[55] Foytack played a year in Japan, although he 'knew it was over.' Brown, Freehan, Horton, and Northrup either resented their release or wanted to play one more year. Warden described it as 'in your blood. (It was] hard to let go even though I realized that a pro athlete must have two careers. Some guys can't stand the end of the limelight.' The transition was easier for some than for others.

Three factors determined a player's ability to adjust. The first was education. Players like Bertoia and Wilson in the 1950s and Freehan, Northrup, Young, and Zepp in the 1970s had university degrees and built second careers upon them. Holdsworth and Warden returned to college and finished their degrees, although Holdsworth had to wait on tables to pay tuition and the Warden family experienced temporary financial hardship when both Carol and Jon returned to school. Holdsworth and Warden built new careers independent from their baseball contracts. Holdsworth became an accountant, Warden a sales representative for *Reader's Digest* after six years of teaching school and coaching.

The second factor was psychological preparation. Lenny Green said: 'You had to remember this was a make-believe world.' Those who planned for the transition fared better. If a player did not get a degree, he needed to establish contacts and gain experience in off-season jobs, usually in sales, that could provide the basis for a new career. Detroit was a good town in which to make connections because sports celebrities were respected and the automobile industry was a male-dominated one. Brown, Davie, Foytack, Freehan, Ginsberg, Gromek, Herbert, Horton, Kaline, Kryhoski, Northrup, and Timmerman, among others, credit their first post-baseball jobs to contacts that grew out of baseball. Foytack built on his baseball career but encountered some early problems because his predecessor, a Pittsburgh alumnus, had taken a salary but sold very little. As Northrup put it: 'Baseball connections helped open doors, but you still have to sell the product.' Some players established businesses that did not succeed. The name was not enough.[56]

Those who had difficulty were players who lacked schooling or those whose careers ended suddenly, often from injury. Roger Kahn's *Boys of Summer* painted a poignant picture of the later lives – some happy, some not so – of the Dodger greats of the 1950s. Jerry Davie's career ended with injury and he admits 'being totally unprepared' after having signed out of high school. Trucks attributed his own difficulty in adjusting to retirement at age forty-two after twenty-five years in baseball to his lack of 'real education.' 'No athlete is ever prepared to leave the sport.' He barnstormed, but made no profit, worked as a batting-practice pitcher with Pittsburgh for some months, and then worked in a series of public-relations jobs. He, like others of his era, is resentful of the small pensions older ballplayers receive: 'We got a few scraps.' Unfortunately, neither baseball nor hockey players of the current generation have been generous in allocating any significant portion of their riches to those who paved their way. Lerchen worked first as a milkman, went into construction, and eventually worked himself up to a post as general superintendent. Most did make a successful transition.

Studies based on samples of former major-league players indicate that about 90 per cent got a new job easily, that players did better than the average American despite myths to the contrary, and that both their baseball fame and their education (which, in turn, depended in large part on their social background) were key determinants in their career patterns. Large numbers remained within professional sports; even if they left sports, contacts made during their career were important.[57]

Table 17 lists post-baseball careers and areas of settlement of Tiger alumni and other major leaguers. Because these are based on alumni records or responses to questionnaires, they are probably slightly skewed to the more successful, but the numbers are large enough to assure that they are generally representative.[58] Twice as many Tiger alumni settled in Michigan and in metropolitan Detroit as had been born there. About half in total settled in the Midwest – half again as many as who had originated there. Players who began their career in the 1960s and spent at least five years in baseball were those most likely to settle in the Detroit area (about half). Contacts and job opportunities served well the 1968 world championship team, many of whom remained to claim a divisional championship in 1972. The 1968 team is probably the most revered by fans, in part because the presence of so many of its members in the area provide a reminder of its glories. They are still featured on WJR call-in shows and were celebrated on their twenty-fifth anniversary in 1993. Timmerman stayed in the area because 'Detroit was a great sports town, with good prospects for former players.' Many other former Tigers, like players from other teams, have settled in Florida. Some had been born in the South, but Florida is a gathering place for retired ballplayers.

Nearly half the Tigers who played in the 1950s continued as managers, coaches, or scouts. The longer they had played, the more likely they were to continue an affiliation with major-league baseball. An exception was Bill Freehan, who had a star's salary and a university degree. He declined a post in the Detroit system because he could not feed his family 'on a minor-league manager's salary.' Tigers with short careers in the 1950s were unique in their continuing presence in the game. The tendency to remain in baseball reflected lack of preparation for other careers and the paternalistic attitude of the Tigers, who were more likely than other organizations to provide sinecures for 'good employees.' The fact that the Tigers had been all white until the 1960s also contributed to a higher number connecting with other clubs.

When they entered careers outside baseball, Tiger alumni were more successful than alumni from other teams. About one-third of those who followed careers outside baseball operated businesses, reached executive levels, or entered professions. Players with short careers and lacking education had to settle for blue-collar or clerical positions. About 20 per cent of players from the 1950s retired before the age of sixty-five, helped by the baseball pension. Bertoia combined his teacher's and baseball pensions to retire early. Although newspapers occasionally recount examples of the impoverished former baseball star,[59] a combination of pensions – albeit not enormous ones for the oldest players – and contacts derived from baseball provided well for most baseball alumni.

Black players, in general, did not fare quite so well as white players. Very few of the first black players found places with any clubs after retirement. After discrimination in the selection of players ended, it continued in the selection of coaches, managers, and executives. Overt discrimination against black talent had ended in baseball by 1960 because exclusion of such talent was too damaging to a team's standing. Discrimination may, however, have been more subtle when it came to selection of marginal players. Sociological literature from the 1970s concluded from statistical analysis of performance indices that black players consistently outperformed their white counterparts on the field. There was no discrimination in either selection of star players or payment to them, but when it came to decisions about who sat on a bench in the majors instead of playing in AAA, white players had an advantage.[60] Willie Horton intuitively sensed this when he walked off the field in 1969. A 1986 analysis indicated a steadily decreasing gap from the 1960s between performances of blacks and whites. Yet, even then blacks constituted a lower percentage of substitutes than they did of regular or star players.[61]

Table 18 compares batting averages, earned-run averages, and years in the minors for black and white Tiger players. The cases are small in number and the differences not statistically decisive, but they are consistent with the general literature. It took a shorter time for whites to advance to the majors, and they had to do less to stay there. Campbell was too optimistic in his affirmation: 'A player has absolutely the same chance of making it regardless of color.'[62] Team-mates were equals and black stars prospered, but unconscious attitudes may have made the road more crooked for the marginal black player.

After their career ended, black players had more difficulty in establishing a second career. Frank Robinson was the first black manager of a major-league team – Cleveland in 1975, nearly thirty years after Jackie Robinson's debut. Front-office positions were not available for another decade. Bill Bruton became a successful business executive, but both Gates Brown and Willie Horton, who admittedly were poorly educated, struggled in a number of businesses. Neither the baseball establishment nor Detroit's business community sought former black stars (see also chapter 9).

The life of a ballplayer was a good one. For stars it was a wonderful life that included acclaim, good pay, a head start in a later career, and a supplementary pension. Only superstars were set for life. Most had to recognize that the limelight was but one stage of life and that it would end pretty quickly. During their careers players had to decide whether they were married to baseball or their wife, or at least learn how to balance their loyalties. They had to remember that the celebrity that fans honored was really still the same guy who had taken tests at school, worried about a mortgage, and was greeted by calls of 'Daddy.' Each player had to decide whether he preferred being a celebrity or a person. Those who settled for the first found that when their batting average dropped, the memories of fans and management were short and the goodbyes quick. Those who kept their perspective had a good start on a further life.

THE ALUMNI ORGANIZATION

The community of players continued after careers in baseball had ended.[63] During the 1970s Al Cicotte, who was made a coach so that he would be eligible for a pension, attempted to build an address list and a social organization to hold dinner dances and golf outings. In the early 1980s Freehan attempted to contact former players. Neither Cicotte nor Freehan received help from the club. In the euphoria of the World Series victory in Tom Monaghan's first year of ownership (1984), Monaghan invited ex-Tigers and Tiger staff on a ten-day trip through Michigan. On the trip Monaghan asked Herbert why there was no alumni organization. Herbert told him that the club had shown no interest and given no support. In February 1985 Monaghan promised support and took Herbert, Ginsberg, Freehan, and Kaline with his staff from Dominos and the baseball club to Florida. Freehan listed certain needs: an office, phone, secretary, postage, and so on. Later that spring, Monaghan took Freehan and Herbert to Campbell's office and asked, 'Do you have any problems with any of this?' Campbell responded, 'No problem.' One thousand letters were sent out. About 500 nationally and 400 'local' players (within four or five hours by car from Detroit) joined. Although Monaghan's financial problems played havoc with the baseball club by the late 1980s, he receives high praise from players. 'Monaghan was the only person [in Tiger management] since 1960 who tried to put anything in the community. What was done before was done by local scouts or players who would do it for free. Scouts and Bertoia organized all-star games for kids at Butzel Field, for example.'

Since then the alumni organization has widened itself. In its first two years, the organization participated in the Equitable [Life] Old-Timers Game, which raised $37,000, less $4000 to purchase uniforms. Tiger management apparently lost interest and dropped the game in 1987. Since then the alumni have played in annual golf outings and old-timers games organized by themselves. They raised about $30,000 for charity in 1994. The 'Toledo Tussle,' made up of amateurs who pay for the privilege of playing against former Tigers, has raised money for the Northwestern Ohio Epilepsy Society and returned 95 per cent of its income to charity. In Grand Rapids, alumni raised money for a children's hospital and visited sick children. At both events, 'old-timers' signed autographs for free. About thirty alumni, whose names appear in this chapter, regularly attend these events. Most played with the Tigers in the era before free agency. They are the antithesis of the selfish athlete. Unfortunately, they have not received support from the new management or from recent alumni.

6

The Era of Personalities, 1969–1977

The decade of the 1970s was a revolutionary one for major-league base-ball. Activity off the field became as important as what happened on the field. The decade witnessed baseball's first modern strike and the intro-duction of limited free agency. A more aggressive journalism shifted attention from action on the field to players' lives and events off the field. A few players gained celebrity status that often derived from off-the-field exploits and carried over to product endorsements in television advertising. Television widened baseball's audience, especially among women. Sports stars were beginning to capture public attention in a way once reserved for movie stars. Although sports figures had been in the limelight for generations, television made them richer and more famous than ever. Not all the ramifications of these changes were immediately apparent. The game itself was, after all, the same, and baseball was pros-pering as never before.

Three hundred thirty million fans passed through major-league turn-stiles during the 1970s, a 47 per cent increase over the 224 million of the 1960s (tables 1, 3, 4, 5, 11, 12, 13 for the following). Per-game atten-dance increased by 18 per cent, from 14,050 to 16,561. During an infla-tionary period costs were rising, but revenues were rising much more rapidly. Per-team revenues increased by 46 per cent from about $6,338,000 in 1974 to $8,884,000 in 1977 and by another 52 per cent to $13,516,000 in 1980 (113 per cent for the decade).[1] The owners pleaded poverty, but a few questioned their plaints. Leonard Koppett wrote that the 'owners are incredibly inept if they lose money on an income of $250 million.'[2] Average ticket prices rose from $3.18 to $4.53 in the decade, but that increase was below the rate of inflation and baseball's tickets remained the cheapest among professional sports. Although television contracts for football were capturing the public eye, baseball was not doing badly. Its broadcast income rose from $1.3 to $3.1 million per team during the decade, with national rights quadrupling. Gate attendance remained much more important than television income (a ratio of 3.6:1 in 1970 and 3.2:1 in 1980), but television income made the difference between profit and loss for most teams.[3] Although golf challenged baseball's former summer monopoly, football was baseball's only serious television rival then; African Americans still preferred baseball to basketball. The World Series on prime time at night propelled baseball's audiences to 60 million in both 1977 and 1978. The classic Red Sox–Reds series that featured Carlton Fisk's famous home run attracted new viewers.[4] Television kept adding unparalleled income.

Baseball was one reason to be optimistic about Detroit despite concerns about crime, racial tension, imported cars, and gasoline prices. In five of the six years beginning with the riot year of 1967, the Tigers were in the pennant hunt at least until Labor Day. Attendance averaged more than 1.5 million annually in the eleven years after the World Series victory and fell below the league average only twice – and then by only 45,000 in 1975 and 1977. It followed Tigers' fortunes on the field more than any annual fluctuations of conditions in the city.[5] Baseball seemed to be the one constant in Detroit's life.

The Tigers struck a new contract with WDIV-TV in 1975. Local broadcast income increased only slowly, but the Tigers had some dreadful teams in the mid-1970s. When the team improved, so did ratings and income. Ticket prices increased more than did the league average ($3.75 box, $3.00 reserve, $2.00 general admission, and $1.00 bleachers in 1970 to $6.00, $5.00, $3.50, and $2.00 in 1979), but the Tigers' most expensive seats were less than the cheapest seats for the Lions and the Wings and less than the average admission to the Pistons. In 1972, a letter to season ticket holders stressed that 'in full support of President Nixon's fight against inflation, we are holding the line on ticket prices.' The 1975 yearbook proudly proclaimed that baseball was the 'best bargain in sports.' It was also a link to happier times in Detroit. The Gehringer/Greenberg years 'helped build a civic pride that lingers still in Detroit.'[6]

Four individuals dominated baseball in Detroit in the half-dozen years following the 1968 championship. These were a sometime organist and former White Sox player, two New Yorkers – one a player, the second a resident – and a fourth who reminded many of a Jim Henson character on *Sesame Street*. They were Denny McLain, Billy Martin, Marvin Miller, and Mark Fidrych, respectively.

THE FALL OF McLAIN

Although Mickey Lolich pitched the Tigers to their World Series victory, Denny McLain had dominated sports in 1968. Honig's history of the American League decided: 'The story in 1968 was McLain.' Falls thought: 'No ball player ever had more going for him than this brash young man had in 1968.'[7] He appeared on *The Today Show*, *The Ed Sullivan Show*, and *The Smothers Brothers*. *Life*, *Time*, and *The Sporting News* printed pictures and profiles of him. Campbell thought he was the most talented individual he had encountered. 'McLain learned to fly quicker than any other student, but he did crazy goddamned things. Lots of players didn't like him, but he put rings on their fingers.' Carol Warden called him 'the most talented human being I ever knew; he excelled at baseball, musical instruments, spoke three languages, bowled 300 in his second game.'[8] His behavior in both 1967 and 1968 sent out warning signals, but the euphoria of McLain's thirty-one victories and the world championship cloaked them.

McLain did not win a game in the last month of the 1967 season after he injured his foot. *Sports Illustrated* thought him 'a paradox' and expected that Joe Sparma and Lolich would make greater contributions than McLain in 1968. Freehan noted in his diary that McLain 'flies in his own world.' Sparma, who had been rooming with him, requested a new room-mate. McLain told *Sports Illustrated* in the spring of 1968: 'I like to travel fast and first class.' During the All-Star break he slept only four or five hours over three days in Las Vegas and Houston, pitching two innings while living on 'greenies.' He abandoned Lolich at the All-Star Game after promising him a flight home. He publicly criticized both Tiger fans and management, referring to himself as an 'Irish god' whose Irish luck would never run out.[9] Team-mates tolerated his antics as long as he and the team were winning. *Sports Illustrated* observed perspicaciously in July of 1968 that 'flakes – even superflakes like McLain – rarely get themselves into trouble, but mighty mouths do.'[10]

Later that year, he deliberately grooved a pitch to Mickey Mantle, who hit it for a home run on his last visit to Tiger Stadium. The Tigers had already clinched the pennant, however. In games that mattered, he admitted throwing deliberately at Boog Powell, breaking his finger, and regretted missing Max Alvis.[11] In an age when athletes were expected to obey the rules, McLain did not. Harwell observed: 'Denny had little sense of responsibility and felt that the rules were made for other people.'[12] Winning covers many sins and luck can prevent a lot of problems, but sometimes luck runs out or the sins are too great.

During spring training in 1969 sports writers and McLain's teammates observed him placing bets over the clubhouse phone in Lakeland. George Cantor said that he and other writers reported the problem to Campbell, who normally did not enter the clubhouse. Falls said that he himself did not know about McLain's gambling but confirmed that other writers knew about it. Who was to question this hero before the age of investigative reporting? Jerry Green, Jim Hawkins, and George Puscas all say that it was not something that they would have written about in 1969. If a similar instance occurred today, they would, however. Campbell remembers: 'McLain was not careful in choosing his friends. Writers said something was going on but there was no proof. Betting was the tip of the iceberg, but I didn't know before the investigations. More and more things started to surface. I don't believe McLain ever threw a baseball game or bet on baseball and still don't!'[13]

The clubhouse incident passed because McLain abided by his own rules in a city that was still celebrating a world championship and trying to recover from the 1967 riot. Sports pages were supposed to bring good news; there was enough bad news in the others.[14] Sports writers were diffident fans. The transition from fan to objective writer was difficult to make. Perhaps, too, McLain's leprechauns were watching over him. Everyone hoped the problem would go away. It seemed to. McLain had another great year (24-9, 2.80) in 1969. *Sports Illustrated* tabbed him as 'baseball's toughest pitcher.'[15] Although the Tigers did not repeat in 1969, it was more because of Baltimore's success – winning 109 games – than any fault of the Tigers.

McLain's Irish luck ran out in February 1970. Three things happened simultaneously. Campbell reported to Commissioner Bowie Kuhn that McLain was having financial problems. McLain claimed then that estimates of $150,000 of personal debt were too high but later admitted that he owed $446,000. A grand jury in Detroit investigating gambling discovered a link between McLain and some gamblers. *Sports Illustrated* was also preparing a major story linking McLain to gambling. On 13 February McLain, accompanied by his attorney, Bill Aikens, met with Kuhn, who described 'Denny' as 'polite, cooperative and a little frightened.' There and in his later memoir, McLain admitted investing $5700 in a bookmaking operation with Clyde Roberts, manager of the Shorthorn Steakhouse in Flint, during his organ-playing booking in 1967, but denied betting on baseball. His attorney is reported to have said to Kuhn: 'We're at your mercy. Whatever you decide, we'll abide by.'

On 17 February the *Sports Illustrated* exposé, 'Downfall of a Hero,' by William Leggett, hit the newsstands. It charged that McLain 'was a partner in a book-making operation during the baseball season and became inextricably involved with a mobster.' That part was accurate enough. It went on to charge involvement with major Mafia figures in Detroit and even claimed that one of them had broken McLain's toes in punishment. There is no substantiation for the latter. Two days later, Kuhn suspended McLain for three months, from 1 April to 1 July 1970. 'The evidence strongly suggested he was more of a dupe than anything else. For his stupidity and greed and for the harm he had done to public confidence in baseball, he clearly deserved a suspension, but I could not find justification for a full-season suspension, let alone a longer one ... In retrospect, the McLain case was a public relations debacle.'[16] No baseball player had been suspended for gambling since 1924.

Rather than running to McLain's support, those Tiger players who would comment judged the suspension too light.[17] Even today, Tiger alumni express little sympathy. McLain had trouble accepting that he was at fault. In 1988 he drew a distinction between 'criminal' and 'illegal activities,' the difference being whether or not anyone was hurt. Campbell supported the suspension, Puscas warned on 15 February in the *Free Press* that McLain's career was in jeopardy, and both the *New York Times* and *Newsweek* were critical of the slap on the wrist. Referring to McLain's plea that 'my biggest crime is stupidity,' the *New York Times* concluded: 'Whether through cunning or stupidity, the brash 25-year-old pitcher from Chicago is on the brink of disaster.' Peter Axthelm in *Newsweek* wrote: 'The sentence was, in a word, a farce.'[18]

The fans were more forgiving. Upon return of the fallen hero on 1 July the *News* observed: 'Denny McLain Wednesday night returned to the warm embrace of a sell-out throng of 53,893 at Tiger Stadium, but the old magic was missing from the arm of baseball's prodigal son.' The crowd was overwhelmingly for McLain, who received three separate ovations – as he warmed up, as he walked to the mound, and with the P.A. announcement that he was the starting pitcher.[19] The magic remained, but the talent did not. McLain won only three games in 1970.

On 26 August 1970 McLain threw his final pitch for the Tigers. The Tigers suspended him for three days and fined him $500 after he threw buckets of water over Watson Spoelstra and Jim Hawkins on 28 August in the Tiger clubhouse. Hawkins recounts:

By then, no one was talking to McLain, who wanted other players' attention. He had a portable phone in the clubhouse, the only one at that time. He was generally pissed off about press coverage. Before the game, he said he would dump water on a writer, and this became a dare. Joe Niekro set me up, sitting me down with my back to McLain. There was a lot of horseplay in the clubhouse, like putting talcum through the fan – childish activities. I didn't like it, but you don't go in there unless you can take it. The press plays jokes on the players, too. The first edition of the *Free Press* printed only two paragraphs about it, but Spoelstra, who was not well-liked, complained to Campbell. Campbell called me, and asked: 'Did McLain dump water on you? Why didn't you tell me?' I replied: 'none of your business.' Campbell said: 'I'm making it my business.'[20]

During that suspension McLain took a gun onto a commercial airline flight, which was a federal crime, and received his third suspension on 9 September. McLain's suspension again drew national attention and little sympathy. Robert Lipsyte suggested a 'cover-up' in the *New York Times* and Arthur Daley, referring to McLain's comment that he was 'double dumb,' wrote: '[It] was an understatement: his dumbness is so monumental as to be beyond arithmetic calculation. Perhaps this is the root of the problem, when management begins to treat star athletes as a privileged class. They produce spoiled brats, like a Denny McLain or a Joe Namath.'[21]

As soon as McLain was reinstated after his one-month suspension, the Tigers sent him packing to Washington on the eve of the World Series. He remained in the hearts and minds of the Detroit fans and press, however. His return to Detroit received major coverage in Detroit newspapers, as did his NL debut in 1972, and his return to AAA in 1973. Falls described him as 'the most memorable man in the game,' about whom he wrote more in one year than about Kaline over twenty-two years.[22] After McLain's career ended, *The Sporting News* ran twenty feature stories on him between 1975 and 1989.[23] McLain was found guilty of racketeering, conspiracy, and drug dealing in 1985 and was sentenced to twenty-three years in prison, although he only served thirty months. After his release he returned to Detroit, where he began a successful broadcasting career.

McLain's star shone brightly but briefly, eventually collapsing on itself. For a while, its aura illuminated Detroit sports. An inability to control his private life destroyed his career and nearly his life. The story of McLain reflected some new directions in sports. He was not just a baseball star, but a celebrity. His off-the-field activities captured as much attention as his on-field performance did. He set himself above the rules, and his arrogance left him vulnerable and isolated when the reckoning came. The tale of a baseball pitcher from Detroit captured major attention in the national press, which was considerably less tolerant than it had once been of the misbehavior of its sports heroes. The lack of tolerance derived from a sense of history – specifically, the shock of the 'Black Sox' scandal of 1919, when White Sox players threw the World Series in return for payments from gamblers. Athletes might get drunk and chase women, but woe betide the player who consorted with gamblers.

There were short-term implications from McLain's troubles. The first was the performance of the team in 1970. For the only time between 1967 and 1973, the Tigers finished below .500. Campbell blamed the McLain 'fiasco' for the team's problems: 'At the start of spring training we had the McLain fiasco which affected players, the whole organization and snowballed ... not conducive to playing good baseball ... Without that could have made a run at the pennant ... Lots of things [were] not made public.'[24] In 1970 Lolich lost 19 after winning 19 in 1969. The team ERA ballooned from 3.31 to 4.09, its highest since 1959. The brightest spot was Al Kaline Day on 2 August, proclaimed by Governor

Detroit's record, 1967–73

1967	91	71	.562
1968	103	59	.638
1969	90	72	.556
1970	79	83	.488
1971	91	71	.562
1972	86	70	.551
1973	85	77	.525

Milliken, chaired by Lee Iacocca, and serenaded by Mel Torme. Cherry Street was renamed Kaline Drive. The best individual performance was the seven hits by Cesar Gutierrez in an extra-inning game against Cleveland on 21 June. Only Horton, in a part-time role, hit .300 and only Northrup hit more than 20 home runs (24). Since basically the same team won 90 games in 1969 and 91 in 1971, one must assume that off-the-field problems contributed to on-the-field problems.

The second result was an eight-player deal with Washington that Campbell describes as 'his biggest and best trade.' It took a full season to negotiate:

Bob Short [Washington's owner] said, 'I want Denny McLain' at breakfast on opening day at the Shoreham Hotel in Washington. It took all season to complete the deal. Few knew about it because the suspension meant that I was not sure the deal could be made. Mayo [Smith] did not know about it despite what television said. Joe Burke and Ted Williams didn't want to make it. We made it in Minneapolis during the playoffs. I insisted Rodriguez be included; Smith was told then. It was a handshake until the suspension was over. Kuhn met us at the Washington airport with McLain and his agent. There were no leaks although 25–30 people knew. Short needed a gate attraction.[25]

Kuhn later wrote that he 'could not believe the robbery. Campbell smiled in spite of himself.'[26] The key players were McLain, Elliot Maddox, and Don Wert, who went to Washington in return for Aurelio Rodriguez, Joe Coleman Jr and Ed Brinkman. Wert had just bought a house in Southfield, but such are the vagaries of baseball trades. The trade made front-page headlines in the Detroit newspapers. Neither Detroit nor Washington fans were pleased with the trade.[27] Washington's fans were either clairvoyant or more dispassionate. Wert played only twenty games for Washington and retired. McLain lost twenty-two of the ninety-six games that Washington lost in 1971 and would win a total of only fourteen major-league games after he left Detroit. Maddox played ten more years, but only one with Washington. Brinkman and Rodriguez anchored the left side of the Tiger infield for four years, and Rodriguez played with the Tigers until 1979. Brinkman was named Tiger of the Year in the division-winning year of 1972, during which he played 72 games without an error, although he hit only .203; Rodriguez led the Tigers in game-winning hits (13) in 1972 and in 58 RBIs in 1973. Coleman twice won 20 games and a total of 88 for the Tigers over five and a half years. He won 20 in 1971, while McLain lost 22.

The third result was the dismissal of Mayo Smith and the hiring of Billy Martin for $65,000 annually. The team was divided, down on itself, and Mayo Smith had lost control. He was also finding solace in alcohol. Campbell concluded: 'Smith knew by then he could not handle the club, which was difficult.' Jon Warden thought he was intimidated by and even physically afraid of some players. Martin hardly fit the image of the conservative Detroit management. Hawkins observed that the 'complete collapse' of the Tigers led to the replacement of 'mild-mannered Mayo' with 'brash, brawling Billy.'[28] I asked Campbell why he picked Martin: 'I liked Billy as a baseball man. He had played for us here. He could take a club and get as much out of a club as anybody. I needed help in a hurry. We met with Mr Fetzer in a cabin up north. I had already told Billy he had the job. Fetzer asked: "Do you know what you are getting into?" I said yes.' George Cantor thought Campbell 'made a deal with the devil to win,' Hawkins that 'he was desperate to win one more time.'[29] Much like McLain, Martin had immediate success, won the hearts of Detroit fans and the press, and quickly self-destructed.[30]

THE MARTIN YEARS

Returning to the condemnation of the Tigers as 'fat cats' that was so common during the 1950s, the press greeted the feisty Martin's appointment with alacrity. Before the Tigers had played a game in 1971, Falls remarked on the 'fantastic job with the players' that Martin was doing.

In August 1972, the *Free Press* credited Martin as the main reason that the Tigers were in the pennant race. The *News* concluded after the team had clinched the division championship: 'One man made the difference – Billy Martin.'[31] The fans were enthusiastic too. In Martin's three years, more than five million fans mustered at the stadium. The team was equally successful on the field, winning 91 games in 1971 and then the Eastern Division championship in the strike-shortened season of 1972.

In his history of the Tigers, written shortly after Martin's tenure, Falls wrote: 'He brought the team back to life, and the town came alive again. The fans loved Billy, they loved the way he argued with umpires – the way he fought for the players.' 1972 was 'a personal conquest for Billy Martin, who fought with everyone and everything in his way.'[32] A more balanced assessment is that of Clete Boyer, Yankee third baseman, who said that Martin 'scares you into winning.'[33] Perhaps Martin did scare the Tigers into winning, and perhaps it was his field generalship, known as 'Billyball,' although a few criticized him for 'overmanaging.'[34] Campbell believed: 'He was a good manager from foul line to foul line.'[35]

Perhaps the team simply won in 1972 because the 1970 record was an aberration and because Baltimore faded in 1972 after having won 109, 108, and 101 games from 1969 to 1971. Although they won only one World Series in those years, Baltimore dominated the American League, sweeping all three divisional play-offs. No manager could have led the Tigers to a championship in those years.

The 1972 season went down to the last weekend, when Boston came to Detroit for a three-game series with a half-game lead. Because of the strike, the teams played an uneven number of games that year. Whichever team won two out of three in the last series would win the division. The Tigers' old nemesis, Baltimore, had defeated Boston 2–1 on 2 October, while the Tigers had defeated Milwaukee 5–1 behind a complete game by John Hiller, who had rejoined the club in July following his heart attack. On 3 October before 51,518 fans, Lolich won his twenty-second game, 4–1, striking out fifteen – 'the best I've pitched all year.' The next day Woody Fryman, acquired in mid-season, won his tenth game before 54,079 cheering fans over Luis Tiant. Kaline, who finished the year on a 22-44 tear, answering a 13 June *Free Press* article 'Kaline's Playing Days Are All But Over,' drove in McAuliffe with the winning run in the seventh inning and caught a fly ball for the final out.

The Tigers had won their division. They lost a meaningless game the next day.

The play-offs opened on 7 October in Oakland. It was a tense series, marked by sudden shifts in momentum and by controversy. The first game matched two twenty-game winners, Lolich and Jim 'Catfish' Hunter, relieved by Vida Blue and Rollie Fingers in the ninth. The game went into the eleventh tied 1–1. Kaline homered off Fingers to give Detroit a 2–1 lead. In the last of the eleventh, however, Sal Bando and Mike Epstein singled off Lolich, bringing in Chuck Seelbach. Gene Tenace bunted to Rodriguez at third, who touched third for a force-out and just missed the double play at first. Gonzalo Marquez, who had batted only twenty-one times during the season, then hit a pinch single to right, scoring pinch runner Mike Hegan. Kaline threw to third, but the throw bounced past Rodriguez; Tenace scored on the error, and the A's won 3–2.

In the second game, 'Blue Moon' Odom pitched a shutout, winning 5–0 behind a four-run Oakland uprising in the fifth. In the seventh inning of that game Lerrin LaGrow hit Bert Campaneris with a pitch. Campaneris threw his bat at LaGrow, prompting Martin to 'lead a charge' from the Tiger dugout. LaGrow was ejected, and Campaneris was later suspended for the rest of the series. Although everybody then denied that LaGrow was throwing at Campaneris, he was – and at Martin's command. Martin signalled LaGrow to 'flip' or knock down Campaneris by making the gesture of pushing his index finger against his thumb to signal a knock-down pitch. For some strange reason, Martin thought that Latin American players could be intimidated. He regularly ordered pitchers to throw at batters. Bill Denehy was his 'hired assassin.' Gates Brown once protested throwing at opponents. Martin yelled, 'You fucking coward.' Norm Cash 'kept me [Brown] from breaking him in half. You can kill somebody, throwing at them.' Martin even ordered Tony Conigliaro knocked down after an earlier near fatal beaning of Conigliaro. 'If he can't see the baseball, then he doesn't belong in the game.'[36] Baseball was more like war than a game when Martin managed.

In Detroit, on 10 October, Joe Coleman pitched a shutout (3–0), setting a play-off record with fourteen strikeouts. Little-used Ike Brown, playing first base in place of Cash because left-hander Ken Holtzman started, got the key hit, driving in Kaline and Freehan in the fourth inning. The fourth game again pitted Hunter against Lolich. Like their first game, their second match-up went into extra innings tied 1–1, this time on home runs by Dick McAuliffe in the third and Mike Epstein in the seventh. In the tenth Marquez again tormented the Tigers. He singled off Seelbach. Matty Alou followed with a double to left. The throw easily beat Marquez, attempting to score, but Freehan, who had been out for three weeks with an injury, could not handle it and Marquez scored. Alou scored on Ted Kubiak's single for a two-run lead and the Tiger season seemed over. Bob Locker came in to finish up for Oakland in the tenth.

The Tigers rallied. McAuliffe singled. Kaline singled. Joe Horlen replaced Locker; Brown batted for Stanley and walked. Freehan then bounced a potential double-play ball to third baseman Sal Bando, who threw to second base. There Gene Tenace, who was playing out of position, dropped the ball. One run scored. Left-hander Steve Hamilton came on to face Cash, who walked, forcing in the second run. The game was tied, the bases were still loaded and nobody was out. Northrup then hit a drive to right over a drawn-in Alou for the game-winning hit, reminiscent of his game-winning triple in Game 7 of the 1968 World Series. The play-off was tied.

Game 5 was another pitching duel, this time between Odom, relieved by Blue in the sixth, and Fryman. McAuliffe, who had singled, scored the first run of the game on a ground-out by Freehan in the first inning. Oakland tied the game in the second on a delayed double-steal, with Reggie Jackson scoring from third; on the play he tore a hamstring muscle, preventing him from playing in the World Series. A controversial call at first base contributed to Oakland's second run. After McAuliffe had made a throw from deep in the hole at shortstop that arrived in time, first-base umpire John Rice ruled that Cash, in his stretch, had taken his foot off the bag and that George Hendrick was safe. Hendrick eventually scored on a single to left by Tenace. It was Tenace's only hit in the series, although he would go on to hit four home runs in Oakland's World Series victory over Cincinnati that year. The Tigers mounted no more threats and lost 2–1. Rowdies showered the field with debris before the game was over, doing Detroit's national image no good.

It had been a pitchers' series. The Tigers hit a mere .198, and Oakland

.224; together the teams scored only 23 runs in the five games. Each team had won its division with pitching and defense. The Tigers hit only .237 and Oakland .240 during the season; the league as a whole hit .239. The Tigers' team ERA was 2.96, more than one full run less than it had been in 1970.

Nineteen seventy-three began well enough for the Tigers. They were in and out of first place until the All-Star Game and in the hunt until a disastrous road trip in late August, coupled with a hot streak by Baltimore. Hiller returned full time to win 10 games and save 38. It was less that the Tigers performed less well than they had in 1972, but that Baltimore returned to their form of 1969 to 1971, winning 97 games. Despite a close pennant race, the story increasingly became Martin and his problems rather than the games.

As with McLain, one personality was subsuming the team. Martin's problems were not new. In May 1971 Horton had taken himself out of the line-up, 'incensing' Martin. It required a meeting with Campbell to settle that. In April 1972 Martin had either punched or shoved a fan. In August 1972 he had led the Tigers in a brawl.[37] Throughout the division-winning year of 1972, he criticized his players in print after losses – Coleman, Freehan, Kaline, Lolich, Northrup, and Seelbach all 'lost' games for him. In his autobiography, he is bitterly critical of most of the Tigers who played for him.[38] As his generally sympathetic biographer John Falkner concluded, 'People did things to Billy Martin; he was nearly always blameless. He never started a fight, drinking was never a problem, he was never fired or divorced for cause.'[39] During spring training in 1973, he clashed again with Horton, and quit (although he later denied that he did) because he did not receive sufficient backing from Campbell. He got into a post-midnight shouting match with rookie Ike Blessitt outside a bar. Blessitt did not make the team.[40] At the Foxfire Lounge in Lakeland, Martin approached the wife of another minor leaguer who was in the washroom at the time, with the come-on 'I want to fuck you.'[41] That player did not make the team either. Most of the worst incidents occurred in or near bars when Martin was drinking.

During a Tigers' road trip and a stretch in which they lost ten of thirteen games, Martin missed a chartered flight from Oakland to Chicago in order to visit Patty Stark, his steady girlfriend in Kansas City. He arrived forty minutes late for the game.[42] The papers reported that he was taking care of 'personal business' or 'business affairs.' He passed out between games on a hot humid day in Chicago. Looking from the press box, Campbell asked, 'Where's Martin?' Campbell called the clubhouse and was told that Billy was sick.[43] Martin had sent girls to players' rooms as rewards and attempted to romance young women fans while in his uniform, and there were rumors about Martin bringing teenaged girls on the plane with him when he managed Texas.[44]

On 3 September, Detroit papers carried the front-page headline 'Martin fired.' Campbell said that the firing came as a culmination to a series of incidents, but he made the final decision after Martin missed the team's flight. 'I decided to fire him after he didn't show up for work. I called him and said I was going to make a change. The decision was made before the spitball incident.' After McLain and Martin, he thought: 'There must be an easier way to make a living.'[45] In Martin's recollections, his dismissal was the result of his challenging of the front office, especially regarding trades. He pointed especially to the Tigers' failure to acquire Deron Johnson, who would knock in 86 runs in 1973; Campbell had not wanted to overrule the negative appraisal of his scouts.[46] Martin's departure, however, had nothing to do with the performance of the team and little to do with disagreements with the front office about personnel. It was the result of his inability to discipline himself.

It *seemed* that Martin had lost his post because he had challenged authority. He had blamed management for the losing streak on WJR radio on 26 August. When he was dismissed, he was under league suspension for boasting about ordering Coleman and Scherman to throw the spitter against Cleveland on 30 August. American League president Joe Cronin notified Martin: 'Your blatant actions and endorsements of such tactics cannot be tolerated.' Martin had complained in print about Cleveland pitcher Gaylord Perry's use of the spitter since April.[47] The spitball incident was either a coincidence or a final rebellious act by a man who knew his time had run out.

Martin remains a controversial figure. His defenders point to his record of turning around teams. The conclusion of the Elias Sports Bureau that Martin was 'the best manager in the history of major league baseball,' responsible for 7.45 wins annually by his teams,[48] is debatable, however. No statistical manipulation of team performance can so accurately measure a manager's effect; too many unmeasurable variables concerning the year-to-year performances of individual players exist. Numbers sometimes conjure illusions of accuracy.[49] Whatever his accomplishments as a manager, Martin was an intense and troubled man. He warned in 1971: 'What I do off the field is my own business.' Upon his firing, he justified himself: 'My record speaks for itself. I'm a perfectionist.' In a 1980 interview, he said: 'Do I question myself? Nobody can judge me. Not you, me – only Jesus Christ.' He also thought that God had held his bat in the 1953 World Series when he got twelve hits.[50] He wore a cross on his baseball cap his entire career, arranged for autographs and tickets for grateful nuns, and assigned 10 per cent of the royalties of his book to the Little Sisters of the Poor. Friends like Bill Reedy, who was with him on that fateful Christmas in 1989 when he was killed in an auto accident, and Jimmy Butsicaris admit his faults but still maintain a great affection for him. Butsicaris described him as a Jekyll-and-Hyde who could come to the house for dinner and play with the kids, but turn mean with alcohol.[51]

Players' assessments are not positive. Although Falkner states that 'several black players' thought he was a racist,[52] the three most favorable comments come from Gates Brown, Lenny Green, and Willie Horton. Green, however, points out that Martin knew enough not to 'mess too much with Horton or Brown, who could have torn him apart.' Brown credits Martin for being 'all baseball' when the game started although he might have been hung over. Horton said: 'Martin gave incentives. He chewed me out but, at the same time, gave me confidence that I could play the game.' His greatest critic was Northrup, who declared: 'Martin was a huckster and a manipulator of the press and fans. After the first year, he would blame players for every defeat, and lost the respect of players. We had a meeting in 1972 and decided to win in spite of him. He was paranoid and schizo, threatened by college grads. He was flat plain ignored in 1972.' More temperately, Tom Timmerman judged Martin 'not a bad manager. The consensus was that we would win in spite of him. Billy didn't like me. Personal likes/dislikes affected his judgment – about pitchers like Seelbach and LaGrow.' (He rode Seelbach, who was an Ivy League graduate.) Fred Holdsworth described Martin as the 'best on-the-field manager I had, but he had no patience and was not good with young players.' Bill Zepp said simply, 'Martin had low people skills.' Hawkins described Martin's 'modus as to get some segment of the media on his side, then the public on his side. When things are going well, he praises the players and then dumps on them. His firing was inevitable.'[53] An umpire, Nester Chylak, described his pattern similarly: 'You fight your own players, the other players, owner, teammates and strangers and then, when you win, and someone wants to know the secret, you say "teamwork."'[54]

No one will ever know whether the Tigers would have won their division in 1972, or whether they would have done better or worse from 1971 to 1973, without Martin. Martin was a skilled self-publicist. He was the first manager to be interviewed regularly by J.P. McCarthy on WJR's morning radio show – a ritual that most coaches and managers from Detroit-area teams have submitted themselves to since. Tiger fans were aghast at the firing. After Martin's dismissal, there was a drug shoot-out outside Campbell's apartment at 1300 W. Lafayette. A bullet barely missed Campbell's head as he was sitting, sipping a scotch. He thought that the fans were shooting at him.[55] Such was Martin's popularity in Detroit. People either loved or hated him, and sometimes they felt both emotions simultaneously.

STRIKE

The third figure who exercised a personal influence on the national pastime was Marvin Miller, who led the first modern baseball players' strike in 1972. Although the strike was brief – only thirteen days – it came as a shock to fans, writers, and probably the players themselves. The 1972 strike would likely not have occurred if Marvin Miller, elected by a vote of 489–136 (with coaches, managers, and trainers among the 'no's'), had not become the lawyer for the players' union in 1966 with the backing of former Tiger Jim Bunning. Pensions were the primary issue. Even activist players 'certainly had no feeling they were setting in motion a bonafide trade union, and could not conceive of a strike in the 1960s.'[56] There was a slow progression. A Uniform Players Contract, the first complete collective bargaining agreement in sports, covering two years, was reached in 1968. It raised minimum salaries of major leaguers from $7000 to $10,000 when 25 per cent of the players were still making less than $10,000. It also increased various allowances and established a formal grievance procedure including arbitration; baseball's commissioner selected the arbitrator until 1970.[57] Players boycotted spring training in 1969 in protest against ownership's reneging on a paltry $150,000 from All-Star Game receipts to the pension fund. *Time* called it a classic test of strength, while maintaining that fans did not sympathize with the players, whose salaries averaged $26,000.[58]

Neither the boycott of 1969 nor the 1972 strike was about salaries, however. Prompted by the announcement of a new $70-million, four-year television contract, players demanded in 1971 an increase from $5.5 million to $6.5 million in contributions to the pension fund by owners. Owners agreed to increase the health benefits for players, but not contributions to the fund. Gussie Busch, owner of the Cardinals proclaimed: 'We voted unanimously to take a stand. We're not going to give another goddamn cent. And if they want to strike, let them strike.' There was, in fact, a surplus in the pension fund. Later, Charlie Finley, owner of the Athletics, pleaded that the owners did not know that there was surplus, but Bob Short, a moderate, said that the owners' intent had been to break the union.[59] A hard-line minority among owners would not adjust their paternalistic ways to meaningful negotiations. Miller believes today: 'Owners and management personnel believed that they were above the law, specifically labor management law. Coming into baseball was like coming into Mars.'[60] Management must have thought that he was from Pluto. A hard-line negotiator from the United Steel Workers, put into the cauldron of antitrust exemptions, Miller was not about to yield points for the 'good of the game.' Judging from their autobiographies in which Miller and commissioner Bowie Kuhn blame each other for the strike,[61] their personal animosity did not help negotiations. After eight days President Nixon proposed use of the Federal Mediation Service, which both sides accepted.

The strike ended quickly when the owners yielded, but the players got a taste of power. As Miller wrote retrospectively: 'The players and the union were never the same again.'[62] Neither was baseball. The national press was generally pro-management. Leonard Koppett was one of the first to insist that the owners were the problem because they would not accept Miller as an equal and gave 'concessions' to the players; he warned that players were still at 'an early stage of assertiveness.'[63]

Tiger management, personified in Campbell, preferred the old way of doing things. Miller, Koppett, and Murray Chass, a sports writer who increasingly concentrated on labor issues in sport for the *New York Times* and *The Sporting News*, regard Tiger management as having been among the most conservative in the 1970s. Chass said that 'Campbell was a nice guy, but a tough businessman who never adjusted.' Miller called him 'a throwback who had the effrontery to tell me who was going to be the player representative for the Tigers. I never met anyone before who told me that the law did not apply to them. Fetzer seemed old when I came in. Campbell attended most of the meetings.'[64]

When players were considering not signing contracts and boycotting spring training in December 1968, Stanley, McLain, and McAuliffe had already signed with the Tigers. McAuliffe and Stanley were embarrassed when Jim Price, Tiger player representative, criticized their signing. McAuliffe apologized: 'I feel foolish ... It never entered my mind that the players might go on strike.' Stanley said: 'I'm with the players. I wish I hadn't signed.' Campbell admitted that he rushed the signings of McAuliffe and Stanley at victory celebrations at the Roostertail and Sheraton because of the possibility of a boycott. He wanted some name players under contract. Stanley said he signed both because he was afraid of Campbell and because he did not believe in strikes.[65] The furor was short-lived because outstanding disputes were settled before the 1969 season began.

That they were not in 1972 surprised contemporaries. In March, the *Free Press* ran articles titled 'Baseball Strike? I Doubt It' and 'Baseball Strike – It'll Never Happen.' On 1 April Detroit newspapers headlined the strike on their front pages. The *Free Press* reported mass confusion in the clubhouse: 'The Detroit Tigers are shocked by news of the strike even though they had voted 25–0 in favor of such a move on March 15. Tiger GM Jim Campbell said, "I think they're being damn greedy ... I'm disgusted with the whole thing."'[66] Jim Hawkins recounts that, an hour before the strike, 'McAuliffe, like a supplicant, asked Martin if they could play cards in the clubhouse. Somehow Kaline got balls and bats to go out to Kathleen High School field where they were like lost little boys, hoping the strike would be settled. If owners had had a modicum of sense, they could have cut the legs out of the union. Players did not want to unionize; they were pushed into it by owners who wanted things like they were in 1906.' Bill Freehan, Tiger representative for a number of years, said that 'it was resistance to change that caused the players' organization and solidified it.'[67] In retaliation, Campbell ordered goods of players and their families – even children's bicycles – taken off the team truck in Florida.[68]

In retrospect, the players' demands seem modest; yet the Detroit press, like the national press generally, was far more critical of players than of management. Falls wrote: 'Ball players are bred in selfishness. It is the nature of their game. They are taught and trained to be paid by what they do as individuals ... The fans will be the innocent victims in this whole mess, as they always are. Not only will they be deprived of diversion which has been an integral part of their lives, but who do you think is going to foot the bill for all the expense of this strike. [Miller] has woven a spell over the players that they themselves do not fully understand.'[69] Asked about his position during the strike, Falls reiterated: 'The company should be allowed to run its business. But if workers run it, everything is backwards.'[70] Hawkins warned in 1972 that fans would remember that the Tigers 'placed more importance on their pension plan than they did on the game and walked off the job at the peak of spring training to prove it.' Fans' memories were short lived, for they cheered the team on in 1972. Today Hawkins admits that he's 'not a union man,' but is now much more critical of management.[71] Campbell recognized that something new had happened: 'From now on, I'm going to have a different feeling when I deal with them. I guess for the first time, I realize we're not dealing with ball players, we're dealing with the union ... This could be the worst thing that ever happened to baseball. It could bankrupt some clubs.'[72] Detroit fans were among few in the nation who supported the strike, perhaps because of high union representation in Detroit.

Newspaper reporters in Detroit were unionized and had struck in 1968. Umpires had struck in 1970 and nobody paid much attention. Why were Detroit sports writers so virulent against the strike? Puscas attributes the vituperance of the press, which was more dispassionate about the 1981 strike, to shock about the first major sports strike. Cantor grants that sports writers lived in a cocoon then and were far too willing to rely on management statements. He cited, for example, Busch's statement that the owners could not afford to satisfy the players' demands. 'Writers did not know any better. We just believed him.' In self-criticism, Dick Beddoes, long-time sports writer for the Toronto *Globe and*

Mail, regretted that sports writers too long deferred to local manage-ment and accepted publicity handouts rather than digging for stories. Jerry Green 'seconds' Beddoes. Even *The Sporting News*, normally pro-management, allowed that sports writers were 'owner-oriented, generally conservative.'[73] Joe Lapointe, formerly of the *Free Press* now of the *New York Times*, believes that the aftermath of Watergate, which occurred the same year as the strike, made graduates of journalism schools more criti-cal of their sources in the future.[74]

Contemporary sports writers and historians of the press have been sharp critics of a long-standing relationship between sports writers and management.[75] Falls, who began writing in 1946, remembered that the Tigers gave meal allowances, free hotel rooms, and free plane rides to writers. 'It took me four years to realize that was payola. I went to my boss at the *Detroit Times* about it. Now you'd be fired for it. Payola of disc jockeys contributed to change.' Puscas remembers a now deceased writer who double-billed his paper and the club. Salsinger prided himself on never going into the clubhouse but was a close friend of Walter O. Briggs. Hal Middlesworth, Salsinger's counterpart at the *Free Press*, told Hawkins: 'Young Man, we sat in the press box and reported what we saw.' Michael Betzold remarked that sports writers suffered the problem of other beat writers, like police writers. If they offended sources, their sources could dry up. He also said that sports writers had been a 'lazy lot' who preserved a 'romantic vision of benevolent owners.'[76]

The profession itself was conservative in admitting new faces. In 1957, Doris O'Donnel, a *Cleveland News* writer who had formerly visited Iron Curtain countries, attempted to cover baseball from the press box in New York and Boston. Her reaction to her treatment was: 'I'd rather see a son of mine drive a bus than be a baseball writer ... I charge baseball writers with discrimination against the fair sex in their own profession ... [They are] snobbish hermits who don't realize the journalistic world around them has changed.' In response, Dan Daniel wrote her an open letter referring to her 'pulchritude' and declaring that 'women are not wholly qualified to be baseball writers.' Bob Addie alone, a Washington writer who had married a former tennis star, chided his fellows for barring her. He called the press box a last 'poor rampart of masculinity.'[77]

Jerry Green described the BBWAA in Detroit as a 'very closed tight organization, like a London men's club.' When McLain was trying for his thirtieth victory in 1968, Dizzy Dean, the last pitcher to win thirty games, was not allowed in the Detroit press box by then president Watson Spoelstra, 'the guardian of the flame after Salsinger.' Radio-TV reporters were separated from newspaper reporters in the press box until the mid-1970s, when the press box was rebuilt and enlarged. Vince Doyle asked Hawkins: 'You mean we are going to be allowed to piss with newspaper writers?' Spoelstra asked Campbell to rescind the arrangement.[78] A woman intern from the *Free Press* covered the Tigers in 1972, but Kuhn banned a woman sports writer, Melissa Ludke of *Sports Illustrated*, from locker rooms in 1975. The Tigers admitted Gail Granik of Channel 4 into the clubhouse in 1979. Campbell complained: 'I am so sick and tired of lawyers that I just don't care anymore. Let the women go in ... Personally, I'm opposed to it.' Steve Kemp was more tolerant: 'It was a little awkward, but I'm sure it was for her, too.'[79]

Metropolitan Detroit concluded in 1978: 'The cosy symbiotic relationship between pro and college teams and their press is obvious.' That same year the *Free Press* sent a city-desk editor to the sports department to ban all 'freebies' and set ethical standards. Both Lapointe and McGraw believe that Detroit sports writers were much too close to management until then. LaPointe describes Falls as being on the same wavelength as Campbell.[80] Falls emphasized that a writer can be 'friendly' but not 'friends or go to the house with players. I almost threw up when I saw a writer hug a player.'[81] Yet Falls, who receives high praise from many younger colleagues – including Cantor, Hawkins, Lapointe, and McGraw – for his 'fresh writing in his prime,' saw no problem in accepting a $1000 interest-free loan in 1973 from Campbell, with whom he was 'friendly.' Campbell and Falls confirmed the loan when it was reported in *Monthly Detroit* in 1982 by Matt Beer and Hillel Levin. But both Ladd Neumann, sports editor of the *Free Press* in 1973, and Herb Boldt, sports editor of the *News* in 1982, said that such a loan violated ethical policies of the newspapers. Jerry Green called it 'the most flagrant violation of conflict of interest I've ever seen.'[82]

The 'chipmunk writers' from New York began to write about a few controversial matters in the 1960s. They were more denunciatory of McLain than was the Detroit press. Nevertheless, in 1972, most sports writers were a part of the baseball establishment. They criticized what they perceived to be harmful to the national pastime. They made little distinction between gamblers and strikers. In fairness, they were not trained to examine financial matters, the owners had a monopoly on financial information, and the players continued a tradition of keeping their salaries a secret. Sports writing had traditionally limited criticism to players' performance on the field or managerial strategy. It preserved a romantic notion of the owners as benevolent sportsmen who were mere custodians of municipal identity. Players had abjured their heroic role and become mere mercenaries.

THE PHENOMENON OF FIDRYCH

The press worried about the effect of the strike on the players' performances and attendance, but their worries were unfounded. After all, the strike delayed the season only two weeks. Baseball attendance in 1973 topped its 1971 level. The game was soon back to normal. Unfortunately, the Tigers were not. They collapsed.

After the dismissal of Martin, Pete Waldmeir suggested that the Tigers hire a black manager because of the changing racial composition of the city.[83] Instead, Detroit hired Ralph Houk, an ex-Marine and ex-Yankee who fit the conservative image of the Tigers. Falls wrote later that Campbell was 'absolutely enamored of the man. Campbell is a conservative, always has been and always will be.'[84] Houk had a reputation for patience and he needed it, for the team sank into the basement in 1974. Symbolic of the decline was Kaline's struggle to reach the 3000-hit plateau – 'I can't reach balls I used to catch ... I don't want to embarrass myself.'[85] He reached the milestone in September, but there were few other highlights. No regular hit .300; no one hit 20 home runs; Kaline, who hit .262, led the team with 64 RBIs. Only Hiller had an ERA below 4.00; he led the team with 17 victories.

Next year's team was even worse. They lost 102 games. Mercifully, the Tigers did not make up three rain-outs or they might have broken their record of 104 losses set in 1952. They lost 19 games in a row, one short of the American League record, and lost 47 of their final 58 games. Horton hit 25 home runs and drove in 92 runs, but no other Tiger hit more than 14 home runs or drove in 60 runs. Lolich led the team with 12 victories, but he lost 18. Detroit was tagged as the city of losers, not only because of its crime rate, but because the Lions, Pistons, and Red Wings were also inept. Things were bleak. It was left to a minor-league pitcher who was not expected to make any contribution to the team in 1976 to revivify the city. That pitcher, of course, was Mark Fidrych, 'The Bird.'

Born on a farm in Northboro, Massachusetts, he was the 232nd player chosen, on the tenth round, in the 1974 draft. After a scout saw him throw one pitch, he signed him for a bonus of $3000 and a $500 monthly salary at Bristol (A). A non-rostered player who stayed in the Tigertown dorm during spring training, Fidrych received a chance in 1976 because the Tigers were desperate for help. The night he was told he was going to Detroit, he took a young woman to the pitcher's mound at Lakeland and celebrated his new salary of $16,500.[86]

His first start was a two-hit victory over Cleveland on 15 May, the no-hitter being spoiled with hits by Buddy Bell and Rick Manning in the seventh. He completed 24 of his 29 starts, won eight straight games between 31 May and 5 July and was 9-2 at the All-Star break. He finished 19-9 with a 2.34 ERA and missed by only one vote unanimous selection as Rookie Pitcher of the Year (Tiger players had to vote for someone from another team). Paul Carey remembers that he recognized that there was something special in that first game Fidrych pitched: 'He had a low-sinker ball with lots of movement that kept the hitter guessing. He himself didn't know where the ball would go either. He was a good pitcher, but his youth, exuberance, natural, obvious joy, that stupid-ass grin, appealed to young people. He had curls, an awkward gait, talked to himself, and gave people hope. My most memorable season was 1976, an electricity you felt. Fidrych was so good for business although the Tigers were a lousy team.'[87] The *Free Press* headlined its story the next day: 'Mark Fidrych Is Unreal.' It called him 'The Bird,' but still seemed a little confused by his antics. Falls saw something special that the fans needed and observed that representatives of the visiting media were wild about him. A major article appeared in *The Sporting News* two weeks later.[88] Stories began in earnest in the Detroit papers in June. He captured national attention after a 28 June Monday night baseball victory 5–1 over the Yanks before 47,855. The next day the *News* headline read: 'The Fidrych phenomenon has swept Detroit like nothing else since Denny McLain.' It editorialized: 'In an era of player greed and owner stupidity, Fidrych has managed to convince us that baseball is a game, not big business, and can be fun.' *Sports Illustrated* ran a major story after his victories over New York and Baltimore, praising his modesty – he did not want to get a big head because his only other job would be at a gas station. Rusty Staub said, 'I've never seen a city turn on like this.'

The next spring *Sports Illustrated* wrote: 'Not since Sandy Koufax has there been a pitcher with such drawing power ... Few rookies have had the impact on the game he had last year.' He had color, which is 'in very short supply in these days of the plutocrat athlete.' The next fall Hawkins wrote in the same magazine: 'No player, perhaps since Babe Ruth, individually has had such an impact on the sport in a single season.'[89] Home and away attendance averaged more than 30,000 for each of his 29 starts, and Tiger attendance increased 40 per cent during the year. The Tigers suffered at the concession stands when he pitched, however, because people would not leave their seats when he was pitching. (Fans usually buy hot dogs and drinks when the visiting team bats.) *The Sporting News* published forty-three major stories on Fidrych between 1976 and 1980, twenty-one after his career had effectively ended; Kaline was the subject of seven stories in that time. *Rolling Stone*, conscious of his following among youth, devoted a cover story to Fidrych on 5 May 1977. He also appeared on the cover of *Sports Illustrated* one month later, on 6 June. Team-mate Fred Holdsworth remembers that 'his innocence was captivating. There was no phoniness. He was like a five-year-old kid in a man's body.' Harwell stressed the importance of television in making Fidrych an overnight celebrity. 'He was a great kid – his naturalness and boyish charm. Girls waylaid him in the hallway, raided barbershops for a lock of his hair. He was really a rock star.'

Stories about the Tigers that year were about Fidrych. During the Tigers' lean years, other sports dominated Detroit sports pages. Even Hiller's save record and a one-hitter by Coleman played second fiddle to Secretariat and Michigan, MSU, and Lions football. Hawkins says he averaged three stories a day on Fidrych, partly because the team was so 'horseshit. Criticizing the team was like picking on a paraplegic. It wasn't their fault – they were just incompetent. People wanted to read about him. He was refreshingly unique and natural.' Charlie Vincent said that Fidrych was 'totally uninhibited. No other baseball season was so much fun.'[90] Fidrych was a relief from the problems of McLain and Martin and the shock of the strike. He reminded people of a mythical era in which baseball was a game played just for fun. He looked like a nerd and every baseball nerd in America who knew that he, save for a bad break along the way, could have been on the mound, striking out batters, loved him.

Unfortunately, Fidrych's career was a short one. His career-ending injury derived in part from his exuberance – chasing fly balls, something that no self-respecting star pitcher would do today. After he injured cartilage in his right knee, he underwent surgery and missed the first two months of the 1977 season. Soon afterward, perhaps because the knee injury changed his delivery, he developed tendonitis. Kaline was perceptive: 'We worry that he will never again be the same.' Ford Hospital was deluged with calls about his operation.[91]

In an abbreviated 1977 season, he won six games (2.89 ERA) and displayed signs of his past magic. He never recovered from his injury, however. His return was front-page news: 'The Bird Back, Loses 2–1.' Green wrote: 'The Bird's return is a tonic for baseball blahs. This sport can use something refreshing to turn the mind from the accumulated failure of the new plutocrats.' *Sports Illustrated* observed that 'Detroit's baseball season began – 51 days late – before 44,207.'[92] Fidrych personified what people wanted baseball to be. They sympathized with his comeback attempts, but he won only four games after 1977. His career was telescoped into a single season. In his own words, 'When it's gone, all you can say is it's gone, and this is what I got out of it.' For a short while Fidrych brought people downtown. The Tigers won 17 more games in 1976 than in 1975 but still finished fifth. For two years, where the Tigers finished did not really matter. The story was Fidrych. Coincidentally, the same year that Fidrych was the big story in Detroit, free agency opened a new era in baseball – which we shall discuss in the next chapter.

It would be a new era in Detroit for other reasons too, as the last players from the 1968 champions and the 1972 divisional champions departed. McAuliffe went to Boston for Ben Oglivie in 1973. Kaline retired after the 1974 season. In August the same year, Cash was released and Northrup sold to Montreal. Hawkins wrote 'An era ended Wednesday.' Cash complained that Campbell had called him and told him that he 'didn't have to go to the ballpark. That seemed a little cold to me, after all the money I made for this team ... It could have been warmer.' Northrup thought there was only a slight chance that he would report. 'It's a mild shock ... but I felt for the last five years that I would be traded.' Puscas predicted: 'There will be more.'[93] Lolich was traded for Rusty Staub in December 1975. Bothered that he had only twelve hours to make a decision about the trade (as a ten-year player he could have vetoed it), he felt hurt: 'In effect, they told me to get lost.' Campbell retorted: 'Getting traded is part of the job.'[94] Horton was traded to Texas for Steve Foucault in 1977. Horton was upset, but Campbell explained that Horton was having problems with Houk and wanted to be traded: 'Probably a big mistake I made was not dismantling the 1968 Tigers in 1969 or 1970. It cost me a couple of years' rebuilding – I should say it cost our people. There were guys I liked because they hustled. I always tried to inform players before a trade but sometimes it just wasn't possible.'[95]

New players were coming up from the farms. The *Free Press* was premature in 1972 when it called the Tiger farm club crop the best in ten years; of the players mentioned, only Tom Veryzer would play regularly for the Tigers. In 1974 Campbell promised that the farm system was 'a hell of a lot better than you think it is.' The slogan then, 'Password 78,' too optimistically envisioned a pennant in 1978. But it was in 1976 that the big advance was made, when the Tigers drafted thirteen players who eventually made the majors – including Jack Morris, Steve Kemp, Alan Trammell, Dan Petry, and Ozzie Smith (who got away).[96] Kemp had been a collegiate All-American at USC, but Tiger scouts also discovered Jason Thompson (1977), who did not play collegiate baseball until his third year and was not among the top four hundred players as identified by the cooperative scouting bureau.

Houk has been praised as an 'experienced and capable skipper' who 'led the rebuilding process, for getting the most out of his players and for being especially good with young players.'[97] Many of his players say, however, that he appeased and alibied for players but provided little leadership.[98] The rebuilding process went on at the minor-league level. In Houk's last year, 1978, Lou Whitaker, Trammell, Lance Parrish, Dave Rozema, and Morris were all making contributions. The Tigers still finished fifth in 1978, but they were one of the most improved teams that year, 'the best fifth-place club in either league.' They won 86 games, twelve more than in 1977 and the most they had won since 1972. The team batting average rose from .264 to .271. Its ERA dipped from 4.13 to 3.64. The Tigers sliced their errors from 142 to 118 while raising the double plays from 153 to 177. The pennant was further away than many expected and more hoped, but the base of the 1984 world championship team was in place.

7

Free Agency and Big Money for Baseball, 1977–1983

On 23 December 1975, arbitrator Peter Seitz ruled that Andy Messer-smith and David McNally were free agents. That decision ended the monopoly that owners held on players' services founded in the reserve clause. It inaugurated a new era in baseball during which players changed teams regularly and garnered million-dollar salaries. As Bowie Kuhn himself admitted after the fact, abolition of a reserve clause that continued in perpetuity from contract to contract should not have been unexpected.[1] Owners have continued to try to put Humpty-Dumpty together again, however. Free agency or its concomitant, a salary cap, was the main issue in four future strikes and two lock-outs. Baseball has always been a business,[2] but recently the business has often dwarfed the game. By itself, the Seitz decision did not guarantee the stratospheric payrolls of today. Those developed from a combination of arbitration decision, free agency, and the simultaneous influx of enormous new sums of money, especially from television. A surge in the popularity of baseball led to expansion in the number of teams, greater gate atten-dance, larger television audiences that included casual followers as well as ardent fans, and, with the introduction of cable television, more tele-vised games. Advertisers underwrote the free-agent bidding wars.

New income allowed owners to squander money as they pleased. Per-club revenue from television more than doubled during the 1970s and then increased ninefold in the 1980s (table 4). Per-club gate attendance topped the 1948 per-club attendance record in 1976 and increased by half in the decade after free agency (table 11). Minor-league attendance also recovered by the mid-1970s after two decades of decline (table 2).

Contrary to popular belief, fans did not pay for big salaries through increased ticket prices. Adjusted for inflation, prices remained stable until the 1990s (table 13).[3]

Players' salaries increased by 50 per cent in the first year following free agency; the rate of increase then slowed but salaries never stopped rising. They increased 3.5 fold during the 1980s and then another 2.4 fold in five years, from 1989 to 1994 (table 16). The differential among players' salaries also increased steadily after the onset of free agency.[4] After a few stars started receiving enormous salaries, more players tested the market. Moreover, free agents' salaries became the benchmark against which other players could negotiate their salaries and turn to arbitration. Arbitrators' decisions constantly pushed up the level of average players' salaries because the test was the salaries of free agents. Arbitration not only preceded free agency, it was also the means to it after both Congress and the courts had refused to overturn baseball's antitrust exemption.

MODIFICATION OF THE RESERVE CLAUSE

There had been a series of challenges to the reserve clause on antitrust grounds shortly after the Second World War (chapter 1). A final court case was brought in 1970. The St Louis Cardinals in 1969 sold the contract of Curt Flood, who had been featured on the cover of *Sports Illustrated* in 1968 as 'baseball's best center fielder,' to the Philadelphia Phillies. Flood refused to report and appeared before the union's executive board on 13 December 1969 seeking support for a lawsuit against baseball. At the time he wrote Kuhn: 'I do not feel that I can be bought and sold irrespective of my wishes. I believe that any system that produces that result violates my basic rights as a citizen and is inconsistent with the laws of the United States and the several states.'[5] Later he explained that 'basic principles of human life were involved.'[6] Kuhn, who, as commissioner of baseball, acted as arbitrator for player-management disputes, refused to invalidate the trade. He complained that Flood was not open to any compromise, but Kuhn's letter of 24 December 1969 to Flood does not indicate any willingness to seek a compromise.[7] On 16 January 1970 Arthur Goldberg, a former Supreme Court Justice, brought Flood's suit to United States District Court, where Hank Greenberg, Jackie Robinson, and Jim Brosnan testified for Flood. That summer the court ruled against him. Two years later, in June 1972, the U.S. Supreme Court upheld the lower court's decision, 5–3. The Court acknowledged: 'Baseball's status in the life of the nation is so pervasive ... that baseball is everybody's business.' After a bizarre introduction showering accolades on the past heroes of the game, the court concluded:

1.   Professional baseball is a business and it is engaged in interstate commerce.

2.3. With its reserve system enjoying exemption from the federal antitrust laws, baseball is, in a very distinct sense, an exception and an anomaly.

3.   Even though others might regard this as 'unrealistic, inconsistent, or illogical,' the aberration is an established one, that has been with us now for half a century, one heretofore deemed fully entitled to the benefit of *stare decisis*, and one that has survived the Court's expanding concept of interstate commerce. It rests on a recognition and an acceptance of baseball's unique characteristics and needs.

Justices William Douglas, who had voted with the plaintiff in *Toolson v. New York Yankees* twenty-five years earlier, William Brennan, and Thurgood Marshall dissented. The national press, which had accepted the need for the reserve clause during the controversies of the 1940s and early 1950s, no longer defended it. The *New York Times* observed that the Court made a mistake fifty years ago and 'now feels obliged to keep on making the same mistake because Congress does not act to repeal the exemption it never ordered.'[8]

The high profile of Curt Flood, growing sympathy in the national press for revision if not outright abolition of the reserve clause, and the 1972 players' strike all increased militancy among players and encouraged a willingness by a few to challenge the existing rules. Richard Moss, who was the union's general counsel then, observed: 'Even though (the lawsuit) was lost, it was an important part of the education of the players. The impact of an overly restrictive reserve system became much better understood through Flood.'[9]

While the Flood case was in the courts in 1970, players had won the right to have an impartial arbitrator rather than the commissioner of baseball decide grievances. Marvin Miller called that 'the most important victory' because commissioners were beholden to owners.[10] Following the 1972 strike and a lock-out in February 1973, binding arbitration was extended to salary disputes for players with more than two years' service. Players and teams each submitted their final offer; the arbitrator had to choose one or the other. The first arbitration cases were heard the next year; awards averaged only $40,839 but would increase annually. Owners apparently believed that they would win most cases, but a few executives were less sanguine. Dick Meyer, of the St Louis Cardinals, told Campbell: 'You have just put the nail in the coffin.'[11]

More important arbitration cases had to do with interpretations of contracts. The first was that of Catfish Hunter of the Oakland Athletics, who filed a grievance after the 1974 season charging breach of contract by the Oakland team because it had not paid part of his salary into an annuity. Arbitrator Peter Seitz agreed that Oakland had indeed breached the contract, which was therefore void, and declared Hunter a free agent on 13 December. Had Kuhn been the arbitrator, it is likely that he would have found some solution short of declaring Hunter a free agent. It was an isolated case decided on a legal technicality. The Detroit newspapers gave it little attention. Leonard Koppett, the first sports writer to concentrate on labor-management relations, 'because the *New York Times* was interested in larger issues,' was one of the few who foresaw 'possible future implications.'[12]

Behaving with their usual avarice, the owners showed what a star could make in a free market.[13] Twenty-three of the twenty-four teams pursued Hunter, and the New York Yankees signed him to a five-year, $3.1 million contract before the year ended. Moss observed: 'It served as a wonderful demonstration that the players should be paid a lot more than they have been paid.'[14] Two decades later Peter Bavasi called the signing 'the defining moment' for 'this mess.'[15]

Later that year the reserve clause was directly challenged. Andy Messersmith, who had won twenty games for the Dodgers in 1974, began the 1975 season without a contract because he wanted one with a no-trade provision. Under Paragraph 10a of the standard players' contract, the Dodgers renewed Messersmith's contract for 'a period of one year on the same terms.' Did the 'same terms' in unilateral renewal include the reserve clause entitling teams to restrict a player to them until they released him? Flood had sat out the 1970 season so that he could become a free agent, eventually signing with Washington in 1971. Rufus Gentry of the Tigers had sat out 1945 but re-signed with the Tigers. No player had played for a season and received free agency at its end. The Dodgers tried to sign Messersmith in 1975, but Miller and Moss were determined on a test case. In case Messersmith signed, they recruited Dave McNally, who had retired during the 1974 season but remained under contract with Montreal, to join in testing the reserve clause.[16] John McHale, the Expos' general manager, went to Billings, Montana, in an attempt to sign McNally, but the die was cast for a test of the reserve provision.

The McNally-Messersmith case, like the Hunter case, came before Peter Seitz. Seitz wanted a compromise. According to John Gaherin, the chief labor negotiator for the owners, Seitz told negotiators on 8 December: 'If there's a decision here, someone is going to get hurt. I'm willing to be of service to you two. I'm willing to say what my impressions are at this moment.'[17] Gaherin warned the owners that they were likely to lose. Encouraged by some of their lawyers, particularly Louis Hoynes, they stonewalled. The players' union over the years has either had better legal advice or owners have ignored legal advice that did not fit their preconceptions. On 23 December 1975 Seitz delivered his decision: 'The grievances of Messersmith and McNally are sustained. There is no contractual bond between these players and the Los Angeles and Montreal clubs respectively ... Absent such a contract, their clubs had no right or power, under the Basic Agreement, the uniform player contract or the Major League Rules to reserve their services for their exclusive use for any period beyond the "renewal year" in the contracts which these players had heretofore signed with their clubs.'[18] Seitz told the *New York Times*: 'I am not an Abraham Lincoln signing the emancipation proclamation ... Involuntary servitude has nothing to do with this case. I decided it as a lawyer and an arbitrator.'[19] Nevertheless, the Seitz decision 'dramatically and irrevocably changed professional sports.'[20]

The owners immediately fired Seitz and brought a lawsuit to overturn the decision. Campbell says that neither he nor most people in baseball realized the implications of either decision.[21] Detroit newspapers ran only brief AP reports. The national press, however, recognized the importance of the decision and displayed little remorse for the demise of the reserve clause in its extant form. On Christmas Day, 1975, the *New York Times* editorialized that 'organized baseball is not quite a slave system as the cliché has it, but its Establishment does suggest the inflexibility of plantation owners on the eve of the Civil War.' *Newsweek* gave the owners little hope of winning their lawsuit and predicted the end of the reserve clause. *Esquire* recalled 'an extended history of feudalism,' but *Time* worried about damage to the competitive balance of the game. The editorial policy of *The Sporting News* attacked free agency. Dick Young, who had been embittered by five newspaper strikes in New York, asked whether freedom was a 'euphemism for more money.' In contrast, Leonard Koppett and Murray Chass, who succeeded Koppett at the *New York Times*, defended the decision in the same weekly. Both of them had become more critical of ownership because the players' representatives were 'more honest and forthright.'[22]

After the owners lost in court in 1976, they locked players out for seventeen days, but Kuhn ordered the camps reopened on 17 March. All players could have become free agents, but the Major League Baseball Players Association recognized the potentially negative effects of a completely free market and agreed to a system that required players to complete six years of major-league service to be eligible for free agency.[23] The owners enjoyed what economists call monopsony power over the players, but the MLBPA could increase wages by restricting the amount of available labor; the result was a bilateral monopoly. A limited supply of free agents would push salaries higher. Chuck Finley, Oakland's owner, anticipated the problem and thought total free agency would be better for owners than a limited market.

On 12 July the two sides reached a four-year basic agreement requiring compensation by draft choices to teams losing free agents. The first free agent re-entry draft was held on 4 November 1976. The New York Yankees, which George Steinbrenner had purchased on 3 January 1973, signed Reggie Jackson for $2.9 million over five years. Nolan Ryan signed the first $1 million one-year free-agent contract with Houston in 1979; David Winfield signed a $25 million contract over ten years with the Yankees in 1980. Ford Frick, former commissioner of baseball, predicted two years before the Messersmith case that 'if the reserve clause goes the prime sufferers will be the players.'[24] He was no better a prophet than he had been a commissioner or sports writer.

The owners had complained that free agency would lead to a great increase in salaries. They were right about that. Payrolls more than tripled before the next strike in 1981. Owners also warned that the competitive balance of baseball would be ruined. They were wrong about that. In all eras, big-market teams (as measured by metropolitan population base) have been the most successful. Competitive differences narrowed in the first fifteen years after free agency. There was more balance among teams in the 1980s than in any decade in baseball's history.[25] The Yankees of 1976–7, helped by the acquisition of Jackson, were the last team to repeat as World Series Champions until the Toronto Blue Jays in 1992–3. Eighteen different teams played in the Series from 1978 to 1992. The end of dynasties and greater competitive balance began with the inauguration of the amateur draft in 1965 and the decline of the Yankees. Eleven different teams played in the Series from 1964 to 1972. Balance was not due to free agency alone.

The 1981 strike resulted primarily from the owners' attempt to undo the free-agency agreement, which expired in 1980. The two sides were unable to agree on player compensation for free agency, but they resolved other issues, played the 1980 season after a brief strike during the spring exhibition season and deferred the question of compensation to 1981. Many owners still thought that the players would not strike. George Steinbrenner laid down the gauntlet: 'Let them strike.'[26] Yet the owners were at the mercy of the players' organization after the courts upheld the Seitz decision. Miller was not about to give up what the players had won. Kuhn described him as 'an old-fashioned nineteenth-century trade unionist who hated management,' feared that the players' organization was threatening to take the game away from the clubs, and tagged the 1981 strike 'Miller's strike.' Grudgingly, *The Sporting News* acknowledged that he was 'the most effective labor leader in the country.' Miller disdained Kuhn and there was 'extreme personal animosity' between Miller and the owners' negotiator Ray Grebey.[27] These personal animosities made matters worse. When the owners unilaterally implemented compensation for free agents after no agreement was reached, the strike was probably inevitable. It was not just about free agency; it was now a power struggle.

On 12 June the players began a fifty-day strike that cancelled 706 games. They returned on 7 August after private negotiations between Miller and Leland MacPhail, president of the American League in late July.[28] The 1981 season was split into two parts. Estimates are that the owners lost $72 million, the players $28 million, and cities $10 million in revenue.[29] Most owners were not used to dealing with unions, which were on the defensive generally in the United States. Chrysler and other industries had forced give-backs, and Ronald Reagan would fire 12,000 air controllers that August during their abortive strike. The atmosphere may have encouraged the owners to be obdurate.

Most sports writers and fans continued to be more critical of the players than of owners; Miller's successor Donald Fehr sniffed in 1985 that the fans were 'relatively uninformed.'[30] Influential national publications, however, either turned blame on the owners or exhibited a disgust with both sides. *Sports Illustrated* titled its lead story 'Strike – The Walkout the Owners Provoked': 'Workers sought to preserve the status quo and avoid a strike while the bosses sought radical change and courted a walkout.' *Time* called the strike 'an outrage, a form of cultural terrorism ... It has subverted that sense of the mystique.' A. Bartlett Giamatti, president of Yale University, wrote on the Op-Ed page of the *New York Times*: 'The strike is utter foolishness ... a triumph of greed.'[31] Impressed by Giamatti's attitude, which they saw as pro-management, the owners selected him as president of the National League and then made him commissioner of baseball in 1989. His major act during a term shortened by a fatal heart attack was the lifetime suspension of Pete Rose for gambling.

The Detroit press was much less preoccupied with the 1981 strike than it had been in 1972, but it remained anti-union. The *Detroit News* editorialized: 'After caving in to all of the player-union demands in recent years [the strike] is a social hurt ... The clubs' position is fair ... [It is] one more example of a powerful union ... unwilling to moderate its appetite.' It was difficult to drum up sympathy for players, when one compared their salaries to the 'average Joe' in Detroit. Defensive of its heroes, the *News* reiterated its 1972 theme that the players weren't the real villains: 'They are a misguided lot, they are being misled by a silky-voiced labor infighter named Marvin Miller ... master of the confused message.' The *Free Press* took a similar tack, although George Puscas criticized obstinate owners.[32] Tiger players put up a unified front, but there was criticism both before and after the fact of the lack of democracy and of voice votes. Established players and representatives from the union dominated meetings.[33]

PROSPERITY AMIDST CONCERN

Many feared that fans would abandon the game, but Joe Falls was correct in predicting that 'baseball will survive.'[34] Baseball survived not only the strikes of 1972 and 1981 but also drug scandals that were afflicting sport by the early 1980s. In 1983 four Kansas City players and Steve Howe of the Dodgers were suspended for using drugs. The next year Ken Moffett, former executive director of the players' union, charged that drugs were a big problem in baseball, especially on the St Louis Cardinals.[35] He retreated under pressure but was proved right the following year. A drug trial in Pittsburgh, in which seven players testified, captured national attention in September 1985. In it Keith Hernandez claimed that 40 per cent of players in the major leagues were cocaine users (Cardinal manager Whitey Herzog later stated that he thought Hernandez was referring only to the Cardinals' team, but agreed that ten or eleven of those players were using cocaine). Twenty-one major-league players received penalties. In that same year former Tiger pitcher Denny McLain was convicted on drug-related charges. The next year former Cy Young Award winner LaMarr Hoyt was sentenced to prison on similar charges. The death of the Boston Celtics' number-one draft choice, Len Bias, from a cocaine overdose caused a sensation the same year.[36] Dwight Gooden, Steve Howe, and Darryl Strawberry were suspended a few years later but played again. Falls thinks: 'Our values are twisted. Hernandez gets a standing ovation after confessing to eight years of drug use.'[37]

Drugs were more available and a part of at least a subculture in America by the late 1970s. Big salaries meant the players had money to indulge any whim, and sycophants who surrounded them led them to believe that they were Nietzschean figures above the laws that bound normal human beings. After a recent study of drug and alcohol abuse in NCAA sports, Dr Gary Wadler concluded: 'Fame, fortune, free time and feelings of invincibility put athletes at risk.'[38]

A revolution had occurred within a generation. Thirty years earlier the revelation that Dr Raymond Forsyth had used novocaine on Newhouser's arm in 1945 created a scandal. A similar furor had surrounded the use of occasional prescription tranquillizers by a 'half-dozen' Tiger players in the late 1950s.[39] Tiger GM Charlie Gehringer had banned both pain pills and beer in the clubhouse in the 1950s. Jim Brosnan and Jim Bouton shocked sports fans in the early 1960s with their announcement of common use of 'greenies' by players.[40] Three Tiger players speak about the use of amphetamines:

Ray Herbert: Trainers got prescriptions for greenies for double-headers in Kansas City. The team doctor would write prescriptions and drugs were kept locked up. The late 1970s and early 1980s is when players start buying it on their own. They were given out a couple at a time in the late 1950s and 1960s. Trainers were very good about it, like a doctor.

Lenny Green: Pep pills were suggested when I hurt my back. Players didn't know the difference from aspirin. Trainers gave them. Alcohol was never regarded as a drug, but there was more abuse of that during the 1960s than any other drugs.

Jon Warden: I could not have spelled cocaine; I never saw any marijuana. Some guys took amphetamines, maybe some did some other drugs but not around the park; and they didn't talk about it if they did.[41]

Ron Leflore was the only Tiger regular to have ongoing drug problems. His trade to Montreal after the 1979 season in which he hit .300 and stole 78 bases was attributed to his missing a team plane, which happened for reasons related to his problem.[42] Campbell euphemistically explained that Montreal 'knew what they were getting.'[43] Although Leflore stole 97 bases, he hit only .257 in 1980 and .246 the following year. His career ended after the 1982 season and an arrest on drug charges.

There was 'private use' of some illegal drugs by other Tiger players and dealing by one girlfriend in a Romulus bar, but players themselves judged that the Tigers were 'cleaner than most.'[44] Except for some hints in *Metropolitan Detroit*, the Detroit press ignored private drug use that did not demonstrably affect performance on the field – an entirely reasonable position, especially in the presence of libel laws.[45] Drugs were not a serious problem on Tiger teams in part because of a staunch management position, enforced by Campbell. In 1984 he announced that the Tigers favored mandatory testing even though the team did not have a drug problem. He also told Gates Brown, then a coach, to report any drug use by players; Brown did not report any players but privately warned any that needed warning.[46] Sparky Anderson, in his inimitable way, put the drug problem in perspective: 'Even if there were three or four on every team, which there aren't, it ain't going to ruin the sport ... In the old days 24 of the 25 guys on every team were drunk. Today nobody hardly drinks anymore and very, very few take drugs.'[47]

The difference between his observations and those of Herzog may reflect the different teams they have managed. Nevertheless, drugs were a *public* problem, involving an illegal substance, whereas past drinking problems involved a legal drug and were covered up by sports writers of the time. Drink had been part of a *macho* subculture and tolerated as long as players could perform the next day. Drugs, strikes, and big salaries meant that players could no longer occupy a pedestal as unselfish, mythical heroes devoted only to the game. They had never been that, but the press and fans had wished them to be. With the image shattered, would fans continue to support sports teams?

The answer was a resounding yes. Despite 'pessimists who thought free agency would hurt' baseball, *The Sporting News* acknowledged that attendance had increased by more than 7.3 million in the first year following free agency. *Sports Illustrated* applauded baseball's 'golden age' when average game attendance reached 20,733 in 1978, half again the 13,869 it had been in 1969.[48] Free agency meant that baseball was on the sports pages year-round. Chass knew that a new age had begun when Mike Torrez's move from the Yanks to the Red Sox dominated the sports pages on a Monday, following NFL games.[49] Although 87 per cent of fans in 1978 thought that there was too much emphasis on money in sports, 73 per cent said they forgot about it when the game began:

'It seems as though nothing can deter American sports fans from their preoccupation with professional sports or from their enthusiasm for it – not even expressed complaints about the commercialization that has occurred, the big salaries paid to the players, the motivations of the owners or the increase in unnecessary violence,' the Yankelovich study says. 'Instead, sports fans ... state unequivocally that, compared to five years ago, they are enjoying professional sports even more now, are rooting harder than ever for their favorite teams, and are more enthusiastic about the star players than they were in the past.'[50]

Before the 1981 strike, attendance was increasing at a record pace. After the strike it declined by 10 per cent in the NL and 6 per cent in the AL. Television audiences declined from a 7.6 to a 6.4 rating.[51] A new attendance record, broken many times since, was set in 1982, however. At the Tigers first workout after the strike ended, 4127 stalwarts attended. Not just ardent fans returned. Historically, fans were those who attended games and fanatically (from which the word derives) rooted for their teams. Television widened the audience. A poll in *Sports Illustrated* in 1980 revealed that half of those who considered themselves baseball fans did not attend games but followed it on television. A Miller Lite study in 1983 concluded: '96.3% of the country plays, watches, or reads articles about sports, or identifies with certain teams and athletes at least once a month ... and nearly 70% of Americans follow sports every day.'[52] ESPN became the first 24-hour TV network for 'sports junkies' in 1978 and soon nearly 400 cable stations reached nearly 15 million homes. Sport has a unique market in that its customers are devoted to the game. Maltreated, disgusted, annoyed, frustrated, they still come back – at least until the 1994 baseball strike. Too much attention has focused on the rise of other sports and the *relative* decline of baseball. It did not and does not really matter if other sports elicit followings so long as those do not detract from baseball's *absolute* following. The general popularity of sports in the 1980s may even have benefited baseball, as women particularly became more interested in both participant and spectator sports.

Although football ratings in the early 1980s averaged 16.5 against baseball's 11.5, baseball's audience share remained larger than that of any other professional or collegiate sport. Its income from television became a steadily greater proportion of total revenues: 3 per cent in 1946, 10% in 1950, 17% in 1956, 28% in 1970, 38% in 1985, and 50% in 1990. National television revenues grew at an annual rate of 17 per cent and local revenues at an annual rate of 13 per cent from 1960 to 1990.[53] Average club home attendance rose steadily from the mid-1960s and doubled in the quarter-century after free agency (table 11). Where did the money come from to pay for free agency? It was from rapidly

Costs and revenues per team (in millions of dollars) 1970–83[57]

	1970	1974	1977	1980	1983
Costs	7.0	6.6	9–10.3	14.3	22.6
Revenues	–	6.4	8.9	13.5	20.1

expanding television income, increased gate attendance, and profits that the owners denied they had been making. The increase in baseball salaries during the 1980s is almost identical with the increased revenue from television. One year before free agency Kuhn had claimed that teams were at best breaking even; yet they were able to spend $24 million for free agents the next year. Roger Noll, who wrote pioneering examinations of baseball finances, found it a frustrating task: 'The sports industry is the most secretive business I know of.'[54] Because financial records of most teams remain secret, one cannot reach exact conclusions about income, costs, and profits or losses. A number of fine works, notably those by Gerald Scully, Andrew Zimbalist, and James Quirk and Rodney Fort, nevertheless provide good estimates of baseball's finances.

Players' salaries were at their lowest percentage of total team revenue in history in the year before free agency (table 3). In the four years following free agency, operating costs nearly doubled from $144 to $267 million and players' salaries increased from about one-sixth to one-fourth of total team revenues. Still, they accounted for only about one-third of the claimed increase in costs. Inflation, travel, advertising, benefits, and a bloated management contributed to rising costs as well.[55] Player salaries, as a proportion of team expenditures, steadily increased in the years following to 40 per cent in 1986, after which collusion temporarily lowered salaries, and reached 50 per cent in 1994.[56] Costs tripled between 1974 and 1983, but so did revenues. The above table on costs and revenues suggests that baseball teams were losing money as a whole, but it shows only operating costs. It does not allow for player depreciation that produced tax savings, or for benefits to other businesses like Budweiser from Busch's Cardinals and Labatt's from the Blue Jays, or to Fetzer's television empire. Noll concluded that the owners were making a true profit of $20 million in 1984 rather than a claimed $41 million loss.[58] Although *Forbes* in 1977 called baseball ownership the 'world's worst investment,' owners made enormous profits from the sale of franchises and payments from expansion teams. Some billionaires probably purchased teams for prestige rather than for an investment. At least until recently, there has always been a 'bigger fool' to take an unwanted franchise. The Mets' capital appreciation was 12 per cent compounded annually 1961–1980; the Tigers' was 8.3 per cent. Franchise values rose more rapidly than did players' salaries or revenue from television.[59] In the 1950s the average sale price of a franchise was $3.5 million, in the 1960s $7.6, in the 1970s $12.6, and in the 1980s $40.7 million. Few other investments paid so handsomely. By whatever means or mirrors, the clubs managed to pay salaries that increased twenty-five-fold in the quarter-century after free agency.

DETROIT'S RESPONSE TO FREE AGENCY

The Tigers entered the free-agency market in 1976, drafting nine players and signing Tito Fuentes, then thirty-three years old and a career .268 hitter. He hit .309 with 190 hits in 615 at-bats for Detroit. In 1977 the Tigers drafted six players, but signed none. The next two years they did not draft anyone.[60] The Tigers also went after Bobby Grich, who moved from Baltimore to California in 1977, but they offered far too little. As Campbell put it: 'I went to war with a switch.'[61] The Tigers also tried to purchase Vida Blue.

Recognizing that he could not outbid rich clubs, Charles Finley decided to sell his remaining stars, as Connie Mack had with the Athletics' franchise a half-century earlier. The Tigers agreed to buy Vida Blue's contract for $1 million, but New York increased its offer to $1.5 million. Boston agreed to purchase the contracts of Joe Rudi and Rollie Fingers for $1 million apiece. Kuhn, egged on by Walter O'Malley of the Dodgers, ruled the deals invalid, claiming they would upset the competitive balance of baseball. *Newsweek* called him the 'village idiot' for doing so.[62] Such sales have become commonplace now.

The inability to get either Blue or Grich convinced Campbell to 'back out of the market. We learned a lesson, there was no limit.'[63] In the immediate aftermath, Campbell said: 'I think the elimination of the reserve clause is going to ruin the competitive balance of baseball.' The next year he promised: 'I don't intend to go hog wild after a multi-million dollar ballplayer and I think we will have more company this year.'[64]

Shortly before his death he stated that he was right about free agency ruining baseball and wrong only in his belief that things could not get worse. The Tigers were as willing as anybody to chase after stars. They withdrew when they realized how pricey they would be.

Fetzer complained in 1983 that 'there has been a tendency [by some owners] to put self-interest against the common interest.'[65] He had summarized his own approach four years earlier:

I've got the authority to go out and spend as much money as any of the owners, and probably more than most of them for baseball players. And I could enjoy the biggest ego ride you ever saw. I could be a hero every day if I went out and spent a million here and a million there.

But what would that do to my peers? What would it do to their payrolls? Some of them couldn't afford it. They don't have the resources. They don't have the town. They don't have the support. What am I doing to them? Do I have an obligation to my brothers or not? It's as simple as that. And I think I do.

I think it's more of a justice to the people of the city of Detroit to see that we have a solid franchise in Detroit that can stand the test of time.[66]

He could indeed have afforded free agents. He could have drawn from his personal fortune, estimated by *Forbes* as $75–$100 million, in addition to $25 million for the baseball club. He also could have used Tiger profits. Although the operating budget increased from $2.8 million to $7 million in 1977 and to $14.8 million in 1982, the Detroit Baseball Club remained a profitable enterprise. The players' payroll in 1977 was about what it had been in the division-winning year of 1972 ($1.25 million) – only half the team's combined television-radio income in 1977 and about 20 per cent of total team expenses. Front-office salaries topped $1 million, and player development added $1.5 million. Fetzer drew annual dividends from the club. The *Free Press* estimated annual profits at more than $545,000 annually from 1980 to 1983, plus tax write-offs of $2.7 million for the stadium in 1979. Campbell's figures reveal higher operating profits of $2 million in 1980 and total revenue of $15.7 million against expenses of $14.8 million in 1982.[67] The players' payroll calculates as only 29 per cent of expenses then.

The Tigers' old paternalistic attitudes towards players mutated to open antagonism in negotiations. George Kalifatis, whom Campbell retained in AAA ball within the Tiger organization for an extra year to finance his law schooling, became an agent with the International Management Group. When he came to the Tigers' spring training, Campbell ordered him to 'stay the fuck away from our clubhouse and our kids.'[68] Campbell had refused to meet with Lolich's agent for two years in 1972–3, sending them to Rick Ferrell. Rusty Staub, obtained for Lolich, became the highest-paid Tiger but wanted to renegotiate his salary in 1979 after driving in 96, 101, and 121 runs from 1976 to 1978. He found himself traded to Montreal. In 1980 Alan Trammell, Lou Whitaker, and Steve Kemp all won arbitration awards. In 1983 Dan Petry, Jack Morris, Whitaker, Chet Lemon, and Larry Herndon won arbitration awards, although Kirk Gibson lost. Arbitrators thought that the Tigers were paying too little. The Tigers ranked twenty-fourth in salaries in the American League in 1979 despite estimated profits by the *Detroit News* of $3 million (presumably including tax write-offs), and twenty-third in 1982. Salaries rose steadily during the 1980s (table 19).

The Tigers also began to sign people to long-term contracts. Trammell at age twenty-two received a seven-year contract for between $2.8 and $3 million in 1980, although Fetzer had proclaimed two years earlier that 'we are constitutionally opposed to the creation of young sports millionaires.' He explained that it was not a new policy, but 'we are building a team.' Milt Wilcox signed for three years in 1981 and Whitaker for two. The Tigers tripled their total payroll from 1977 to 1981, while baseball payrolls as a whole increased by a factor of 2.4 (tables 16, 19). Trammell's salary was renegotiated in 1984 for a nine-year contract approaching $5 million; Petry, Morris, Evans, Whitaker, Lemon, Herndon, and Parrish signed multi-year contracts as well.[69] Detroit did not make a major free-agent acquisition until Darrell Evans for the 1984 season, but they were astute in locking up young players at reasonable costs and increased their payroll as their income increased from both television and gate receipts. Campbell prided himself in balancing the books. Despite economic problems and fears about crime within Detroit, the metropolitan base for the team was 4.4 million in 1980 versus 3 million in 1950 – below only New York, Los Angeles, and Philadelphia in both those years.[70] Allowing for the missed games in 1981 during the strike, Tiger attendance in the early 1980s averaged 50 per cent more than it had in the mid-1970s. Local television revenue doubled in that time (tables 5 and 12). The *Detroit News* editorialized that the cities and the suburbs too often regarded themselves as separate but were brought together by the Tigers. The neighborhood around Tiger Stadium remained 'one of the safest in town' and there were no reports of attacks on anyone attending games.[71]

The Tigers did trade two promising young players who offended management. The first was Kemp, whose arbitration award of $600,000 stunned both the Tigers and the newspapers. Falls asked, 'Where does this insanity end?' Campbell was shocked at the award – the highest that year – and decided that the Tigers could no longer afford Kemp.[72] On 27 November 1981 Kemp was traded to the Chicago White Sox for Lemon. The previous May the Tigers had traded Jason Thompson, who had hit 77 home runs over the last three years, to California. In 1982 both trades looked bad for the Tigers as Kemp hit 19 home runs and drove in 96 runs and Thompson hit 31 home runs and drove in 105 runs, but this was the only big year either had after leaving the Tigers.

Detroit made good choices about whom to keep and whom not to keep. The Tigers acquired Aurelio Lopez from the St Louis Cardinals in December 1978 and Herndon from the San Francisco Giants on 9 December 1981 – important cogs in the 1984 championship team – for minor leaguers or players near the end of their careers. Tiger drafts were more successful during the 1970s than during any other period. Their first-round draft choices included Tom Veryzer (1971), Lance Parrish (1974), Tom Brookens (1975), Pat Underwood (no. 1 overall in 1976), Kemp (no. 2 overall in 1976), and Gibson (1978). The 1975 draft brought Rozema (round 4) and Whitaker (5). The 1976 draft produced Trammell (2), Petry (4), and Morris (5) as well. Despite computerized scouting, the amateur draft has always been a lottery. Only twenty (one-third) first-round draft choices from 1975 to 1977 from all teams were in the majors in 1980 and only 55 per cent of first-round draft choices from 1977 to 1986 ever made the majors.[73]

The club might be said to have participated in free agency in another way as well. It hired Sparky Anderson to manage the team in mid-1979. Anderson had won pennants with Cincinnati in 1970 and 1972 and the World Series in 1975 and 1976; he was dismissed after two second-place finishes in 1977 and 1978 when Cincinnati won 88 and 92 games respectively. Anderson replaced Les Moss, who had been appointed manager when Houk retired in 1978 – a reward for years of service in the Tiger organization. Moss had managed the 1976 Montgomery (AA) team that included Brookens, Morris, Parrish, Rozema, and Trammell. Campbell explained at the time why he replaced Moss. 'I've been too loyal. I kept the 1968 team too long. I screwed myself and I screwed the whole organization.'[74] Years later he said: 'One of the hardest things I had to do in my life was to dismiss Moss. But he lacked charisma and the Tigers took an awful beating in Seattle. Anderson was in Anaheim when we went there and that's when it hit me. I called [George] Kell, who said "do it." I asked Kell to come to my room for breakfast and asked him to see Anderson at once about his interest because there was an unclear deal with Cincinnati and I didn't want to tamper. Sparky managed for a day without a contract. I guaranteed to his wife what he made in Cincinnati.'[75]

The *Free Press* hoped that Anderson would put more life into a 'lethargic' ball club, and 'revive baseball passion in this town.' Hired for five and a half years, Anderson received about $110,000 compared to Moss's $35,000. It was unfair to Moss but a 'brilliant surprise to all.'[76] When Anderson was hired the Tigers had had fifteen managers and three interim managers since 1952.

Anderson had a reputation as a tough manager, 'My Way or the Highway.' At Cincinnati, where Bob Howsam wanted a clean image, he had strictly enforced a no-mustache rule. There was immediate speculation that Rodriguez and Thompson, who refused to shave their mustaches, would be traded. They were, whether it had anything to do with mustaches or not. He eliminated stripes on Tiger socks as 'sloppy.' Leflore told him, 'I'll think about it.' Anderson responded: 'Hurry up because the game starts soon.'[77] He had some problems with players in 1980, but a series of team meetings and trades made it clear who was in charge.[78] At first he banned cords and Levis, but later allowed both them and wives on road trips for the first time. He brought his boyhood friend Billy Consolo as a coach in 1979. He was a celebrity, a traditionalist who fit the Tiger image, and was a master with the press. On arrival he predicted correctly a pennant in 1984, although in 1984 he denied that he had a specific five-year plan. That is remembered better than his prediction of ninety wins in 1980, which the team did not attain.[79] On the occasion of his becoming the third-winningest manager (behind John

McGraw and Connie Mack), 'This Week in Baseball' reminded viewers of Anderson's pennant in 1984. That has become a part of baseball lore. In his first decade the Tigers were a great success, suffering no losing season until 1989 and tying New York for most victories in the American League from 1980 to 1988.

MARKETING THE TEAM

The Tigers were a conservative organization, headed by Campbell, who made no secret of his hatred of free agency and agents. He was a tough negotiator who intimidated many players. Stanley was 'scared' of him, Kip Young 'terrified.' Holdsworth said that if a player used an agent Campbell would make life miserable for him, and Underwood described him as 'very distant and unable to relate to young ballplayers.'[80] The Tigers judged talent well, however. If the team did not sign free agents, neither did it lose any key players. Detroit was among the most successful teams in baseball in the decade soon after free agency was introduced.

The club took a traditional approach to the game. It opposed the designated-hitter rule.[81] It was slow to market baseball, but it began to make some changes during the 1970s. As we saw in chapter 3, the Tigers had approached television rights in a rather amateurish way, appointing 'Doc' Fenkell, who had no experience in either television or advertising, to sell time to advertisers. After the Tigers' last-place finish in 1974 and with not much hope for 1975, Fenkell worried about future sales and suggested selling rights to a television station. He approached WWJ-TV, where Peter Kitzer envisioned Detroit Tiger baseball as a way of raising the station's image as well as making money. Negotiations went on for some months and ultimately WWJ, later WDIV-TV, offered the Tigers $6 million for five years. WJBK-TV came in with an offer of less than $3 million. The deal was announced the Friday after Thanksgiving, 1975.

WWJ-TV lost money in the first year but by the third year 'made a lot of money and continued to do so all through the contract.' The station gradually learned how to market the team, not understanding at first the full value of Tiger baseball and being timid in charging advertisers. Later they tied general marketing for the station with the Detroit Tigers, carrying promotions for other programs during the games. Kitzer chose Al

Kaline over Larry Osterman to share announcing with Kell, although Osterman worked for Fetzer, because Kaline was a personality who could market the games. Kaline made personal appearances for the station and the Tigers, as well as fulfilling an announcer's role. This dual role of announcer and promoter would become a problem later regarding radio announcer Ernie Harwell's duties. Kitzer was less concerned about Kaline's skills than his personality. As he put it, 'an audience will put up with a non-broadcaster if the guy is well known. Both Kell and Kaline were sensational guys.'[82] Television writers criticize Kaline, but the audience loves him.[83] WDIV-TV made money, the Tigers made money, and the audience increased with both the increased popularity of baseball and the success of the Tigers on the field in the 1980s. In the first year of the contract forty-six games were shown in Detroit and forty on an out-state network consisting of Cadillac, Kalamazoo, Lansing, Saginaw, Sault Ste Marie, and Toledo, Ohio. WJR continued to broadcast Tiger games on radio. The station lost the Pistons and the Red Wings because Fetzer insisted on all Tiger games being carried and there were nineteen conflicts during the season. Baseball was still *the* sport in Detroit.

Campbell believed that the best way to draw fans was to put a successful team on the field. The club did hire Lew Matlin to organize special nights and on-the-field promotions. In 1972 Autograph Day allowed children to get autographs before the game from their favorite players. Helmet Day was inaugurated in 1973, and special SEMTA buses brought fans from the suburbs, on whose residents the team increasingly depended. Polish American night outdrew Free Bat Day (36,377 to 24,824) in 1976. That year special nights included ones for the American Legion, Elks, Fan Club, Kiwanis, Knights of Columbus, Lutherans, Navy, Polish Americans, Shriners, and Windsor.[84]

The club deliberately kept ticket and concession prices low to stay within the reach of the average fan.[85] It was not the Tiger management's style to put on a 'Hot Pants Night' to honor the fashion of the time, as Oakland did in a game against Kansas City in 1971. (Organizers had expected five hundred women to take advantage of the reward of two free ducats for parading on the field in hot pants; they were surprised when five thousand did.) Nor would the Tigers sponsor a '10 cent Beer Night,' as Cleveland did in 1974 when 25,000 fans drank 60,000 beers and 500 fans ran on the field, prompting players to defend themselves with baseball bats. Beer was Detroit's most profitable concession, and the bottom line was also important in Detroit. One would not expect the Tigers to sponsor a 'Disco Demolition Night,' as Chicago did in a game against Detroit in 1979. The Tigers' organist played music that suited Campbell more than it did young fans. But neither would one have anticipated Public Relations Director Hal Middlesworth to nix a Fan Appreciation Night, like that held in most cities. Yet he did.[86]

One might have expected some outreach to the African American community as its percentage of the population of Detroit progressed from 29 per cent in 1960 to 44 per cent in 1970 to 63 per cent in 1980 (table 10). Instead, the club relied on white suburbanites. That was a dangerous course as tensions between the city and the suburbs increased. The metropolitan/city disparity in income was the highest in the nation at $33,241 to $21,556 in 1983. Hourly wages in Detroit were above the national average, but the median income of whites was half again as high as that of non-whites ($20,658 vs. $13,695) and their unemployment rate less than half (7.4% vs. 15.5%) in 1979. Twenty-two per cent of city residents were living in poverty in 1980 and that proportion rose rapidly in the next few years. Joe Louis Arena, Central Industrial Park (Pole-town), the People Mover, and $500 million of HUD money were signs of improvement downtown, but the closing of Stroh's, Vernor's, and Hudson's and the loss of 21 per cent of industrial operations from 1977 to 1982 were evidence of serious problems.[87] The city's financial problems and the perspective of African American residents would not become an issue until the next decade. The horizon appeared bright in 1980.

8

The Golden Age of Detroit Baseball

One of the charms of baseball has been its historic dimension. Fans debate how players of one era would have performed in other years. Some like H.G. Salsinger believed that Ty Cobb was the greatest player ever and that the dead-ball era demanded strategy that the home run obliterated. Others pointed to the Ruthian years as baseball's heyday, or to 1941 when Joe DiMaggio hit safely in 56 consecutive games and Ted Williams was the last player to hit .400, or to the 1950s, the era of Mickey (Mantle), Willie (Mays), and the Duke (Snider). A possibly apocryphal story about Cobb, who denigrated the modern game and contemporary players,[1] is illustrative. Asked shortly before his death what he would hit against contemporary pitchers, he responded, '.270.' 'Only that?' 'You have to remember that I'm over 70 years old.' If audience, wealth, and working conditions are the test, there can be no doubt. The true golden age of baseball in America was between the 1981 and the 1994 strikes. In Detroit, it was the decade of the 1980s.

Baseball, like all sports, captured wider interest during the prosperity of the 1980s – perhaps because of a wish to return to happier times after the Vietnam War, Watergate, and stagflation. The success came despite predictions of gloom and doom after the 1972 and 1981 strikes and despite owners' complaints of impending poverty and a bleak future for baseball.[2] Baseball teams have a strong incentive not to appear too profitable because they engage in collective bargaining and receive indirect subsidies in the form of low stadium rents and favorable tax treatments. In 1985 the owners claimed that most teams were in the red to the tune of $2 million per team. After they were forced to open their books, however, an economist at the Brookings Institute, Roger Noll, concluded that baseball was quite profitable.[3] It should have been. More people attended games and more watched them on television than ever before. Drum-beating enthusiasts cheering on the home team raised average club attendance in the minors to record heights (table 2). Network television gave baseball teams more money than they had ever dreamed about. Baseball was rich, successful, and arrogant. So was the Detroit Baseball Club.

Detroit fielded its most successful teams in history during that decade, winning one world championship, one divisional pennant, and staying close enough in other years to entice fans. Memories of the riot of 1967 and of the grisly homicides that etched Detroit on the map as Murder City faded as fans flocked to the stadium. Local television of Tiger games received the highest ratings in the country, and 'Detroit Tiger Baseball' enriched local television channels. The club made more money than it ever had.

The Reagan/Bush era was good to baseball throughout the nation. Total attendance for the 1980s was 460 million against 330 million during the 1970s. Attendance before the 1994 strike projected to 600 million for the 1990s. Per-game attendance was one-third higher in the 1980s than it had been in the 1970s and increased by another third in the early 1990s to 28,302 fans – more than double what attendance had been during the 1950s and 1960s. The average major-league franchise drew 2.5 million fans in 1993 (table 11). Baseball's revenues doubled every five years after 1977, when they were about $235 million. They exceeded $1 billion for the first time in 1988, topped $1.5 billion in 1991, and were approaching $2 billion annually before the 1994 strike. Per-team revenues increased more than tenfold in two decades, at an annual rate of 11.7 per cent, while costs rose at an annual rate of 9.5 per cent.[4] *Financial World* estimated baseball's total operating profit at over $100 million annually from 1987 to 1993.[5] The average baseball franchise was appraised at $120 million in 1991 (an annual increase of 18 per cent since 1976). The New York Yankees were worth the most, $185 million, Pittsburgh the least, $70 million, in 1994.[6]

Free agency permitted players to take an increasing proportion of these enormous new riches. From a low of 17.6 per cent of team revenues in 1974, salaries and bonuses reached 41 per cent in 1983, fell back temporarily during the owners' 'collusion' in the late 1980s, and were about 48 per cent in 1993 (table 3). Salaries tripled in the early 1980s and then doubled from 1989 to 1992 (table 16). The average player became a millionaire in 1992, receiving payments like those commanded by movie and rock stars.

Television was the genie that permitted these new riches. Total rights increased geometrically from $80 million in 1980, to $278 million in 1985, to $350 million in 1987, to $707 million in 1990 (table 4). The estimated share of broadcast revenues within baseball's total revenue rose from 28 per cent in 1970 to 50 per cent in 1990. That was less than the 60 per cent share for football but twice that for basketball and hockey. More than 2500 games were being shown nationally by 1987 – about half of them on cable or superstations, with more than half of American homes linked to cable.[7] The biggest broadcast contract in history, and one probably not to be matched soon, came in 1990 when CBS paid more than $1 billion and ESPN $400 million over four years for national rights to baseball; CBS radio added another $50 million.

To put these astronomical figures in some perspective and to understand their impact on the financial structure of the game: revenues from television in 1985 exceeded baseball's total revenues in 1977. The 1990 contracts assured baseball twice as much money as it had at the beginning of the 1980s, even if every team had opened its gates and let every fan in free during the 1990 season. Per-team broadcast revenues in 1990 were nine times what they had been in 1980, fifteen times what they had been in the year before free agency, twenty times what they were in 1970.

After losing scads of money,[8] television moguls regretted the 1990 contracts too late. They should have been warned by the $50–$75 million bath that ABC had taken on the 1984 Olympics. But local television stations were making money on baseball, ratings were 'better than ever with good demographics' throughout the 1980s, and the seventh game of the 1986 World Series had attracted a record 34 million viewers and a 55 per cent audience share. To reach that audience for thirty seconds advertisers paid $275,000.[9] CBS needed a showcase and sports were big in America. ESPN became the largest cable TV network in 1983 with 28 million subscribers. An all-sports radio station was inaugurated in Denver in 1986, WFAN in New York was a huge success by

1990, and by 1993 one hundred such stations and ESPN radio were drawing large audiences.[10] Broadcasting had extended the audience for sport and then had to pay enormous sums to reach it. Bowie Kuhn attributed the 'tremendous leap forward of the popularity of baseball' in 1983 to 'the leadership of John Fetzer,' especially his vision of showcasing baseball's spectaculars of the All-Star Game and the World Series on prime-time television.[11]

Fetzer, who was born in Decatur, Indiana, on 25 March 1901, was an old man and frail when the 1980s began. Without heirs save for a nephew, he decided in 1983 to dismantle his financial empire and establish a foundation. Carl Lee, his confidant, had talked with him for some years about how to sell off holdings. They decided that baseball would be the first. Two native Detroiters, Tom Monaghan and Mike Ilitch, both of whom had made fortunes selling pizza, wanted to buy the team they had once wanted to play for. Campbell, who had 'considerable input in the sale,' had misgivings about Ilitch and steered Fetzer to Monaghan. The sale price of $54 million before the 1984 season began represented a tenfold increase in the price of the franchise since 1956. It was considerably more than the average price for other franchises that changed hands around the same time, for Detroit was a very healthy franchise. Campbell had suggested that a reasonable price would be $46–7 million, but Campbell was a parsimonious man; Fetzer expected at least $50 million.[12] Monaghan may have paid more than a prudent investor would have because being a part – much less owner – of the Tigers had been a 'boyhood dream.' After obtaining the Detroit franchise, he confessed: 'There is nothing more that I want now.'[13] Ownership of the Tigers brought prestige as well as potential profits, as it had to Walter O. Briggs. Fetzer, in turn, sold to Monaghan because he believed that Monaghan had the right philosophy: 'Monaghan will serve the best interests of the city of Detroit and the fans of the Tigers.'[14]

Detroit newspapers originally reported that Monaghan had paid $40 million cash and financed $13 million of the sale. When they later reported that it was 90 per cent financed, nobody paid much attention.[15] Doc Fenkell insisted that Monaghan had borrowed the $40 million from the National Bank of Detroit. 'He put zero money in.' Leverage was the watchword of the 1980s. Many conglomerates paid a later price for over-extension – the most famous being those of Donald Trump. Troubles would arise later because of Monaghan's other financial ventures, but the ball club maintained autonomy at first. As president of the club, Campbell remained in charge. 'I'll run it by Tom but the final decision will be mine.' Haase remembers that the baseball club's executives met weekly. Sometimes Campbell had one vote and sometimes he had one more than the total of the other executives assembled. The club's management met with Domino's representatives only once annually.[16]

Because the business of baseball has received so much recent attention, because of pleas of poverty from Detroit's management during the stadium controversy, and because of the unique financial records available, we need to consider the financial health or illness of the Detroit Baseball Club during Monaghan's stewardship in some detail (tables 20, 21). Expenses rose but revenues increased more. The result was that the Detroit Baseball Club made a profit every year that Monaghan owned it. Campbell made sure that it did.

The club had a total revenue of $13.5 million in 1980. Record attendance and post-season play in 1984 produced revenue of $31.7 million, an amount not to be matched until 1987. By 1991 the club was raking in $48 million and was projected to take in $55 million had there been no strike in 1994. Revenues increased at an annual rate of $2.3 million during the 1980s and by $4.5 million in the first four years of the 1990s. Still, Detroit's revenues were only about average for baseball during the 1980s. Detroit had become a middle-market franchise, after having been among the richest during the Briggs era. Although revenues increased more rapidly in the 1990s than in the 1980s, they did not keep up with those of baseball as a whole. By Monaghan's last year Detroit had $10 million less to spend than did the average franchise. There were legitimate concerns about Detroit's ability to compete in the future. There was no problem with the bottom line, however. The Detroit Baseball Club showed a profit every year for sixty straight years before the strike year of 1994.

In 1980 the Tigers made a profit of $2 million. The World Series year of 1984 brought profits of $7.8 million, making Detroit the second most profitable franchise in the majors.[17] Campbell's records show a net income of $2.2 million in 1985, but the *Free Press*, which obtained records filed with the state, reported profits of $4 million in both 1985 and 1986.[18] That difference may result from the 'net income' versus 'cash flow' methods of accounting. The key difference as it relates to the Detroit club's records is the exclusion of depreciation and of amortized tax credits from net income.[19] For the years for which we have club records (1987–91), depreciation and amortization claims amounted to $7.5 million; Campbell's records put the difference at $0.5 million in 1982. If we use the more conservative net-income method of accounting, the club's own statement of finances, prepared for club buyers in 1992 and certified by Arthur Andersen & Co. of Ann Arbor, reveals that the Tigers made $7 million 1987–8, broke even 1989–90 because they allotted $10.7 million in those years as provision for grievance damages from collusion, and made $5.4 million in 1991. *Financial World* reported a net operating income of $3.2 million in 1992. During Monaghan's tenure the Detroit Baseball Club showed a profit of more than $30 million even after paying off collusion damages of $10.8 million. Cash-flow accounting would make the profit about $10 million higher at $40 million in nine years. Stadium renovation funds also were paid off ahead of schedule. Domino's received benefits from its association with the Tigers, and the club eventually sold for a $30 million profit. Net-income figures fit with the $22 million that Campbell and Schembechler say that they had saved to put towards a new stadium before 1991, when money began to be funnelled to Monaghan Enterprises (chapter 9). According to Noll's analysis, the club remained profitable in 1992 and 1993, even excluding the $3 million received from the Colorado and Florida franchise entry fees; Noll expected the team's first real losses to occur in 1994, even before the strike made matters worse.[20] Profits continued although expenses had mushroomed – from $2.9 million in 1962 when Campbell became general manager to $29 million in 1982 and to almost $48 million in 1991, Monaghan's last year as owner.[21]

The biggest single item in the club's expenses was players' salaries. At $3.7 million they constituted one-third of the budget in 1980, rising to one-half ($12 million) in the pennant year of 1984 and 55 to 60 per cent in 1991–2. Although the team compiled winning records after 1978, its payroll was near the bottom of the league until 1984 (table 19). The team was young and major-league salaries depended on years of service more than performance in a single year. During the 1980s players with ten or more years of service made about six times as much as players with a single year; the difference would rise to twelve to one in 1994.[22] Moreover, Campbell's reputation as a tough negotiator was a justified one. The payroll increased by only 10 per cent after the 1984 championship. It was among the highest in the league in 1987–8, when salaries in the league as a whole were artificially held down by collusion and many Tigers had long-term contracts. Despite rising one-third from 1989 to 1991 to half of total revenues, the payroll remained below the league average and below Campbell's projections until new owner Mike Ilitch attempted to buy a pennant. During the 1980s, Detroit's payroll (from an admittedly low base) rose twice as fast as salaries in the league as a whole – at about $1.5 million annually. It doubled from 1989 to 1994, increasing by a total of $20 million in five years and swallowing up all the riches from the 1990 national television contract.

The second largest item was 'stadium payroll and upkeep' ($3 million in 1980, an average of $4.4 million 1987–90). Because of later claims that the stadium was 'falling down' (chapter 10), let us be clear here that the city was responsible for and paid major maintenance costs. The Tigers' contribution was primarily for the salaries of employees at the stadium. The team spent very little on regular maintenance; paint jobs were neglected. There was no attempt to make the stadium a showcase, as it had been during the Briggs reign, because Tiger management had determined to get a new stadium. The budget for the ballpark decreased from 28 per cent of total expenses in 1980 to 10 per cent in 1990. Neglect allowed claims of an old, decaying stadium to become a self-serving prophecy.

Administrative costs tripled during the decade but were always below the league average.[23] Campbell thought that working for the Tigers was a privilege and preserved a tight-knit organization of loyalists. 'If you want to leave, there are no fences around here.'[24] Despite press criticisms of this 'tight-fisted autocrat,' most former employees judge benefits and pay to have been 'not bad.'[25] Long hours – a day in the office followed by attendance at night and weekend games – were the rule. Childless and divorced, Campbell lived in an apartment on the sixteenth floor at 1300 Lafayette, about two miles from the stadium. Stories about the light in his office at the stadium burning at midnight typified his total dedication to Tiger baseball.

Two areas where the club's parsimony had negative consequences

were player development and public relations. In the present era of baseball a club can undertake to improve its team either by signing free
agents or by developing a strong farm system. In big-market cities like
New York where revenue far exceeds any reasonable costs, teams can
gamble on free agents, needing perhaps only half to produce. For a mid-
dle-income team, which Detroit was during the 1980s, a less expensive
course is to develop its own players. That is how Detroit built its world
championship teams of 1968 and 1984, each of which won a second
divisional championship. Detroit averaged only about $1 million on
player development in the first half of the decade; it became each year a
decreasing proportion of expenses. With the team's payroll rising from
long-term contracts, Campbell and Fenkell deliberately limited other
administrative expenses. Careful monitoring of the total payroll was 'the
key to profitability.'[26]

Budgets for 1987 to 1991 do not distinguish between player procurement (primarily the purchase of contracts) and player development, but,
historically, the club had spent nearly as much on procurement as on
development. These expenses together totalled $3.4 million in 1987, ris-
ing to almost $5 million in 1991. Of those, let us estimate $2 million to
$3 million for development – scouting and minor-league salaries – for
the years 1987–91. The range of expenditures among major-league
teams for development was from $5 million to $14 million in 1993.[27]
The Tigers apparently ranked at or near the bottom in spending for the
future. Good judgment as well as money is necessary to a successful farm
system. The Tigers lacked both. Their collective draft choices of the
1980s rated dead last in later performance among all teams.[28]

The other area that the club neglected was public relations (less than 3
per cent of expenses through 1985, after which it becomes obscured
within 'general administrative expenses'). From the time of Briggs, the
club had assumed that putting a winning team on the field was enough
to draw fans. Ardent fans go to see bad teams, and pennant winners
attract some who want to be associated with winners. Most potential
fans fall somewhere in-between. Detroit lagged in special events that
might have attracted to the ballpark some of the millions who watched
'Tiger Baseball' on television. The club report of 1992 shows that promotions raised attendance by 25 to 50 per cent (appendix 6). Better public relations might have prevented some of the public-relations gaffes

made during the stadium controversy as well. In the euphoria of winning teams and fan adulation, management fell behind the times.

The money to pay rapidly increasing expenses came from two principal sources. Attendance swelled and television revenues poured in. Attendance averaged 1.9 million fans for the decade. It exceeded two million in 1984, 1985, 1987, and 1988, after reaching that figure only once before, in 1968. Excluding the shortened strike year of 1981, attendance averaged more than two million from 1980 to 1988. It was above the league average in eight years. As in other decades, performance on the field, rather than economic fluctuations within the city, determined attendance patterns.[29]

Detroit lost 800,000 people or 44 per cent of its population between 1950 and 1990. The Detroit Baseball Club prospered because most of its fans came from the affluent environs.[30] The Tri-County area, exclusive of Detroit, increased its population by 1.7 million between 1950 and 1990 (table 10). It had two and a half times as many people as the city proper did in 1984, after having surpassed Detroit's population only in the late 1950s. The Detroit Metropolitan Area was still the sixth largest Standard Metropolitan Statistical Area (SMSA) and the second largest single-team SMSA in the United States in 1990. The metropolitan area boasted a median household income of $36,099, 18 per cent greater than the national average in 1991.[31] The area around the stadium was safe. So long as suburbanites identified with the city and would venture downtown for baseball, if not for shopping, the club had a sufficient population base. Since the days of Cobb sports had been an important part of a city that was like a small town in many of its tastes. Both Detroit newspapers expanded sports coverage in 1985 and 1986, which was deemed crucial in deciding readership wars.[32] Sports personalities dominated Detroit as movie stars did Los Angeles. The Lions, Pistons, and Red Wings all had mediocre teams or worse for two decades until the Pistons reached the NBA finals in 1988. Baseball was not the only game but it was *the* game in town. 'This is simply a baseball town. Always has been, and it always will be.'[33] The Tigers provided pride when the city had little else to feel proud about. Average ticket prices rose about 40 per cent during the decade, but they were still less than half what tickets for the Lions cost, and, adjusted for inflation, less in 1990 than they had been in 1970. With general admission at $6.50 and reserved seats at $8.00 in

1989, the average fan could afford to take his family to a game. The bleachers allowed an inexpensive outing for young people.

Attendance accounted for 55 per cent of club revenues in 1980. In 1984, for the first time, it accounted for less than half (47 per cent), but if concession revenues are added to attendance revenues, patrons at the ballpark still supplied the club with more than 60 per cent of its revenues. Broadcast revenue surpassed total income from the ballpark for the first time in 1989, exceeding gate receipts the year before.

The greatest source of *expanded* revenues was television. These came from both local and national contracts. Detroit's income from its contract with WDIV-TV quintupled during the 1980s (table 12). In addition, the Tigers received $750,000 in rights from WJR in 1984; that became $1.5 million in the late 1980s and $3 million in a new five-year contract in 1990. The club also received fees from PASS, the local sports cable channel which succeeded Pro-Am and debuted on 17 April 1984. These reached $3.1 million in 1991, although they were probably less than they should have been when PASS became a part of Monaghan's empire in 1987. It was not uncommon for television stations to get bargain rates from baseball clubs when the ownership was the same – as with Turner Broadcasting and the Atlanta Braves.[34] Detroit also shared in national television revenue, which provided about two-thirds of its total broadcast revenue during the 1980s (tables 12, 21, and appendix 6). Its total revenue from television and radio went from $14.4 million in 1987 to $24.9 million in 1991. Its income from television in 1987 exceeded the club's total expenses in 1982. Still, that was about $12 million less than the New York teams received from local contracts.

Tiger baseball went into the homes of millions of metropolitan Detroiters who never ventured to the downtown ballpark. Metropolitan Detroit was the seventh-largest television and sixth-largest radio market in the nation, with 1.7 million homes and 4.5 million people.[35] Tiger baseball had the highest local ratings of any baseball team from 1982 to 1987 (table 22). Its 'share of audience' was more than 40 per cent of television sets turned on. On one May Wednesday night in 1984, the Tigers went head to head with a Pistons NBA playoff game and *Dynasty*. The Tigers still grabbed a 42 per cent share of the metropolitan Detroit audience. The next night, with less competition, baseball captured a 52 per cent share.[36] PASS increased its subscribers from 75,000 to 600,000 in five years and to 750,000 in 1991, the fourth-largest cable baseball audience among AL cities.[37]

'Tiger Baseball' not only had a large audience; it had good demographics. Competing against summer reruns, it was the main vehicle for reaching women and 'young male demos [audience] that are so difficult to reach in Spring and Summer months.' Ranked high among young males, among women, and in households with income over $35,000 a year, Tiger Baseball and television linked the suburbs to Detroit and probably fostered a greater sense of community between them than did anything else:

Is it 1987 already? Or is it 1937? Because it looks and feels the same at Michigan and Trumbull ... The Tigers have played here all our lives, and nothing has changed ... Tiger Baseball is a communal experience. It is the common bond that connects us all, men and women, rich and poor, black and white, from downtown to Grosse Pointe. It is communal through time as well, uniting generations of Detroiters. Baseball is the #1 sport in a sports-crazy town. Sport is a common bond. Our teams foster a sense of unity in a population that is diverse ... Sports help to define the rhythm of our lives, giving them order.[38]

Baseball was important to the television station as well. WDIV went from third to first among Detroit television stations. Their executives attribute that success to 'Tiger Baseball.' By interweaving other programs with baseball and by running promotions for other shows during games, they forged an identity of the station with baseball. Al Ackerman, sports anchor of WDIV, had praised Tiger wins with 'Bless you, boys.' WDIV copyrighted the slogan, which became a password in Detroit in 1984. Even Ronald Reagan was pictured holding up a t-shirt with 'Bless you, boys' on it. Sponsors usually bought forty-five games at $100,000 to $150,000 per spot, although WDIV reserved some spots in September in case the team was in the thick of the race and the station could charge more. In 1988 there were approximately four thousand 30-second spots – twice the number for the Pistons and the Wings. The spots brought more income than did those during any basketball game, even when the Pistons were in the NBA finals. The range of advertisers illustrate the wide reach of baseball, which no longer had to rely primarily on beer companies as they had during the 1950s (* = 3 or more spots): Farmer Jack,

UAW, Miller,* Chevrolet,* Hygrade, McDonalds,* General Motors, Highland Appliance, J.C. Penney,* Helme Tobacco, Wang Computers, Elias Bros., Art Van, KFC, K-Mart, Coke, Domino's, Wheaties, Goodyear, Detroit Edison, Metro Chevrolet dealer, Standard Federal.

WJR sold radio spots at $600 per minute, which would have produced $2 million more in income than the rights they paid if all were sold. WJR's overall audiences were at their peak in 1984–5 as listeners stayed tuned to the station before and after baseball games. Baseball's television audience in Detroit diminished only in the 1990s. The Tigers were suffering on the field at the very time that the Pistons and Red Wings were enjoying success, and the proliferation of sports on cable television glutted all but the most ardent fans. Compared to other cities, baseball nevertheless continued to fare well on Detroit television. In 1989 Detroit audiences were behind only those in Cincinnati and Pittsburgh. Tiger baseball had slipped to a 13 per cent rating and a 25 per cent audience share in 1991, but it still ranked fifth among prime-time summer shows. *Cheers* had the highest rating at 15 per cent. Women composed 43 per cent of Detroit's baseball audiences in 1991, but they were only 36 per cent of those who watched basketball, 27 per cent of those who watched football, and 23 per cent of those who watched hockey.

WORLD CHAMPIONS AGAIN

Detroit had record attendance and television ratings and profits during the 1980s for the simple reason that it had a record eleven straight winning seasons, 1978–88. They were the only team in baseball without a losing season during those years. They tied the Yankees for the most wins (780) between 1980 and 1988 and had the most wins (696) 1981–8. Prorating victories during the strike season to a full season, the Tigers averaged 90 wins a year 1980 to 1988. They won one world championship, one divisional championship, and missed winning the second half of the 1981 strike-shortened split season on the final weekend.

Detroit went to Milwaukee on the final weekend needing to win two out of three to win the second half. Unfortunately, Milwaukee won the first two games, and the Tigers (29-23) finished 1½ games behind Milwaukee. Gibson, whom Anderson hailed as 'the next Mantle,' carried the team in the second half, hitting .375 after .234 in the first half; he finished the season with a .328 average. He was a rough-and-tumble sort, more like Pete Rose than like Mantle. He was also a controversial figure in his early years, criticized for not signing autographs and for his vulgarity. He offended Tom Monaghan by saying 'fuck' in front of children. Paul Carey observed that he 'stirred people to do better but he could be a real bastard.' When he returned to the Tigers in 1993, Anderson remarked: 'I never knew anybody who wanted to win so much.'[39] Tiger hitting was generally unimpressive in 1981 as they finished ninth in runs scored, but the pitching improved considerably with an ERA of 3.53, from 4.25 in 1980. Morris, Petry, Wilcox, and Rozema, with Lopez in relief, became the foundation of the staff of the 1980s.

The Tigers led the league in ERA in 1982 but finished fourth. Their pitching could have been even better had it had not been for Lopez's sore shoulder and Dave Rozema's injury during a brawl on 14 May with Minnesota that finished his season; he had injured himself earlier in a juvenile shoving match.[40] The Tigers were 35-19 in June but then proceeded to lose 15 of 17 games and 22 of 29 before the All-Star Game. Relief pitching and clutch hitting were problems. They lost twenty-seven games from the seventh inning on, including three straight on last-inning home runs, 8–10 July.

The Tigers finished second in 1983 and won 92 games – the most victories since their 1968 world championship team. They outscored their opponents by 110 runs (789–679). Whitaker (.320), Trammell (.319), Enos Cabell (.311), and Herndon (.302) topped .300. Parrish hit 27 home runs, Lemon 24, and Herndon 20. Parrish knocked in 114 runs, Morris won 20 games for the first time (20-13, 3.34), and Petry just missed (19-11, 3.92). The Tigers had improved but were not favored to win the pennant in 1984; *The Sporting News* picked them fourth, *Baseball Digest* uniquely anticipated a pennant. John Fetzer apparently did not see a pennant on the horizon either, for he sold the club to Tom Monaghan after the 1983 season.

The team gave the owner two big presents in his first year. One was the prestige of a world championship. The other was a home record and league-leading turnstile count of 2.7 million. Unlike the 1968 champions, who were famous for their last-minute comebacks, this team won early. They won a team-record 104 games, although their winning percentage of .642 was second to the 1934 champions (.656). They raced to a 35-5 record start by 24 May, swept Kansas City (3–0) in the playoffs and defeated San Diego (4–1) in the World Series. The Tigers were the first team to be in first place from wire to wire since the great 1927 New York Yankees. Morris pitched a no-hitter against Chicago on the first Saturday of the season on national television – the first no-hitter by a Tiger pitcher since Bunning's in 1958. Morris won 19, Petry 18, Wilcox 17. The most remarkable performance was that of Willie Hernandez, acquired with Dave Bergman for John Wockenfuss and Glenn Wilson before the season. He appeared in 80 games, finishing 68, winning nine, and was 32 for 33 in save opportunities. Bergman hit .273 in a part-time role and hit two game-winning home runs against Toronto. Detroit entered the free-agent market to sign Darrell Evans, who hit a home run in his first at-bat at Tiger Stadium.[41] The Tigers finished first in runs scored with 829, first in home runs with 187, first in ERA with 3.49, and were stingiest in runs allowed (643).

Despite the great start, there were some scary times. After their 35-5 start the Tigers split their next 22 games, allowing Toronto to close to within seven games by the All-Star Game. They faced a treacherous stretch in August too. Within twelve days, they played five doubleheaders. Kansas City swept the first one, in Detroit on 5 August, culminating a four-game sweep. Detroit journeyed to Boston's Fenway Park for consecutive doubleheaders the next two days. After losing two of the first three games, they fell behind 4–0 in the final game before rallying to win, 7–5, on a two-run home run by Parrish in the eleventh inning; Lopez won his ninth game in relief without a loss. They lost six of nine again in early September and went to Toronto with a mere 5½ game lead. Though they trailed in each game, they swept the series as an atrocious Toronto bullpen failed to hold leads. The Tigers suffered slumps during the season but always seemed to win when they had to. Often it was one of the cast of extras who contributed the key hit. Bergman hit a three-run home run, after fouling off seven pitches from Toronto's Roy Lee Jackson in the tenth inning on 4 June on national television. On 7 September he hit another three-run, tenth-inning home run, this time off Ron Musselman, to defeat Toronto again.

To the consternation of some downtown businessmen who hoped that three playoff games in Detroit would boost business, the Tigers swept the playoffs against Kansas City, which had won the Western

Division with only 84 victories, fewer than fifth-place Baltimore in the East.[42] Continuing their regular-season modus of striking early, the Tigers jumped to a 2–0 lead in the first inning of the first game at Kansas City; Morris breezed to an 8–1 victory supported by fourteen hits and three home runs, one each by Herndon, Trammell, and Parrish. In the second game reserve outfielder John Grubb doubled home two runs in the top of the eleventh to give the Tigers a 5–3 victory. Wilcox pitched a three-hit, 1–0 shutout in the final game, with Lemon scoring the only run on a botched double play in the second.

The Series lacked the drama of 1968. Detroit scored a run before anyone was out in the first inning at San Diego on 9 October. The Padres answered with two runs in their first but did not score again. Herndon hit a two-run home run in the fifth to give Morris and the Tigers an opening 3–2 victory. The Tigers jumped to a 3–0 lead in the second game on five first-inning singles, driving out Ed Whitson, but Andy Hawkins and Craig Lefferts held the Tigers scoreless the rest of the way. Kurt Bevacqua, who averaged only two home runs over his eleven-year career, hit a three-run home run in the fifth as San Diego defeated Petry, 5–3.

On 12 October the Series returned to Detroit. The Tigers walked to victory in the third game, drawing a Series record eleven bases on balls. Marty Castillo, who hit a total of eight home runs in his major-league career, gave the Tigers a 2–0 lead with a home run in the second. Wilcox was the winner; Hernandez gained the save. Trammell, who was named MVP in the Series, hit two-run home runs for the Tigers in the first and third innings of the fourth game as Morris pitched a complete game for a 4–2 victory. The Tigers led 5–4 in the bottom of the eighth in the fifth game. Gibson, who hit .367 with nine RBIs in the post-season, then hit a three-run home run to put the game away. Mary Schroeder, a *Free Press* photographer, captured Gibson's fist salute as he rounded the base path. The now-famous photo appeared on the front page of the *Free Press* the next day. Lopez won the final game in relief before 51,901 fans. Only in the first game had a San Diego starter completed three innings.

The players were heroes. But so was the manager. Falls wrote: '84 belongs to Sparky Anderson; he is the unquestioned leader of the Tigers.' Anderson had been hurt by his dismissal after the Reds' championship teams: 'They questioned me after Cincinnati. I was called a "push button manager," but no one will question me again. I got fired for finishing second in Cincinnati.' An AP report on 15 October, however, resurrected the image of a push-button manager: 'There is no strategic magic in managing what many had called a mechanical team – wind them up and watch them win.'[43] His pitching coach Roger Craig, who received much of the credit for developing the Tigers' pitching staff, gave Anderson mixed praise: 'I've never seen anyone who gets so high at one moment and so low the next, but he has great rapport with his players and is an expert at motivation, he wants to be the best manager in history of baseball ... Sparky is an impulsive man, and, believe me, the coaching staff worked hard over the years to temper much of his impulsiveness.'[44] Most managers get more credit than they deserve when their teams win and more blame than they deserve when they lose. Everything broke right for the Tigers in 1984. Many players had career years. It was the last pennant the Tigers have won.

SHORT-LIVED EUPHORIA

As with the 1968 championship that followed a riot, the 1984 championship came at an opportune time. The percentage of Detroit's citizens living in poverty reached a new high of 42 per cent in 1984, up from 22 per cent in 1980, when it was twice the national average, and 15 per cent in 1970 (table 10). Hudson's, Stroh's, and Vernors had all recently closed, schools were more segregated than they had been in 1960 and one-quarter of high school graduates could not pass proficiency examinations. Detroit maintained the highest murder rate in the country, suffered a 'hunger emergency' in 1982 and had lost one-quarter of its population and one-third of its jobs since 1970. Half of the residents of the east side had vanished over thirty years – 'the most extreme depopulation of any urban area in America.'[45] About a hundred homes were being razed every week while only eighteen permits for single-family dwellings were issued within the city in the *decade*.[46] State and federal funds were drying up as Mayor Young's influence declined in Lansing after the (Governor William) Milliken years (1969–82) and in Washington under the Reagan administration.[47]

The championship temporarily buoyed the city. When the Tigers clinched the 1984 pennant, Joe Falls wrote that its victories 'extend over time ... [Its] celebration is a way for this city to let everyone know that Detroit is alive and well, vibrant as ever.' Pete Waldmeir hoped that the 1984 championship victory would bring the city together as the 1968 championship, following the 1967 riots, had. The *News* reprinted Jerry Green's article about 1968 from his book *Year of the Tiger*: 'Following the Tigers is part of the texture of life in this community. The great moments are woven into the fabric of Detroit.' The *Free Press* was proud that baseball had at least temporarily banished thoughts of crime, unemployment, recession, and soup kitchens: 'The boys on the baseball field, bless them, brought unbridled joy to school kids and to occupants of nursing homes, to white-collar workers and to people in food stamp lines, to cops and to crooks, to priests and sinners, to baseball fans and to human beings who wouldn't know Kirk Gibson from Kirk Douglas.'[48]

The *New York Times* and *Newsweek* linked Tiger fever with a resurrection of downtown, booming auto sales, and the success of ethnic festivals. Despite ambivalence about the racist past of the Detroit Baseball Club, the *Michigan Chronicle* heralded Tiger successes, linking them to Chrysler's comeback as signs of Detroit's resilience.[49]

Optimism did not last, however. Even the victory celebration turned sour. Although police had announced special preparations for crowd control when the pennant was clinched, they seemed unprepared after the World Series and lost control. Hooligans took over from the fans. The *New York Times* at first reported: 'The victory was a happy distraction ... in Detroit where unemployment was 14% and there were crime problems.' It mentioned only 'scattered vandalism.' As the hour got later, things got worse and so did press reports. The final *AP* report read: '34 arrests, one dead, dozens injured.' Few of those arrested had attended the game, but the pictures of burning police cars and taxis appeared in national newspapers and in magazines. A photograph of seventeen-year-old Kenneth (Bubba) Helms, an eighth-grade dropout from Lincoln Park, in front of a burning police car, became the image of Detroit's celebration.[50] The *Detroit News* correctly editorialized: 'The police were unprepared and the mayhem in Detroit could have been avoided'; the rampage was by 'marauders ... young goons playing chicken with each other.'[51] But the damage to Detroit's precarious image had been done.

Other victory celebrations got out of hand – after the University of Michigan's NCAA championship, after San Francisco's Superbowl victory when two died, after Montreal's Stanley Cup. There were two differences, however. First, violence elsewhere did not happen under the very eyes of the assembled national press. Watching a burning police car, a visiting writer advised Joe LaPointe: 'That is not good for Detroit's image.' Second, other cities did not have the same reputation for crime and violence. A nationwide public-opinion poll, conducted by WDIV and the *Free Press* that autumn, came on the heels of a month of unusually heavy national publicity about Detroit, including auto talks, the violent aftermath of the World Series, and eight hundred fires around the city on Devil's Night and Hallowe'en. It revealed that two-thirds of the one thousand adults surveyed rated Detroit worse than other large cities, giving it the worst image of seventeen major cities surveyed. The appraisal of 348 people who had lived in Michigan or visited Detroit was not better. Half cited economic problems in Detroit, while one-third listed crime and violence to explain their rating.[52]

Had the hooliganism after the 1984 championship been an isolated event, it might have been dismissed as just that. Unfortunately, problems in and around the stadium were of long standing (chapter 4). The 1980s began no better than the 1970s had ended. A few in the stadium (they were not necessarily fans) threw cherry bombs, nuts and bolts, even bullets, when the Yankees were in town in May 1980. Falls wrote: 'Our town suffered another black eye last night.'[53] The next month, rowdies pelted Gorman Thomas of the Milwaukee Brewers with bottles. Campbell closed the bleachers: 'I'm just god-damned fed up. It's dangerous. It gives the city a bad name.'[54]

Concession workers blamed the problem on alcohol sales, which produced the Tigers' biggest concession profit. When the club reopened the bleachers, it stopped beer sales after the sixth inning of a doubleheader's second game and when single games ended. It also reduced the size of a draft from 14 oz. to 9 oz., though it did not decrease the price accordingly. A year later the Tigers sought an ordinance against bringing bottles into the ballpark, but found there was no legal basis for that. Problems continued. Someone set a fire in the stadium an hour and a half after a win over Minnesota in August 1981. Two years later Anderson had to appeal for sanity over the public address system after the crowd threw beach balls on the field and the umpires threatened to forfeit the game.[55]

As part of the 'wave' in 1984, bleacherites had chanted: 'Less filling, tastes great,' in tune with a popular Miller commercial at the time. In May 1985 one part of the bleachers was chanting: 'Fuck you,' the other side: 'Eat shit.' Campbell again ordered the bleachers closed. Joe Falls summarized the problem:

In Detroit, again, we've got a problem in our ball park. The fans have acted so poorly in the bleachers at Tiger Stadium that Jim Campbell, president of the Tigers, had to close the bleachers in center field.

How many of you, when you're thinking about the 1984 World Series, remember that burning police car instead of Kirk Gibson's home run off Rich Gossage in the final game? Unfortunately, we've created the image of rowdiness in Detroit.

I know there are rowdies everywhere, but ours seem worse than most. They've become so obsessed with shouting profanities in the bleachers that Campbell had to put a lock on the section.

Campbell did this for one game in 1980. Then, there were so many fights that the bleachers became almost a battleground. He shut down the bleachers section following a night in which 17 people were arrested for getting out of line.[56]

The *Chicago Tribune* praised Tiger Stadium as a place to play baseball, but complained: 'Detroit fans have one of the worst reputations in either league.' The *New York Times* thought that the problem was 'drunken fans.'[57] The problem everywhere was drunken fans, but Detroit's image suffered again. Detroit newspapers soon ran features on racism in Detroit's metropolitan area and the contrasts between thriving suburban malls and a moribund downtown.[58]

A DIVISIONAL CHAMPIONSHIP

Hopes remained high for more pennants. Anderson had promised that the team would be even better in 1985.[59] It was not to be. The Tigers had good teams in 1985 and 1986 but not good enough. They won 84 games in 1985, twenty fewer than in 1984, and 87 in 1986, finishing third both years. They hit 202 home runs in 1985 and 198 in 1986. Evans hit forty home runs, leading both leagues in 1985, and was the oldest player to hit that many home runs. All four Tiger infielders, Evans, Trammell, Whitaker, and Darnell Coles hit at least twenty home runs in 1986 – the first time any infield had done that. Gibson added 28 and Parrish 22. Trammell and Whitaker scored 200 runs between them that year. Pitching, fielding, and the supporting cast fell off dramatically, however. By the end of the 1985 season, the team was playing sloppy baseball. Anderson complained: 'I've never seen worse baseball ... It was downright dangerous for us to get on base'; the players did not 'know what seventh-graders do.'[60]

The year 1987 began inauspiciously for the Tigers. They were 9-20 in Florida and began the season 11-19, falling eleven games behind by the end of May. A surge in late May and June put them back in the race. From 16 July until 26 September the Tigers and Blue Jays were never separated by more than 1½ games.

The season came down to a home-and-home weekend series from 25 September to 4 October in two countries between baseball's two winningest teams.[61] A single run decided all seven games. The Blue Jays won the first three (4–3, 3–2, 10–9), each time coming from behind and winning the last two games in their final at-bat. In the third inning of the first game, Bill 'Mad Dog' Madlock crashed into Tony Fernandez at second base, breaking Fernandez's elbow.[62] In the second game Tanana, who had been banished from the rotation after allowing 28 runs in his previous 27 innings, shut out the Blue Jays for seven innings. The Tiger bullpen, which had blown ten saves in its last twenty opportunities, could not hold the lead. Dickie Noles, obtained from the Cubs the previous week, gave up hits to Jessie Barfield and Rick Leach. Manny Lee tripled off Hernandez and after two intentional walks, Mike Henneman came in. Lloyd Moseby hit a perfect one-hop potential double-play ball to Whitaker. Trammell was covering second, but Whitaker chose to throw home and bounced the throw to the plate as Lee scored the winning run. The Tigers roared to a 9–4 lead in the third game but the bullpen again collapsed. Pinch hitter Juan Beniquez hit a bases-loaded triple off Noles over a leaping Trammell, and Toronto won 10–9. Its bullpen had won its eleventh game among Toronto's last nineteen. The Tigers salvaged the last game in Toronto 3–2 on a Gibson home run in the thirteenth inning. That seemed mainly a face-saving gesture because the Tigers still trailed by 2½ games.

The Blue Jays left the door open by losing three straight at home to Milwaukee. Although Detroit led the league with 225 home runs and 896 runs scored and Toronto hit 215 home runs and scored 845 runs, pitchers dominated the final series in Detroit (combined ERA of 1.51). The Blue Jays were without both Fernandez and catcher Ernie Whitt, who was injured in the Milwaukee series. The first game began as a slugfest. Lee hit a three-run home run for the Blue Jays; Scott Lusader and Trammell answered with Tiger home runs. Defense was the key to the game, however, as the Tigers scored two unearned runs and turned five double plays. Evans scored the winning run after he kicked the ball out of Rance Mulliniks's glove at third. Doyle Alexander won his ninth straight (4–3) after being obtained from Atlanta in mid-August for John Smoltz. Jim Clancy lost for the sixteenth time in twenty decisions to the Tigers.

The second game featured a remarkable pitchers' duel between Morris, who went nine innings, and Mike Flanagan, who pitched eleven. The Tigers won the game in the twelfth inning (3–2) when a hard shot by Trammell ticked off Lee's leg with the bases loaded. Roger Angell captured the game's atmosphere beautifully: 'That game felt like a leftover World Series classic from our childhood, fought out in the slanting autumn sunshine between two principals who ... seemed a little larger than life ... "That game on Saturday – " Jack Morris said later on ... "was the best I've seen in the last five years. I knew damn well Mike was never going to give in, but I knew I wasn't going to be the one to die out there either. If they hadn't pulled us out, we'd still be there, waiting for the other man to fall."'[63]

Incredibly, the Tigers were in first place – one week after they seemed buried. The Blue Jays needed to win Sunday to force a play-off. They did not. Herndon hit a home run that barely cleared the left-field screen in the second inning and Tanana's slow stuff frustrated the impatient, fastball-hitting Blue Jays. The Blue Jays were excoriated for 'choking.'[64] They had lost the 1985 AL play-off to Kansas City after leading 3–1 and would lose the 1991 play-off to Minnesota. They became free of the choke label only after winning the World Series in 1992 and again in 1993. MVP winner George Bell had only three hits in the final week. Trammell finished the season hitting .343 with 28 home runs and 105 RBIs. Both *Sports Illustrated* and the Detroit papers thought he won the

MVP award in the final week. Bell might have won it because some writers voted before the final weekend.

The Tigers journeyed to Minneapolis on 7 October to play a Minnesota team that had won only 85 games – thirteen fewer than the Tigers had – but had the best home record in the majors (56-25). Alexander held a 5–4 lead going into the bottom of the eighth of the first game, but he and three relievers could not hold it. Minnesota won 8–5 behind two home runs by Gary Gaetti. The Tigers gave Morris, who had been born in St Paul, Minnesota, a 2–0 lead in the second game, but Minnesota triumphed 6–3. Back in Detroit on 10 October, the Tigers lept to a 5–0 lead in the third but needed a two-run home run by Pat Sheridan in the eighth to come from behind 7–6. That was the Tigers' last gasp. They lost at home to Minnesota the next two days, 5–3 and 9–5.

The Tigers came close in 1988 although they won ten fewer games. They were in first place longer than any other team and held the lead for three months from late June until 5 September. Then the Tiger offense faltered. Tiger starters hit only .203 with seven home runs from the All-Star Game to Labor Day. Detroit lost the lead during a 4-19 collapse in late August and early September when Boston was playing only .500 ball. In a four-game sweep over Detroit, Milwaukee scored more runs (24) than Tigers had hits (18). At season's end, Detroit had scored only 703 runs against 896 in 1987 (there was a decline in league scoring generally from a team average 794 to 704). In 1989 the team completely collapsed, falling to last place, 14 games behind sixth-place Cleveland, 30 games behind division-winning Toronto. It won 29 fewer games (59) than in 1988 – the greatest fall-off in Tiger history. The time of troubles had begun.

9

A Franchise in Decline

Detroit has been a troubled franchise in the 1990s. An average home gate of more than two million from 1983 to 1989 became one and one-half million over the next six years, half a million below the American League average for those years. The team never won more than 85 games and finished a total of 79 games below .500 from 1989 to 1995. The climax of ineptitude occurred in the final three games of the 1995 season, when they did not score a run. The club lost money for the first time since the Depression. It had to borrow money from the league to meet its payroll in 1992. Banks forced its sale that August. Two different owners, Thomas Monaghan and Michael Ilitch, threatened to move the team to sunnier climes. The estimated value of the franchise declined by $16 million in the two years after Ilitch bought the team,[1] causing him to regret having bought it.[2] Suddenly, the 'best baseball town in America' was near the bottom of the league in attendance and earnings. The only ones who did not suffer were Tiger players, whose salaries tripled from 1989 to 1994; average major-league salaries increased by 235 per cent (tables 16, 19) during that period. Baseball as a whole enjoyed record annual attendance (70 million) and revenues (nearly $2 billion) until the 1994 strike. What went wrong in Detroit?

ISOLATION FROM THE COMMUNITY

The Detroit Baseball Club had long neglected Detroit's African American community that had come to dominate politics in Detroit.[3] Confident that winning teams were enough to draw crowds, it treated fans with disdain. An old management lost touch with fans and young ball-players. When it tried to revitalize by bringing in new people, office squabbles created indecisiveness and confusion. Financial problems that arose out of other parts of Monaghan's enterprises drained the club financially. When new owner Mike Ilitch infused new capital, an untrained management squandered it on free-agent flops. A series of public-relations disasters, culminating in the botched dismissal of popular announcer Ernie Harwell, irritated its most loyal followers. A younger, more critical media asked questions about the direction of the club that had not been raised before. A bellicose mayor alienated suburbanites and outstaters. A few highly publicized incidents in the downtown area magnified their fear of coming to the downtown stadium and psychologically separated them from the city. The club became separate from the city, and the wider metropolitan community divorced itself from the city.

The racist legacy of the Briggs years left Detroit's African American community suspicious of the club. Some African Americans attended games and rooted for local hero Willie Horton, but no other black star captured the public fancy until Cecil Fielder. Dr Edward Turner remembered being called 'nigger' while attending games both as a child and an adult. 'One can feel the racism. The history of the organization is there in the black community.' Tom Walker, sports writer for the *Michigan Chronicle* in the 1980s and now for the *Port Huron Times Herald*, observed: 'There was a long history of a color line and neglect, if not enmity, toward the black community that needed to be addressed.'[4]

The Tigers did little to gain support from the African American community, although Detroit had the highest percentage of African Americans in any city by 1980. They constituted almost 80 per cent of Detroit's citizens in 1990. Many African American Detroiters were too poor and too preoccupied with poverty to worry about attending ball games (about one in five received public assistance), but many more were not. More than 35,000 African American households had incomes between $30,000 and $75,000 in 1984. Metropolitan Detroit had the highest disparity between metro/city income in the nation, but African American Detroiters had the highest household income ($16,403) among African Americans in any major city.[5] They attended Piston

games when the Pistons played in downtown Cobo Arena; and basketball tickets cost more than baseball ones.

The absence of African American fans at baseball parks was not pecu-
liar to Detroit. The *New York Times Magazine* ran an article in 1987
entitled 'Where Are the Black Fans?' It estimated that 17 per cent of
fans at basketball games were black, at football games 7.5 per cent, and
at baseball games 6.8 per cent. It described an earlier 'black romance'
with baseball at the turn of the century and again with the appearance of
Jackie Robinson, but abandonment afterward. Brent Staples, author of
the article, concluded: 'The source of discord, I think, is the mythology
of American sport in general and of baseball in particular ... It carries
with it a racism that is at the very heart of baseball and may never be got-
ten at.'[6]

Three years earlier the *Detroit News* had addressed the issue of the lack
of black fans, perhaps prompted by an article by Walker in the *Michigan
Chronicle*. The *News* attributed their absence to the fact that the Tigers
were the last team to sign a black player, management's distance from the
community, prices, and blacks' preferences for basketball and football.
When asked about the paucity of black fans, Campbell said: 'I hadn't
noticed it ... We run a baseball club. Our seats are available to anybody
who wants to buy them. Besides, what's enough or not enough black fans
or any other kind of fan?' Later, he explained: 'We do for black fans
exactly what we do for whites.'[7] That answer did not encourage change.
'With a history of exclusion, one needs to make an effort to show one is
included. They [management] don't know how to communicate or what
to communicate. The idea that everybody is equal is insensitive to the history and issue.' Campbell's idea of recruitment was to ask Gates Brown to
try to sell season tickets during the off-season.[8]

Irwin Cohen recalled conversations about how to get black fans by a
management that 'generally had attitudes that typified their age.' Doc
Fenkell recalled little communication between the club and the black
community over three decades. 'The mentality of the management prevented cultivation of black fans.'[9] Charlie Vincent, who was honored on
Afro-American Night, charged that a Tiger executive had referred to
blacks as 'those people' long before Ross Perot said 'you people.' He
called for the Tigers to reach out to blacks, but warned 'there's not much
the Tigers can do about erasing lifelong prejudice.'[10]

African Americans who were Tiger fans could be ambivalent about the club. The *Michigan Chronicle*'s reportage during the 1984 championship drive indicates that ambivalence. The sports section ran headlines: 'Black Fans Struck with Tiger Fever, Too' and 'Blacks, Whites Put Aside Differences and Call Truce.' In the same issue, however, Danton Wilson announced that he would not 'pull for a team consciously disconnected from the city which houses it.' Earlier that summer, the *Chronicle* had criticized the club for ignoring the community and failing to 'reach out.' Disaffection increased when popular coach Gates Brown, the most visible black member of the organization, 'resigned' in November 1984 after having been offered a mere $2000 raise from his $38,000 salary. The *Chronicle* called it 'a slap in the face of Detroit's black community.'[11] Campbell said that Brown 'disappeared' for a month after the season, but management had tolerated peccadillos by others. Brown believes that he was eased out because 'Sparky Anderson wanted "yes-men" as coaches and I didn't kiss managers' asses. The Tigers got me out of prison but how long does a man have to pay his dues?'[12] Vada Pinson, a black who had played for Anderson in Cincinnati, replaced Brown. Like Brown, Pinson made appearances at inner-city sandlots, but he was a new face in the community. Lonnie Peek Jr, chairman of the Concerned Citizens Council, attributed Brown's dismissal to the racism of Tiger management.[13] Tiger management was insensitive, residing in a cocoon.

A few African American fans tried to establish a greater link between the club and community by organizing an Afro-American Night. Modelled after Lutheran Night or Shriner's Night or a host of others, it honored Ron Leflore in 1979. John Hearst, former Alpha Phi Alpha president, purchased $5000 worth of tickets, but the organizers did not sell enough tickets to satisfy Tiger management. Campbell snorted: 'It fell flat on its face.'[14] The club did not make any special accommodations, failing even to provide a microphone; nor did it offer any free tickets to children from the inner city. Lew Matlin and Dr Turner, who were contacts between the African American community and the club, accused each other of rudeness or worse.[15] Although the club hosted a Black Shriner's night a few years later, no Afro-American Night occurred again for a decade.

Dr Turner and Dr Charles Adams, pastor of Hartford Memorial Baptist Church, approached the Tigers in 1987 about renewing the Night.

The club ignored them for a year and a half. A year after the first letters, Jeff Odenwald apologized for the delay, blaming the illness of an employee for the lack of communication.[16] The following May, Vincent wrote an article, after talking to Dr Turner, entitled 'Many Blacks Color the Tigers as Racist.' Odenwald told Vincent that he was 'perplexed' by the lack of blacks in Tiger Stadium: 'There are not a lot of blacks coming to Tiger Stadium, but then there are not a lot of blacks going to ball-parks around the country.' Vincent reported: 'But Jeff Odenwald and Edward Turner have never spoken to each other. Both have telephones. I managed to reach both of them on the phone Monday. I went to Odenwald's office and spent 45 minutes with him. I met with Turner in my office for almost an hour.'[17]

That article prompted communication from the club to Dr Turner and an agreement to hold another special night (now African-American Night). The second annual event drew about 8000 African Americans, including 1000 children who received free tickets. Reverend James Holley commented that their attendance was a way of saying, when the club was threatening to move out of Detroit, 'We want you to stay in the city and the stadium.'[18] Under Ilitch, the Tigers declared a Negro League Tribute Night for 8 July 1995, three years after one in Chicago had attracted 50,000 fans for a commemoration of the 1941 Negro World Series. In March 1996 John McHale Jr expressed 'concern' about the lack of African American fans and promised 'efforts' to attract them.[19] The club's outreach occurred only after fans had begun to desert the ball-park, and the club needed community support for a new stadium.

Management often seemed bent on driving white fans away too. Drinking fountains did not work. After complaints, management allowed fans to get water at concession stands but charged for cups. After more complaints, they dropped that charge but never advertised 'free water.' 'Rude' was the most polite word that the press and fans used to describe stadium personnel. Ushers chased children from vacant seats in late innings but took 'tips' to seat adults there when season box-holders did not show. They sold prime tickets returned by players to 'friends' rather than to the general public. One wag observed: 'The ushers shook hands so much, you thought they were running for office.'[20] Matlin and Snyder, in charge of stadium operations, attribute the inability of Tiger management to deal with abuses to a strong employee union that challenged all disciplinary action, but management did little to make their customers want to come. Cohen, who had responsibility for group sales and tours, acknowledged that others in the front office 'did not want to be bothered with fans. We were selling baseball and boredom.'[21]

After the Divisional Championship of 1987, the Detroit Baseball Club decided it would not make the same mistake it had made in 1984 by letting victory celebrations get out of hand. They made a different mistake. They hired over zealous security people who quickly offended fans and whose actions did not improve Detroit's national image a whit. Newspaper photographs showed fans being frisked. Those who bought tickets for the bleachers during the play-offs were middle-class, middle-aged people, who raised a ruckus about their treatment. Snyder admitted that 'security used very bad judgment. They were underpaid, with a high turnover.' The Tigers 'corrected the problem,' but their aloofness remained even when the team was struggling.

Two publicly reported instances are illustrative of management's arrogance. Two season-ticket holders brought a guest with them. Bill Haase refused to exchange the season tickets for two elsewhere so the three could sit together – even though the crowd totalled only 18,000 and the Tigers were in last place! 'There are certain rules you have to live by,' explained Haase. Two years later a fan from Westland complained that his seats were obstructed (verified by sports writer John Lowe) and that there were no vendors. Haase said that there was a customer-relations office in the left-field seats but made no apologies. Paul Carey commented: 'What a great change now [1993] – smiling ushers helping people, handing baseballs to fans. Campbell forbade tossing baseballs into the stands for fear a scramble could cause a lawsuit.'[22]

The club report to prospective buyers was disingenuous in its glowing description of the club's involvement in community relations. It contributed to charities, but few outside the organization thought that the club contributed anything else to the community. They did nothing, were 'totally uninvolved,' or 'just plain absent.'[23]

The problem was not just management. It was the contemporary selfish athlete. Mobility and money meant there were fewer ties to the community. Since the 1960s, the club had maintained a 'Speaker's Bureau.' Athletes could make a few extra bucks speaking to social clubs, and charitable organizations could ask for someone to come gratis. Matlin, who ran the bureau, mentioned several Tigers who had made appearances: 'Timmerman, Cash, Brown, Horton, Kilkenny, Ruhle, Blesset, Stanley, Petry, Lolich, Rozema, Arroyo, Wilcox, Fielder. Lolich insisted on no publicity about his charity work.' Most had played in the 1960s and 1970s. Tiger alumnus Dave Tobik (1978–82) helped to feed 68,000 monthly in Project Hope, founded after the 1967 riot. By the late 1980s, Anderson and Fielder were the only visible contributors. 'Some players would not go out unless they were paid. Many would not go out at all.'[24]

THE PRESS

The Detroit media historically confined criticism to the team's performance on the field. A younger generation was beginning to ask questions about the club's relationship to the community, but the media were having internal problems. Walker was denied access to the Tiger press box on grounds that the *Michigan Chronicle* was only a weekly. It was not a matter of space because the refurbished press box was cavernous. The panjandrums had admitted Walker's predecessor Frank Sanders, whose reportage had been of the traditional variety – about players and the game on the field. Walker was concerned with wider issues. He had addressed an NAACP meeting about lack of Tiger outreach to the community and lack of African Americans in the front office. He had also written about the exclusion from the press box of reporters from the only African American Detroit newspaper.

Tom Henderson washed the media's dirty linen in public. His article from *Metropolitan Detroit* is worth quoting at some length because it reveals both the close ties between some of the media and Tiger management and a shared insensitivity to potential African American supporters of the team:

In Detroit sports circles, the BBWAA is literally the lock and key to covering the Detroit Tigers, and along with membership comes virtual country club treatment by the team. BBWAA reporters can talk to ball players on the field before the game, in the locker room after the game. There are ticket privileges for their families, and members can join Tiger officials and scouts for free full-course meals in the executive dining room. Most important, they are guaranteed entry to the Tiger Stadium press box – a two-level aerie above the diamond ...

Every other baseball team in the league issues its own season-long pass to local reporters, letting them into the press box and locker room whether or not they're BBWAA members. The Tigers alone leave those decisions up to the baseball writers. They have succeeded in making the Detroit chapter of the BBWAA probably the most powerful in the country ...

Of all the BBWAA's critics, Joe LaPointe has been the most vocal. [Ed] Browalski's membership policies, LaPointe charged, were arbitrary at best, keeping his old buddies on the roster even though they no longer covered baseball, while keeping out working reporters from weekly or monthly journals ...

The problem, they say, goes beyond the association's meetings, right to the door of the Detroit Tiger management. 'You're looking at a Tiger Stadium system-wide malaise,' LaPointe explains. 'It extends through the ushers, to the ticket sellers ... It's an attitudinal problem at Tiger Stadium. The attitude of the [Detroit BBWAA] and the public relations department is very much in tune with the traditional attitudes of the people who have run Tiger Stadium since nineteen-ought-one' ...

Walker had first approached the BBWAA chair personally to ask for membership. 'I talked to Browalski in the spring about getting proper press credentials,' he recalls. 'He said I had to work sixteen games during the season.' Walker then obligingly proceeded to work twenty-four games. 'We never went two issues without a Tiger story' ...

LaPointe's revelations were greeted by groans and exaggerated sighs from the BBWAA members in attendance. Their disgust was not with the editor of one ethnic weekly denying access to the editor of another. They were disgusted with LaPointe – even after Browalski lamely explained that the *Polish Daily News* had access because of a grandfather clause in the local bylaws ...

Later Joe Falls, the veteran sports reporter at *The Detroit News*, proposed a round of applause for Browalski.[25]

WJR personalities like Sonny Eliot regularly visited the press box as did Jim Hawkins, retired sports writer of the *Detroit News*, and friends of writers. The Lions and Pistons granted Walker access. A (white) Washington editor of National Public Radio, for whom Walker had done freelance writing, described the BBWAA's policy as 'patently absurd.' Within a month of Henderson's article, Walker was admitted to the press box, but only after intervention from the mayor's office.[26] Some Detroit writers remain critical of the BBWAA's conservatism:

McGraw: 'It was a middle-aged boys club with Ewald buddies of all. The base-ball group was the most absurd group I encountered. In annual meetings they would purge you (the word they used) like Stalinist Russia. I felt depressed that the meetings were so negative.'

LaPointe: 'The Detroit BBWAA acted as a third arm of baseball; it is an orga-nization that needs to be shook up. As soon as writers are in the organization, they do not speak out. There was a split among writers in Detroit, not between young and old, but between liberals and conservatives. Joe Falls was an impor-tant force in the BBWAA.'

Vincent: 'The BBWAA has been a little clique, a good-old-boy network that prevents a newer, younger perspective.'[27]

Relations between the media and management in Detroit could hardly be described as 'flammable' then as they would become nationally by the early 1990s.[28] A group within the media, however, was beginning to challenge cosy relations within the BBWAA and between it and the club. No longer could Tiger management depend on writers being on the same wavelength as Campbell.

Nationally, the media were asking questions about the lack of African Americans in management positions in baseball. Although their absence had struck acute observers two decades earlier,[29] it was Al Campanis's interview on Ted Koppel's *Nightline* in April 1987 that brought the mat-ter to the forefront. When Koppel asked this Dodger executive why there were no blacks in positions of authority, including no black manag-ers in the major leagues then, Campanis replied: 'I truly believe that they may not have some of the necessities to be a field manager or perhaps a general manager. I don't say all of them, but how many quarterbacks, how many pitchers do you have that are black?'[30] A survey later that month revealed that there were only 17 African Americans and 13 His-panics in baseball's 379 top jobs.[31] The only black managers had been Frank Robinson (Cleveland 1975–7, San Francisco 1981–4); Maury Wills (Seattle 1980–1); Larry Doby (Chicago White Sox, 1978 for 87 games), Bill Lucas had been general manager at Atlanta before his death in 1979. All twenty-seven Tiger leading executives were white. The *Michigan Chronicle* editorialized: 'Al Campanis virtually spit in the grave of Jackie Robinson when he talked of the inability of blacks to pay their dues ... Consider the Detroit experience. The Tigers have never even come close to considering a black manager, much less an executive in the office. Campanis is associated with the most liberal organization in baseball, can you imagine what some of the old line Tigers had to say when they let their hair down?'[32]

The local chapters of both the NAACP and Operation PUSH met with the Tigers. Reverend Holley, one of the negotiators for PUSH, recalls: 'Campbell made you feel good but we felt he wasn't going to do anything. We asked them why they didn't sponsor Little League baseball, advertise on black media, give blacks concessions for contracts. The city was not in the stadium.'[33] Campbell agreed in June 1987 that the Tigers would join an affirmative-action plan and hired the first African American in the front office – Michael Wilson as comptroller. Campbell wanted 'to be fair but not to be rushed' and wanted 'the right person' (a phrase strikingly familiar to the explanation for caution in signing black players three decades earlier). Later that year, Chuck Stone became the first black manager in the farm system. The Tigers again promised to hire more minorities and women in 1994.[34]

Minorities had increased their front-office positions in baseball to nearly 15 per cent by 1993, but they were concentrated among a few clubs. Retiring National League President Bill White lamented his 'inability to further minority hiring in baseball' and 'was angry and bitter at having to deal with racists and bigots in baseball.'[35] For those who wondered who might be included among the racists and bigots, Marg Schott, owner of the Cincinnati Reds, stepped forward. A few months after White's observations, other owners suspended her for racist comments. They suspended her less because of their new social consciousness than because the press brought her behavior to public attention. Schott had been making regular and blatant racist statements (including 'nigger') to owners and at community gatherings in Cincinnati for years.[36] A year later an executive with the New York Yankees resigned after referring to Bronx youth as 'monkeys.'[37]

The racist views expressed by Campanis and Schott were national embarrassments in which Detroit was only indirectly involved. Because of the ethnic make-up of Detroit, the issue was more sensitive there than in some other cities. Tiger management had always believed that it and baseball could operate in a vacuum, separate from social issues of the age. They were finding that this was no longer possible.

MANAGEMENT

Overt racism in baseball was rare by the 1980s, but it remained an old-boy network. Nowhere was this more true than in Detroit. Campbell, Alice Stone (long-time secretary of Campbell and vice-president/assistant to the president by 1991), Snyder (stadium operations), Fenkell (public relations and broadcasting), Hoot Evers (scouting and player development), and Harry Sisson (finance) were all products of the (Walter) Briggs era. Don Lund (farm director) and Alex Callam (finance) joined the club in the early 1960s. Everyone was in his or her sixties. Dan Ewald took charge of public relations in 1978 after having been a local sports writer. Only Haase, who joined the Tigers as business manager in 1975 and became vice-president, operations, in 1978, represented new blood. He was an ex-marine.

The organization was paternalistic and either close-knit or incestuous, depending on one's perspective.[38] It was not innovative. Campbell made no secret that he preferred baseball the way it was before the days of free agency and marketing. The main duty of the public-relations officer was to distribute press releases to the media. Players described management as distant and old-school.[39] LaPointe summed up the attitude of much of the Detroit press about management: 'Tiger management was insular – half-bright, never let fresh air in. Haase tried to act more conservative than the old ones, running things with military precision. Community relations begin with customer relations, and they were abysmal. The club was run like a navy ship. Campbell was stuck in the 1950s.'[40]

The Tigers had been slow to adapt to new marketing in the 1950s and the 1960s. So too were they in the 1980s. They were among the last to accept credit cards. While people stood in lines in the rain to buy tickets, meter maids ticketed their cars. Cohen became so disgusted with management's refusal to make any innovations in marketing that he stopped wearing his World Series ring in 1988. David Cope, director of marketing and advertising for Baltimore, summarized the approach of the old guard: 'Ilitch's people don't have to do too much to improve things. Formerly, they operated under the axiom, "Open the gates and they will come."' Haase excused the lack of promotions: 'Detroiters don't like gimmicks. Fans did not even stay for free gifts on Fan Appreciation Day, the last day of the year.'[41] Campbell, however, recognized that changes needed to be made: 'I was a one-man game too long. I saw the handwriting of people getting older. We were conservative. Some people might have been kept on too long. We were slow on public relations. I recognized the necessity of bringing in new people. By the late 1980s, we were going through a major transition.'[42] He was astute in recognizing that change was necessary, but unsure about how to change.

The club soon went through an upheaval unlike any since Fetzer had become sole owner. The first attempts to integrate new personnel were not successful. Lund hired Bill Lajoie as a scout. Lajoie worked his way up to chief scout and then general manager. He clashed with Anderson, Campbell, and Bo Schembechler, and even Tiger announcer Paul Carey. Lajoie refused to speak to Carey for many months when Carey, hearing a rumor about an upcoming trade, wished him good luck with Atlanta. Lajoie demanded: 'Where did you hear that?' Tiger announcers were not part of the inner circle and were expected to keep their place. Schembechler dismissed Lajoie soon after Schembechler became president.

Campbell hired Jeff Odenwald as vice-president of marketing, radio, TV and public relations in November 1987. Odenwald had worked for the Reds, the Mariners, and the Cubs, and won a peer award for best marketing efforts in 1984. He was universally disliked by other Tiger executives, who sarcastically tabbed him the 'wizard' and resented intrusions into their turf. Odenwald also did not know Detroit, whatever marketing talents he had. That would prove a disability in his decision about what to do with an aging Ernie Harwell. Joseph McDonald joined the club as vice-president in August 1986 to head Detroit's scouting and minor-league operations, replacing Hoot Evers, who had died in office after being ill and 'semi-retired for some time.' He too clashed with the established executives. Campbell bemoaned some of his appointments: 'They did not work out, but I don't want to bad-mouth anybody in particular.'[43] Campbell's health was deteriorating then; Rick Ferrell, Campbell's 'right-hand guy,' had retired. Lines of authority broke down.

Tiger minor-league operations and drafting were a disaster in the 1980s and the early 1990s. The only pitchers from Tiger farms who were regulars on any team in the majors in 1986 were Morris and Petry.[44] Henneman joined the Tigers in 1987, but they traded away young prospects who later blossomed – John Smoltz, Ken Hill, and John Hudek – for older players. The first farmhands to become regulars after Glenn Wilson and Howard Johnson in 1982 were Travis Fryman and, for a time, Milt Cuyler in 1991. The last first-round draft choice to have an impact was Gibson. Lund, Evers, Lajoie, McDonald, Joe Klein, and Anderson all had input at various times, sometimes simultaneously. Some of these people were not even speaking to each other except in formal meetings. Confusion, jealousies, and an inability to integrate new personnel were at the heart of the Tigers' failure to rebuild.

The one appointment that might have made a difference was that of former University of Michigan head football coach Bo Schembechler as the Tigers' twelfth president on 8 January 1990 after he had become a member of the board of directors on 22 January 1989. He had connections with both Monaghan and Campbell. He had known Campbell since college days. Monaghan had bought him a pizza franchise in Ann Arbor when he had been offered the coaching job at Texas A&M in 1982. Campbell recalled:

We knew I was going to retire, probably at age 70, although maybe I would continue in an advisory capacity. We considered appointing Roger Staubach, but that passed. Bo and Tom were friends. Bo wanted to leave football because his wife Millie wanted him to get a front office job after open-heart surgery. Monaghan was the one who suggested Bo, but I was enthusiastic. The deal was in the works in 1987. Monaghan would not put somebody in who was not compatible with me. I was a friend of Bo, even though we didn't see each other much. Most winning teams now are not run by baseball people. You mainly need someone who can handle finances and people. There was no one in the organization who I thought could really take over.

Schembechler confirms that Millie encouraged him to get a front-office job. Furthermore: 'I would not have considered going to the Tigers without Jim Campbell.' Schembechler brought in fresh ideas about recruitment and training of players.

I had to try to sell people on: (1) New ways of drafting and recruiting. The dismal farm system proved that. (2) Improving poor teaching on the farms where coaches were just ex-ballplayers. I insisted on three coaches (hitting, pitching, managing) on each team. (3) Upgrading of training facilities, especially weights. Every injury of a minor league player had to be on computer within 24 hours. Some injured players had not seen a doctor in the previous year. (4) Widened scouting. This was not a big money operation. I went to Venezuela to consider setting up a camp down there. You need scouts who know the Caribbean. (5) Concentrating on athletic ability. Our great athletes are football and basketball players, not baseball players. You need to look for athletes who just miss making it in their chosen sport. We emphasized speed. The old guard was still there so it was hard to change. Former ballplayers, largely uneducated, are often not good teachers. There were too many old timers as coaches, managers, or scouts, with no knowledge of modern methods of teaching or conditioning. They were kept in the system because they were good, loyal people. Drafting was not well studied. My problem as baseball executive was that I was interested in building the team. Piss on public relations. I know how to build a team.[45]

The Tigers had been living in another age with regards to recruitment and development of players. Schembechler never got a chance to try his ideas about player recruitment and training because he quickly became embroiled in controversies over Harwell's contract and the building of a new stadium. A year later, Monaghan dismissed him in conjunction with the sale of the club.

THE DISMISSAL AND RETURN OF ERNIE HARWELL

People identify teams with announcers, their primary contact with the team. The decision by Tiger management and WJR to bring to an end Ernie Harwell's tenure as Tiger radio announcer was not unreasonable, but they bungled it. It became one of the greatest public-relations gaffes in the history of sports. The Detroit media's handling of it deserves no prizes either.

Harwell was an institution in Detroit baseball. In *Voices of the Game*, Curt Smith described him as a 'lyricist, poet, and historian ... Listeners hear his disarming voice – and they are reminded in a twinkly way, I believe, somehow like personae from a Pepsi commercial, how constant baseball/America remain in a strange and turmoiled world.' Harwell had raised a generation of Tiger fans to Detroit baseball and received regular praise in the Detroit press.[46] Like Walter Cronkite, who was acclaimed the most trusted man in America, listeners believed him. He probably could have been elected to public office had he chosen to run. His Ford Frick National Press Award had hung in the Baseball Hall of Fame since 1981. A decade later, on 5 December 1991, he was named to the National Sportscasters Hall of Fame.

Born on 25 January 1918 in Washington, Georgia, he was seventy-two years old when his five-year contract with the Tigers expired in 1990. Most announcers, like baseball executives, worked from year to year without contract. Paul Carey had no contract with either the Tigers or WJR during his last sixteen years.[47] There had been no public discussion, however, of contracts or of when Harwell might retire. Thus, his announcement on 19 December 1990, in a press conference held at Tiger Stadium and carried live by WJR, that he had been 'fired,' effective the end of the 1991 season, came as an enormous shock. 'I'm just going to tell the truth. If it hurts feelings, well, that's what the truth does. I wanted to go farther. I wanted to work more years ... There is some hurt ... but I don't want to whine and I really don't feel bitter.'[48] Carey announced that he would retire following the 1991 season on the same day that Harwell held his press conference.

The outrage of the local press, the national press, and fans was immediate and vicious. Monaghan was called a 'dough-brain,' Schembechler 'the Grinch of Whoville,' and the Tigers' explanation that it was a 'business' matter likened to the description of business by Marlon Brando in *The Godfather*. Polls showed between 97 and 100 per cent of fans opposed to the decision. Bumper stickers and billboards appeared in support of Harwell. Fans chanted 'We want Ernie' at a Red Wings game. RPM Pizza, owner of Domino's franchises in Detroit, cancelled advertising with WJR. Mitch Albom, multi-year winner of the AP award for finest sports columnist in America, wrote: 'What the Tigers did ... was one of the most shameful acts I have ever witnessed from a sports franchise ... They took a man who was a national treasure and told him to start packing. They took a man who literally has taught baseball to hundreds of thousands of fans, summer after summer, they told him he was too old, his time is up.'[49] Tiger management offered little explanation.

Schembechler told the assembled press that Harwell was 'only an announcer.' Tiger executives later talked about declining skills, WJR executives about declining ratings.[50] A column by Joe Falls on 6 January attributed the firing to WJR station manager Jim Long, but the next day, Pete Waldmeir, countered: 'No radio executive on earth could fire a baseball team's broadcaster without the express advice and consent of the team,' which provided a $15-million advertising package for WJR.[51]

All was not what it seemed. Harwell had suggested, at the time of the signing of his previous five-year contract, that it would be his final one. Everyone has a right to change his mind, and Harwell's health was good. Nevertheless, WJR and the Tigers thought Harwell could be eased out by simply not renewing his contract. Long did not fire Harwell, but Long, Fenkell, and Odenwald had been discussing how to get rid of Harwell for at least a year. Campbell investigated how other clubs with long-standing announcers, like Bob Prince of Pittsburg, had handled 'retirement.'

Declining ratings or Harwell's skills were not the main issues. The principal dispute was with Harwell's insistence that he was strictly a play-by-play announcer and did not have to do gratis promotions for the Tigers or WJR. That combined with 'private things' – which might be translated as personal animosity towards him by the decison makers. Harwell acknowledges that he did not feel obliged to do more than report games. WJR and Tiger executives were of one mind in condemning the 'private' as opposed to the 'public' Harwell.[52]

The decision not to renew Harwell's contract had been made before the 1990 season had ended, but he did not know that. Soon after the season ended, he took his lawyer-agent Gary Spicer with him to negotiations. Spicer infuriated Schembechler by demanding a much higher salary and another five-year contract when others were pushing Schembechler to dismiss Harwell outright. Schembechler had decided on one more year before the meeting. He had called in Odenwald, Fenkell, and Long, telling them, 'If you think you're going to saddle me with this, you have another think [sic] coming. We will give him a year to go around and say good-bye, give him more money than he ever made, and let him do pre-game shows the next year.' Despite his antipathy towards Spicer, Schembechler let his original offer stand. Harwell refused the deal at first: 'I'm a play-by-play announcer, not a Harwell scrapbook. I want to be reevaluated after a year.'[53]

Schembechler stuck to his guns, and in December Harwell signed a terminal one-year contract with the Tigers and WJR. When Harwell asked Ewald for a press conference the day after he signed the contract, the Tigers and WJR fully expected him to announce that he had accepted a one-year contract and that he would retire after the 1991 season. Had they any doubts about his intentions, the Tigers would not have lent him the stadium and WJR would not have carried the press conference live. Harwell snookered them. He announced that he had been 'fired.' Spicer gave the Harwell slant on things to Jerry Green before the news conference, but an assistant editor refused to allow Green to print it. Presumably Harwell anticipated the resulting furor. Schembechler felt betrayed: 'If he hadn't had a contract, he would not have announced that last year after what he did. Harwell thinks he's right, that's his business.'

Carey entered the picture after a phone call from Green attempting to clarify the impending announcement. Carey knew nothing about it. He and Harwell worked together well but were not close friends. 'Ernie was wonderful to me but a very private person.' In response to a query at Harwell's press conference, Carey announced that he too would retire after the 1991 season. The timing made it seem that he had quit in support of Harwell, but he had decided independently to finish his career. Carey denied at the time that he gave Harwell hand signals about the ball's flight during night games, but Harwell later admitted that he and Carey 'helped each other out.' On a few occasions Harwell mixed up names, but so do we all. Cohen put it well: 'Ernie was no longer a .400 hitter but he was still a .300 hitter.'[54]

The press loved him. Reporters uniformly describe him as warm and decent. Walker remembers Harwell putting his arm around him after he received his pass to the Detroit press box. The media commonly reported Harwell's salary at $150,000 and did not mention that he had signed a contract in December 1990. Falls alone reported in January that Harwell's salary had been $177,000 since 1986 (and would be $202,000 in his final year) and criticized Harwell: '[He] did not do right by the people who have paid his salary for the past 31 years.'[55] Two writers who praised Harwell as a person admitted that the media overreacted. Jerry

Green judged: 'We reflected the mood of the people. Objectivity? No.' Vincent thought the media 'didn't handle it even-handedly, maybe not even rationally.'[56] Like a good general, Schembechler took the blame. It was another nail in the coffin of Tigers public relations.

Fan dissatisfaction and media antagonism doomed new Tiger announcers Rick Rizzs and Bob Rathbun. Harwell was broadcasting CBS's radio Game of the Week in 1992 as 'a good way to wind down a career.' The *Detroit News* ran a story greeting the new announcers: 'Broadcast Experts Give Harwell the First Round.' The group of experts were students from the SPECS Howard School of Broadcasting. Green termed the article 'terribly unfair and inaccurate. Amateurs and want-to-bes criticizing qualified professionals. These two quality broadcasters had enough to overcome – the memory of Ernie and the mood of the fans – so that there was no cause for that kind of journalism.'[57] Rizzs and Rathbun knew what they were up against. As Rathbun said: 'Nobody could have replaced Ernie in that atmosphere, even Ernie.' Rizzs opened his broadcast: 'Folks, I'm sitting in the chair of a Hall-of-Famer, Ernie Harwell, and Bob is sitting in the chair occupied for nineteen years by Paul Carey. Gentlemen, I hope you're both listening and we both hope we can continue in the great tradition of broadcasting such as the two of you.'[58] They hoped for a good start to take the heat off, but the Tigers lost six straight at home. Harwell had encouraged Rizzs to apply for the job ('I'm through here'), but by the summer of Rizzs and Rathbun's first year, Harwell was looming over their shoulders, not as a ghost but as a live person.

Ilitch realized that something had to be done to restore public relations damaged by the firing of Harwell, the stadium controversy, and arrogance towards fans. By July rumors were flying that Harwell would return. On 23 July in Anaheim, Rizzs asked Harwell about the rumors and Harwell responded: 'I have to keep my options open.' 'I realize now that I irked Rathbun and Rizzs with my answer, but it would not be fair to myself to say that I wasn't interested. I would not have worked for the old regime but management changed.' By August, Spicer and Ilitch had conversations that resulted in Ilitch offering Harwell a contract to be paid by the Tigers. Ilitch asked Rizzs and Rathbun if they wanted Harwell back. They were reluctant, but agreed when Ilitch admonished: 'We must correct a wrong.' Rizzs voluntarily gave up two innings from the six innings in his contract. Harwell explained his return: 'Out of sight is out of mind and I have enough ego that I want to be a part of things. Once you're off the air, you're forgotten.'[59] Falls correctly worried that Harwell's return 'would overshadow them and would be the same as moving them out.' He also criticized Harwell for trashing the club, with whom he had signed a contract in 1990. But nobody paid much attention.[60]

The trio did not get along. They blame one another but agree that they barely spoke beyond what was necessary. They lunched once in Farmington but otherwise avoided social contact. Harwell had his friends during another farewell tour and went his own way. Bob Talbert reported that Harwell was 'too nice' to mention, in his recent book, treatment by the other announcers: 'Congenial Harwell often asked them out to dinner, lunch, but they refused.' Rathbun denies that 'absolutely,' as he does the claim that he ever said or that Rizzs ever said to him: 'We may have to work with the man but we don't have to talk to him.' Talbert never even telephoned Rathbun in all the time that Rathbun was in Detroit. Someone was leaking strange stories to a media friendly to Harwell.[61]

On air, Carey and Harwell reported separate innings, while the other usually remained silent and occasionally left the booth. Harwell was a rich storyteller and low-key in the style of Heilmann. As Van Patrick could not replace Heilmann, neither could Rizzs and Rathbun replace Harwell. Harwell had a mellifluous southern twang, while Carey had the 'voice of God.' Rizzs was louder than Rathbun, but their voices sounded alike. They were under pressure to be more promotive of the team and home-towners.[62] Rizzs's signature 'Good-bye Baseball' became tiresome when the ball was flying out of the park at Tiger games at a rate of 350 per season, 1991 to 1993. It was especially tiresome when the Tigers trailed by a half-dozen runs as they often did. WJR's ratings declined. Long, however, attributed rating problems more to the success of the Blue Jays and the decline of radio generally than to the tandem broadcasting Tiger games.[63] If some reporters praised the broadcast team for its hard work, by 1994 criticism exceeded sympathy. Both Detroit newspapers complained that they talked too much and were not getting any better.[64] Although their contract ran through 1995, they knew their jobs were in jeopardy in 1994. Gary Vitto and Mike Dietz told Rathbun in July that the club was seeking new announcers as part of a renewed five-year arrangement with WJR to broadcast Tiger games, but that Rathbun would be moved to television. At 4:45 p.m. on Friday 15 December 1994, in a conference phone call, Rathbun learned of his dismissal. He was bitter: 'Never once did anyone say, "Bob, we don't like the way you do this." I thought these people were my friends, who I thought were up front and honest. If they said there are others who don't like you and we can't protect you, I would not have bought a house.'[65] WJR sports reporter, and voice of University of Michigan football, Frank Beckman and Lary Sorenson replaced the R&R team and received positive initial reviews.[66] Harwell continued to do promotional spots and some television work. Whatever Rizzs's and Rathbun's weaknesses, they were never forgiven for replacing Harwell. Their dismissal was part of a general housecleaning that continued in 1995.

FINANCIAL PROBLEMS

The alleged 'firing' of Harwell and media criticism of management drove fans away. Radio and television ratings declined as did attendance after 1988. Although local television ratings remained above the league average, WDIV-TV passed on the right of first refusal in 1995 after their long association with the Tigers; WKBD-TV became the new carrier in a five-year contract that left the Tigers responsible for selling 80 per cent of the spots.[67] The Tigers had some bad teams after 1988, but they had respectable ones in 1991 and 1993. Still, neither ratings nor attendance recovered the way they had in the past. The statistical association between home attendance and winning, discussed in earlier chapters, retained during that period but was weaker than for any other five-year period tested.

Detroit's other sports teams, the Red Wings, the Lions, and the Pistons, which had languished in the 1970s and 1980s, were posting winning records by the 1990s. The Pistons won the NBA championships in 1989 and 1990. The Red Wings had a core of ardent season-ticket holders, who provided a base for what *Financial World* estimated was hockey's most valuable franchise ($125 million) in 1995. Baseball was no longer the most important game in town, and it depended on hundreds of thousands of fans who attended only a few games a year, but were less willing to come to the stadium.

Detroit was increasingly separate from the larger metropolitan area that provided the bulk of baseball fans both at home and at the gate. In a 1986 interview Mayor Young told the Canadian Broadcasting Corporation: 'I'll be damned if I let them collect guns in the City of Detroit while we're surrounded by hostile suburbs and the whole rest of the state ... where you have [Ku Klux Klan] and vigilantes practising in the wilderness with automatic weapons. I am in favor of everyone disarming and I am opposed to the unilateral disarming of Detroit.' Young attributed the region's 'racial antagonism toward Detroit' and his 'regrettable reputation as the agent of hostility between the city and the suburbs' to that statement and a 'one-dimensional' injurious book on Detroit. That book was Chafets's *Devil's Night*, which was excerpted in the *New York Times Magazine* in 1990 and provided background for a *Prime Time Live* story about corruption in Detroit.[68] Whatever the cause, Detroit was becoming an 'impoverished island surrounded by prosperous suburbs ... with a cultural and emotional gap as wide as any that divides hostile nations.'[69]

Gregg Berendt, former mayor of Grosse Pointe Farms, emphasized that Detroit had been one of the few communities in the United States where people identified themselves by the metropolitan area. Travellers called themselves 'Detroiters' rather than saying they resided in Grosse Pointe or Troy. Suburbanites talked about going 'downtown,' not 'to Detroit.' Berendt thought that was changing by the 1990s, with suburbanites less willing to go 'downtown' and identifying less with the city proper.[70] In this atmosphere the Joanne Was incident, in which a group of teenaged African American girls attacked a white woman from Farmington Hills and her daughter in front of the Omni Hotel, galvanized the media. It increased antagonism towards both the city and Young after he sided with the perpetrators.[71] Bill McGraw believed that it still has 'an enormous lasting effect on downtown. Greektown has not yet recovered. Young sent a message to the suburbs: "You are not safe and we do not care."'[72] Young's unpopularity in the suburbs had been building since the CBC interview in 1986.

Amidst all this turmoil, the club remained financially solvent. Two factors changed that. One was the collusion award made after players filed a grievance against owners for conspiring in 1985 and 1986 to restrict free-agent movement and salaries. The other was the financial crisis arising out of Monaghan's other enterprises.

The owners had sought to curtail the salary arbitration system and to introduce a salary cap in 1985. That resulted in a two-day strike (6 and 7 August). After dropping their demand for a salary cap, the owners obtained a concession that players would be eligible for arbitration only after three years of service instead of two. The next month Commissioner Peter Ueberroth personally addressed ownership, calling for restraint in salaries.[73] Sixty-two major-league players, including Kirk Gibson, filed for free agency after the season. It was not a great crop of free agents, but only five, all of whom their original team had shown no interest in signing, received offers from other teams. The next year, a much better crop of seventy-nine free agents found few offers. That year Jack Morris, finding no takers in the free-agent market, settled for arbitration, which raised his Tiger salary to $1.85 million for 1987.[74] Why did no one want to sign a pitcher who had compiled the most victories and pitched the most innings during the decade? Two arbitrators, Thomas Roberts and George Nicolau, in three separate judgments, charged the owners with 'collusion' to suppress free-agent salaries in violation of the Basic Agreement. A 1990 settlement cost owners $280 million. Detroit's share of the collusion payment was $10.8 million, allocated to the income statements of 1989–90. Final awards to Detroit players included Parrish $1,786,666; Evans $692,541; Gibson $615,336; Herndon $396,996; and Wilcox $25,000.[75]

The provision for grievance damages came while Monaghan's other enterprises were running into financial problems. Campbell recalled: 'TSN, Monaghan's holding company, got all of the Tigers' extra cash during his tenure. I was told, "It's all Tom's money." I could call Doug Dawson at TSN to get cash flow, but for a year or two they weren't returning phone calls.'[76] Monaghan had overextended, got caught in the real estate recession, and business at Domino's had slowed. In Monaghan's own words: 'I spent money like a drunken sailor. I thought I could have everything in the world and everything in the next world too.'[77] He purchased Drummond Island for about $28 million, eventually selling it for $3.5 million, bought more than a hundred antique cars, Frank Lloyd Wright furniture, a helicopter, and was building a $5 million house. Tiger management met with Commissioner Francis Vincent in June 1990 to discuss financial problems. Despite allocating collusion payments to 1989 and 1990, Fetzer Inc. (the formal corporation title of the Detroit Baseball Club) had to borrow against 1992 advance ticket sales to make final payments. Later that year the club had to borrow up to $5 million from the league to make payroll.[78] Had it failed to pay salaries, every player on the team would have become a free agent because of breach of contract. Ultimately, the banks forced Monaghan to sell the club, for $83 million. The club had been good to Monaghan. His profits in the sale of the club were $29 million, and it made profits of about $40 million during his stewardship (tables 20, 21). That was not a bad return on his purchase price of $54 million.

Ilitch purchased the club on 26 August 1992. There are both psychological and economic reasons for ownership. After graduation from Cooley High School and four years in the service, Ilitch signed with the Tigers and played on their farm teams for three years. Ilitch had wanted to buy the Tigers in 1984. The Ilitch family purchased both the Detroit Red Wings and Olympia Arenas, Inc., the management company for the Wings in 1982. The family purchased the historic Fox Theater in Detroit in 1987, renovated and reopened it in 1988, and in 1989 moved Little Caesar's Pizza headquarters to the adjoining ten-story office building, investing $50 million in the Fox Center.[79] He had shown a commitment to the City of Detroit. Despite White Sox owner Jerry Reinsdorf's complaint, 'I don't know why anybody in their right mind would buy a baseball team,'[80] most operations were profitable. There were also tax advantages to such a purchase. Up to 50 per cent of a club's purchase price could be allocated to players' contracts, which in turn can be depreciated over a five-year period, as can 'other tangible and intangible assets' (appendix 6). The Tigers had a net operating loss of $3–$5 million during Ilitch's first year (table 23). It lost about $15 million in 1994, when the big national television contracts ended and the strike shortened the season, but tax benefits would have cushioned the blow. Ilitch claimed cash losses of $40 million and $56 million in book losses for 1994–5, but *Financial World* estimated operating losses at only $5.4 and $5.3 million for 1994 and 1995 respectively.[81]

Ilitch swept out the old guard. Three weeks before the sale became official, Monaghan fired Schembechler by fax – an odd way of firing the president of a company. Monaghan then called Campbell, who was in Cooperstown, to tell him of Schembechler's dismissal. Campbell said: 'Let's talk about it when I get back.' Monaghan responded: 'Well, by the way, I've got to let you go too.' Campbell made clear at the time: 'I did not resign or quit. I'm mad.' Later he said: 'I didn't expect it, but it was Tom's right to do what he wanted to. It was clear that he had reached an agreement to sell the club.' Schembechler 'never had a written contract at Michigan; I counted on the integrity of the people I dealt with. That's the last time I did that.'[82] Ilitch denied knowledge of the firings, but dismissal of Campbell and Schembechler was part of the agreement. Monaghan, not Ilitch, would be responsible for any breach of contract. The expected lawsuit came. That same week, Schembechler hired Joseph Golden, an expert in wrongful discharge, claiming that he had been guaranteed employment for ten years until age seventy. Monaghan dismissed the agreement as 'a few figures on a napkin.' A sealed settlement was reached in 1993 to Schembechler's satisfaction.

Campbell and Schembechler had recognized the impending financial crisis. Anticipating a sale, they protected other executives. Only Walker, Klein, and Anderson had three-year contracts. Campbell and Schembechler issued 'letters of understanding' to other executives in the early summer of 1992, granting them a year's severance pay if dismissed. The day that Ilitch took over, executives were called to a meeting. Lawyers interviewed people one on one. Some were crying after the interviews. About a third were let go the first day, another third soon afterward, including long-time secretaries. Before Fetzer sold the club, he issued to executives three-year contracts that were never renewed.[83] Fetzer of course did not have the financial problems Monaghan did, but the difference shows how openly baseball had become another kind of business.

The new regime did not know a lot about baseball, but they did know about business. They immediately inaugurated a series of new promotions. On Monday nights, kids under fourteen could run the basepaths after the game. Tuesday's fans received mementos. Business cards brought discounts on Wednesdays. Fireworks illuminated the sky on Fridays. There were give-aways in the fourth inning, celebrity singalongs in the seventh inning, and a bleacher chicken dance in the ninth. The Tigers may have had more give-aways than any team in baseball after previously having the fewest. Bleacher seats were made available in advance and by phone (previously, they were available only at the park). Fans were guaranteed the best available seats through TicketMaster. Waiters served patrons in the Tiger 'den,' which had 3750 box seats from dugout to dugout with more comfortable seats. Tickets there cost $20. Family bargain days increased from thirteen to twenty; pizzas and soft drinks came in packages with tickets. Mike Dietz, director of marketing, announced: 'Our number one goal was to make Tiger Stadium a fan-friendly place.'[84] Ticket prices, which had been unchanged from 1986 to 1990, however, rose from $8.50 to $12.00 for reserved and $10.50 to $15.00 for box seats by 1994. The average cost for a family of four attending a major-league baseball game (including parking, tickets, and concessions) skyrocketed from $52.48 to $118.03 from 1988 to 1994.[85] For the first time, fans at the gate were feeling the repercussions of baseball as business.

The new crowd spent money with abandon for free agents and home-run hitters. The Tiger payroll increased by 63 per cent from 1992 to 1994, rising from seventeenth to sixth in the league (table 19). It was $7 million above the average for the other four teams with the poorest winning percentage. Henneman and Fielder made $4.3 million in 1993, Phillips, Mike Moore, Mickey Tettleton, and Whitaker made $3 million plus, Bill Gullickson and Eric Davis $2 million. Fifteen Tigers made more than $1 million in 1994.[86] Of those only Henneman and Fryman had graduated from the Tiger farm system since 1980. Two free-agent pitchers, Tim Belcher and Moore, the latter of whom the *Chicago Tribune* called the most over-paid pitcher in baseball at $3.3 million,[87] never managed an ERA lower than 5.22. We can only speculate about the reasons for the search for a quick-fix, but Anderson's impatience with losing teams and the hope to marshall fan support for a new stadium probably contributed.

The Tigers could not stop the opposition from scoring, but they hit home runs. With 51 home runs in 1990, Fielder averaged 40 for the four years before the strike, and Tettleton 31 over the three years; Rob Deer hit 71 home runs in two and a half years with the Tigers, but hit .212. The team averaged 185 home runs in the four years before the strike, and hit 161 in the shortened 1994 season. Their opponents averaged 161 home runs from 1990 to 1993. Had the strike not shortened the 1994 season, 1000 home runs might have flown out of Tiger Stadium from 1990 to 1994; the actual total was 934. The Tigers were among the top three teams in runs scored every year 1990–4, but they were no better than third-last in runs allowed.

Between their last-place finishes in 1989 and 1994, the Tigers were only two games below .500. They won seven straight 19–26 August 1991 to put them in first place. They then lost nine of twelve while Toronto won twelve of fifteen to end that race. Henneman (10-2, 2.88, 21 saves) injured his arm in the stretch run. At the time, fans and the media called for the Tigers to 'rent' a free-agent relief pitcher. We now know the reason that they did not. The club had no money.

Although the Tigers had lost sixteen straight in spring training, lost their opener 9–4, and lost again to Oakland 12–7, giving up nine runs and seven walks in one inning, they raised hope with a tremendous offensive surge in 1993. Detroit had not scored twenty runs in a game since 1937, but did it twice in a week, 20–3 over Seattle following a 20–4 demolition of Oakland in the home opener. A week later (23–25 April) the Tigers outscored the Twins 45–10 over three games. In August they shocked the Orioles 15–1, 15–5, and 17–11, becoming the first team in this century to score forty-five runs over three games twice in the season. They won three of four from the Blue Jays 10–13 June to take a three-game lead and attracted 158,323 for the series. The following week they drew only 18,000 on Tuesday and Wednesday night each. Suburbanites and outstaters would no longer venture to a deserted downtown on weeknights; the Tigers played exactly half their home games in daytime the next year. Eighteen games above .500, they blew a 7–1 lead to Baltimore on 20 June 1993, beginning a ten-game losing streak, the first nine on the road. Recovering in late August they won seven straight to move within four games of first place. By month's end they had scored ten runs for the seventeenth time, but they faltered again in September. The problem was pitching, especially relief pitching; the combined ERA of the six main relievers was 6.31. All were gone a year later.

Although the Tigers were picked for last in 1995, they surprised pundits by closing to just three games back on 5 July. They lost four straight at home to California immediately after the All-Star break, however, with the bullpen losing two late-inning leads. Eight straight losses and eighteen of twenty-two dashed hope. During the latter stretch, forty-two relief pitchers made appearances; in thirty-five of those, the opposition scored a run. The team ERA of 5.49 for the year was the highest in Tiger history, but was topped in 1996, at 6.42 (unofficial).

A slugfest with the White Sox on 28 May typified the Tigers of the nineties. They squandered a 7–1 lead despite hitting seven home runs – two by Curtis, Fielder, and Gibson, one by Whitaker. All were solo home runs. The White Sox hit five home runs and won 14–12. The teams set a major-league record of twelve home runs by both teams, breaking the record first set on 23 June 1950 by Detroit and New York. They also established an AL record of twenty-one extra-base hits. Anderson won his 2160th game in July 1995, putting him third among all managers behind only John McGraw's 2840 and Connie Mack's 3776. He could take solace in that and in the fact that the Tigers finished four games ahead of the Blue Jays, but no pride in the 60-84 record. Sparky despaired of the pitching, telling his pitching coaches: 'You don't have enough smarts to straighten this out. This is unstraightable [sic].'[88]

By the end of July, management gave up the 1995 season, trading its best starting pitcher, David Wells, for three minor leaguers. Fielder was critical of management for quitting when the team was only four games out of a wild-card berth. McHale countered that the team had to balance being competitive with smaller salaries. Other clubs unloaded star players with big salaries as well – Jim Abbott, Bobby Bonilla, David Cone, Ken Hill, and Bret Saberhagen also changed teams. Detroit sent Henneman to Houston for Phil Nevin, a former number-one pick overall, on 10 August. The next day, Gibson announced his retirement. Before the season began, the Tigers had signalled a rebuilding effort by trading Tony Phillips to California for a younger, less expensive Chad Curtis. Klein noted: 'Detroit has tried for a decade to win with veterans, and for the most part it hasn't worked.'[89]

Whitaker and Trammell set an AL record for team-mates playing in 1915 games together (later raised to 1918) on 13 September 1995. Fittingly, Whitaker hit a three-run game-ending home run in the ninth for a 5–3 decision over Milwaukee. The only Tigers with 2000 hits, 2000 games played, and 200 home runs have been Kaline and Whitaker; among other major-league second basemen only Joe Morgan achieved such numbers. Trammell accumulated four Gold Gloves, Whitaker three. Trammell played on six All-Star teams, Whitaker five. After weeks of rumor, on 27 September the *Detroit News* announced that Anderson would not return. A press conference on 12 October confirmed his departure after a 1331-1248 record in Detroit and a career

2194 victories, five pennants, and three World Series championships. At the conference Anderson observed: 'Since '84 we didn't win nothing and they loved me forever.'[90] Campbell called Anderson the 'best manager I had because of the way he handles men,' but Sparky does not suffer losing well. During the team's troubles in 1989 he went home with what Leonard Koppett described as 'what amounted to a nervous breakdown.' Anderson admitted that he nearly quit in 1989 because 'God didn't put me on this earth to finish fifth. God put me on this earth to win.' He has a reputation of preferring veterans and being impatient with younger pitchers. He clashed with many of Ilitch's men, particularly Gary Vitto. McHale had signalled a change in April 1995: 'We do need somebody who's in touch with the younger players.'[91] The Tigers appointed forty-three-year-old Buddy Bell, Cleveland infield coach, to succeed Anderson on 9 November. One era had ended. A new one was beginning.[92]

Before the 1995 season began the Tigers hired John McHale Jr from Colorado as president of the club. After the season they appointed thirty-two-year-old Randy Smith general manager. Smith had earlier been with McHale at Colorado, most recently at San Diego. Coincidentally, Campbell died the next day (31 October) in Florida. For the first time since the firing of Campbell, winner of a 1983 Citizen/Sportsman Award 'for his total dedication to the game of baseball in the City of Detroit,' baseball people were again in charge of the club. It was a time for rebuilding but also for integration of the 'ballclub with the fans, sponsors and community.'[93] Modern general managers could not limit their concerns to putting a good team on the field, as Campbell once had.

The city was looking to the future as well despite some trials. Beer, whisky, and pop bottles, lighters, baseballs, batteries, and a metal napkin holder pelted from the stands on opening day, 1995. The *Free Press* headline read 'Opening Day Disgrace,' the *News*'s 'A Total Embarrassment.' 'Detroit, once a proud city, took another one in the heart.' Although fans vented their frustrations at players and owners in other cities, Detroit received national attention.[94] Los Angeles had to forfeit its game to St Louis on 10 August after souvenir balls struck the field. That was the first forfeit since Disco Demolition night in 1979, but it did not receive the coverage that Detroit's opening day did.

Following a fatal attack on Eletha Word on the Belle Isle Bridge after two minor traffic accidents at 2:00 p.m. on 19 August, the national press again blistered Detroit. *Newsweek* headlined its story 'The Shame of a City.' National television featured the attack, but neither it nor *Newsweek* reported that many people called police on cellular phones and cooperated in apprehending the assailant.[95] The *New York Times* printed a picture of a deserted downtown Detroit in June. *Financial World* ranked Detroit twenty-ninth of thirty city in management in 1994 after rating it worst in 1993.[96] Downtown still had about eighty empty buildings as well as vacant storefronts. Young's dream twenty years earlier of the Renaissance Center and big, dramatic projects had not turned the city around.

A new mayor symbolized hopes for better times. Dennis Archer promised better relations with the suburbs and the state. They, in turn, welcomed a friendlier face in the mayor's office. Housing prices within Detroit rose for the first time in real dollars since the 1950s. New housing sprang up, especially along the riverfront, and a dozen more projects were planned over a wider area, including Harmonie Park and the Woodward Corridor. Detroit was experiencing its biggest housing boom since 1950 and median prices rising.[97] Chrysler built a new $750 million plant and there was a $2 billion commitment to Detroit's Empowerment Zone. Devil's Night fires declined from 182 in 1994 to 61 in 1995 – about an average night in Detroit – while 35,000 volunteers participated in an effort to maintain neighborhoods. Devil's Night was the lead story on ABC and second on CNN in 1994; it passed with little comment in 1995. Crime declined about 6 per cent – more than the decline nationally – although Detroit was still eleventh among 201 cities (100,000 population) in violent crime and random slayings remained high.[98] After decades of squabbling, a tentative agreement for a new stadium in Detroit raised hopes for a revitalized downtown. The early 1990s were not a happy time in the history of Detroit baseball, but there was reasonable hope that the second half of the decade would be better.

10

The Stadium as Symbol

Tiger Stadium has been more than a place to play major-league baseball. It has served as an icon of baseball in Detroit. On the same site for a century, in its present form for half a century, it has linked present and past. It brought suburbanites to downtown and has been part of the identity of 'Detroit' for those living throughout the metropolitan area. This elderly citizen symbolized better times in Detroit and was a meeting place for generations, joined in memories of Tigers' victories and hopes for future glories. Built in a different era, it seemed to some an anachronism that needed replacement. Others regarded its proposed replacement as the destruction of the past. Controversy over the stadium reveals a number of the themes discussed here earlier.

The Detroit Tiger Baseball Club considered a new stadium with luxury boxes and increased ticket prices essential to its ability to remain competitive on the field during an era of stratospheric salaries. Business wanted a new stadium to revivify the downtown. Developers sought construction contracts. The mayor's office wanted revitalization of downtown and a permanent symbol of the Young era. Some African American leaders envisioned jobs that a large construction project might bring. Groups who insisted on a sense of history and the preservation of Detroit's heritage allied against them. Joined in opposition were those who did not believe that public funds should subsidize a millionaire and those who did not care whether or not Detroit had a baseball team. Out-staters, becoming more distant from Detroiters and more powerful within the state legislature, opposed their taxes being spent on Detroit's problems. Who did the baseball team belong to anyway – Tom Monaghan and his successor Mike Ilitch, the City of Detroit, Detroiters, or its fans everywhere? The community was split.

Public financing of professional sports stadiums and complexes is now the norm. Cities have invested $3 billion in them – $1 billion between 1992 and 1995 – and provided an annual tax subsidy of $500,000.[1] Advocates have agreed since the 1950s that construction costs have become too large for any private investor.[2] They also argue that sports teams foster pride in communities, which should not just root for them but financially support them. They claim too that teams and stadiums bring indirect revenues in the form of tourist dollars and jobs and are integral to urban renewal. Critics challenge the economic benefits of new stadiums, criticize subsidies to 'rich men' who own them,[3] and question this use of public funds during a period of budget deficits, tax revolts, and urban decay. Even when there is a willingness to raise public funds, there is debate about whether the city, the metropolitan area, or the entire state should bear the costs.

New Comiskey Park in Chicago, Baltimore's Camden Yards, and Cleveland's Jacobs Field are among new stadiums that have been funded at taxpayer expense and drawn large crowds; the last two seem to have revitalized the area surrounding them. Although a new stadium is now planned, the Detroit Tigers will play at Tiger Stadium, which opened the same April day in 1912 as did Fenway Park, at least until 1998. They remain the oldest functioning major-league ballparks in America. Yet, there have been many calls for a new stadium in Detroit for forty years. Secret plans and negotiations for a new stadium began within a year of Tom Monaghan's purchase of the team in 1983. A new stadium has been the subject of vigorous and bitter public discussion for a decade. Debate over it gives insights into the financial problems and the political implications of public funding in one decaying American city. It speaks to the importance of symbols in American popular culture. It also provides an example of successful civic action that turned the political tables on the main players. A central question has been why a ballpark with an honored history and once acclaimed as one of, if not the very, best in the nation needs to be replaced.

Briggs Stadium (renamed Tiger Stadium in 1961) was dedicated on 22 April 1938. The stadium was the first in the majors to be completely double-decked, with all seats roofed with the exception of the center-field bleachers. It was Walter O. Briggs's showcase and recognized as one of baseball's finest parks for decades. Red Smith of the *New York Times* called it 'the handsomest in the American League, rated one-two with Wrigley Field.'[4] Gene Mack, artist for the *Boston Globe*, regarded Briggs Stadium as the 'dream field of the majors. If Detroit has the best ball park, it's true that it probably has the best fans as well.'[5] Curt Smith, author of the classic *Voices of the Game*, wrote: 'As a Red Sox fan, let me admit it [Tiger Stadium was] the best damned park in America.'[6] As late as 1974, *Sports Illustrated* observed: 'Tiger Stadium is one of the last of the old, majestic, steel-graded ball parks.'[7]

Even while Briggs Stadium was receiving national praise, Tiger management had concerns about the stadium. Jim Campbell claims that 'as early as then [1950s], concrete was falling, toilet facilities were bad, the concourse was narrow, the clubhouse small. It was one of the three best stadiums in the 1940s but was deteriorating.'[8]

The first cry for a new stadium came not from Tiger management, however, but from Detroit business and civic leaders who sought a wider use for the stadium. As early as 1948, there was a proposal for a large municipal stadium to bring the Olympics to Detroit (appendix 7 for a general chronology). *Free Press* columnist Lyall Smith argued that the money should be spent instead on facilities for high school athletes.[9] In 1956, this theme of community athletics was resurrected. Councilman Ed Conner then proposed a hundred-thousand-seat stadium to serve all of Detroit's sports teams – the Tigers, the Lions, the University of Detroit, and high school championships – somewhere in the 'outlying section of the city; then we could get rid of Briggs Stadium, which doesn't belong in the heart of the city anyway.' Mayor Albert Cobo, gave 'serious consideration' to a city-owned park, a proposal that the (football) Detroit Lions supported, but the City Council split 4–4 and the proposal died.[10]

In the early 1960s, a committee led by Fred Matthaei attempted to lure the 1968 Olympics to Detroit. The bid promised an Olympic stadium to be built in Detroit or an adjacent suburb. John Fetzer spent $25,000 for a study that suggested razing the old stadium for parking and building a new one in Corktown where the Father Kern housing project is located today.[11] When Iron Curtain countries chose Mexico City as a more neutral site, hopes for an Olympic Stadium faded.[12] Both

Mayor Jerome Cavanagh and Councilman Billy Rogell, shortstop on the pennant-winning team of 1935, opposed using public funds for the venture because of the city's financial problems and more pressing needs in the community;[13] nevertheless, Cavanagh formed a Mayor's Committee in 1966 to study the stadium question. In July of 1967, the committee recommended a 60,000-seat 'enclosed stadium at the fairgrounds [in north-east Detroit],'[14] but the riot in the same month put that project on hold. By the 1960s, questions of whether public funds should be used for sports facilities, whether such facilities should be in downtown Detroit or follow demographics to the suburbs, whether parking was adequate, and what incentives the community should offer to keep sports teams had become public issues, involving not just the city but the state as well. All of these questions would return a quarter-century later.

During the late 1960s a variety of proposals emerged. Cavanagh wanted a domed stadium along the riverfront near the Convention Center to invigorate downtown. The state recommended a domed stadium off East Seven-Mile Road, near Detroit's northern city limits, which would be more accessible to outstaters. A Detroit Renaissance committee, formed after the 1967 riot, promoted a riverfront stadium as part of a large redevelopment project to revitalize downtown.[15] On 15 September 1971 the stadium authority announced a forty-year bond issue to raise $126 million, and on 30 November the *News* reported that John Fetzer had promised to move to a multi-sport domed stadium on the riverfront. Early in 1972 a provisional lease was signed between the Detroit Tiger Baseball Club and the city. The 1972 Tiger yearbook included drawings of the stadium: 'A revenue bond issue of $126 million is contemplated for the project, of which $85 million is earmarked for the stadium and parking. The bonds are to be supported by stadium rents, a hotel-motel tax and horse racing revenue.'[16] At the annual Tiger press party, Fetzer announced the signing of a forty-year lease, which the *News* concluded 'virtually guarantees a stadium, planned for three years, will be built.'[17]

Presaging civic action groups of the late 1980s and 1990s, television talk-show personality Lou Gordon queried whether the stadium could be completed for the costs proposed. After Wayne County's credit rating had been lowered, a financial analyst from Grosse Pointe, Mark Allen, and attorney Ron Prebenda filed a lawsuit to stop the sale of bonds. On

1 June Judge Blair Moody ruled that the Tigers were getting too cushy a deal. A week later the Michigan Supreme Court ruled that Detroit and Wayne County officials had misled the public about the actual costs. That killed the project. In September 1971 Pontiac residents voted in favor of building a stadium in that city. Two years later, on 19 September 1973, stadium construction began, and the Lions played their first game at the Silverdome in Pontiac on 23 August 1975.[18]

White residents had fled the city after the 1967 riot, and fear – bordering on paranoia – about increasing crime in Detroit inhibited suburbanites from visiting Detroit. City officials feared an exodus by Detroit's other sports teams.[19] In 1976–7, while rumors were flying that the Red Wings intended to join the Lions in Pontiac, Mayor Coleman Young and the Detroit Red Wings entered into negotiations about a new hockey arena. Federal funds and local public revenue bonds permitted the construction, at a cost of $58 million, of Joe Louis Arena, which opened on 27 December 1979. Although Fetzer had promised to keep the Tigers in Detroit, Tiger executives, particularly Jim Campbell, increasingly complained about structural problems at Tiger Stadium and the need for extensive repairs.[20] Was this a prelude to relocation?

When Fetzer announced, on 28 September 1976, a $15 million renovation program funded by the Tigers, the Detroit newspapers were fulsome in their praise of Fetzer for his loyalty to the city and for the commitment of his own money.[21] About then, public criticism of blackmail used by owners elsewhere to demand subsidies for their stadiums was appearing for the first time.[22] Good citizen Fetzer received a quick reward. In October the City of Detroit offered to buy the stadium for one dollar and lease it back to the Tigers, if the city received federal funds of $5 million to refurbish it. Young announced approval of the $5 million federal grant on 13 July 1977. In April 1978 the City of Detroit purchased Tiger Stadium for one dollar, and the Tigers leased it back from the city.[23] Campbell observed that this would make the park 'one of the finest in the country.' Mayor Young stressed that no tax money was involved. The 1978 *Tiger Yearbook* promised: 'Financing is arranged to relieve taxpayers of any liability.'[24] To supplement the federal money, the city sold renovation bonds of $8.5 million at 8⅞ per cent interest over twenty years; in return, the Tigers agreed to play in the stadium for at least thirty years with three optional ten-year renewals. That thirty-year commitment was reported at the time, but would be forgotten a decade later when a new stadium began to be mooted.

Precisely who initiated the transfer of ownership is unclear. Council members of the time Erma Henderson and Billy Rogell remember that the initiative came from Mayor Coleman Young, but Young claims that it was Fetzer's idea. Young stated: 'Fetzer was unwilling to put more money into this. We [city officials] were not seeking ownership. We were seeking to maintain it. Fetzer first proposed the deal to me. He agreed to give the stadium to the city, [President Jimmy] Carter was then giving money to cities. We put in $17 million. In long run, we were ahead. We got more from the ticket surcharge than structural maintenance cost.'[25] The city's original application for the $5 million capital economic development administration grant, signed by Mayor Young himself, asserted: 'Tiger Stadium, the City of Detroit's major athletic facility since 1911 [sic] is a structurally sound stadium, and with renovation will revitalize the significant city landmark.'[26] The City of Detroit had conducted successful negotiations with the Red Wings and unsuccessful negotiations with the (basketball) Pistons, who followed the Lions to Pontiac in 1978. Young condemned that move: 'The departure of the Pistons ... was a symbolic gesture ... further evidence of the suburbs' raid on Detroit, the looting of the old community in the interests of the new.'[27]

It is likely that the city initiated discussions to guarantee that the Tigers would remain in the city and to obtain federal money for other urban development near the stadium. The Detroit Baseball Club received an immediate tax break, relief from the annual maintenance bill, and public funds for the proposed $15 million restoration. The Detroit club's own analysis in 1992 of the stadium lease arrangement emphasized the advantages to the club:

In April 1978, the City of Detroit (the 'City') purchased Tiger Stadium from the Tigers and entered into a lease arrangement with the Club. The lease runs through 2008, with renewal options for three successive ten-year terms.

From 1978 when 30 year lease began, until 1989, the Tigers paid the city $150,000 a year to rent the stadium. Additionally, the Tigers collected 90 cents for every ticket sold. That surcharge money and the annual $150,000 payment was used to help pay off $12.1 million in city-sponsored bonds, which had been sold to investors to help pay for $18 million in renovations to Tiger Stadium. Since January 1989, when the bonds were paid off, the Tigers have not been required to pay rent, nor will they pay any through the expiration of the lease in 2008.[28]

The Tigers were disappointed with the renovations, however. Rossetti Associates, in charge of the project, discovered that there was need for more substantial repairs than anticipated and that those were more expensive had been than anticipated. A new press box was built to replace the one destroyed by fire in February 1977, the light towers were replaced, new broadcast booths were built, a $2 million computer scoreboard was installed, and about 10,000 upper-deck bleacher seats were replaced. Still much was left undone: 'Tiger officials expected to get forty private booths they could sell to high-paying corporate customers and a number of other modern appointments. Instead, the stadium got new wiring, new plumbing, new seats and new paint. The loges, the escalators and the glass tubes remained only blueprint promises ... With proper maintenance, *the stadium would last thirty years from the time it was renovated*'[29] (author's emphasis).

Another bond issue, this time for $3.6 million, was issued at 13¼ per cent interest in 1982 and the ticket surcharge was hiked from $0.50 to $0.90 to subsidize it. Eighteen million dollars were eventually spent and paid for by fans through the ticket surcharge, not by the city or the club. According to the club's own report in 1992, a mayor's press release in 1991, and a review of documents by the *Free Press* in 1991, the Tigers' annual rent was only $150,000. Their maintenance costs were as little as $100,000 per year – much less than commonly assumed and much less than the Lions paid to maintain the Silverdome – because the city, which received the ticket surcharge, paid up to 80 per cent of maintenance costs.[30] Still the Tigers were unhappy. Jim Campbell reached the conclusion that further renovation was useless: 'We did not want to send good money after bad. There was no end to maintenance.' The team needed a new ballpark.[31]

It was Mayor Young, however, who made the first public suggestion of a new stadium – a domed one – in 1983. Campbell scoffed at the idea, pointing to other priorities and a need to fix up the old stadium.[32] Monaghan promised never to tear down the stadium: 'As long as I own this team, we will not build a new stadium. We'll keep fixing it up and making it look as good as possible ... It reminds me of the stadium at Cooperstown.'[33] The Detroit press too favored preservation. After a tour of other stadiums in the country, Joe LaPointe praised Tiger Stadium. In an editorial, the *News* attacked domed stadiums as 'godless stadia.' The *Chicago Tribune* stressed the importance of Tiger Stadium in Detroit and quoted Campbell concerning the team's commitment to stay in it: 'You couldn't rip us out of here now ... The Stadium and the land under it was sold to the city for $1 in 1977 and leased back to the Tigers for 30 years. That should keep Tiger Stadium in business at least until 2007, with another 30-year option.'[34]

Campbell was being economical with the truth. On 30 June 1985, three days after the *Tribune* article, he addressed two hundred ardent followers at the Mayo Smith Society's annual luncheon at Carl's Chop House. 'They're going to have to build a new stadium in this city. It could be in the same neighborhood. It looks good now, but, to be realistic, it's a tired old building.' Six months later, in January 1986, he told a group of reporters in Grand Rapids, 'It's an old, old edifice; it's old underneath. In five, ten, or fifteen years Tom Monaghan is going to have to sit down with the city and make a decision on a ballpark.'[35] In 1985, Campbell had commissioned an internal report to analyze problems with the stadium, estimate how long the stadium would last, and determine what options were open to the club. The lease was not seen to be a problem. The report, which recommended construction of a new stadium, was given to Monaghan by Campbell early in 1986, but already in 1985 Tiger management 'had set a course for a new stadium.'[36] Beginning in 1984, Young began visiting Monaghan 'as his guest' at spring training for three or four consecutive years to discuss a new stadium. These talks remained a secret. Young always preferred a dome, like that in Toronto.[37] Talk about a new stadium seemed mostly that – talk – in 1986. The press gave it only intermittent attention. It was another full year before it became clear that the club was actively investigating a new stadium.

The *News* published a series of stories about the possibility of a new stadium at the beginning of August 1987. Changing his mind from his column of the previous year in the *Free Press*, Joe Lapointe decided that the Tigers did need a new stadium: 'My relations with the club had always been at arms length. I found myself on their side, and felt uncomfortable about it. The Tigers had treated people rudely and made things as uncomfortable as possible at the park. They have been high-handed. They were one of the last to get modern public relations. There is a time for something new. There were 20,000 good seats and those are wonderful, but there is a serious fall-off after that. The posts, the lines at the concessions and seats that don't face home plate were a problem.'[38] This new climate prompted Betzold to return to the fray. In his 'Tiger Town' column of 23 August, he defended Tiger Stadium and asked readers' opinions. Three weeks later, he reported that the mail ran 5–1 in favor of keeping the park, and the few in favor of a new stadium were all 'saying they want one with real grass.'[39] A high-school chum of Betzold, Frank Rashid, called him about the column. Betzold in turn called his friend Robert Buchta to explore the possibility of saving Tiger Stadium. On 2 September 1987, at Buddy's Pizza, Frank and Kevin Rashid, Betzold, Buchta, and Jerry Lemenu founded the innocuous-sounding 'Tiger Stadium Fan Club.'

They had neither money nor a political base, but they proved to be a sharp thorn in the side of the club and the mayor's office. They began with a conviction that Tiger Stadium was 'a great place to watch a ballgame' and a disbelief that it was structurally unsound. They also believed that an older sense of history and community had been neglected since the 1960s.[40] They might have agreed with Bruce Kuklick's later description of the importance of Shibe Park in Philadelphia: 'a steel structure that provided historical coherence to peoples' lives,' a 'fanciful landscape' with handed-down stories and beliefs from one generation to the next. The *New York Times* believed that Tiger Stadium occupied 'a special place in the hearts of many residents.' *Inland Architect* praised it: 'As one of three remaining Golden Age artifacts, its existence should be assured if only because so many have been lost. Those parks had unmatched character and priceless histories, but lamenting their demise is not mere nostalgia. They offered a quality of experience, a type of action, and a view of the game that current stadia cannot match. They were good citizens, economical of land and gentle to their neighborhoods.'[41]

During the process, the Fan Club became more politicized, raising larger issues and recognizing baseball as a form of political action. They concluded that Young wanted a monument to himself, that there had been cozy relationships between developers and the mayor's office in the past, and that there were too many needs in a poor city to use public funds for a palatial stadium to replace a perfectly serviceable one.

They struck a chord. The question of whether public funds were integral to urban renewal or were merely a subsidy for millionaire owners was capturing national attention. *Sports Illustrated* found that only 38 per cent of sports fans supported subsidies for stadiums in 1978. A study by the *Baltimore Sun* concluded that taxpayers had 'shouldered a large share of the burden for supporting the team' and that few benefits had accrued to the Baltimore economy. Public stadium authorities were reported to be losing $23 million a year. Robert Baade wrote widely cited articles criticizing public funding and questioning claims of economic returns from these stadiums. *Newsweek* in 1987 published a biting condemnation of public funding of sports stadiums: 'Each stadium-building city may have its own motives and its own price but two results are almost assured. The cities will lose money and team owners will make more. No politician wants to appear a loser.'[42]

The Stadium Fan Club held its first meeting and opened a post-office box in September 1987. In a meeting of 9 November 1987 organizers made an important early decision to begin a process nominating the stadium for the National Register of Historic Places, a designation achieved a year later. That brought in support from heritage groups. *Free Press* reporter Bill McGraw covered the November meeting and wrote a front-page article about the group on 12 November. Detroit's *Metro Times* ran a major story in December. Over the Christmas holidays, the Fan Club decided to give the stadium a 'great big hug' on opening day, 20 April 1988. It published its first newsletter in January 1988, by which time it had eight hundred members.[43] Boston had held a seventy-fifth anniversary for Fenway Park the previous year, but the Detroit Baseball Club had let the anniversary of Tiger Stadium pass the same year unnoticed and were reluctant to cooperate in the 'hug.'[44] Although turnout for the hug on a rainy day was small and the Fan Club spent $20,000 it did not have, it brought attention to the movement in the *Christian Science Monitor*, the *New York Times*, and the *Wall Street Journal*. Radio stations WCXY and WCSX offered to co sponsor the hug and the *News* editorialized: '"Root, Root, Root for the Home Park" – Tiger Stadium may not be pretty. It may not be modern. But it is Detroit. The stadium has forged a relationship with the fans and the city, something that no domed stadium or artificial turf playing field has managed to do. So if you are one of the lucky ones who attends today's game, please sign one of the petitions.'[45] The Fan Club was learning how to capture media attention.

While the Fan Club was organizing and attracting attention, owner Tom Monaghan was awaiting an engineering study concerning the cost of shoring up the foundation and superstructure of the existing stadium. In a letter to Frank Rashid in November, Peggy Shine, public affairs coordinator for Domino's Pizza, wrote: 'We have not made any decisions regarding its development. Ideally, we'd love to preserve Tiger Stadium ... We will keep you informed of the feasibility study's results and any other information regarding the future of this stadium.' Sometime that same month, the Turner Construction Company submitted a study to the City of Detroit recommending less than $6 million of improvements, of which $1 million was for structural steelwork. But that's not what was reported. John McDevitt, who handled finances for Monaghan Enterprises and Domino's, had become spokesperson regarding the stadium. He and Campbell disliked each other, so there was little communication between Domino's and the ball club.[46]

In January 1988 McDevitt announced that the Turner study indicated a total price tag of $45–100 million to preserve the park and $4–5 million annually to maintain it. A new park was necessary. That same month Michael Rohde, Domino's Farms senior project manager, threatened that the Tigers might move to Tampa Bay where Monaghan could get a new stadium free. Two days later, Monaghan, in a front-page story in the *News*, refused to disavow the possibility of a move: 'Anything is possible.' On 22 January, the *Free Press* quoted Mayor Young: 'It's obvious the damn thing [stadium] is falling down.' On 4 February at a news conference to welcome Southwest Airlines to City Airport, Young announced: 'We're re-building a city and there comes a time when we need a new stadium, and the only question is whether it's now, five years from now or ten years from now.' He expected the ball club and the state to 'help the city to pay for it' and challenged 'impractical nostalgia buffs' to put 'money in the pot.' Two weeks later, he promised: 'We're going to build [Monaghan] one downtown – the best baseball stadium anywhere.'[47]

Convinced that both the mayor's office and spokespersons for the Tigers and Domino's were deliberately dissembling about the costs of renovations, Buchta and Rashid took the offensive. They wrote a public letter on 24 January 1988 to Monaghan demanding disclosure of feasibility studies and a pledge to keep the stadium in Detroit. On 2 February McDevitt, in a meeting with Fan Club representatives, admitted that there was no written study of the stadium and that the $100 million would include a 'fabric roof.' He maintained that the basic structural renovation would still cost $45 million. Two weeks later the Fan Club formally requested relevant documents from the city, but received no reply.[48] They issued a public statement at the mayor's office on 5 February demanding disclosure: 'Tiger Stadium is a public building. Both renovation and replacement would almost certainly involve public money. Even the highest cost estimates of renovation are far less than the cost of a new stadium. And thus far no studies have been released about the structural integrity of Tiger Stadium. The public has a right to this information before any decision is made about the future of the ballpark.'[49]

A number of Detroit newspaper columnists and radio and television stations picked up the scent and began to question the terminological inexactitude of officials' statements and the concealment of studies.[50] The May issue of *Detroit Monthly* hit the newsstands on 20 April 1988, the same day as the 'hug.' In it McDevitt conceded that the $45–100 million figure was 'really a number we developed internally. It's based on different remodelling concepts.' He refused to name the engineer who was telling him that Tiger Stadium faced extensive structural problems, but challenged the interviewer to 'bring your own structural engineer to look around the stadium.' *Detroit Monthly* did precisely that. Lev Zetlin was hired to do an on-site evaluation of Tiger Stadium and concluded that it was structurally adequate. In his opinion, it could 'last indefinitely' if it were 'properly maintained,' but the stadium's current maintenance position was 'neglected.'[51] In the same week, both the *News* and the *Free Press* wrote articles and editorials stressing that the stadium was structurally sound and safe. On 31 July the *News* published excerpts from the Turner Construction report that it had obtained under the Freedom of Information Act. The report showed that the Turner Construction Company had recommended renovations of $6 million, not the enormous figures quoted by Tiger officials.[52] Ralph Snyder, in charge of stadium operations, was never allowed to see the Turner report. Privately, he described McDevitt's $45–100 million estimate as 'a set of phantom figures. They could not know the state of the stadium. McDevitt never talked to me, I was never even introduced to him.'[53] After public disclosure of the real recommendations of the Turner report, that report, which heretofore had been quoted as definitive by Tiger management and the mayor's office, was dismissed as a 'mere band-aid.'[54] Councilman Mel Ravitz charged that the only reason that Young wanted a stadium was so that it could be named after himself.[55]

The Tigers were running into trouble on other fronts as well. The state senate passed Bill 866 containing an amendment from Senator John Kelly (D, Detroit). That prohibited any funds from the governor's proposed $800 million bond issue being used for a professional baseball stadium in Michigan. Kelly had introduced the amendment in cooperation with the Fan Club. The state legislature's actions reflected its growing animosity towards Detroit and Young's diminishing influence there after Milliken's governorship. Outstate attitudes also reflected racial divisions in the state. 'Detroit' came to symbolize poverty, crime, and African Americans that outstaters wanted to leave to their own devices. Yet, the suburbs are linked economically to the city and their economic problems are, at least in part, attributable to the decay of the inner city.[56]

On 13 October 1988 the state board of review approved the Fan Club's petition to place Tiger Stadium on the National Register of Historic Places, despite opposition from Detroit's legal counsel. After the legislature formally endorsed the recommendation, registration prevented any federal funds from being used to demolish Tiger Stadium or construct any other structure on the site at Michigan and Trumbull. Cutting off this source was important because federal money had provided for the 1978 renovations and would have been needed for any major new development. In January 1989, the last of the bonds from the 1978 renovations were paid off and phase-three renovations, planned from 1978 to 1980, were put 'on hold' until a determination was made of whether to renovate or build a new stadium. The city held a series of meetings with the Detroit Baseball Club during the winter of 1988–9 concerning financial arrangements. HOK Sports Facility Group began a design study and presented a recommendation for a new open-air stadium at a cost of $118 million in March 1989. The mayor went to Lake-land, Florida, meeting with Governor James Blanchard and Monaghan to discuss the HOK report.[57]

In all the public discussion there was very little mention of where all this money was to come from. In March, Blanchard made it clear that he had not promised any funds for the stadium. The Detroit city council passed a resolution in support of keeping Tiger Stadium by a 5–2–2 vote on 21 April. A phone survey of eight hundred households conducted from 27 March to 7 April. 1989 showed substantial opposition to a new stadium. Statewide, only 20 per cent favored any allocation of state funds to support construction costs. Uniquely in the city proper were people in favor of using state funds, and 75 per cent of Detroiters favored renovation of the existing stadium.[58] In Corktown, around the ballpark, residents who had business interests wanted to preserve Tiger Stadium, but the new gentry complained about congestion. Public funding was increasingly being cut off. Where was the money to come from?

The city had none. The Tigers did not have any money either. Campbell and Schembechler had carefully built up a $22 million sinking fund to be used as a starter for a new stadium, but that money was disappearing fast.[59] Bill Haase, point man for Tiger Stadium, described the situation: 'Everybody concurs that we must kill discussions of renovations because commitment is to a new stadium. Money is going to Domino's. They promise to transfer money the next day. But, [Alex] Callam [Tiger treasurer] says, you don't answer the phone. By end of '89, I realized that the stadium was not likely to happen because of financial problems. I looked in the pot and there was no gold there. Mayoral and gubernatorial elections meant there were small windows of opportunity between those to get things done.'[60] Mayor Young said flatly: 'I always assumed the Tigers would pay for the stadium.'[61] Everybody was broke. Everybody expected somebody else to fund the stadium.

The only way a new stadium could have been financed is if the Tigers had elicited widespread public support for the new venture. Not only did they not do that, but they also alienated their fans and the press. After the single meeting with McDevitt from Domino's, the Tigers refused to meet with the Fan Club. George Cantor criticized management for not meeting with representatives of the Fan Club: 'By refusing to meet with the Fan Club or discuss the Cochrane Plan, the Tigers feel they can deny it a certain credibility. But there are issues involved here that go a lot deeper than baseball nostalgia.'[62]

In March 1988 Monaghan had pretended that it was the mayor alone who wanted the new stadium and that he'd 'go along with it along as the rent didn't go up.' He then refused, however, to reveal what rent he was paying – which had been only $150,000 per year, and would be zero in another year.[63] Domino's, the baseball club, and the mayor's office were all caught in false and contradictory statements about the cost of renovations, the structural safety of the park, and potential financial sources. Both Campbell and Bo Schembechler admitted in retrospect that they either 'mis-spoke' or used 'poetic license' about the stadium falling down. Snyder, in charge of stadium operations, emphasized its structural solidity, although 'much work needed to be done.'[64] The Detroit Tigers were a walking public-relations disaster. They compounded their public-relations problems when they refused to extend popular announcer Ernie Harwell's contract. The Detroit press and fans of the ball club were looking for blood after Harwell's press conference.

During the last half of 1989, two young architects who were Fan Club members – John and Judy Davids – worked feverishly to prove that Tiger Stadium was salvageable. On 22 January 1990 they unveiled a color booklet with plans for a major renovation of the ballpark for $26 million. Their plan, which became known as the Cochrane Plan (named for one of the streets bordering Tiger Stadium), probably did not allocate sufficient funds for repair of deep structural problems, particularly of outdated wiring and plumbing.[65] Neither Monaghan nor his staff would ever glance at it despite numerous attempts to contact them by John Davids, who had redesigned Monaghan's private box. Nevertheless, it was not a useless exercise. It prompted club executives to admit publicly that they were committed to a new stadium and that renovation was no longer a consideration.[66] By refusing even to view the plans, the Tigers alienated the press. If an inexpensive option was available, why would the Tigers not even consider it? Why did they demand enormous amounts of public funds and claim that the existing stadium was in ruin? The reaction of Detroit's *Crain's Business* was typical: 'The Detroit Baseball Club, as we all know, is a private business owned by Thomas Monaghan. But it isn't quite like most businesses. People identify with, even love Detroit's baseball franchise ... The fan-club proposal seems to be a detailed, well-thought out plan to renovate Tiger Stadium. The Tigers' reaction is puzzling. Strictly from a customer-relations standpoint we wonder why any business would brusquely snub an intensely loyal bloc of customers.[67]

The Tigers were on the defensive. Their hole card was a threat to move to another city.[68] When the Tiger Stadium Fan Club obtained a copy of the 1978 lease between the Tigers and the city in autumn 1990, that card was revealed to be a deuce and deuces weren't wild. Although legal opinion differed, the consensus was that the Tigers had no escape clause in the lease and were bound by it until the year 2008. They could be released only if the Detroit city government agreed.[69] That agreement might be forthcoming for a new stadium within Detroit, but it was not going to be granted for the Tigers' departure.

The only remaining source of funding was county government. County Executive Ed McNamara and his deputy Mike Duggan approached Campbell, Haase, and Schembechler in December. The county told them that they were there to help build a stadium. They would prefer it to be in Detroit, but it could be raised in a suburb. The Tigers insisted on the city, however. Schembechler emphasized that 'there was absolutely no thought of the Tigers going outside the Detroit area. Even the suburbs were not politically possible. Because the Lions and the Pistons were gone, the Tigers couldn't leave.'[70] Nor did the lease allow it. The county made special efforts to get the press back on its side, revealing the sites considered by leaving plans on a table for reporters to see.[71] If they were to float any bond issues, they had to have the press's support.

Before a firm proposal could be tendered, however, club spokespersons made two more blunders that alienated public opinion. In a rather off-handed comment to someone whom he apparently assumed was an out-of-town reporter, Monaghan referred to Detroit as 'one of the worst baseball cities' in America and asserted that fans' perception about crime make the location a liability.

Detroit NAACP President Art Johnson declared that a relocation of the Tigers 'would be the most serious insult to race relations in this region that I have seen.' Young called Monaghan's statement a 'racist perception of the city of Detroit.'[72] Metro Times characterized Monaghan as 'the only capitalist in America to publicly trash his place of business when he stated that Tiger Stadium is perceived by fans to be located in a high crime area.' It referred to the week of Monaghan's remarks as Fan Alienation Week.[73]

That week had hardly passed when Schembechler gave an address at the Economic Club of Michigan that came to be known as the 'Rusted Girder Speech.' In it, Schembechler invoked heroes of the past, promised to rebuild the farm system, and mentioned imminent financial problems. He concluded with the theme of a building that was collapsing: 'It's unfair for you to think you can shackle us to a rusted girder in Tiger Stadium and win, because it's not going to work.' He ruled out renovation, demanded that the community provide a new ballpark, and implied that, without one, the Tigers might have to depart. Haase 'had no idea what was coming.' Schembechler had spoken extemporaneously.[74] Although the audience applauded, the furor in the press was immediate. The Tigers were accused of grabbing for the public pocket and told to leave the 'bull' behind; Schembechler was condemned for acting like the 'god' he had become at the University of Michigan.[75] The Fan Club highlighted internal contradictions of his comments: 'The most amazing assertion in Bo Schembechler's Economic Club harangue was his complaint that more than half the seats in Tiger Stadium have obstructed views. Since the Tigers for years have marked about 3,000 seats as obstructed-view, that means Bo has discovered about 23,000 more in his short tenure as club president.'[76]

In a board meeting the previous year, the club had decided that there was to be one spokesperson for the stadium, and that was to be Schembechler. Since he was already being blamed (wrongly) for Harwell's dismissal, Schembechler was a poor choice to be front man. *Esquire* (July 1991) included Monaghan and Schembechler on their list of 'most annoying people' in America. Communications with the mayor's office were breaking down.[77] Tiger executives were unused to public criticism and did not know how to respond.

The county hoped to raise money from two sources. A 1971 state law allowed counties with a population of more than 1.5 million to collect a 5 per cent hotel tax for stadium construction; that revenue could support a bond issue.[78] Senator John Kelly and others, however, introduced in Lansing on 14 March an amendment to the Building Authorities and Revenue Bond Act outlawing such bonds to be issued for constructing a new professional baseball stadium. The second hope was to create an enterprise zone that might be eligible for federal funding. Duggan promised developers the moon: 'Tax breaks, expedited building permits, zoning exemptions. Tell us what it will take ... We're going to the State and the city to make this a development-friendly zone.'[79]

By the spring the Tigers became pawns in a political game between McNamara and Young. County and city officials fought publicly over who was in charge and where the stadium would be located.[80] Young said, 'Under no circumstances will I allow the county to go ahead without the city ... I don't know what the county has but a lot of nerve.' A temporary truce was reached in July when Alfred Taubman and a group of business leaders recommended the establishment of a Detroit / Wayne County Stadium Authority to spearhead development of a new stadium and surrounding area. Although some of the press enthused about a development that might revitalize Detroit, the funding and location remained contentious. Polls opposed taxpayers' money being used for a stadium.[81] Haase recognized that 'the club had to put in some money politically and should. Without it, there is no public support.'[82] Newpapers demanded: 'Where is Monaghan's money?'[83] The answer was there was no Monaghan money. His financial situation had reached crisis proportions by 1990–1.

Detroit was becoming more isolated from the white enclaves around it and from the state. The Joanne Was incident frightened suburbanites. Famous, long-standing downtown restaurants like the London Chop House, the Pontchartrain Wine Cellars, and Galligan's closed their doors. So did the Statler Hilton hotel. Any public funding depended on cooperation by the city, county, state, and the Detroit Baseball Club. Political antagonism between these bodies and their constituencies made such cooperation impossible.

The last hope for local public funding during the Young administration and Monaghan's ownership was dashed in March 1992. At a meeting of the Fan Club in the summer of 1991, someone suggested a ballot initiative to restrict city funds for the stadium. Out of that emerged the Common Ground Coalition, a group of religious and community leaders with connections to downtown Detroit.[84] They gathered enough signatures for a referendum. On 17 March 1992 Detroit voters approved by a 63–37 per cent margin an ordinance banning the use of any city money for building a new stadium. That vote was a severe setback not only to the baseball club, but also to the Wayne County officials who had counted on Detroit's support for a financing package.

After purchasing the club, Ilitch replaced Tiger executives with his own people, who immediately took a new tack. Within weeks, Ilitch met with the Fan Club and examined the Cochrane Plan, on 24 September 1992. The Fan Club's newsletter reported the meeting was 'cordial, detailed and productive' - Ilitch and Tiger officials expressed interest in the potential of the plan for meeting the club's needs.[85] Ilitch, however, made clear the following June his commitment to a new stadium. He promised $150–200 million to pay for a new stadium if about $200 million of public money was provided for the lands and roads.[86] The press rallied to his support. Charlie Vincent summarized the new situation: 'Grass-roots activism is a wonderful concept, but it doesn't really accomplish much any more. The truth of the matter is – in our county – nothing talks so loudly as money. And Ilitch's money began screaming the day he said he would pay for the construction of a stadium out of his pocket.'[87] In November 1993, Detroit Democratic Representative Morris Hood introduced a bill for a new Tiger Stadium that had the blessing of the team, city officials, and the governor's office. The state was to provide $100–250 million for roads, land, demolition of buildings, and parking lots. But taxpayers were no more willing to dig into their pockets than before. Seventy-nine per cent of Michigan taxpayers opposed state dollars for the stadium at the end of the year. Early in 1994, there was still opposition from 67 per cent of all voters, 71 per cent of outstate voters, and 61 per cent from the tri-county area.[88]

On 23 March 1994 Ilitch released details of his plan for the development of Foxtown that the *News* enthused 'would give the city its greatest boost since Henry Ford II raised the Renaissance Center.'[89] It received front-page headlines in both Detroit papers. After a visit to Baltimore, Cleveland, and Chicago, Mayor Archer gave his support for the stadium; Council voted its assent 5–2.

Nevertheless, the project depended on public funding from the state, and questions remained. Joe Stroud, editor of the *Free Press*, queried why this plan was a 'better use of the money than the possible alternatives.' Four days later the *Free Press* complimented Ilitch's vision of 'a new Detroit [which] would bustle with the vibrancy it knew in the 1950s ...

But it is just that: a vision.' Pete Waldmeir pessimistically concluded that outstate voters 'don't really give a hoot about sending anything to Detroit – particularly when it's going to help a rich man get richer.'[90] Bill McGraw asked some fundamental questions about public funds being used for this project and the way they had been used to subsidize Ilitch's Fox Theater project.[91] The stadium bill stalled in committee in June 1994 after legislators complained that they were being asked to approve money for a stadium without costs or details about where the money would come from.

By June Ilitch was musing that it might be cheaper to build in Romulus. Six months later, Lisa Ilitch Murray threatened that the Tigers might leave south-east Michigan altogether despite her father's promise 'never to move' when he bought the club.[92] Mayor Archer announced in December that there would be no more serious talk about a future stadium until the major-league players' strike had ended. Disgusted with the strike, a *News* editorial criticized 'socialism' in baseball; it should not be 'a money machine for exploiting the masses.'[93] Ilitch announced in January 1995 that he could no longer commit $150 million of his own money, but on 8 February new president John McHale Jr announced that a new stadium would be 'a priority.'

On 14 September 1995 McHales's hopes reached fruition with the announcement of a deal with the state for funding, details of which were announced a week later. The nine-member Michigan Strategic Fund Board voted 8–1 to grant $55 million 'for the purchase of land and infrastructure around the baseball club's proposed new stadium' on a twenty-five-acre tract off Woodward Avenue, above Grand Circus Park. Cost was estimated at $230–250 million, of which the Tigers would pay half – more than any other club has paid up front. *Sports Value*, a newsletter published by *Financial World*, predicted that Ilitch might receive a quick return on his investment, estimating that the value of the franchise could increase from $83 million to $205 million with a new stadium. Both the Red Wings and the Pistons top lists of franchise value in their respective sports in 1995, so the Detroit market can be a profitable one.[94] The city announced its participation with a $35 million share (later raised to $40 million) on 27 October, by refinancing existing Downtown Development Authority Bonds, the issuance of which was announced on 4 December. The club has to negotiate a fifteen-year lease and open the publicly owned stadium by 1 October 1999 or pay the state back. The open-air stadium is to be of 'classic design,' with natural turf and about 10 per cent of its 42,000 seats in the bleachers. Although the *Detroit News* supported the project, the *Free Press* initially continued its editorial opposition on the basis of possible cost overruns, unlikely stimulation of jobs, historical preservation considerations, and 'blackmail by sports teams.' The fan club and Michigan Taxpayers United also opposed funding as 'corporate welfare.' State Senator George Hart and the fan club filed suit on 2 November to halt the use of state money, quoting the State Constitution that 'no money shall be paid out of the state treasury except in pursuance of appropriations made by law.'[95] It also opposed any city bonds for the project. On 5 January 1996 Archer announced that the club had obtained $140 million in financing and that the city council had approved (7–2) a $40 million bond issue as part of a $160 million issue by the Detroit Development Authority, whose boundaries were extended to include the stadium site. But the Fan Club also presented 10,000 signatures (needing 8107) to force the city's funding onto a 19 March ballot.

This time the attempt to forbid the council from issuing bonds failed decisively, 108,310 to 24,982 (81%–19%). The *Free Press* switched its editorial position to support for the stadium project. The *Michigan Chronicle* and African American church leaders supported it as well.[96] On the final Sunday before the ballot, Ilitch, Archer, and Young attended church rallies, culminating a $600,000 advertising blitz that promised ancillary benefits, no new taxes, and 'what was best for Detroit.' Although the Fan Club had 10,000 members, it could spend only $20,000 and was politically isolated. Two days later Judge James Giddings in Ingham County ruled that similar revenues from Indian Casino gambling 'are essentially private funds' and 'never became state funds subject to appropriation.' Both the *Free Press* and the *News* advised the Fan Club not to be 'obstructionist' but to serve as a 'continuing watchdog' over the project.[97] The Fan Club did appeal, however. On 5 July 1996 the State Appeals Court ruled, 3–0, that the governor's use of state funds was legal. The Fan Club appealed that decision to the state Supreme Court, which declined to review the Appeals Court decision on 14 August. Six days later, the Detroit Lions announced their intention to move to a new $225 million domed football stadium next to the baseball one.

In June 1996 Robert Buchta summarized his feelings about the Fan Club's efforts:

Whatever the outcome of the stadium fight, I think the Fan Club has accomplished a good deal. By winning the city ballot initiative in 1992 and continuing to question the propriety of raising taxes for a statium, we marshalled public pressure on local and state governments to limit the kinds and amounts of public dollars for a private sports enterprise. To the extent that we focused attention on the drawbacks of Monaghan's proposal for a stadium in a self-contained island apart from the rest of the city, we may have contributed to his decision to sell the team. Although we continue to question the wisdom of any new stadium investment, at least the Ilitches favor a genuinely urban setting. And in the final analysis we may have helped to add five years or more to the life of a classic ballpark. Perhaps the greatest beneficiaries of that five-year grace period are the children whose earliest baseball memories will now be rooted in the same sights and sounds and smells their grandparents thrilled to.

Penury of the city and of Monaghan Enterprises, grass-roots politics by the Tiger Stadium Fan Club, and divisions over a host of political and social issues between Detroit, the outlying tri-county region, and out-state Michigan had doomed the Monaghan-Young project. The 1995 deal was possible only because of improved relations between the mayor's office and Lansing. Dennis Archer made a conscious effort to improve relations between Detroit, the suburbs, and the state. *Newsweek* noted: 'To those beyond the city limits, he [Archer] offered an end to the racial demagoguery of the Young Era and an approach based on regional cooperation.' Gregg Berendt, then mayor of Grosse Pointe Farms, observed: 'Archer recognized that "Detroit" is not just the city but the surrounding community as well.'[98] Ilitch, unlike Monaghan, was willing to put up substantial capital of his own. Nevertheless, outstate polls and the Republican caucus in the legislature still opposed public funding. State support came through administrative decree rather than by referendum or legislative vote.[99] Club, city, and state reunited in a venture deemed essential to the preservation of major league baseball in Detroit and the vitality of the city center. A sports-entertainment complex, it is hoped, will provoke 'synergy' around it.

It has been more than a decade since the Tigers embarked on a project to obtain a new stadium. Cleveland had the only municipal stadium in the country in 1950; now only four teams lack them.[100] Six municipal stadiums were built in the late 1980s; Camden Yards, the new Comiskey Park, and Cleveland's sports complex have been built in the 1990s. In 1995 Wisconsin voters approved money for a new stadium in Milwaukee and the Washington state legislature voted to build a new one in Seattle. Cincinnati voters approved funding the same week that Detroiters did and a privately funded enterprise in San Francisco is being debated. All of these ventures face court challenges from taxpayer groups. Baltimore's $230 million stadium was 90 per cent publicly funded from an instant lottery and a $0.10 tax on tickets. The Arlington, Texas, park received 75 per cent public funding with a half-cent city sales tax. Cleveland's $460 million project ($290 million for the sports complex and $170 million for baseball) had 50 per cent public funding originally from a county sin tax on alcohol and tobacco. Cost overruns may push the public share to 70 per cent. Chicago's $150 million park received 100 per cent public funding. Funding of two different Baltimore stadiums (Memorial in 1954 and Camden Yards in 1992) received criticism. John Feinstein wrote: 'If you cut through all the political mumbo-jumbo and hype, what had happened was simple, Edward Bennett Williams, then the team's owner, had blackmailed the State of Maryland into building him a new ballpark. How had he managed this? By threatening to take the team elsewhere.'[101]

The House Subcommittee on Antitrust Monopolies in 1989 concluded that owners used threats to move to another city 'to extort concessions from local taxpayers.'[102] Franchises can move. Stadiums are fixed by their nature. A number of recent critics have questioned the economic benefits of the new sports stadium: 'The vast majority of stadiums built in the last three decades ... cover the operating costs of hosting a team but not the fixed costs ... Construction cost overruns on average have been 73%.'[103]

The Detroit Baseball Club's prospectus for buyers demonstrates that revenue enhancement was the principal reason that the club wanted a new stadium:

A new stadium would allow for several possible revenue enhancements, including club seating, luxury sky boxes, the provision of stadium run and supervised parking, elimination of obstructed view seats, wider concourse areas, increased concession selling, and increased signage areas. Several new stadiums have been built recently, resulting in a substantial attendance increase for the home club.

From a revenue standpoint, the Tigers' seating breakdown of 22% box seats and 21% bleacher seats compares unfavorably to the League average of 36% and 6% respectively. A new stadium would likely include a higher percentage of box seats and fewer bleacher seats.

The prospectus estimated that 100,000 more fans would produce $1 million in revenue. Attendance had increased by an average of 62 per cent in the first five years of new stadiums (1960–82), and luxury boxes would provide additional income. The loss of the big national television contracts in 1994 resulted in a significant loss of income for baseball. Luxury boxes have become the source of new revenue, accounting for 20 per cent of team revenues. Unlike other gate receipts, they are not shared with the visiting team.[104] Teams lacking such revenue are doomed to be among the poorer clubs, hard-pressed to compete on the field in this era.

A new stadium received community support for a different reason. An outspoken African American leader in Detroit made clear that he favored using public funds for the new stadium – although he stipulated that African Americans should get construction contracts – because it was crucial to the vitality of downtown. Arthur Johnson, president of the NAACP, criticized the Fan Club, which had been viewed as defenders of downtown interests, for obstruction and being 'disloyal to the city.' Newspaper columnists have supported a new stadium because they fear the departure of the team, which would be a 'disaster even to the suburbs.' A stadium 'might not save downtown, but without it, downtown Detroit would be lost.' The loss would be 'a mortal blow to downtown.'[105]

A scientific poll revealed that 85 per cent of Detroiters agreed: 'It's important to Detroit's image and psychology to keep the Tigers in Detroit.'[106] Sports have helped define Detroit's community and reminded people of better times in Detroit. Tiger Stadium has been the most familiar building in the state, resurrecting images of heroes like Cobb, Heilmann, Gehringer, and Cochrane. Icons are not easy to abandon, but keeping the team in Detroit has become the paramount concern. The classic design of the proposed park attempts to link the present with the past.

Epilogue:
The 1994 Strike and Its Aftermath

The 1994 season might have gone down in history as one of baseball's greatest, remembered like that of 1927 or 1941. It was a season of offensive fireworks with teams on a pace to hit more home runs and score more runs than anytime since 1930. Tony Gwynn was hitting .394 when the season ended. Matt Williams, Ken Griffey Jr, and Frank Thomas threatened to break Roger Maris's record of sixty-one home runs. Thomas was challenging Ruth's season marks for walks, runs scored, and total bases. Amidst all the offense, a bespectacled pitcher, Greg Maddux, achieved a 1.56 ERA, one full run less than any other qualifying pitcher and nearly three runs below the league average. Instead, the season ended abruptly on 12 August with baseball's eighth work stoppage since 1972. Team owners cancelled the season and all post-season play on 14 September. For the first time since the First World War abbreviated the 1918 season, there was no major-league baseball after Labor Day. For the first time since 1904, there was no World Series. Nineteen ninety-four was just the 'Year of the Strike.'[1]

Thirteen years earlier, *Metropolitan Detroit* had warned that what threatened baseball was 'greed, greed, just plain greed.'[2] Greed seemed to have swallowed up the game for good in 1994. The prosperity of the 1980s had not brought labor peace. The strike was rooted in avarice and the players' and owners' ascending mutual distrust. Collusion, which the owners never admitted, embittered the players, who long had distrusted their employers. The owners, for their part, felt that they had lost every battle. The atmosphere got chillier and greedier. After an abortive thirty-two-day lockout during spring training, 1990, Bud Selig (Milwaukee) and Jerry Reinsdorf (Chicago White Sox) 'immediately thought 1994 was going to be the year and they'd have to do things differently ... They needed to get their way this time.'[3] On 28 August 1992, in response to a question about how the owners could get what they wanted, Reinsdorf replied: 'You do it by taking a position and telling them we're not going to play unless we make a deal and being prepared not to play one or two years if you have to.'[4] The owners had wanted a salary cap in 1990, but Commissioner Fay Vincent intervened to take that off the table and to wring out a collective bargaining arrangement that would be due for renewal in 1994. On 7 September 1992 he resigned under pressure from hard-line owners. Exactly three months later baseball's magnates voted to reopen economic aspects of the 1990 collective agreement. They reached an internal agreement about revenue redistribution among clubs on 18 January 1994 but linked that to players' acceptance of a salary cap in a 14 June proposal to the players. A confrontation loomed.

The sorry tale of the negotiations – or lack thereof – that captured attention in all major newspapers need not be retold here.[5] Federal arbitrators were brought in without success. Congress threatened legislation to revoke baseball's antitrust exemption, but never passed any. The players' association expected the owners to fold as they had in the past. Donald Fehr, lawyer and chief negotiator for the association, admitted that he might have waited until the last week of the season to call a strike if he had known that the owners would not budge.[6] This was a power struggle. The strike ended after the players' association filed an unfair-labor-practices complaint with the National Labor Relations Board, which in turn filed for an injunction that was granted by U.S. District Judge Sonia Sotomayor on 30 March 1995.

The national press had become impatient with both sides before the strike began. George Will wrote: 'The owners spent the 1980s proving themselves dishonest and dimwitted ... Players are privileged to be temporary participants in a great cultural institution ... the owners are privileged to have temporary custody of that institution.' *Newsweek* admonished a sport that is 'slowly committing suicide with crass commercialism, growing disregard for fans and bad business sense.' *Time* condemned the 'governance and power relations' of baseball.[7]

The strike was headline news both in newspapers and on network television, which condemned both sides. The *AP* warned: 'The damage to baseball could be incalculable ... Baseball will lurch into an uncertain future with all deliberate greed.' It was a 'dispute between two gluttonous sides,' 'a weigh-in.'[8] 'The game is drunk with power.' 'Never before has the naked power struggle between the players and owners been so heedless and so self-destructive.' 'Fans everywhere are disgusted at the greed that may be destroying America's game.'[9] An *AP* poll indicated that a few more fans blamed the players than the owners, but a majority damned both in polls, in letters to editors, and on talk shows. As the *Free Press* observed: 'The owners live such fortunate lives; the players live such fortunate lives. They should have been able to solve this.' A week later, when the season was cancelled, the *Free Press* printed a tombstone with R.I.P. etched on it. The end of the strike was again headline news, but columnists like Mike Albom, letters to newspapers, and fan behavior at opening games evidenced a general disgust. The *Detroit News* warned: 'The game that can't solve its own problems again will be exposed for the mess it's become.'[10] A seventy-three year old who had played baseball in the backyard with her brothers and grandfather expressed poignantly the hurt felt by many: 'Baseball has lost its soul and it lost my heart.'[11] By 1994 everyone knew that baseball was a business. They were shocked that it seemed to be only a business.

There was an economic problem that needed to be addressed. The end of the national television contract after the 1993 season meant that the biggest source of *shared* revenue among teams would be cut by more than half. Large-market teams would have a permanent advantage over smaller-market teams. Small-market teams like Minnesota, Montreal, and Pittsburgh had produced successful teams through their farm systems; both New York teams had squandered money without buying success. Nevertheless, only big-market teams could afford to keep star players, necessary to maintain success. Arbitration awards, which were based entirely on a player's performance without consideration of a club's revenue, had doubled the salaries of those players who won arbitration cases in 1990. Owners could have decided to share local television revenue with visiting teams as they did gate attendance. Such sharing had been proposed in the 1950s but came to naught (chapter 1). Or they could have split the gate with visiting teams (a common practice early in the century) without linking such sharing with a salary cap. The agreement two years later (21 March 1996) to share a percentage of all local revenue was not linked to a salary cap.[12] Bud Selig, chief negotiator for the owners, claimed that they were only trying to preserve competition, stability, and fan affordability,[13] but they had increased ticket, concession, and parking fees at the very time that they had all the riches from the 1990 television contract. Billionaire owners, squabbling among themselves while pleading altruism, elicited little sympathy from fans who were paying higher prices while they were reading and hearing about the enormous profits of this unregulated cartel. The press had educated fans about the business of the game for over two decades.

Millionaire players – and there were more than three hundred of them in 1994 – were no better placed to marshall support from fans. Resistance to a salary cap protected the highest salaries in the game, not the earnings or pension of a journeyman. The players' association, with private entrepreneurship within the collective agreement, was unlike any other striking trade union outside of sport. Fehr's sneer and arrogance on television bytes did not improve public relations. Superstars made more money in a year than the average fan could make in a lifetime. Sixteen of them received more than $5 million in 1993. They still insisted on being paid to sign autographs and then tried to evade paying taxes on that income. The IRS claimed that Darryl Strawberry had collected one million dollars over five years but paid no taxes. Hall of Famer Duke Snider pleaded guilty to tax evasion in 1995. As popular as Lou Whitaker has been in Detroit, his motoring to negotiations and to camp in his limousine was not easily digested.[14] A few hundred people could not figure out how to divide a $2 billion pie of revenue.

Multimillion-dollar players were part of the selfishness of the 1990s. President Clinton thought the strike was 'a metaphor for what's wrong with this country sometimes. A lot of money controlled by a few people who can't decide how to divide it up.'[15] A corporate CEO's remuneration, on average, had been thirteen times that of the lowest-paid worker in 1960. Many of them were making 135 times a worker's pay in 1995. In big companies, the average salaries and benefits reached $5 million despite the firing of workers (euphemistically termed 'downsizing').[16] Players were part of *The Winner Take All Society*, described by Robert Frank in 1994. That did not make the strike any easier to stomach. Most fans wanted a pox on both their houses.

The pox came in the form of financial losses. Attendance for the abbreviated season fell from 70 million to 50 million. Cancellation of the play-offs and World Series sharply reduced media income. Teams collected, on average, $11.5 million, instead of an expected $19.8 million.[17] Networks lost more than $100 million in advertising revenue, owners something between $600 million and $800 million, and players $350 million. The licensed sports industry, which was a $13.8 billion-dollar business in 1994, $2.5 billion of which derived from baseball (up from $450 million in 1987), suffered a major decline.[18] Free agents got less in 1995. At least ten of them took cuts of $2 million; Tettleton's was $1 million. The average baseball salary declined by 5 per cent in 1995, but was still $1.1 million (table 16). The average Yankee took in more than $2 million. Players technically won the strike, but only stars could be certain of commanding the same salaries as before. The gap between rich and poor teams and between stars and other players was greater in 1996 than ever before. One hundred players received more than half of the total payroll.[19] No one won. Baseball lost.

Fans had always come back after previous work stoppages. Not this time, at least not immediately. During the month of July 1994, when the strike was merely threatened, those calling themselves baseball fans declined from 33 to 26 per cent of the American public. A Reuter/ABC poll in April 1995 revealed that only 28 per cent considered themselves baseball fans, down from 44 per cent in the year before the strike. Seventy-nine per cent of respondents asserted that labor disputes 'have taken the fun out of the game'; a majority was 'disgusted.' At the end of the 1995 season, 56 per cent of fans still had a 'less favorable' view of pro sports than they had the summer before.[20] In 1960 baseball was Americans' favorite sport; by 1972 it had fallen behind football; by 1995 it was behind basketball too, with the allegiance of only 12 per cent after 34 per cent in 1961 and 24 per cent in 1971.

The owners were determined to play the 1995 season with 'replacement' players if necessary. Only Peter Angelos of Baltimore refused to follow that course. The Toronto Blue Jays resisted because they would have had to play their home games in Florida owing to an Ontario law (since rescinded by a Conservative government) that forbade the replacement of striking workers. A majority of fans said that they would be 'unlikely to attend one game' under such circumstances. Sacrificing

$150,000 in salary, Sparky Anderson refused to manage replacement players: 'I cannot bargain my integrity.'[21] He had been battling with management anyway. Fans stayed away from spring training games. The Tigers drew about 2000 per game instead of the 6000 to 7000 of the previous year; spring-training crowds were down by about two-thirds generally. The *New York Times* stopped printing schedules and box scores, and WABC radio sued the Yankees for $10 million of expected lost revenue from 'sham' games.[22]

When the season did begin with the regular players, fans vented their annoyance by showering fields with debris on opening day or by simply staying home. Crowds were down from 1994 at twelve of the fourteen openings. They were off 25 per cent in the first month and 20 per cent at the All-Star Game. At the end attendance was 20 million (28 per cent) below 1993's record. In contrast, minor-league attendance increased by 10 per cent in 1994 and 30 per cent from 1990 to 1995 (table 2). Television ratings for the All-Star Game were the lowest in twenty-eight years; fans cast 5.4 million ballots for player selection, down from 14 million the year before.[23] Teams offered discounts and launched massive public-relations campaigns in an attempt to placate their customers. The Tigers halved bleacher tickets to $2.50 ($1 for those fourteen and younger), arranged corporate tie-ins, and offered 'family value packages' for Mondays to Wednesdays, with four tickets, soft drinks, and hot dogs or pizza slices for $24, discounted from $60. Harwell advertised the package on radio. Tom Boswell of the *Washington Post* thought players 'nicer' after the strike.[24] At least they were less belligerent.

Baseball had lost its innocence and heroes. As luck would have it, Cal Ripken Jr offered fans someone to admire. He turned out for work every day, had played for the same team his entire career, and signed autographs without charge. He epitomized old-fashioned values. On 6 September 1995, before the home crowd at Camden Yards, he broke Lou Gehrig's 'unbreakable' mark of playing in 2130 straight games. Fans and the media rallied to him as a symbol of an imagined simpler time when players played for the love of the game and, as A. Bartlett Giamatti had believed, 'baseball was a public trust.' Both *Sports Illustrated* and *The Sporting News* acclaimed him 'Sportsman of the Year.' For a time players' heroics, pennant races, and a new wild-card race were the main items on sports pages.

Fans had voted with their feet by staying away from ballparks, but in the comfort of their homes they had not lost interest. Local television ratings and those of ESPN (the only national outlet for the regular season in 1995) were stable in 1995. The New York–Seattle play-off excited fans across the nation and the last four World Series games finished in the top ten of most watched television hours of the week, even if the ratings were lower than the 20.2 average achieved from 1990 to 1993. All-sports radio stations increased to 148 in 1995; ESPN reached a record 60 million subscribers (90 million worldwide in 1995).[25] The networks apparently retain faith in baseball's drawing power. NBC and ABC had pulled out of the Baseball Network in June, blaming executives for 'a trail of broken promises.' NBC's president then predicted: 'I can't imagine being involved in baseball the rest of this century.'[26] Yet, in November, baseball signed a $1.68 billion contract through the year 2000 with NBC, ESPN, and Liberty Sports. The Saturday afternoon Game of the Week would be restored after a two-year absence and all play-off games would be televised by staggering the starting times. ESPN and Prime Liberty Media Cable would expand night coverage. It was remarkably good financial news for baseball.

Detroit rose from last in attendance to eleventh in the American League in 1995. Major-league club attendance averaged more than 25,000 in 1995. Seven clubs topped 30,000 and fourteen (half) exceeded 24,000.[27] Cleveland's first pennant race in four decades and a new stadium restored fan excitement in that city weeks before it learned that it would lose its NFL franchise. The sale of the St Louis Cardinals' franchise brought $150 million and Pittsburgh, despite big losses and the lowest attendance in baseball, sold for $90 million. After a 25 per cent decline in team merchandise revenue from 1993 to 1995, marketing revenue increased in 1996, as did attendance. By September 1996, *News-week*, *Sports Illustrated*, and the *New York Times* were lauding baseball's resiliency.[28] Fans came back after every other work stoppage, but none was like the 1994 strike. Baseball's last commissioner, Fay Vincent, presciently warned in a press conference at Fairfield, Connecticut, on 21 February 1991: 'Baseball is poised for a catastrophe and it might not be far off.'[29] The catastrophe struck, but by 1996 baseball seemed on the road to recovery. Whether the owners and players will botch things again remains to be seen.

TABLES

TABLE 1
Major-league paid regular-season attendance, 1930–60 (in millions)

Decade	Attendance	Year	Attendance	Percentage increase/decline
1900s	50	1930	10.1	–
1910s	56	1933	6.1	–40%
1920s	93	1940	9.8	61
1930s	81	1943	7.5	–23
1940s	135	1945	10.8	44
1950s	165	1946	18.5	71
1960s	224	1948	20.9	13
		1950	17.5	–16
		1953	14.4	–18
		1955	16.6	15
		1960	19.9	14

Sources: Celler Commission (1952), 1616; 'Retrospective' in TSN, *Baseball Guide* 1979. The (official) *Baseball Guide* publishes annual figures, as did *The Sporting News* in its annual January review during the 1940s and 1950s; the last are often slightly different, perhaps because they are preliminary. Thorn and Palmer, *Total Baseball* (668), calculates figures by decade. Attendance figures since 1901 for all teams have been compiled in Quirk and Fort, *Paydirt,* and in *Total Baseball* (1995), 106–9.

TABLE 2
Minor-league total attendance, 1930–95*

Year	Paid attendance	Number of leagues	Clubs	Average club attendance
1930	11,100,000	25		
1933	7,200,000	14		
1940	15,100,000	44	310	48,700
1943	5,800,000	9	66	87,900
1945	10,656,000	19	85	125,400
1947	40,505,210	52	406	99,800
1948	40,949,028	58	452	90,600
1949	41,872,762	59	464	90,301
1950	34,534,488	58	446	77,400
1952	25,301,253	43	324	78,100
1955	19,042,825	33	243	78,400
1960	10,974,084	22	152	72,200
1965	9,887,000	19	138	71,600
1970	10,726,470	20	150	71,500
1975	11,021,848	18	137	80,400
1981**	16,178,790	17	152	106,400
1985	18,380,000	18	168	109,400
1990	25,244,569	16	164	153,900
1993	30,022,761	16	169	177,600
1994	33,355,199	16	172	193,900
1995	33,126,934	16	172	192,600

Sources: For the years for 1930–45, see Celler (1952), 1616; these were 'estimates.' For 1947–60, see Objoski, *Bush League*, 27. The Celler Commission lists slightly lower figures but within 2 per cent for 1947–51. For 1965–95, see National Association of Professional Baseball Leagues' Office.

* Includes both regular-season and playoff games through 1960. Only regular season thereafter. Record regular-season attendance was in 1949: 39,782,717.
** 1980 was year of Mexican League players' strike.

TABLE 3
Salaries/bonuses as percentage of total expenditures, 1929–93

Year	Salary share*(%)	Minor-league share** (%)
1929	35.3	10.3
1933	35.9	10.9
1939	32.4	7.5
1943	28.9	15.3
1946	24.8	5.4
1950	22.1	12.6
1974	17.6	13.3
1977	20.5	11.3
1980	31.3	11.4
1981	39.1	n.a.
1983	41.1	10.9
1989	31.6	12.6
1991	41.2	n.a.
1993	48.5 (est.)	n.a.

Sources: Zimbalist, *Baseball and Billions*, 87; Noll, 'Baseball Economics.'

* Salary share through 1950 includes salaries to coaches and managers and is a share of total expenditures, not revenues. Benefits are not included.
** Total expenditures on minor-league system. Through 1979 the share is based on total expenditures.

TABLE 4
Baseball's total broadcasting revenues, 1933–90 (in thousands of dollars)

Year	Local rights	National rights	Total rights	Average per club
1933	18	0	18	1
1939	885	0	885	55
1946	838	0	838	52
1950	3,365	0	3,365	210
1955	6,123	1,185	7,308	383
1960	9,355	3,174	15,779*	783
1965	15,970	5,950	25,670*	1,096
1970	21,850	16,600	38,150	1,310
1975	26,495	18,000	44,495	1,854
1980	38,650	41,575	80,275	3,088
1985	116,900	161,000	277,900	10,688
1990	342,100	365,000	707,000	27,192

Sources: Horowitz, 'Sports Broadcasting,' 287; Scully, *Business of Baseball*, 108.

* The Yankees, who had separate national contracts, are not included.

TABLE 5
Detroit Tigers' attendance figures, 1945–96

Year	Attendance
1945	1,280,341
1946	1,722,590
1947	1,398,093
1948	1,743,035
1949	1,821,204
1950	1,951,474
1951	1,132,641
1952	1,026,846
1953	884,658
1954	1,079,847
1955	1,181,838
1956	1,051,182
1957	1,272,346
1958	1,098,924
1959	1,221,221
1960	1,167,669
1961	1,600,710
1962	1,207,881
1963	821,952
1964	816,139
1965	1,029,645
1966	1,124,293
1967	1,447,143
1968	2,031,847
1969	1,577,481
1970	1,501,293
1971	1,591,073
1972	1,892,386
1973	1,724,146
1974	1,243,080
1975	1,058,836
1976	1,467,020
1977	1,359,856
1978	1,714,893
1979	1,630,929
1980	1,785,293
1981	1,149,144
1982	1,636,058
1983	1,829,636
1984	2,704,794
1985	2,286,609
1986	1,899,437

TABLE 5 (*Continued*)
Detroit Tigers' attendance figures, 1945–96

Year	Attendance
1987	2,061,830
1988	2,081,162
1989	1,543,656
1990	1,495,785
1991	1,641,661
1992	1,423,963
1993	1,971,421
1994	1,184,783
1995	1,180,979
1996	1,168,610

TABLE 6
Detroit Tigers' profits, 1938–51

1938–44	$ 516,000
1945	192,000
1946	469,000
1947	197,000
1948	255,000
1949	33,000
1950	113,000
1951	297,000
TOTAL	$2,072,000

Source: *TSN* (7/18/56), 6–8.

Note: Figures are based on records made public in 1956 at time of sale.

TABLE 7
Detroit Tigers' profits, income, and expenses, 1952–6

Profits

	1952–56	1952	1953	1954	1955	1956
Major-league operations	2,682,266	420,691	327,668	474,622	879,712	579,712
All operations (net profit)	851,518	(26,265)	43,639	114,572	529,962	189,610
Net after taxes	442,621	(26,265)	43,639	86,465	257,191	96,645

Income (in thousands of dollars)

Year	Gate	Radio/TV	Concessions	Other	Total
1956	1,675	403	297	205	2,581
1955	1,872	348	351	338	2,908
1954	1,512	328	239	351	2,430
1953	1,285	316	189	367	2,157
1952	1,429	320	203	303	2,256
1951	1,479	201	164	100	1,944
1947	1,540	175	184	34	1,933

Expenses

Year	All (exclusive of player salaries)	Player development	Stadium depreciation
1956	1,795,272	459,263	120,407
1955	1,773,035	397,594	157,811
1954	1,695,485	413,683	150,136
1953	1,483,456	310,628	149,371
1952	1,610,484	468,285	149,069

Source: Celler (1957), 1297–8, 2032–5, 2048–53. 1947 and 1951 income figures are from private records of Jim Campbell.

Note: For the period, before taxes New York Yankees made nearly $4 million, Cleveland more than $2 million. P. 2032 shows net profit as $189,610 in 1956 vs $529,862 on p. 1298, which is probably an error since it is almost identical with 1955. P. 1298 shows $81,591 as after-tax profit, but p. 2032 shows $96,645. Precise profits were a mystery even to Congress.

TABLE 8
Detroit Tigers' payroll and players' salaries, 1929–57
(in thousands of dollars)

Detroit payroll
(Including coaches and manager)

Year	$	Rank in league
1951	625	n/a
1950	549	2nd
1946	505	2nd
1943	173	7th
1939	297	2nd
1933	139	8th
1929	186	7th

Players' salaries

	1947	1950	1951	1952	1953	1954	1955	1956	1957
Total	477	452.5	539	380	335	279	292	362	395
Mean	n/a	18.1	n/a	14.6	13.4	12.1	12.1	14.5	n/a
Median	n/a	15.0	n/a	13.1	13.0	10.0	9.3	13.0	n/a
Detroit rank in league	n/a	2nd	n/a	3rd	4th	6th	5th	5th	n/a

Sources: Celler (1957), 2056; Celler (1952), 965, 1610; *TSN* (1/14/59) for 1957–8; *TSN* (7/18/56), 6, for 1951. Records of Jim Campbell for 1947.

TABLE 9
Detroit Tigers' won-lost records, 1945–96

Year	Position	W-L	Percentage	GA/GB	Manager
1996	5	53-109	.327	39	Buddy Bell
1995	4	60-84	.417	26	Sparky Anderson
1994	5	53-62	.461	18	"
1993	3T	85-77	.525	10	"
1992	6	75-87	.463	21	"
1991	2T	84-78	.519	7	"
1990	3	79-83	.488	9	"
1989	7	59-103	.364	30	"
1988	2	88-74	.543	1	"
1987	1	98-64	.605	2	"
1986	3	87-75	.537	8½	"
1985	3	84-77	.522	15	"
1984	1	104-58	.642	15	"
1983	2	92-70	.568	6	"
1982	4	83-79	.512	12	"
1981	4	60-49	.550	2	"
1980	5	84-78	.519	19	"
1979	5	85-76	.528	18	Les Moss–Sparky Anderson
1978	5	86-76	.531	13½	Ralph Houk
1977	4	74-88	.457	26	"
1976	5	74-87	.460	24	"
1975	6	57-102	.358	37½	"
1974	6	72-90	.444	19	"
1973	3	85-77	.525	12	Billy Martin–Joe Schultz
1972	1	86-70	.551	½	Billy Martin
1971	2	91-71	.562	12	"
1970	4	79-83	.488	29	Mayo Smith
1969	2	90-72	.556	19	"
1968	1	103-59	.636	12	"
1967	2T	91-71	.562	1	"
1966	3	88-74	.543	10	Dressen-Swift–Frank Skaff
1965	4	89-73	.549	12	Chuck Dressen–Bob Swift
1964	4	85-77	.525	14	Chuck Dressen
1963	5T	79-83	.488	25½	Bob Scheffing–Chuck Dressen
1962	4	85-76	.528	10½	Bob Scheffing
1961	2	101-61	.623	8	"
1960	6	71-83	.461	26	Jimmie Dykes–Joe Gordon
1959	4	76-78	.494	18	Bill Norman–Jimmie Dykes
1958	5	77-77	.500	15	Jack Tighe–Bill Norman
1957	4	78-76	.506	20	Jack Tighe
1956	5	82-72	.532	15	Bucky Harris
1955	5	79-75	.513	17	"
1954	5	68-86	.442	43	Fred Hutchinson

TABLE 9 (*Continued*)

Year	Position	W-L	Percentage	GA/GB	Manager
1953	6	60-94	.390	40½	Fred Hutchinson
1952	8	50-104	.325	45	Red Rolfe–Fred Hutchinson
1951	5	73-81	.474	25	Red Rolfe
1950	2	95-59	.617	3	"
1949	4	87-67	.565	10	"
1948	5	78-76	.506	18½	Steve O'Neill
1947	2	85-69	.552	12	"
1946	2	92-62	.597	12	"
1945	1	88-65	.575	1½	"

TABLE 10
Demographic statistics, Detroit area

A. Population of City of Detroit
to Second World War (in thousands)

1890	206
1900	286
1910	466
1920	994
1930	1569

B. Population of Detroit area (in thousands)

	1940	1950	1960	1970	1980	1984	1990
Detroit population	1623	1850	1670	1511	1203	1127	1028
% black	9	16	29	44	63	–	76
% below poverty line	–	–	–	15	22	43	32
Wayne, Oakland, Macomb Counties	2377	3016	3762	4200	4044	3916	3912
Tri-County population*	754	1167	2092	2689	2841	2789	2885
	754	1167	2092	2689	2841	2789	2885
% black			4	4	5	–	6

Sources: U.S. Census; Neithercut, *Detroit Twenty Years After*, tables 1–5; Robert Buchta supplied some figures from the U.S. Census.

* Wayne, Macomb, and Oakland population less Detroit.

TABLE 11
Major-league paid regular-season attendance, 1948–96 (in millions)

A. Total attendance and club average attendance

Year	Total attendance	Attendance per club
1948	20.8	1.30
1955	16.6	1.04
1960	19.9	1.24
1965	22.4	1.12
1970	28.8	1.20
1975	29.8	1.24
1976	31.3	1.31
1977	38.7	1.49
1978	40.6	1.56
1984	44.7	1.70
1988	53.0	2.04
1990	54.8	2.11
1993	70.3	2.51
1995	50.5	1.80
1996	60.1	2.00

Sources: Zimbalist, *Baseball and Billions*, 52; TSN, *Baseball Guide* (1978–96); *USA Baseball* (10/1/96).

B. Per-game attendance per decade

1920s	7,548
1950s	13,392
1960s	14,050
1970s	16,561
1980s	21,792
1990–1993	28,302
1994	31,612
1995	25,260
1996	26,889

Sources: *Sport* (6/95), 82; *USA Baseball* (10/1/96).

TABLE 12
Detroit Tigers' broadcasting revenues, 1952–91

A. Local television revenues (in thousands of dollars)

1952–54	$320
1955	350
1956	400
1959–64	600–650
1965–77	1000–1200
1978–79	1300
1980	1450
1981	1500
1982	1700
1983	2000–2500*
1984	3950
1985	4000
1986	4400
1987	5000
1988	6000–7000*
1989	n/a
1990	7900
1991	8200
1992–93 (est.)	8200

Sources: Before 1965: Celler (1957), 2048–52; newspaper
reports. 1965–88: Quirk and Fort, Paydirt, 506. 1980–91
supplemented from club records. See also tables 20–21.

* The higher figures were suggested by Peter Kitzer of
WDIV. These were 'more' to 'substantially more' than reported; we might assume they were higher for other years as well.
In addition, there were radio rights and, from 1983, cable
television payments that reached $3.1 million in 1991.

B. Total radio and television revenues (in thousands)

1980	$ 3,050
1984	9,025
1985	8,000
1987	14,387
1988	16,915
1989	19,592
1990	23,649
1991	24,884

Sources: Records of Jim Campbell and Detroit Baseball
Club's prospectus.

TABLE 13
Average baseball ticket prices, 1920–96

Year	Box	General admission	Overall	Overall (1990 prices)
1920			$ 1.00	$ 5.46
1939			1.20	6.55
1946			1.40	7.65
1950	$ 2.40	$1.20	1.60	8.74
1960	n/a	n/a	2.05	9.11
1970	n/a	n/a	3.18	10.79
1980	n/a	n/a	4.53	7.23
1984	7.71	3.33	5.93	7.51
1985	8.19	3.48	6.21	7.60
1990	10.26	4.47	7.95	7.95
1994	n/a	n/a	10.45	9.40
1996	n/a	n/a	11.20	10.07

Sources: Table adapted from Zimbalist, *Baseball and Billions*, 52; Scully, *Business of Baseball*, 105; *TSN* (2/3/54), 11; *Toronto Star*, 4/6/94; *USA Baseball* (11/25/96).

TABLE 14
Place of birth of Detroit Tigers and all major-league players (percentages)

A. Detroit Tigers

	Decade career began				
	1950 or before*	1960s	1970s	1980s/90s	All
Michigan	13%	14%	10%	4%	11%
Other Midwest	19	27	26	17	22
Northeast	19	21	16	11	17
South	23	16	17	25	21
West	10	5	9	6	8
California	11	7	17	30	15
Non-U.S.**	4	9	6	6	6
Total cases	125	56	70	47	298

* Year career began. Includes only players who spent equivalent of one full year on Detroit Tigers' major-league roster.
** 13 of the 17 players in this category were from Latin America.

B. All major-league players (from the nineteenth century to 1990)

	Total	Percentage of U.S.-born	Percentage of total
Michigan	374	3.0	2.8
Other Midwest	3279	26.0	24.2
Northeast	4067	32.2	30.0
South	2480	19.6	18.3
West	1068	8.5	7.9
California	1348	10.7	9.9
Non-U.S.	937	–	6.9

Source: Compiled by Society for American Baseball Research (SABR).

TABLE 15
Baseball career patterns of Tiger alumni, 1940–90

Median	Decade career began					Total
	1940s	1950s	1960s	1970s	1980s	
Number of players with Tigers more than one year	63	79	67	81	69	359
Number of players with Tigers one year only	12	74	47	55	61	249
Years in majors of players more than one year with Tigers*	9	8	8	9	7	8.5
Years with Tigers of players more than one year with Tigers	5	4	4	4	3	4
Years in majors, all Tigers	9	7	7	7	7	7.5
Years with Tigers, all Tigers	4	2	2	2	1.5	2
Years in minors (before 1st major-league appearance)*	3	3	3	2.5	3	3
Years between marriage and beginning of ML career**	−1	1	3	1	3	1.5
Average number of children**	2	3	2	1.5	1	2.5

Sources: Players selected from Smith, *Tiger S.T.A.T.S.*; players with fewer than ten game appearances and pitchers with fewer than 45 innings pitched excluded. Major-league career information from Thorn and Palmer, *Total Baseball*. Minor-league career information from *Detroit Tiger Yearbook(s)* in Harwell Collection in Detroit Public Library and the personal collection of Dr Peter Dembski.

Note: Players who were with the Tigers less than one year are excluded; thus, the bias of the table is for lengthy career but the same bias applies for all decades.

* Medians
** Unmarried excluded

TABLE 16
Major-league players' salaries: Minimum and mean, 1950–96

Year	Minimum salary	Mean salary
1950	$ 5,000	$ 14,000
1952	5,000	13,600
1953	5,000	14,580
1954	5,000	14,740
1955	5,000	14,870
1956	5,000	14,750
1967	6,000	19,000
1968	10,000	n/a
1969	10,000	24,909
1970	12,000	29,303
1971	12,750	31,543
1972	13,500	34,092
1973	15,000	36,566
1974	15,000	40,839
1975	16,000	44,676
1976	19,000	51,501
1977	19,000	76,066
1978	21,000	99,876
1979	21,000	113,558
1980	30,000	143,756
1981	32,500	185,651
1982	33,500	241,497
1983	35,000	289,194
1984	40,000	329,408
1985	60,000	371,157
1986	60,000	412,520
1987	62,500	412,454
1988	62,500	438,729
1989	68,000	497,254
1990	100,000	597,537
1991	100,000	851,492
1992	109,000	1,028,667
1993	109,000	1,076,089
1994	109,000	1,168,263
1995	109,000	1,110,767
1996	109,000	1,172,736*

Sources: Major League Baseball Players Association for
1967–95; Celler (1957), 1413; (1952), 965, for 1950s. Median
salary was $11,000 in 1950 and 1952; $12,000, 1953–56.

* Preliminary, usually higher than final figure.

TABLE 17
Post-baseball occupations of major-league players and Detroit Tigers, 1950–90 (percentages)

	Tiger alumni					All players*			
	Career began 1950s		Career began 1960s		Career began 1970s/80s and completed	Career began 1950s		Career began 1960s	
	Years in majors		Years in majors			Years in majors		Years in majors	
Occupation	Under 5	Over 5	Under 5	Over 5		Under 5	Over 5	Under 5	Over 5
Pro sports (incl. scouts)	37	45	11	21	24	15	32	9	29
Non–pro sports	7	4	–	9	–	7	3	9	3
Media	–	4	4	12	3	1	4	1	8
Self-employed (bars, stores)	3	5	22	18	15	13	11	11	18
Professional (teachers)	10	2	7	–	–	10	4	11	2
Executive (sales)	13	11	11	9	9	9	11	10	5
Sales	3	15	22	21	35	17	17	20	21
Employee	13	5	15	3	3	9	6	9	7
Blue-collar (constr./clerk/farm)	13	2	7	3	6	19	10	19	8
Other (govt.)	–	4	4	6	–	1	2	1	0
Totals	30	140	28	34	34	163	301	234	214
					(Absolute numbers for the following)				
Retired (prev. occ. included above)	3	27	–	4	–	6	6	–	–
Died	3	16	4	3	–	40	24	4	7
Not given	3	1	2	2	8	60	12	25	6
Unidentified/still active	–	–	–	–	0	15	8	3	33
Total cases	39	141	30	43	42	269	343	263	227

Areas living in
(after baseball; %)

Michigan	24	27	8	55	33	3	7	2	3
Other Midwest	15	13	42	6	15	21	22	17	21
North-east	9	14	12	24	8	17	16	17	13
South	29	27	27	9	28	28	27	22	19
West	12	12	12	3	8	11	9	14	12
California	3	7	–	–	8	16	14	19	23
Non-U.S.	9	1	–	3	0	5	4	9	10
Totals	34	86	26	33	39	258	286	243	172

Sources for Tiger alumni: F. Smith, *Tiger Tales and Trivia* (1988); *Tiger S.T.A.T.S.*, 261–75; Marazzi and Fiorito, *Aaron to Zuverink; Aaron to Zipfel.* Twelve former Tigers were identified as coaching in the majors in 1991 by Smith (*S.T.A.T.S.*, 275). Marazzi and Fiorito books are also sources for 'All players.'

* No geographical area given for managers, coaches, instructors, and many scouts. Based on 40% random sample of players listed in Marazzi and Fiorito, *Aaron to Zuverink*, for players whose careers began in 1950s and Marazzi and Fiorito, *Aaron to Zipfel*, for players whose careers began in the 1960s

TABLE 18
Performance of black players

A. Comparison of career statistics of black and white Tiger players

	Median batting average						Total cases
	1930s	1940s	1950s	1960s	1970s	1980s	
Black	–	–	.263	.257	.274	.257	32
White	.269	.265	.255	.241	.257	.248	140
Total	.269	.265	.256	.244	.263	.252	172
	Median earned-run average						
Black	–	–	3.70	3.67	3.78	4.06	10
White	3.45	3.97	3.97	3.81	3.77	4.39	105
Total	3.45	3.97	3.90	3.78	3.78	4.25	115

B. American League: Black position players

Hitters	1955	1965	1975	1985
All	8%	27%	31%	36%
Starters	16	38	44	44
Stars*	20	54	62	52

* Top 25 in batting average

Notes: Selection as in table 17. Career statistics at end of
1993 year in Thorn and Palmer, *Total Baseball*, and TSN's
Baseball Register. Black players spent 3.1 median years
in the minors during the entire period; white players
spent 2.4.

TABLE 19
Detroit Tigers' mean salaries, 1978–96

Year	Salary	Ranking in league
1996*	$ 877,640	21st
1995	1,029,737	18th
1994	1,535,868	6th
1993	1,265,317	10th
1992	942,284	17th
1991	850,109	12th
1990	675,898	11th
1989	506,246	15th
1988	612,326	2nd
1987	534,986	4th
1986	466,653	10th
1985	406,755	8th
1984	371,332	10th
1983	263,899	17th
1982	174,134	23rd
1981	160,561	19th
1980	86,988	21st
1979	63,377	24th
1978	61,012	23rd

Source: Major League Baseball Players Association

* Unofficial

TABLE 20
Budgets of Jim Campbell, 1980s (in thousands of dollars)

	1980 (actual)	1984 (actual)	1985 (estimated)	1989 (projected)
Income				
Home attendance	$ 6,300	$12,500	$ 9,260	$13,820*
Road attendance	1,350	2,350	2,125	2,970
Concessions	2,300	4,600	3,700	4,500
National TV	900	4,100	3,000	3,000
WDIV-TV	1,450	3,250	3,300	4,300
WJR-Radio	650	975	1,000	1,600
Cable TV	50	700	1,000	1,800
Other	450	3,225	915	1,270
Total income	13,450	31,700	24,300	33,260
Expenses				
Team total	3,730	12,000	13,700	26,080
− Mgr/coaches/trainer	315	460	400	400
− Active players	2,350	9,200	11,600	23,210
− Other	1,065	2,340	1,700	2,470
Stadium payroll & upkeep	3,025	4,500	4,200	5,710
Administration	2,235	4,000	3,100	4,210
Public relations	375	600	600	810
Player procurement	750	1,250	1,200	1,630
Player development	1,285	1,500	1,500	2,040
Total expenses	11,400	23,850	24,300	40,480
Net income	$2,050	$7,845	$2,167**	($7,220)

Source: Records of Jim Campbell dated 2 March 1985. He underestimated actual income and overestimated expenses for 1989. Cf. table 21. Total income in 1982 was $15,682,000; expenses were $14,818,000 for net income of $864,000. Cash flow was $1,396,000 according to Campbell's records.

* 100,000 loss in attendance would cost $675,000 in 1986, $916,000 in 1989.
** While other figures for 1985 are estimates, this net income figure represents actual income.

TABLE 21

Detroit Baseball Club income statement, 1987–91

	1987	1988	1989	1990	1991
Revenue					
Home game receipts	$15,173,170	$15,519,058	$12,182,056	$11,633,732	$15,390,177
Visiting clubs' share	(3,026,074)	(3,094,145)	(2,404,164)	(2,318,556)	(3,068,299)
American League's share	(340,433)	(464,123)	(392,316)	(318,801)	(460,245)
Net home game receipts	11,806,663	11,960,790	9,385,576	8,996,375	11,861,633
Road game receipts	2,773,027	3,173,392	3,437,096	3,438,051	4,205,966
Playoff receipts	1,667,648	–	–	–	–
Total game receipts	16,247,338	15,134,182	12,822,672	12,434,426	16,067,599
Television and radio	14,387,000	16,915,194	19,592,121	23,649,236	24,884,223
Concessions	3,318,307	3,085,215	2,297,369	2,551,036	3,195,458
Royalties and promotions	459,101	760,904	1,297,814	1,590,060	2,492,474
Advertising and other	440,819	443,013	564,298	677,834	891,367
Spring training receipts	221,250	272,494	328,743	86,926	329,080
Total revenue	35,073,815	36,611,002	36,903,017	40,989,518	47,860,201
Revenue growth	17.4%	4.4%	0.8%	11.1%	16.8%
Operating expenses					
Team	15,199,137	17,385,664	17,967,119	21,276,600	28,638,597
Stadium	5,090,276	5,059,037	3,256,452	4,130,995	4,749,382
General and administrative	4,853,922	4,880,292	5,418,947	5,499,673	6,416,878
Player procurement and development	3,427,528	3,815,914	3,942,742	4,379,084	4,913,711
Amortization of players' contracts	979,009	694,229	732,401	1,669,491	1,900,676
Gain on sales or release of players	105,256	12,848	(171,835)	(9,569)	(5,979)
Total operating expenses	29,655,128	31,847,984	31,145,826	36,946,274	46,613,265
Income from operations	5,418,687	4,763,018	5,757,191	4,043,244	1,246,936
Depreciation and amortization	1,299,893	1,032,973	1,057,759	1,962,297	2,152,362
Free cash flow*	6,818,443	5,632,444	6,525,652	5,625,515	2,686,536
Provisions for grievance damages	–	–	2,716,150	8,056,613	–
Interest income (expense)					
Interest income from parent company	623,009	908,700	1,007,010	1,116,281	1,221,931
Other interest income	0	173,088	739,054	822,671	476,154
Interest expense	(247,450)	(272,328)	(230,888)	(1,048,050)	(1,693,757)
Total interest income	375,559	809,460	1,515,176	890,902	4,328
Income (loss) before provision (credit) in lieu of income taxes	5,794,246	5,572,478	4,556,217	(3,122,467)	1,251,264
Provision (credit) in lieu of income taxes	2,360,000	1,900,000	2,900,000	(1,278,000)	(4,160,000)
Net income (loss)	$3,434,246	$3,672,478	$1,656,217	$(1,844,467)	$5,411,264

Source: Detroit Baseball Club prospectus. Monaghan's attorney's brief in the Schembechler/Monaghan court case put club net losses (not cash flow) at $1.6 million for 1992. *Crain's* (7/26/93), 1, 30.
* A number of small items are excluded from this table that make up a part of 'Free Cash Flow.'

TABLE 22
Detroit Tigers' local broadcast ratings, 1980–90

A. Local television ratings

Year	HH rating	Total homes (000)*	Men (000)	Women (000)
1990	19			
1989	16			
1987	20	–	–	–
1986	19	350	278	233
1985	23	410	337	275
1984	25	440	370	277
1983	20	352	300	219
1982	20	354	307	199
1981	18	319	259	147
1980	20	326	256	171

Source: WDIV brochure

* Out-of-home viewing adds 9% to adult audience. Pre-game show is tops in nation.

B. WJR Radio share of weekly night audience and rights

1984	28.6	$ 750,000
1985	22.4	750,000
1986	11.6	1,500,000
1987	13.7	1,500,000
1988	12.4	1,500,000
1989	9.1	1,500,000
1990	12.1	3,000,000

Sources: *DN* (12/21/90); *FP* (4/13/85); *Crain's* (7/23/90),
31.

TABLE 23
Detroit Tigers' and league revenue and expenses, 1993
(in millions of dollars)

	Detroit	League average
Gate	$18.9	$23.8
Media	30.3	27.7
Stadium	4.0	9.0
Total revenue	55.6	63.4
Player costs	43.6	35.8
Operating costs	61.0	52.3
Income	(5.4)	6.0
Franchise value	87.0	107.0

Source: *Financial World* (5/10/94), 52. These figures should be regarded as estimates. Monaghan's attorney's deposition in the Monaghan/Schembechler court case projected Detroit losses as only $3 million in 1993. Noll, 'Baseball Economics,' claims that Detroit was profitable in 1993. He may have factored in tax write-offs that are not considered in the above.

Notes: League proportion of income: 39% gate; 42% media; 10% stadium; 9% other. Detroit proportion of income: 31% gate; 56% media; 8% stadium; 5% other.

APPENDICES

Major League Steering Committee Report (1946, excerpt)

These people who charge that baseball is flying a Jim Crow flag at its masthead – or that racial discrimination is the basic reason for failure of the major leagues to give employment to Negroes – are simply talking through their individual or collective hats. Professional Baseball is a private business enterprise. It has to depend on profits for its existence, just like any other business. It is a business in which Negroes, as well as Whites, have substantial investments in parks, franchises, and players' contracts. Professional Baseball, both Negro and White, has grown and prospered over a period of many years on the basis of separate leagues.

The employment of a Negro on one AAA league club in 1946 resulted in a tremendous increase in Negro attendance at some games in which the player appeared. The % of Negro attendance at some games at Newark and Baltimore was in excess of 50%. A situation might be presented, if Negros participate in Major League games, in which the preponderance of Negro attendance in parks such as the Yankee Stadium, the Polo Grounds and Comiskey Park could conceivably threaten the value of the Major League franchises owned by these clubs.

The thousands of Negro boys of ability who aspire to careers in professional baseball should have a better opportunity. Every American boy, without regard to his race or his color or his creed, should have a fair chance in Baseball. Jobs for half a dozen good Negro players now employed in the Negro leagues is relatively unimportant. Signing a few Negro players for the major leagues would be a gesture – but it would contribute little or nothing towards a solution of the real problem. Let's look at the facts.

(1) A MAJOR LEAGUE baseball player must have something besides great natural ability. He must possess the technique, the co-ordination, the competitive aptitude, and the discipline, which is usually acquired only after years of training in the minor leagues. The minor league experience of players on the Major League rosters, for instance, averages seven years. The young Negro player never has had a good chance in baseball. Comparatively few good young Negro players are being developed. This is the reason there are not more players who meet major league standards in the big Negro leagues.

(2) About 400 Negro professionals are under contract to the 24 clubs in four Negro leagues. The Negro leagues have made substantial progress in recent years. Negro baseball is now a $2,000,000 business. One club, the Kansas City Monarchs, drew over 300,000 people to its home and road games in 1944 & 1945. Over 50,000 people paid $72,000 to witness the East-West game at the White Sox Stadium in Chicago. A Negro league game established the all-time attendance record at Griffith Stadium in Washington. The average attendance at Negro games in the Yankee Stadium is over 10,000 per game.

These Negro leagues cannot exist without good players. If they cannot field good teams, they will not continue to attract the fans who click the turnstiles. Continued prosperity depends upon improving standards of play. If the major leagues and big minors of Professional Baseball raid these leagues and take their best players, the Negro leagues will eventually fold up, the investments of their club owners will be wiped out and a lot of professional Negro players will lose their jobs. The Negroes who own and operate these clubs do not want to part with their outstanding players. No one accuses them of racial discrimination.

(3) THE NEGRO LEAGUES rent their parks in many cities from clubs in Organized Baseball. Many major and minor league clubs derive substantial revenue from these rentals. (The Yankee organization, for instance, nets nearly $100,000 a year from rentals and concessions in connection with Negro league games at the Yankee Stadium in New York and in Newark, Kansas City and Norfolk.) Club owners in the major leagues are reluctant to give up revenues amounting to hundreds of thousands of dollars every year. They naturally want the Negro leagues to continue. They do not sign, and cannot properly sign, players under contract to Negro clubs. This is not racial discrimination. Its

simply respecting the contractual relationship between the Negro leagues and their players.

Summary: Your Committee believes that the relationship of the Negro player, and/or existing Negro leagues to Professional Baseball is a real problem – one that affects all Baseball – and one that should have serious consideration by an Executive Council.

There are many factors in this problem and many difficulties which will have to be solved before any generally satisfactory solutions can be worked out. The individual action of any one club may exert tremendous pressures upon the whole structure of Professional Baseball and could conceivably result in lessening the value of several Major League franchises.

Your Committee does not desire to question the motives of any organization or individual who is sincerely opposed to segregation or who believes that such a policy is detrimental in the best interests of Professional Baseball.

Your Committee wishes to go on record as feeling that this is an overall problem which virtually affects each and every one of us – and that effort should be made to arrive at a fair and just solution – compatible with good business judgement and the principles of good sportsmanship.

Source: TSN (2/25/78), 43.

First Dates That a Black Player Played for Each Major-League Team

Team	Player	Date
Dodgers	Jackie Robinson	4/15/47
Indians	Larry Doby	7/5/47
Browns	Hank Thompson	7/17/47
Giants	Hank Thompson	7/8/49
Braves	Sam Jethro	4/18/50
White Sox	Sam Hairston	7/21/51
A's	Bob Trice	9/13/53
Cubs	Ernie Banks	9/17/53
Pirates	Curt Roberts	4/13/54
Cardinals	Tom Alston	4/13/54
Reds	Nino Escalera	4/17/54
Senators	Carlos Paula	9/6/54
Yankees	Elston Howard	4/14/55
Phils	John Kennedy	4/22/57
Tigers	Ossie Virgil	6/6/58
Red Sox	Pumpsie Green	7/21/59

Source: *TSN* (8/5/59), 19.

Detroit Tigers' Owners and Presidents, 1901–1996

OWNERSHIP

1901 James D. Burns, hotel operator and Wayne County Sheriff, becomes owner and president of charter Tiger franchise in American League.

1902 Samuel F. Angus, insurance entrepreneur, buys franchise; Frank J. Navin enters business office as bookkeeper.

1904 William Hoover Yawkey, son and heir of William Clymer Yawkey, Michigan lumber and ore magnate, buys franchise for $50,000. Navin and Edward G. Barrow, team manager, get $5,000 and $2,500 in stock, respectively, for arranging sale.

1905 Yawkey buys Barrow's interest for $1,400.

1907 Navin acquires remaining interest from Yawkey for $40,000 and becomes president.

1920 Walter O. Briggs, Sr., and John Kelsey, auto industrialists, each buy 25% from heirs of Yawkey for $250,000 each after his death on March 5, 1919.

1927 Briggs becomes half-owner, buying Kelsey stock from his estate.

1935 Briggs gains complete ownership and becomes president, acquiring Navin's stock from his estate after his death on November 13, 1935.

1952 Briggs' stock goes into estate following his death on January 17, 1952; Walter O. (Spike) Briggs Jr. becomes president.

1956 On October 1, 1956, all stock sold under court order by Briggs' heirs to syndicate of 11 radio/television investors headed by John

E. Fetzer, Fred A. Knorr, and Kenyon Brown for $5.5 million. Knorr is made president, succeeded by Harvey R. Hansen (April 19, 1957) and William O. DeWitt (September 30, 1959).

1960 John E. Fetzer buys out Brown group and becomes president on October 11, 1960.

1961 Fetzer becomes sole owner on November 14, 1961, purchasing interest held by Knorr estate after Knorr's death on December 27, 1960.

1978 Fetzer becomes chairman of board, yielding title of president to then general manager, James A. Campbell.

1983 Thomas S. Monaghan purchases Fetzer's interest as a sole owner on December 1, 1983.

1992 Michael Ilitch purchases Tigers from Monaghan, August 26, 1992.

CLUB PRESIDENTS

1901	James D. Burns	1957–9	Harvey R. Hansen
1902–3	Samuel F. Angus	1960	William O. DeWitt
1904–7	William H. Yawkey	1961–78	John E. Fetzer
1908–35	Frank J. Navin	1978–90	James A. Campbell
1936–52	Walter O. Briggs, Sr	1990–92	Glenn E. (Bo) Schembechler
1952–56	Walter O. Briggs, Jr		
1957	Frederick A. Knorr	1992–	Michael Ilitch

Sources: Detroit Baseball Club press release; Media Guide (1996).

APPENDIX 4

Detroit Tigers' Broadcasters and Stations, 1943–1996

Years	Radio	Stations
1943–50	Harry Heilmann	WXYZ
1951	Ty Tyson–Paul Williams	WXYZ, WJBK
1952	Van Patrick	WKMH, WJBK
1953–5	Van Patrick–Dizzy Trout*	WKMH
1956–8	Van Patrick–Mel Ott*	WKMH
1959	Van Patrick–George Kell*	WKMH
1960–3	Kell–Ernie Harwell**	WKMH, WJR
1964	Harwell–Bob Scheffing**	WJR
1965–6	Harwell–Gene Osborn	WJR
1967–72	Harwell–Ray Lane	WJR
1973–91	Harwell–Paul Carey	WJR
1992	Rick Rizzs–Bob Rathbun	WJR
1993	Rizzs–Harwell–Rathbun	WJR
1994	Rizzs–Rathbun	WJR
1995–6	Frank Beckman–Lary Sorensen	WJR

	Television	
1947–52	Ty Tyson–Harry Heilmann–Paul Williams	WWDT-TV; renamed WWJ-TV
1953–5	Van Patrick–Dizzy Trout*	WJBK-TV
1956–8	Van Patrick–Mel Ott*	WJBK-TV
1959	Van Patrick–George Kell*	WJBK-TV
1960–3	Kell–Ernie Harwell**	WJBK-TV
1964	Harwell–Bob Scheffing**	WJBK-TV
1965–6	Kell–Ray Lane	WJBK-TV
1967–74	Kell–Larry Osterman	WJBK-TV
1975	Kell–Osterman–Don Kremer	WWJ-TV
1976	Kell–Osterman–Kremer–Al Kaline	WWJ-TV
1977	Kell–Osterman–Kaline–Joe Pellegrino	WWJ-TV
1978	Kell–Kaline–Pellegrino–Mike Barry	WWJ-TV
1979	Kell–Kaline–Barry	WDIV-TV
1980–94	Kell–Kaline	WDIV-TV
1995–6	Kell–Kaline	WKBD-TV

	Cable	
1981–3	Larry Adderley–Hank Aguirre–Norm Cash	ON–TV
1984	Larry Osterman–Bill Freehan	PASS
1985	Osterman–Freehan–Jim Northrup	PASS
1986–92	Osterman–Northrup	PASS
1993–4	Northrup–Jim Price–Harwell	PASS
1995–6	Harwell–Fred McLeod–Price	PASS

* Simulcasts
** Alternate radio/television

Jim Campbell's Scouting Book (c. 1961, excerpts)

SCOUTING OBJECTIVE

Professional baseball offers great opportunity to that young man who has ability and desire and who is willing to make the sacrifices necessary to reach his goal in life. Our scouts should *sell* professional baseball and the Detroit Tigers. Compare baseball players' earnings with earnings in any other industry. Compare the pension plan that is available to Major League players with pension plans of other companies, unions or industries. Professional baseball does not have to take a back seat to any business, industry or profession under any circumstances. SELL professional baseball and SELL the Detroit Tigers because we have one of the very fine organizations in our profession.

Our objective continues to be to sign and develop players for the Major League club. We are not interested in a player unless you feel he has a chance to play in the Majors or high minor leagues. Concentrate on the outstanding prospect and devote most of your time and attention to this particular type player.

Responsibilities of chief scout: weekly communication with all scout supervisors, personally scout 'key' prospects, at least by telephone, evaluate scouting personnel, 'constant touch' with home office.

Responsibilities of scout supervisor: all area scouting, weekly report to chief scout and weekly communication with scouts, personally scout all 'top prospects.'

Responsibilities of scouts: own territory, reports to home office. This includes all rules, assignments to 9 geographic areas, minor leagues and colleges. Sub-scouts are paid on basis of success of recommendations: $100 for a signing; $750 if reaches Majors (1962).

[*Summary of benefits*: Scouts were included in group health (about 50% paid), life insurance ($7500 paid by club), pension (83% by club) if paid $3000 annually. Both free-ticket and expense policy could be described as 'frugal' but reasonable. Scouts were cautioned about sporting forms that cost 40¢.]

TEN TIPS ON SCOUTING

1. Groundwork Is Important

A big league prospect usually shows baseball ability at the age of 15 or 16. Whenever a boy of 15 or 16 years of age is considered by you to have ability you should immediately try to make a friend of the boy, and also whenever possible, become a real friend of the boy's family. Keep contact with the boy and his family and study the boy's attitude with regard to his family and friends. If there is any particular person you feel guides the boy's affairs, or in whom the boy has confidence, you should cultivate that person as well as the boy, and implant confidence in them in your judgment and ability to direct the boy's future.

The boy's confidence in you should be built up gradually and his friendship developed over the period between his discovery by you and the time when he is about to graduate from high school. Usually this is at about 18 years of age. When you have watched his ability develop from age 15 to 18, you should have a very good idea as to whether or not he has the ability you anticipated him to develop. Care should be taken NOT to promise anything you are not certain you can produce. Great injury may be done a boy and your own scouting reputation may suffer if a youthful prospect is allowed to build up great expectations which you are unable to fulfill. Should the boy decide to go on to college, you are in a position to tell him you can get him into college. Encourage him, let [him] know you are his pal. Never try to boss him but help him and hold his friendship and the friendship of his family.

If he does go on to college, you have a better chance to follow his development.

When you have scouted a boy through his high school and his college days, from say 15 years of age to 21 or 22 and you have become close to him during this period, he should give you an edge when he is ready to sign. Of course, what very often happens, money enters the picture and you have the competitive scout who walks in cold and sells himself and his organization. Now you must work to keep your boy and to get him to see your offer. This is where your years of building up confidence in yourself by the boy and his family pays off. If he believes in you, you have an edge.

There is a knack of handling boys. You must not hurt him in any way nor do one thing that will get him down on you from the time you first meet him until he signs. When a boy likes you he will listen to you. When he does not like you, your chance to get him is not good.

2. Signing Technique

When the time has arrived for signing of a first year player, one of the most important things to find out is what is on the player's mind, his parents', and also if there is an advisor outside of his family.

In most cases, they will ask you all sorts of questions and now is the time you must be careful in answering these questions to the benefit of the Tiger organization. Never talk about anything which will give them ideas which may complicate matters.

Be careful about making a definite offer and do not make your offer until you are convinced that the boy is ready to sign. Don't just submit a figure for someone else to top. And don't leave a contract with any player you think anything of to sign and mail to you or write to a player regarding terms. They will simply peddle it to some other club. Sometimes you have to work 24 hours or more on a boy ready to sign, but if you like him, stay with him until the deal is closed.

3. Rely on Your Own Judgment

A scout should go strictly on his own judgment. If you like a young player, make up your own mind and then stick to it ...

4. Relations with Coaches

You must be friendly with the coaches at all costs. Never argue or get sore even when you have lost out. On the other hand, you should realize that unless you know the individual thoroughly you cannot always trust coaches or would-be-advisors. Unknown to you a coach may be working for some other scout or club ...

5. Subscouts

A very important item is your choice of subscouts. If you cannot get an honest one you are better off not having any. A subscout is always a type looking for a higher rating and he is always trying to get acquainted with men from other organizations. In trying to get an in, he will divulge all he knows. Some subscouts will deal with all clubs. Your subscouts must be honest and sincere. If he is not, you are better off without him ...

6. Scouting Conversation

... A boy may unexpectedly prove to be far better than you had thought (so be careful of what you say).

7. Not Ready to Sign

Never accept a player's statement that he is not ready to sign, that he is going to college but that, if he changes his mind, he will contact you. You will very likely read somewhere about a week later than the player has signed with someone else ...

8. Character

You must give some regard to more than just physical ability. Baseball is a game of elimination. There are only 500 major leaguers holding regular jobs each year. You may question how a player with ability could eliminate himself. The answer is: bad habits, wrong attitude, family or other troubles. You may then ask how you can tell a lad won't go wild on you. If he was a good boy at 18, you may be sure he will not go too far wrong

– not if he has spirit and character. Get these set in a boy and you have a big percentage, without both he will not go far.

9. *The Outstanding Prospect*

In scouting for the Tigers you are, of course, looking for the outstanding prospect. Devote your time and efforts to finding and signing this type player. When you believe you have located him, ask yourself why you believe this particular boy is a major league prospect. Is he a good living lad, does he have great spirit, a good body, can he run, throw and hit, does he have great hands and great instinct, a good attitude and disposition? If a boy has all these things, you have a prospective super player. This is your dream. When you see that super prospect you must make your boss get him. Ask for leeway as to price and, if your boss won't go as high as you think he should, make him. Never be too conservative with the player you REALLY like.

10. *Sales Highlights*

A. Sell the idea that we are only seeking quality players.
B. Tigertown –
    (1) Explain in detail the value of instruction at Tigertown.
    (2) The importance of training in Florida.
    (3) Give examples of personal and individual instruction by our specialists.
    (4) Plant seed of personal angle pertaining to our housing, dining and recreation facilities.
C. Elaborate on the personnel of front office as well as system managers.
D. Point out the Detroit policy of seeking the best facilities possible in all of our minor leagues.
E. Business opportunities after playing days. The contacts gained during playing career will aid immeasurably the chances of embarking on a new career.
F. Our stadium one of the finest in the land. Its facilities for player and fan best money can purchase.
G. Sell the hitters on the advantages of right and left fields and the excellent hitting background at Tiger Stadium. Ted Williams called

Tiger Stadium the best major league park in the country to hit in.

H. Prove to them by mentioning names of players who have come up rapidly through the Tiger Farm System that the opportunity to advance is just as good in this organization as in any other, if not more so and, after the boy reaches the top, his salary with the Tigers will exceed that he would get with any other club.

I. Sell yourself as a representative of a fine organization.

Know all your sales points thoroughly.

COOPERATIVE SCOUTING AGREEMENT (1965)
[Addenda]

Detroit Tigers Bulletin (#33, July 8/65), Memo from Edward G. Katalinas to All Scouts:

All of our scouts must adopt a new attitude and a hard-nosed philosophy regarding the signing of players. The draft rule was adopted primarily to cut down bonuses in all aspects. Many of our scouts are still clinging to the idea of a 'give-away package,' – *anything to sign a player.*

The quality prospect will always receive a reasonable bonus and be a satisfied player. It is the average and chance prospect that concerns us when it comes to contract. We must be realistic in our approach and evaluate his future on a dollar basis. When we add the many supposedly small and medium bonuses, plus expenses, the end of the year report is alarming. This is the area which scouts must condition their thinking – low drafts and free agents fall into the class of being given an opportunity.

Detroit Tigers Bulletin (#38, Sept. 7/65), Memo from Edward G. Katalinas to All Scouts:

We want all of our scouts to 'wrap up' the scouting season by September 15, 1965. Unless a scout has a special assignment, his reports and voucher should be in this office immediately after date mentioned.

The draft rule has altered our scouting procedure. It is not necessary to visit prospects or work at public relations. Please refrain from *all travel.* Keep your communication lines open by *correspondence.*

Detroit Baseball Club Prospectus
(1992, excerpts)

Investment Considerations. Unique Investment Opportunity with Substantial Scarcity Value. The Tigers present a potential investor with the opportunity to join a select group of owners of one of the 26 well-established and nationally recognized Major League Baseball ('Major League' or 'MLB') franchises. Major League franchises have appreciated substantially over time. In the 1976 Major League expansion, the costs of the Mariners and Blue Jays franchises were $6.25 million and $7 million, respectively, compared with the $95 million paid [for Seattle] in 1992, a compound annual growth rate of almost 18%. Fundamental reasons for this appreciation include increasing attendance, the growth in revenues from television and other media, the limited number of prime franchises available, and the prestige associated with ownership of a sports franchise.

Attractive Baseball Market with Significant Potential for Increased Attendance. The Detroit Metropolitan Area is the sixth largest Standard Metropolitan Statistical Area ('SMSA') and second largest single-team SMSA in the United States. The Detroit Metropolitan Area boasts a median household income of $36,099, 18% greater than the national average. In addition, Detroit is the eighth largest television market and sixth largest radio market in the nation. Although the Tigers ranked 12th in the American League for home game ticket sales in 1991, they had the second highest paid attendance for away games, suggesting that significant potential for increased ticket revenue exists in the Detroit market.

Substantial Revenue Enhancement Opportunities. By moving the Tigers to a new, strategically located stadium in an area with higher fan concentration, a future owner could leverage off of strong fan support to increase revenues by providing expanded concessions, club seating, substantially more luxury sky boxes, parking facilities, and public and private stadium clubs.

Tax Advantaged Purchase Structure. The current owner of the Tigers anticipates a stock sale eligible for a §338(h)(10) election under the Internal Revenue Code, allowing an acquiror to write up certain assets without triggering a taxable event for the acquiror. Generally, up to 50% of the Club's purchase price can be allocated to player contracts. Club's purchase price can be allocated to player contracts. For tax purposes, player contracts are generally depreciable over a five-year life. There are numerous other tangible and intangible asset that can be depreciated or amortized for tax purposes. These include local media contracts and concession contracts which are typically amortizable over the lives of the contracts. The resulting level of potential non-cash deductions would suggest that the Club would generate tax benefits of substantial value to certain acquirors.

Television and radio income for years ended December 29, 1991 and December 30, 1990

	1991	1990
Distributions from Major Leagues Central Fund, net	$13,672,193	$13,692,878
Local television income	5,115,000	5,060,000
Cable television income, net	3,097,030	2,896,358
	21,884,223	21,649,236
Local radio rights	3,000,000	2,000,000
	$24,884,223	$23,649,236

Promotional events' effect on attendance (club report)

Year	Non-promotion weekend game	Promotion weekend game	% Increase	Non-promotion weeknight game	Weeknight game	% Increase
1991	22,213	27,680	25%	16,621	24,964	50%

Broadcasting contract summary (club report) ($ in thousands)

Contract	Station	Expiration	Estimated Tigers revenue 1992	1993	Number of regular games broadcast in 1991
Network	CBS	1993	$10,428	$11,063	1
Local TV	WDIV–TV	1994	5,040	5,002	48
Network cable	ESPN	1993	3,846	4,231	31
Local cable	PASS	1991	–	–	70
National radio	CBS	1993	512	538	4
Local radio	WJR	1995	3,250	3,500	162

Broadcasting. The Detroit television market ranks as the eighth largest in the United States, according to *Arbitron Research*. In addition, Detroit is the sixth largest metro radio market.

Local Broadcast Television. WDIV-TV will broadcast a minimum of 47 regular season games through the season and five spring training pre-season games.

Local Cable Television. Tigers games are cablecast on PASS to 200,000 premium equivalent cable subscribers and 500,000 basic cable subscribers throughout Michigan and parts of Indiana and Ohio ... Under the terms of the contract, PASS pays the Club $.18 per premium equivalent subscriber and a flat fee of $10,000 for each game televised on PASS. Over the 1991 season, Tigers games carried by PASS averaged 220,000 subscribers per game. In addition, the Tigers revenue from PASS during 1991 was $3.1 million. Pursuant to an American League revenue sharing agreement, each team must contribute 20% of their cable television revenue to a fund which is divided equally among the 14 American League teams.

Corporate Sponsorship and Logo Promotion. Advertising revenue has grown at a compound annual rate of 19% from 1987 to 1991.

The Tigers will receive approximately $850,000 from sponsors for these events. The estimated expenses associated with these promotions is $675,000.

Local Radio. The Tigers radio network is comprised of over 38 statewide markets, covering 98% of Michigan's population. Tigers games have been broadcast on WJR radio in Detroit since 1964.

Concession sales per capita

	1991	%
Gross sales		
Food and beverage	$4.00	61.7
Beer	1.70	26.2
Novelties	.78	12.1
Total	$6.48	100.0
Club revenues		
Food and beverage	$1.32	20.4
Beer	.56	8.6
Novelties	.28	4.4
Total	$2.06	31.8

For each additional fan who attends a Tigers home game, the incremental revenue to the Club equals the ticket price plus, on average, increased concession revenue of $2.06 less the surcharge of $0.90 per ticket and the share paid to the road team and the American League.

Chronology of Stadium Controversy, 1956–1996

1956 • City-owned park proposed by Ed Connor
1960 • 'Briggs' renamed 'Tiger' Stadium
mid-
1960s • $200,000 repairs; $100,000 upkeep annually; study of stadium in Corktown
1920s • Olympic bid – first considered 1948
1967 • (July) Fairgrounds proposed by Mayor's Committee; Detroit riot
1968 • (January) Lions call for new stadium
1969 • Riverfront, Pontiac, or Fairgrounds?
1970 • (July) Wayne County Stadium Authority bill approved by Milliken
1971 • $126m bond issue
1972 • Fetzer signs 40-year provisional lease for stadium
    • Yearbook has sketches
    • Lou Gordon and attorneys oppose bond issue
    • (June) 'General Obligation' bonds struck down by Judge Moody and Supreme Court
1975 • Lions move to Pontiac
1976 • (September) Fetzer announces $15m renovations
    • (October) City offers to buy stadium for $1
1977 • (February) Pressbox fire
    • *TSN* values stadium at $8m
1978 • (April) City buys stadium for $1; team leases it for 30 years
    • $8.5m city bond issue paid for by 50¢ ticket surcharge

1980s • Renovations

1982 • $3.6m additional bond issue, paid by additional 40¢ ticket surcharge

1983 • Mayor Young proposes domed stadium

1985 • Internal discussions by Tigers and decision to seek a new stadium

1986 • Monaghan approves new stadium

1987 • (July) Campbell calls for new stadium, supported by Joe Lapointe in *Free Press*
   • (August) Bechtold column demands preservation
   • (September) Tiger Stadium Fan Club founded
   • Turner Construction examines structural base of stadium

1988 • (January) McDevitt claims $45–100m needed for repairs.
   • (January) Young says we will build a new stadium; old one is 'falling down.' Dominos spokesperson threatens move to Tampa Bay
   • (February) Fan club meets with McDevitt
   • (20 April) First stadium hug *Detroit Monthly* publishes report stating stadium is sound
   • (June) State blocks funds
   • (July) Turner study published
   • Phase 3 renovations put on hold ($2.5m)

1989 • (January) Stadium bonds paid off; Haase says team is committed to new stadium
   • (March) Mayor, Governor Blanchard, Tigers meet in Lakeland
   • Monaghan endorses new stadium
   • (March) Five plans unveiled
   • (December) County executives meet with Tigers

1990 • (22 January) Cochrane Plan unveiled
   • City and Tigers both encounter budget problems
   • Haase realizes there is no money for stadium

1991 • (March) State blocks county bond issue
   • (22 April) 'Rusted Girder' speech
   • (Spring) Controversy between city and county
   • (1 August) Detroit / Wayne County Stadium Authority established

1992 • (March) City referendum bans use of city funds for stadium

- (August) Michael Ilitch purchases team
- (September) Ilitch meets with fan club
1993 • (June) Ilitch promises own money to build stadium if state provides matching funds for development
1994 • (March) Foxtown development plans revealed..Polls still oppose using state funds
- (June) Threats to move team
- (August) Strike; stadium put on hold
1995 • (September) State provides $55 million for land and infrastructure
- (December) City council approves issuance of city bonds.
1996 • (January) Detroit Tigers announce their financing obtained; fan club collects 10,000 signatures to force city financing onto 19 March ballot
- (21 March) Judge Giddings upholds legality of state funding
- (5 July) State Appeals Court rules that governor's use of state funds is legal
- (20 August) Lions plan to move to new domed football stadium next to new Tigers' stadium

Notes

INTRODUCTION

1 This description of baseball by Harold Seymour early in the century still holds true. *Golden Age*, 91.
2 *Esquire* (8/44), 58. A recent history of baseball in the first half of the twentieth century is White, *Creating the National Pastime*.
3 *The Sporting News* (10/26/84).
4 Eitzen and Sage, *Sociology of American Sport*, 16; Ball and Loy, *Sport and Social Class*, 9.
5 DiMaggio, *Lucky to Be a Yankee*; Spalding, *America's National Game*; Smith, *American Dream*.
6 *Newsweek* (6/29/81), 13.
7 Quoted in Reston, *Collision at Home Plate*, 249.
8 Mitch Albom in *Detroit Free Press* (4/12/94).
9 *Detroit News* (1/20/70).
10 Child, *How to Play*, preface.

CHAPTER 1 Baseball in Postwar American Society

1 A masterly study of the war at home and on the front is *World at Arms* by Gerhard Weinberg.
2 Quoted in Fountain, *Sportswriter*, 262; *The Sporting News* (4/19/45), 10 (hereafter *TSN*).
3 *TSN* (2/8/45), 1; (1/4/45), 2; (1/18/45), 8.
4 Ritter, *Glory of Their Times*, 188; Voigt, *American Baseball*, 257; Thorn and

Palmer, *Total Baseball*, 617; review of wartime baseball in *USA Today Base-ball Weekly* (hereafter *USA Baseball*) (8/22/95), 18–23.

5 *TSN* (7/26/45), 3.

6 Goldstein, *Spartan Seasons*, 8; Goldstein states that Greenberg was drafted then. He had been drafted and discharged the previous year, then re-enlisted. Hugh Mulcahy, a pitcher for the Philadelphia Phillies, was the first draftee after Pearl Harbor, on 8 March 1941. Only two major leaguers died in service – Elmer Gedeon and Harry O'Neill. They had played between them only six major-league games. *USA Baseball* (8/22/95).

7 James, *Historical Baseball Abstract*, 180.

8 *TSN*'s front-page story of 21 June 1945 was headlined 'Greenberg gives new flag punch to Tigers.' Detroit papers also ran big stories. 47,729 fans welcomed him back in Detroit against the Philadelphia Athletics on 1 July. *TSN* was full that summer of stories about returning stars. Other mentions of returning Tigers in *TSN* are on 16 July (33) and 30 August (60).

9 Annual statistics with season highlights for the Tigers are given in a useful paperback put together by Fred Smith, *Tiger S.T.A.T.S.* Newhouser was the last AL pitcher to lead the league in wins, strikeouts, and ERA in the same year (1945).

10 In 1967 again the Tigers would play a doubleheader for the pennant, this time with the California Angels, but that year they needed a sweep and lost the second game.

11 Virgil Trucks states that his arrival a week before the Series was pure coinci-dence. Washington, not base commanders, had to approve all discharges and his discharge was in order before the Tigers clinched the pennant. Interview, 3/25/94. Charlie Grimm, manager of the Cubs, called Trucks the difference in the series. He was 'as fast as Feller,' pitched two no-hitters in the minors, and won 25 games while striking out 418 batters in Andalusia in the Alabama-Florida League in 1938. Various clippings in Harwell Collec-tion, Burton Historical Collection, Detroit Public Library.

12 Quoted in Falls, *Detroit Tigers*, 102.

13 Originally it was scored a two-base error on Greenberg; later, the official scorers changed it to a double but only after newspapers had printed accounts of Greenberg's 'error.' Falls states that movies showed that the ball hit a drainpipe. *Detroit Tigers*, 105.

14 The quotation is slightly different but the sense the same in Falls, *Detroit Tigers*, 101, and Mead, *Even the Browns*, 236.

15 *TSN* (1/5/49), 61.

16 Objoski, *Bush League*, 27.

17 Celler Commission (1952), 963; *USA Baseball* (8/22/95).

18 *TSN* (11/2/46), 2; (2/3/54), 11; for a rough equivalency multiply 1950 prices by 5.5 for 1990 prices. Zimbalist, *Baseball and Billions*, 52.

19 Miller, *Baseball Business*, 3–5.

20 *Total Baseball*, 668.

21 *Detroit News* (hereafter *DN*), 7/2/39. Frank Navin, then principal owner of the Tigers, predicted that night baseball would be the end of baseball; Lieb, *Detroit Tigers*, 43.

22 Quoted by Joe Falls in *Detroit Free Press* (hereafter *FP*), 4/19/74. The installation apparently cost $400,000; *TSN* (11/26/47).

23 Betzold and Casey, *Queen of Diamonds*, 67.

24 Interview with Basil 'Mickey' Briggs, grandson of Walter and son of 'Spike.'

25 Detroit night attendance in thousands was as follows: 1948, 629;1949, 375; 1950, 616; 1951, 421; 1952, 433; 1953, 354; 1954, 434.

26 *TSN* (10/30/76), 7.

27 *Total Baseball*, 671.

28 Horowitz, 'Sports Broadcasting,' 302; *TSN* (4/15/51); (1/3/51), 4.

29 *TSN* (4/4/62), 1.

30 Voight, *American Baseball*, 3: 292. *US News* (5/30/52, 16) estimated that 40 per cent of attendance was women and children, but it is not clear on what evidence that is based. Sommers estimates 35 per cent of attendance was female in the 1970s; *Diamonds Are Forever*, 192, 226. There are a lot of impressionistic data in the literature; the fact that a number is given does not mean that it is an accurate. Jim Campbell, Tiger executive for forty-two years, said: 'Without a doubt there were more women attending games after the war, and kids too' (interview). As contrary evidence, a survey conducted by the Baltimore Orioles in 1954 listed only 4 per cent as 'housewives'; employed persons were not distinguished by gender; *TSN* (1/25/58), 7. James Miller concluded that few women attended games in Baltimore but that they listened to games on radio; *Baseball Business*, 16. More women followed baseball than football in the 1960s; Guttmann, *Sports Spectators*, 143. For the social composition of crowds before the war, see Voigt, 'Counting, Courting, and Controlling,' 92 129, Reiss, 'Social Profile'; Guttmann, *Sports Spectators*, 145. Although they disagree about the social strata, they agree crowds were predominantly male. Better distinction could be made in

the literature between those who sat in bleachers and those who purchased reserved seats.

31 James, *Historical Baseball Abstract*, 206. He also attributes the rise and fall of attendance to the types of pennant races (190).

32 The decline is one-fourth from 1949 to 1953, not one-third from 1948 to 1956 as Rader states, *In Its Own Image*, 52. His figures are repeated in Roberts and Olson, *Winning Is the Only Thing* (109). Attendance declined by 74,133 in 1956 but had risen in 1954 and 1955. The decline 1948–56 is one-fifth. The error is crucial because it implies that television played a greater role than it did. Attendance began to decline *before* there were many television sets and increased along with television viewing during the 1950s. The National League counts only paid and present at the ballpark; the American League counts paid 'no shows'; Zimbalist, *Baseball and Billions*, 202.

33 *Collier's*, 'Are the Major Leagues Strangling Baseball?' (3/10/51), 18–19ff; *US News*, 'Baseball Is in Trouble; High Costs, TV Are Blamed' (3/30/52), 16; *Newsweek*, 'TV Can Kill Baseball' (6/8/53), 69; *Fortune*, 'Is Baseball a Dying Business?' (7/53), 70; *Business Week*, 'Can Baseball Survive TV?' (12/5/53), 101–8; *Newsweek*, 'Where's Baseball Headed?' (4/18/55), 90; *Baseball* 'Television Must Go or Baseball Will' (11/52); *Baseball* soon folded (James, *Historical Baseball Abstract*, 212). There are similar articles in *Sport*. Daley's excerpt in Harwell Collection.

34 *TSN* (8/27/47), 1; Miller, *Baseball Business*, 6. The first televised major-league contest was a doubleheader between visiting Cincinnati and Brooklyn on 26 August 1939, narrated by Red Barber.

35 *TSN* (5/21/47), 1; (1/5/49), 2.

36 Bianculli, *Teleliteracy*, 55.

37 *TSN* (4/4/62), 1; Bianculli, *Teleliteracy*, 55; Miller, *Baseball Business*, 7–8. Spigel, *Make Room for TV*, 32. The price of television sets had decreased from about $440 in 1948 to $240 in 1954.

38 *Baseball*, 7.

39 Rader, *In Its Own Image*, 60.

40 Horowitz, 'Sports Broadcasting,' 285, 304. I know of no such analysis for the 1950s.

41 *TSN* (4/29/59), 8.

42 (1952), 186–190, 308. Televisions entered homes in the North-east first, in the South last. Only in 1955 did a majority of households in all regions have televisions. Spigel, *Make Room for TV*, 32.

43 Ebbets Field had spaces for only 700 cars nearby; Rader, *American Sports*, 288. The number of automobiles in the United States doubled from 32 million to 65 million, 1942–62. *TSN* (4/4/62), 1.

44 Kahn, *1947–1957*, 3–4. This dominance did not help attendance in New York, and it may have hurt it elsewhere. Paul Richards attributed American League problems to both television and Yankee dominance; 'American League Is Dying,' *Look* (2/17/59), 41–4.

45 Kahn, *1947–1957*, 3–4.

46 (7/15/55), 12.

47 Bluthardt, 'Fenway Park,' 44.

48 A statistical analysis of various factors affecting attendance in 1977 concluded that population base was the most important factor – more so than team performance, per capita income, racial composition, ticket prices, age of stadium, or presence of other sports teams. Markham and Teplitz, *Baseball Economics*, 68.

49 Population figures are from the Celler Commission (1952), 1594.

50 See *TSN* (8/23/45), 1, (1/17/46), 2, and (8/24/48), 1, for earlier attempts to move the Browns and (5/16/51), 1, and (12/3/51), 3–4, and for revenue sharing. Walter O'Malley of the Dodgers called proposals, also supported by the Cardinals, 'socialistic' in the May issue. Zimbalist gives an excellent concise history of revenue sharing (*Baseball and Billions*, 57). For the move to Baltimore, see Miller, *Baseball Business*, 27–31. For Veeck's comments on promotions, see *Hustler's Handbook*, 27. The Browns showed a profit, despite small crowds, by selling players; *TSN* (7/18/56), 6.

51 Kahn, *1947–1957*, 328–9; Zimbalist, *Baseball and Billions*, 126. For the successful marketing of the Dodgers in California, see Sands and Gammons, *Coming Apart at the Seams*, 24–6. New York's City Council considered building a 50,000-seat stadium in Queen's to keep the Dodgers. See testimony of Abe Stark, president of the Council, and of Walter O'Malley; Celler (1957), 1817, 1851–6.

52 Smith, *Voices of the Game*, 245. See also Horowitz, 'Sports Broadcasting,' 303–4.

53 *TSN* (10/28/53), 1.

54 Falkner, *Great Time Coming*, 26.

55 The 'debut was quite uneventful,' said Arthur Daley of the *New York Times*; about 14,000 of the usual opening crowd of 25,623 fans were black; *TSN* (4/23/47), 3. The New York press generally ignored Robinson's debut in Jersey

City; Kahn, *1947–1957*, 26–31. Black newspapers had the original signing on the front pages, white newspapers on the back; Tygiel, *Baseball's Great Experiment*, 78. Detroit white newspapers carried only one-paragraph releases from AP. For trivia buffs, the first black pitcher signed to a major-league contract after the war was Dan Bankhead, who debuted 27 August 1947 against Pittsburg at Ebbets Field.

56 Simons, 'Robinson and American Mind,' 40.

57 The fullest and best discussion of integration is by Jules Tygiel, *Baseball's Great Experiment*. He emphasizes moral considerations. In his essay on 'Black Ball,' in *Total Baseball*, he refers to Rickey's 'bold plan to integrate organized baseball,' but attributes a variety of motivations to him (556). Guttmann (*Whole New Ball Game*, 128–9) considers Rickey a 'modernizer.' Rogosin (*Invisible Men*, 207) attributes more cynical motives of money and control. *TSN* speculated that it was a purely 'legal move' in response to the Quinn-Ives anti-discrimination law of 1 July 1944 for New York; (11/1/45), 12. Harold Parrott, travelling secretary of the Dodgers, years later, remembered that Rickey had told him that 'blacks are a great pool of talent and we'll be winners'; *TSN* (2/3/73), 46. Falkner states: 'Since the middle of the war, [Rickey] had been planning to introduce black talent as part of his scheme to revolutionize and revitalize the Dodger system'; *Great Time Coming*, 104. Arthur Mann, Rickey's assistant, reported that Rickey told directors and stockholders in 1943: 'We are going to beat the bushes ... and might include a Negro player or two.' There was a carefully drawn six-step plan including the 'right Negro off the field.' Mann believed that 'the motivating force was and always had been better baseball players.' *Saturday Evening Post* (5/13/50), 19–21, 118–20. Jackie Robinson tells us only: 'Mr. Rickey had to move cautiously and with skill and strategy' (Robinson and Dexter, eds, *Baseball Has Done It*, 67). The Rickey papers at the Library of Congress unfortunately shed no light on motivation. He reportedly told black newspapermen in the spring of 1945, however, that he was 'more for your cause than anybody else you know,' but integration must be a 'matter of evolution not revolution'; quoted in *TSN* (4/12/45), 1. As Roger Kahn points out, Rickey was only a minority shareholder and needed the support of other owners as well; their role has rarely been acknowledged; *1947–1957*, 26–31.

58 Rogosin, *Invisible Men*, 171.

59 Wiggins, 'Wendell Smith,' 5–29; Simons, 'Robinson and American Mind,' 54–5; Rogosin, *Invisible Men*, 180–1.

60 Tygiel, *Baseball's Great Experiment*, 35.

61 Quoted in Scully, 'Discrimination,' 227, from *Pittsburgh Courier* (2/25/33) and (7/25/42). See also Rogosin, *Invisible Men*, 193.

62 Interviews: Murray Chass, Marvin Miller.

63 *TSN* (5/21/42), 14; (11/1/45), 12.

64 Quoted in Simons, 'Robinson and American Mind,' 44–5.

65 *TSN* (5/21/47), 14; (7/16/47), 16. In 1954 *TSN* warned about recruiting in the Caribbean lest the present 'ethnic mix' in baseball be disturbed; (2/10), 10.

66 *TSN* (2/25/48), 1, 12.

67 The meeting and the destruction of evidence was reported in an interview with Arthur Mann, Branch Rickey's assistant, by the *Saturday Evening Post* (5/13/50), 19–21, 118–20, and by Dan Daniel in *TSN* (9/4/46). Baseball writers ignored those revelations.

68 *TSN* (12/27/51), 5. Quoted by Wendell Smith, who attended the camp.

69 Historical review in *San Francisco Chronicle* (3/1/93). San Diego had a working agreement with the Cleveland Indians, owned by Veeck.

70 Kuklick, *To Every Thing a Season*, 146.

71 Miller, *Baseball Business*, 13; Sommers, ed., *Diamonds Are Forever*, 185; *Ebony* (6/61), 35–42.

72 Miller, *Baseball Business*, 122. The hiring of Emmet Ashford, the only black umpire in professional baseball then, was announced in *TSN* (12/24/52), 9. The Cubs' coach was profiled in *Ebony* (6/62), 81–4; Ashford was stopped by the Secret Service on opening day in Washington because they did not believe there were any black umpires; Gerlach, *Men in Blue*, 276.

73 *TSN* (1/5/49), 6.

74 Ibid. (2/22/61), 10.

75 Halberstam, *Summer of '49*, 54–5; Kahn, *1947–1957*, 189–90; *Our Sports* (1953), 59. *Our Sports*, begun in 1953, called itself 'The Negro's Own Sports Magazine.' In Arthur Mann MSS, Library of Congress.

76 *TSN* (12/10/52), 7.

77 Ibid. (8/3/55), 3.

78 For Pittsburgh, see ibid. (8/11/62), 31; try-outs at the Dodgers camp are reported in ibid. (4/12/45), 1. Harry Reick, of the black newspaper the *Pittsburgh Courier*, suggested in 1942 that Pittsburgh sign stars of the Homestead Grays of Pittsburgh including Josh Gibson, now a Hall of Fame member. He received a brush-off from William Benswanger, then

president of the Pirates. Attempts to integrate the Boston Braves in 1944 and the first attempt to force try-outs of black players in New York in 1945 also failed.

79 *Time* (11/5/45), 77.

80 Quoted in Simons, 'Robinson and American Mind,' 42.

81 Ibid., 61–3.

82 *TSN* (1/26/49), 1, 2, 12; (8/3/55), 3; (8/24/55), 14.

83 See Robinson and Dexter, *Baseball Has Done It*, 68–9, 77; Kahn, *1947–1957*, 34–6. Kahn states that Walker apologized to him in 1976. Tygiel, *Baseball's Great Experience*, 170–1; *Saturday Evening Post* (5/13/50), 19–21; *TSN* (5/7/47). All agree who the organizers were; there is some disagreement about who and how many supported it.

84 Woodward's story was reprinted in *DN* (5/9/47) and is my source. See also *TSN* (5/21/47), 3; Tygiel, *Baseball's Great Experiment*, 187–8, who believes the strike threat was exaggerated. Falkner (*Great Time Coming*, 165–6) and Kahn (*1947–1957*, 34–6) do not. Robinson was also asked, 'Which of white boys' wives are you dating?' Besides the racist complications of this image of the insatiable black male, this comment did not show much confidence in white players' wives, but players missed that point. Hugh Casey's cure for bad luck was to 'find me the biggest, blackest nigger woman I could find and rub her teats to change my luck.' He said this to Robinson, apparently without even realizing its offensiveness; Robinson and Dexter, *Baseball Had Done It*, 67.

85 *Post* (5/13/50), 19–21, 118–20. George Lerchen remembers that Hornsby remained a baiter of blacks when he was manager of Cincinnati in the early 1950s (interview). Bragan and Stanky's opposition did not prevent them from becoming managers.

86 *TSN* (2/3/73). Reported by Harold Parrott, travelling secretary of the Dodgers.

87 Quoted in Simons, 'Robinson and American Mind,' 52.

88 Tygiel, *Baseball's Great Experiment*, 304. In professional football, which integrated later, black and white team-mates generally accepted each other. 'They aren't Negroes, they are Packers'; Kramer, *Instant Replay*, 28. John Gordy spoke of remaining prejudices, but found them less among players than others; Plimpton, *Paper Lion*, 186–9.

89 Flood, *The Way It Is*, 34–43; Robinson and Dexter, *Baseball Has Done It*, 67–8; Dolson, *Beating the Bushes*, 90–107; Miller, *Baseball Business*, 121;

Tygiel, *Baseball's Great Experiment*, 318–39; *Ebony* (6/62), 81–4; *Sports Illustrated* (hereafter *SI*) (7/1/68), 72–7 and (7/22/68), 28–41. Regarding 'gentlemanly behaviour' on the field, see *TSN* (3/7/46), 8; (6/22/57), 2. Robinson and Dexter, *Baseball Has Done It*, 67.

90 Twenty-nine per cent of major leaguers had attended a college in 1941, whereas only 20 per cent of males 18–24 were in college in 1949. Reiss, 'Social Profile,' 233. Two samples for the 1960s indicate that a slight majority had attended college in the 1960s. Charnovsky, 'Major League Players,' 48.

91 Fountain, *Sportswriters*, 247–55; Roberts and Olson, *Winning Is the Only Thing*, 28–9. Young's remarks appear in *TSN* (9/18/54), 16; *TSN* (11/16/46), 2. See also defense of racist slurs as 'normal hazing,' *TSN* (5/21/46), 14.

92 Tygiel, *Baseball's Great Experiment*, 336. Scully ('Discrimination,' 233) computes an annual 2.2 per cent increase of black players as a percentage of all players in the National League, but only 0.6% in the American League; from 1960–71 it was 1.4% annually in the American League, 0.6% in the National League.

93 Jennings, *Balls and Strikes*, 174–8; Scully, 'Discrimination,' 261–3. The Rand Corporation, as reported in the *Detroit Free Press* (9/21/86), concluded: 'Position by position black players in the big leagues tend to outperform their white counterparts ... While there is equal pay for equal work, there is [*sic*] unequal opportunities for equal abilities.' Flood wrote that 'blacks had to be better than whites'; *The Way It is*, 71. In 1962, blacks represented 19 per cent of players but 21 per cent of salaries; *Ebony* (6/62), 81–4.

94 The 1879 reserve rule is printed in Dworkin, *Owners versus Players*, 46.

95 Conot, *American Odyssey*, 395–400.

96 Reported in *TSN* (4/25/46), 1.

97 Ibid. (5/23/46), 1; (6/5/46), 1. Roberts and Olson, *Winning Is the Only Thing*, 58.

98 *TSN* (4/25/46), 3. In the same issue, Vincent Flaherty of the *Los Angeles Examiner* made sarcastic remarks about the whole thing; J.G. Spink opposed the union but supported a minimum salary; *TSN* (5/23/46), 10. Salsinger also attacked the national labour laws generally: 'An outsider can invade a man's property, incite his employees, say what he likes'; *TSN* (6/19/46), 5–6.

99 Emanuel Celler Papers, Library of Congress MSS, box 1.

100 *Newsweek* (8/19/46); *TSN* (8/28/46), 10. *TSN* later praised the pension plan 'to protect the old player from becoming a public charge,' but reiterated its condemnation of the Guild; (2/19/46), 14.

101 Quoted in Zimbalist, *Baseball and Billions*, 17. For the early history of the organization, see also Miller, *Baseball Business*, 13, 83; Korr, 'Marvin Miller'; Lowenfish and Lupien, *Imperfect Diamond*. *TSN*, in front-page stories, called the pension plan a 'welfare set-up' and referred to players as 'those platinum-plated peons'; (1/27/54), 1; (2/24/54), 1.

102 For a legal expert's view of this litigation, see Irwin, 'Historical Review of Litigation.' Much of the following discussion is based on this source. Buchta argues that the antitrust exemption 'originally limited player salaries,' but, since free agency was introduced, has maintained 'baseball's control of the location and number of franchises; 'Baseball's Anti-Trust Exemption,' 1–2. A short review of court cases is most accessible in *Total Baseball*, 642–6. See also Guschov, 'Exemption of Baseball.'

103 Irwin, 'Historical *Review of Litigation*,' 294.

104 *US News* (8/3/51), 2; *NYT* (8/1/51), (5/23/52). Extracts from newspapers in *TSN* (8/15/51), 6, and in Celler Papers, box 1.

105 *NYT* (11/10/53). Similarly, see UP report on District Court ruling, *FP* (2/21/53).

106 *DN* (7/11/93); Dworkin states that the 1922 decision was based on baseball being a 'game' (*Owners versus Players*, 55). See also *TSN* (5/29/53), 12; *SI* (8/24/64), 26.

107 Celler Papers, box 1. Celler expected an adverse decision in the Toolson Case too; *FP*, 2/22/53.

108 Frick's testimony is in Celler (1952), 23–119; Wrigley's, 734–6; Hutchison, 840; Spink, 893–9; Garver letter, 601–2.

109 Both letters in Celler Papers, box 1.

110 Quoted in *TSN* (5/29/57), 12; (6/12/57), 8.

111 Irwin, 'Historical Review of Litigation,' 295.

112 *US News* (7/18/58), 53; *Business Week* (6/29/57).

113 Zimbalist, *Baseball and Billions*, 62. See also Celler (1952), 1321 ff.

114 *TSN* (7/18/56), 8.

115 Ibid. (1/13/51), 6; Kahn, *1947–1957*, 328–9; *TSN* (8/14 and 8/21/57). Detroit is discussed in chapters 2 and 3.

116 Bill Veeck discovered the tax loophole that existed until 1976; *Veeck*, 340ff. For an explanation of how it worked, see Quirk and Fort, *Paydirt*, 89–124.

117 Noll, 'Baseball Economics,' 31.

118 Celler (1957), 1413; (1952), 965; *TSN* (2/12/47), 1. See also table 16.

119 *TSN* (2/12/47), 1; (1/19/49), 10; (2/12/58), 1. See also (12/10/46), 1; (2/21/46), 1; (6/2/46), 10; (2/15/50), 14; (2/23/54), 11; (8/15/56), 1; (1/6/60), 1. For similar reactions in national magazines, see note 33 above. Writing a history of baseball in 1959, Danzig referred to the present 'stratospheric salaries.' *History of Baseball*, 5.

120 Celler (1952), 186–90, 308, 894. Giles is quoted in *TSN* (2/28/51), 1.

121 *Who's Who in the American Association* annually listed dozens of players in that AAA league who had more than ten years in professional baseball during the late 1940s and 1950s. George Lerchen provided me with copies of *Who's Who*. See also *TSN* (11/24/54), 2.

122 Fans narrowly voted (154–143) that salaries were not too high in a *TSN* poll (2/7/51), 3. They thought Williams's salary was, but Musial's was not. This probably had little to do with the performance and much to do with the respective popularity and press image of those two stars.

123 Quoted in Tygiel, *Baseball's Great Experiment*, 336.

124 *TSN* noted: 'TV made its first appearance on a grand scale'; (1/5/49), 6.

125 Statistics are taken from his article in *TSN* (8/30/50), 1.

126 *TSN* (2/4/60) and (4/13/60), 26; Horowitz, 'Sports Broadcasting,' 303; Smith, *Voices of the Game*, 245. Smith argues that the National League was more protective of home attendance by restricting live television, but the difference between the two leagues was primarily due to the Yankees' policy of showing most games. For his view of Dizzy Dean, see pp. 129–30.

127 *Total Baseball*, 672.

128 Zimbalist, *Baseball and Billions*, 57.

129 *TSN* (6/28/50), 1–2; (12/3/51), 3–4; (5/16/51), 1. Miller, *Baseball Business*, 27. Veeck had also proposed a return to a 40 per cent gate share for visiting teams. Zimbalist, *Baseball and Billions*, 57.

130 *TSN* anticipated the problem even before television became a factor: (5/19/48), 6, and in a major story, 'At the Crossroads' (12/16/50), 14.

131 *TSN* worried, however, about the lack of qualified major leaguers: (8/6/47), 12. In every era, there have been concerns that there were shortages of talent, although the players per male population ratio in the United States was the highest in history during the 1950s at 1:210,000 white males (1950); in 1960 the ratio was 1:220,000; if black males are included the ratios are 1:186,000 and 1:197,000. *USA Baseball* (5/19/93), 42; SABR

(Society for American Baseball Research) unpublished paper.

132 Celler (1952), 28; (1957), 1901–3; *TSN* (2/27/53), 13. There was a one-third turnover in major-league rosters from April 1957 to April 1958. *TSN* (2/26/58), 1.

133 *TSN* (8/4/48), 1. *TSN* observed that others would follow.

134 *Total Baseball*, 664.

135 Reprinted in *TSN* (5/23/56), 6.

136 Sullivan, *The Minors*, 233–6; Horowitz believes the decline 1949–57 was 'largely attributable to nation-wide major-league telecasts'; 'Sports Broadcasting,' 284. Some minor-league subsidiaries were profitable for their major-league sponsors; United States, 'Broadcasting' (1953).

137 In 1962 the minors were reorganized into 'rookie,' A, AA, and AAA leagues, with each major-league team supporting five minor-league teams and paying salaries over $800 monthly, some manager's salaries, and spring training expenses.

138 Game lengths were 1:49 in 1905 and 1:48 in 1943. For these and the other times listed, see James, *Historical Baseball Abstract*, 206, and *TSN* (8/12/56), 1. Television commercials may have contributed to the lengthening of games, but so did the increasing walks, strike-outs, and 'deep counts.'

139 Wills was drafted by the Tigers from the Dodgers. Before the Tigers could assign him to their AAA farm, he had to clear waivers from all other clubs. No major-league club claimed him, but Spokane in the Dodger organization did. Campbell said: 'That was one of my mistakes' (interview).

140 A concise analysis of reciprocity between television and sports appeared in *Psychology Today* (4/77), 64.

CHAPTER 2 The Briggs Era of Detroit Baseball

1 This history is based on Detroit Baseball Club press releases, especially the one of 15 December 1961, in the Harwell Collection; on the history in the club's 1975 Yearbook; and on the account in Lieb, *Detroit Tigers*. There are errors in the press releases, which may be typographical.

2 A list of owners and presidents is given in appendix 3.

3 Ten years later, on 18 June 1911, the Tigers overcame a 13–1 deficit against the Chicago White Sox in Detroit to win 16–15. The comeback began with four runs in the fifth inning. That remains the largest deficit overcome. The best guide to records is TSN, *Baseball Record Book*.

4 Bluthardt, 'Fenway Park'; the parks were Shibe Park, Forbes Field, and a new Sportsman's Park (1909); Comiskey Park and League Park in Cleveland (1910); a new Polo Grounds and Griffith Stadium (after a fire) in 1911; Crosley Field and Fenway Park (1912); Ebbets Field (1913); Wrigley Field (1914); and Braves Field (1915).

5 Interview with 'Mickey' Briggs, grandson of Walter.

6 Ibid.

7 *Life* (3/17, 24/52), 136–8, 63–4. Contrast Stump's fawning 1960 biography with his recent one: Cobb with Stump, *My Life in Baseball* (1960); Stump, *Cobb* (1994). The latter was the source for the movie *Cobb*. For years Cobb did not speak to Heilmann, who won four batting championships in the 1920s, because he believed that Heilmann cost him championships. Only two players attended Cobb's funeral. Recounted by Shirley Povich of the *Washington Post*. Reprinted in the *Kitchener–Waterloo Record* (1/18/95).

8 *DN* (6/7/69), (7/14/85).

9 For his attitudes to broadcasting, see Harwell, *Tuned to Baseball*, 179. Paeans to Cobb in *TSN* (5/24/51), 3–4, and (10/5/53), 13. The latter by Salsinger's successor Watson Spoelstra began as a feature about Al Kaline but emphasized the greatness of Cobb. Salsinger was in good company with the BBWAA award; prior recipients included Grantland Rice, Damon Runyon, and Ring Lardner; *TSN* (11/2/68), 28.

10 The following discussion is based primarily on Conot, *American Odyssey*, except where otherwise cited.

11 Cleveland had complained that Detroit was not a major-league city in 1901. Lieb, *Detroit Tigers*, v–vi.

12 Résumé in *FP* (11/25/84); see also 'Our Car: The Road Behind,' *DN* (1/7/96).

13 *FP* (6/8/32).

14 Chrysler press release (12/29/53).

15 Mickey Briggs interview.

16 Earlier, the Davidson Freeway had taken workers from Detroit to the Highland Park Chrysler plant.

17 Conot, *American Odyssey* (379) gives the figure of 25,000 but Darden mentions 39,000; *Detroit, Race and Development* (68).

18 Quoted in Conot, *American Odyssey*, 386.

19 What little headway that was made came to a halt with the election of

Albert Cobo. Darden et al., *Detroit, Race, and Development*, 156–8; Young, *Hard Stuff*, 145.

20 Darden, *Detroit, Race, and Development*, 11. Detroit would hold only one-sixth of the wealth of the metropolitan area in 1980 after having more than half of it during the 1950s.

21 Chafets, *Devil's Night*, 18. Sales of the downtown Hudson's store steadily declined from a peak of $154 million after first Northland and then Eastland opened. It closed in 1983.

22 *DN* (10/11/45); similarly, see *DN* (4/18/49).

23 Angell, *Five Seasons*, 122; *TSN* (4/20/49), 12; (7/11/51), 12.

24 *NYT* (1/21/52).

25 Quoted in *DN* (7/25/53).

26 *NYT* (8/5/56).

27 The editorial page of Detroit newspapers annually commented on opening day: e.g., *DN* (4/12, 4/17/55); (4/10/59); (3/22/78); *FP* (6/17/76). Six different stories appeared in *FP* (4/17/67).

28 *SI* (7/1/68), 75; (4/7/69), 69.

29 WDIV brochure, 1984.

30 *FP* (4/12/94).

31 League attendance figures are listed in Celler (1952), 1616–17.

32 *TSN* (1/15/58); for population base, see Celler (1952), 1594.

33 *FP*, obituary (1/18/52); *NYT* (1/21/52); interview, Walter Briggs III.

34 *TSN* (7/11/51), 7–8.

35 Ibid. (8/11/48), 1.

36 Celler (1957), 2035.

37 Interview: Walter Briggs III.

38 Interview: Mickey Briggs.

39 Quoted in Zimbalist, *Baseball and Billions*, 33, from *NYT* (7/31/90).

40 *DN* (7/9/56); *TSN* (7/18/56). The general profitability after the war was confirmed by both Jim Campbell and Mickey Briggs. The Celler Commission shows a slight loss for 1952 after Walter O's death, but stadium rental from the football Lions, which is not listed under 'income' might have put the team in the black even then. Detroit newspapers reported financial problems and worried about attendance (e.g., *DN* (5/21/41), (12/22/53), but Watson Spoelstra, successor to Salsinger as sports editor of *DN* admitted that they were just 'guessing' about profits and player salaries. George Puscas also said they would 'guess' and 'check' with management. Trucks

was reported as making $18,000 in *TSN* (12/26/51). He remembered that he was making $28,000 then. Interviews: Puscas, Spoelstra, Trucks. *TSN* also admitted that before the Players Association under Miller gave 'leaks,' reports of salaries were 'mere guesswork' (5/14/84), 14.

41 *TSN* in 1960 claimed that the Tigers had the highest payroll in 1949 (2/8/60), 50. The Detroit press generally reported salaries of $450,000 to $500,000, but there were estimates as high as $600,000. Part of the problem arises from whether coaches and managers are included. Some tables in Celler include them, others do not. But reporters were 'guessing' and even contradicted themselves. Total major-league salaries were listed as both $5,500,000 and $8,000,000 for the same year. *TSN* (1/21/48), 10; (4/20/49), 12; (12/26/51), 1; (12/24/52); *FP* (3/6/50), (1/16/59).

42 Interview: Mickey Briggs. Newsom's cut is reported in Falls, *Detroit Tigers*, 97, Newhouser's in *TSN* (11/14/51), 2, and *Sport* (1952; in Harwell collection). According to tax records, Greenberg was paid $38,500 and Gehringer $20,000 in 1937. As president, Walter Briggs received a salary of $24,000; *DN* (4/7/39).

43 Interview: Trucks. We will discuss player-management relations in more detail in a later chapter.

44 George Lerchen, who played with Gentry, told me the amount that was at issue.

45 Wakefield used his bonus money to purchase Briggs's stock. Interview: Mickey Briggs.

46 Interviews: Mickey Briggs, Jerry Davie, George Lerchen.

47 *TSN* (4/20/49), 6. Press criticisms were regular. In an editorial, *TSN* blamed his lack of success on the 'evils of big bonuses'; (6/14/50), 14. Salsinger – generally no friend of players – however, noted that he had produced in 1943 and 1944 after his bonus; *TSN* (5/19/48), 13. *FP* attributed the firing of manager Steve O'Neill to problems with Wakefield (5/1/50).

48 Interview: Mickey Briggs.

49 Berkow, *Hank Greenberg*, 170–1.

50 Ibid., 174. Salsinger defended management through the press debates. See also *TSN* (1/1/47), 11; (1/15/47), 2; (1/29/47), 2; (2/5/47), 2.

51 Hill, *I Don't Care*, 37; Kuklick, *To Every Thing a Season*, 114. In his acceptance speech at the Hall of Fame, Kell modestly said: 'I suspect George Kell has taken more from the game than he could ever put back'; quoted in Westcott, *Diamond Greats*, 35.

52 Smith, *Tiger S.T.A.T.S.*, 285; James, *Historical Baseball Abstract*, 185.
53 Interview: Mickey Briggs.
54 *FP* later referred to the preference for the 'home-grown' Houtteman and Gray (7/3/56).
55 *TSN* (7/25/51), 11; (8/8), 3; (1/21/53), 5.
56 *FP* (5/12/53).
57 The number of Tiger farms 1941–52 were as follows: 11, 8, 2, 3, 2, 7, 11, 16, 14, 9, 8, 7; *Total Baseball*, 664.
58 *FP* (1/4/41). See also *DN* (1/5, 1/16/40); *FP* (5/16/39); (1/17, 1/18/40); (1/4/41).
59 *FP* (1/16/40). See other accounts in *FP* (1/4/41); *DN* (1/16/40).
60 *TSN* (11/10/48), 6. See also his similar remarks in *DN* (10/29/48).
61 See Hank Greenberg in *TSN* (1/19/57), 1; Paul Richards in *Look* (7/8/61), 41–4. Celler (1957), 1833–4, 1901–3. George Kell recounts 'totally illegal arrangements' by Connie Mack's A's, which owned both the Lancaster and the Wilmington franchises in the same league; Wilber, *Love of the Game*, 203.
62 Published in *TSN* (11/3/48), 3; see also *DN* (9/1/48), *FP* (10/28/48); *TSN* (9/18/48), 1. The Celler Commission investigated the Detroit-Dallas arrangement: (1952), 316–19.
63 *TSN* (11/3/48), 3; *DN* (11/25/50).
64 Interview: Lerchen. The contracts substantiate his account.
65 Figures supplied by Campbell.
66 *TSN* (1/3/46).
67 Interviews: Davie and Lerchen.
68 *TSN* (6/14/49), 10; *FP* (6/22/49). All the proceeds from the annual exhibition game went to the Detroit Amateur Baseball Federation.
69 *TSN* (1/28/53), 16.
70 Celler (1952), 2035.
71 Interview: Fenkell.
72 *FP* (3/19/50).
73 *DN* (11/25/50).
74 Ibid. (6/4/47).
75 Ibid. (1/16/49); (5/12/49).
76 *TSN* (11/8/50), 1.
77 Interview.
78 Bak, *Cobb Would Have Caught It*, 104. Joe Falls said that he never heard the phrase 'No jiggs with Briggs' in the press box; the lack of blacks on the team

simply was not talked about; interview. Years later the *FP* reported that Walter Briggs had said no blacks would ever play for him (9/21/86). See also the condemnation of Briggs in Tygiel, *Baseball's Great Experiment*, 286.

79 *Queen of Diamonds*, 71.

80 Henry Ford was a notorious anti-Semite whose *Dearborn Independent* between 1920 and 1927 published the long-discredited Zionist *Protocols* and regularly blamed Jews for a host of problems in the United States and in the world. In 1938 he accepted the Iron Cross from Hitler.

81 Interviews with the people mentioned in the two preceding paragraphs.

82 Tygiel, *Baseball's Great Experiment*, 224; *FP* (7/9/51).

83 *MC* (4/28/51); see also earlier story (4/21) querying Tigers' policies.

84 *DN* (5/8/45); see also (8/4/41) and (8/8/42). Like Walter O. Briggs, Salsinger had been born in the nineteenth century.

85 Ibid. (8/27/47).

86 *FP* (7/24/53), (7/25/53).

87 *FP* (2/24/94). Excerpt from *Hard Stuff*.

88 Tygiel *Baseball's Great Experiment*, 131; *DN* (8/10/46); *MC* (4/20/47); interviews: Keith and Young.

89 Originally reprinted by Wilber, *Love of the Game*, 349. Additional information from interview with Gromek.

90 Interview in *FP*; quoted in Betzold, *Queen of Diamonds*, 71.

91 Interviews: Brown, Holley, Turner.

92 Grier and Cobbs, *Black Rage*, 23–39.

93 *FP* reported that another 1000 fans were there but not counted. If so, that would be the largest crowd in Tiger history (9/27/48).

94 Ibid. (6/25/50). That home-run record was broken in a 28 May 1995 slugfest, which Detroit lost to Chicago 12–10. Twelve home runs were hit then, seven by Detroit.

95 Tigers won-lost records by month were: 6-3, 16-9, 21-9, 16-13, 18-13, 18-11, 0-1.

96 *FP* (7/10/51); see also Smith, *Voices of the Game*, 35.

97 The incident was originally told me by Lew Matlin, confirmed by Harwell (8/30/94).

CHAPTER 3 Transitions and Adaptation in the 1950s

1 The title of the article by M. Eckhouse on the Detroit Tigers in the *Encyclo-*

pedia of Major League Baseball Team Histories is 'Detroit Tigers: The Connection of Detroit Baseball and Stability,' 140–82.

2 Falls, *Detroit Tigers*, 110.

3 The first major article on Kuenn in *TSN* appeared 5/27/53. His rookie accomplishments are reviewed in *TSN* (10/7/53).

4 Boone had 63 over those three years. These and other statistics about game-winning RBIs were compiled by Larry Amman and provided by SABR.

5 *FP* (6/12/54).

6 Ibid. (9/25/57).

7 Interview: Virgil Trucks. Only 2215 fans attended Trucks's no-hitter in Detroit because of a hero's parade for General Douglas MacArthur (Falls, *Detroit Tigers*, 110). Later judgments about MacArthur were much harsher; see Manchester, *American Caesar*.

8 Saves did not become a part of baseball's official statistics until 1973.

9 Interview: Ralph Snyder.

10 Between 1952 and 1960 the Tigers ranged from first (1955) to seventh (1960) in runs scored and first (1956) to last (1960) in batting average but they never ranked above third (1958) in runs allowed.

11 Thorn and Palmer, *Total Baseball*, 2191–92.

12 *TSN* (12/17/52), 2; (6/24/53), 9; (1/26/58), 2; (6/4/58), 4. Smith, *Tiger S.T.A.T.S*, 286–91. The *FP* published a box on performances of traded players and concluded the Tigers had not done well (8/16/52). The Tiger average age was still 27.6 in December 1952.

13 Interview: Mickey Briggs.

14 *TSN* (3/23/49), 11; (5/18/49), 16.

15 Interviews: Trucks and Joe Ginsberg.

16 The 'kitchen cabinet' of Spike's sons encouraged the Wertz/Garver trade. Interviews: Mickey and Walter III. Wertz had led the Tigers in game-winning RBIs, 1949–52. He had tried first-base with the Tigers but the experiment lasted only a week.

17 *FP* (7/31/51), (8/12/51).

18 *Post* (1956), 19–20, 46–7, excerpt in Harwell collection; Golenbock, *Wild, High, and Tight*, 134–5.

19 McLain wrote that Cash could not make 9:00 a.m. workouts because he threw up until 10:00 a.m.; *Strikeout*, 34. His problems were confirmed in anonymous interviews. He drowned off his boat after drinking at the Shamrock Bar on Beaver Island in October 1986.

20 See interviews with Jim Campbell and Rick Ferrell in *Bengal Tales* (2/94) and (5/94) about both trades. Verified in interview with Campbell. See also Pluto, *Curse of Rocky Colavito*. Cash was described as 'versatile' and was not expected to be a regular; *TSN* (4/20/60), 3.
21 *DN* (6/24/86).
22 Interview: Campbell.
23 *FP* (10/3/60).
24 *TSN* (11/24/48); *FP* (4/16/50), (7/2/52). Interviews: Newhouser, Kell in Audio-visual Collection, National Baseball Library. George Lerchen recalls that Rolfe would ask Charlie Keller, acquired from New York, 'Is that the way we did it with the Yankees?' Interview.
25 *DN* (4/9/90).
26 *TSN* (11/17/48), 3.
27 Steve Gromek and Red Wilson both praised Hutchinson, Wilson saying there were 'no good managers' after Hutch.
28 *DN* (9/30/54). *Sport* (7/55), 35.
29 *FP* (4/5/79); updated and expanded by Falls in *DN* (4/9/90). See also *FP* (5/2/59) and (5/3/59).
30 Ryan, *Wait Till I Make the Show*, 71–2.
31 Interviews: Bertoia, Davie. *TSN* observed that coaches were 'not as important as people believe' and that cronyism was often the basis of selection'; (11/17/62), 10. Curt Flood, from the National League, wrote: 'I can recall no effective instruction.' He admitted that Sain was an exception; *The Way It Is*, 60–1.
32 Lolich named Sain, a 'psychiatrist,' an exception; *Sport* (8/79), 37–42. Later he credited Gerry Staley, an older, fellow pitcher with teaching him the sinker ball; *Bengal Tales* (1/94). McLain also praised Sain; *Nobody's Perfect*, 47. For the mental aspect of pitching, see Craig, *Inside Pitch*, 33 ff.
33 Complaints of Tiger complacency were common in the sports sections in the 1950s. Each manager was expected to put a stop to it. *FP* (4/16/50); *DN* (6/25/56), (7/18/56); *TSN* (8/1/56); *TSN* (1/11/50), 3.
34 Interviews.
35 The following account is based primarily on interviews: Mickey Briggs, Campbell, 'Doc' Fenkell, Carl Lee. They are consistent. See also *TSN* and Detroit newspapers, especially during 9/55 and 7/56. There are many contradictory reports in the papers because reporters had to make guesses and depend on leaks; Bill Veeck's account is in *Veeck*, 314–18.

36 *FP* (9/15/55) reported Olson's share as 24%, Mitchell's 10%, Sisson's 10%, and Gehringer's 10%, but some of the latter depended on outside financing. Mickey Briggs believes that Gehringer's monetary contribution was only a token.

37 Interview. *FP* (9/16/55) correctly reports unanimous rejection by the sisters. Watson Spoelstra and others incorrectly reported a split between the older and younger sisters; *TSN* (9/26/55). A myth of a split was believed by grandsons until recently when an aunt revealed that it was a unanimous decision.

38 *TSN* (3/7/56).

39 *TSN* (2/1/56), 1, 2; *DN* (4/12/56).

40 In the closed and prejudiced world of baseball at that time, Jacobs was an outsider because he was Jewish. He had given a refund of $25,000 to Walter Briggs because of excess profits from concessions in 1936. That story of the refund spread through the league and gave him a base for concessions rights elsewhere. His financial role is confirmed by both Briggs and Campbell. There was a later investigation by the House Crime Committee of his loans. *DN* (6/16/72); see also *FP* (5/15/59).

41 *DN* (4/12/56); *FP* (7/4/56).

42 Interview: Walter Briggs III.

43 Falls, *Detroit Tigers*, 117.

44 *DN* (7/10/56).

45 *TSN* (3/10/79), 36.

46 *FP* (9/26/83). Regarding his interest in broadcast rights, see interview in *Metropolitan Detroit* (4/81), 37.

47 Ibid. (2/6/57); see also Veeck, *Veeck*, 314–15. I suggested the possibility of a leak. Fenkell believed there could have been one. Carl Lee said, 'I've wondered about that.' Mickey Briggs does not believe that there was one.

48 Interviews: Lee, who was with Knorr; Fenkell, who was with Briggs.

49 *DN* and *FP* (6/28–29/56); *TSN* (7/4/56), 10; *TSN* (1/16/53), 11; (1/22/57), 7.

50 See Detroit papers (4/20–27/57); *NYT* (4/27/57); Knorr was quoted in *TSN* (7/25/56), 4; Veeck, *Veeck*, 318. Mickey Briggs claims that his father was promised a place 'as long as he wanted one.' Both Lee and Fenkell stressed the Knorr-Fetzer rivalry and Fetzer's attempts to gain control from the early days. Interviews.

51 Veeck's refers to 'that rich man's confidence' that he would always be in control; *Veeck*, 315–18.

52 *FP* (7/4/70).

53 *Absent Friends*, 84.

54 Harwell attributes DeWitt's dismissal to having the Tigers' ground crew work on his house in Grosse Pointe. He also recounts his general cheapness, counting vitamins in the clubhouse and asking for cash instead of the shoes normally given for a radio interview. *Tuned to Baseball*, 70–2. Campbell says that work on the house was minor. It was his alienation of everybody that led to his firing. He was deemed 'more autocratic' than Billy Evans; *TSN* (5/4), 3.

55 Major stories appeared in *DN* (9/27/55) and *FP* (5/15/59). *FP* was commenting on a lead story in *Sports Illustrated*, 'The Tiger Is Underfed.' But *Look* regarded the Tigers as 'one of the richest franchises'; (7/8/61), 68. Management was the source of most 'guesstimates' about profitability and salaries. Interviews: Puscas and Spoelstra.

56 *FP* (5/15/59), (11/5/61). Interview: Lee. They had been paying only $13–24,000 in state, federal, and property taxes before income tax, 1952–6; Celler (1952), 2035. Veeck was the first to depreciate contracts to save income tax; Veeck, 340; Quirk and Fort, *Paydirt*, 91–103.

57 *FP* (12/2/58).

58 *DN* (1/22/32); (2/17/37); (12/14/39); (1/24/41); (2/2/50); (2/10/50); (8/6/54).

59 *TSN* (6/5/46), 1.

60 *FP* (2/1/56).

61 (4/23/58), 1. The next year the *FP* was claiming $1 million had been spent, beginning with Wakefield. *TSN* (2/8/58) reported that the Tigers had spent $185,000 annually since 1950, but that seems high.

62 Bertoia's bonus was not $25,000 as reported at the time but $10,000 plus $1000 for his mother to visit her relatives in Italy, plus off-season tuition at Assumption College in Windsor; Turner, *Heroes, Bums, and Ordinary Men*, 34–8; confirmed by interview.

63 Typewritten reports in Harwell Collection; see also *TSN* (1/20/62), 3.

64 See criticisms in 'Kaline No Super Star Yet,' *Baseball Magazine* (3/59), 23, 87–8; 'The Torments of Excellence,' *SI* (1957); 'The Al Kaline Mystery' (by Joe Falls), *Sport* (1964); the latter two clippings are in the Harwell Collection. He was voted 'least talkative' Tiger, *TSN* (1/6/54), 1. *TSN* also won-

dered whether he would be 'good' like Gehringer or 'go for the big bucks'; (10/26/55), 22. Butler, *Al Kaline*, 36–42.

65 *Bengal Tales* (2/94), 4. Confirmed by interview. Voight observed that Kaline 'charmed a generation of Tiger fans'; *American Baseball*, 252.

66 *FP* (8/26/59). 1959 was a particularly successful year for night baseball. For comparison with other teams, see *TSN* (12/9/54), 16.

67 *TSN* (10/31/56), 1; (1/15/58), 16.

68 *DN, FP* (6/2/59). Even a woman writer was condescending in tone, *FP* (5/31/59). Both Watson Spoelstra and Lyall Smith were negative towards the initial announcement; *DN, FP* (4/26/59). Hudson's fiasco is reported in *FP* (6/23/63). A 'history' of Ladies Day in Detroit is presented in *DN* (5/31/65).

69 *TSN* (3/14/56), 25; (4/3/57), 10; (4/23/59), 15; *FP* (9/13/59).

70 *TSN* (2/9/55), 8; (4/13/60), 26.

71 *DN* (1/28/60); *TSN* (2/3/60), 19; Smith, *Voices of the Game*, 222.

72 Harwell, *Tuned to Baseball*, 69; *The Babe Shined My Shoes*, 205; Smith, *Voices of the Game*, 227. For Kell's role, see Bak, *Cobb Would Have Caught It*, 332; Wilber, *Love of the Game*, 207.

73 Hill, *I Don't Care*, 215. Paul Carey called Van 'imperious'; he thought that Ott was 'one of the nicest people I ever met.' Interview.

74 Quoted in Smith, *Voices of the Game*, 35–56.

75 Tygiel, *Baseball's Great Experiment*, 328–9.

76 Interviews: Baxter, Williams, Young.

77 Young, *Hard Stuff*, 42–3; Rich, *Coleman Young*, 68–72.

78 *DN* (4/24/58); McHale said there were twenty-two black players at Tigertown. Hansen mentioned both twelve and seventeen in the minors. The management was a bit confused.

79 *DN* (4/30/58).

80 *MC* (5/3/58).

81 Ibid. (4/26/58); see also (4/19/58). By the opening of the baseball season, the question was clearly being mooted.

82 *TSN* (2/5/58), 25.

83 Interviews: Brown, Davie, Young. Falls wrote: 'A lot of black fans refused to accept him as true black'; *DN*, 10/13/84.

84 Young, *Hard Stuff*, 42–3. For a critical view of Hoover and the FBI, see Gentry, *J. Edgar Hoover*. The Communist party in the United States did have links with Moscow, but the FBI confused protests with plots. Kiehr et

al., *Secret World*. The report was acquired under the Freedom of Information Act; a copy was given me by Rev. Hill's daughter, Mrs Bermecia McCoy.

85 *NYT* (6/6/58), *FP* (6/6/58); *DN* (6/15/58); Spoelstra in *TSN* (6/25/58), 8.

86 *MC* (6/14/58). There was controversy in *MC* as to whether a threatened boycott was the proper way to proceed. Cf. (5/10, 6/7/58).

87 Interview: Campbell. Doby played center field and conversed with African American fans, who were concentrated in the lower right-center-field bleachers.

88 Scully, 'Discrimination,' 234–5; years 1960–71.

89 That practise was commonly known. To the best of my knowledge the first reporting of it was by Pete Waldmeir years later; *DN* (2/5/92).

90 Interview: Green.

91 At first *TSN* blamed economic problems but later acknowledged that recalcitrant segregation was a factor: (2/7/62), 10; (3/28/62), 11, (4/4/62), 13. Objoski reports 'sheer economic reasons'; *Bush League*, 220. A new Southern League, composed of cities from the Southern Association and the Sally League, emerged in 1964.

92 *DN* (12/18/54); *NYT* (2/16/58); *FP* (2/17/61); *TSN* (4/4/62), 13.

93 Interview: Campbell. His memory was faulty because the Bull Conner incident occurred after the Birmingham Barons were no more, but he probably remembered similar incidents.

94 Interview: Harwell.

95 *DN* (4/1/53); Tiger yearbook, 1958. Campbell called Michigan 'the breadbasket'; interview.

96 *TSN* (1/29/59), 11; *DN* (6/14/59).

97 *TSN* (1/1/58), 1.

98 Thorn and Palmer, *Total Baseball*, 664.

99 Celler (1957), 2035; *TSN* (2/8/58), 24; *FP* (5/15/59). Interview: Campbell. Average bonus payments per team were $281,000 annually, 1958–69. The peak was 1961 with $470,000 spent per team for a total of 1486 players; that amount exceeded average payrolls. Figures derived from *Flood v. Kuhn* court records and calculated in Scully, 'Discrimination,' 238.

100 *TSN* (12/2/53); (11/9/55); (1/21/59); (12/22/62).

101 Interview. Freehan referred to Campbell as 'farm director' then, when he was 'general manager,' but that reveals the attention that Campbell continued to give to the farm system.

102 *FP* (6/20/63); Joe Falls in *TSN* (4/6/63), 35. In 1965 eighteen of the twenty-six players on the Tiger roster were from the farms; four others were acquired by trade for former farmhands. Jim Northrup would soon join the team. *FP* (4/21/68).

103 Interviews: Campbell, Lund. See also Jerry Green about the Tigers' problems with both the draft and free agency; *DN* (2/11/80). Lund mentioned Rowe's problem.

104 *TSN* (2/8/58), 24.

105 Markham and Teplitz, *Baseball Economics*, 50–2.

106 Celler (1957), 2484.

107 Casey Candaele, aged thirty-three; quoted in *SI* (7/25/94), 77.

108 Scouting appointments for the Caribbean announced in *FP* (11/24/59); *TSN* (11/25/59), 5. Interviews: Campbell, Snyder.

109 Interviews: Lund, Snyder.

110 *FP* (7/1, 9/9/66).

111 Thomas, 'Baseball's Amateur Draft.' The author compiled career records of draftees in four offensive categories and four pitching ones to rate draft success.

CHAPTER 4 Community Problems and a World Championship

1 Celler (1952), 23–119, 125, 1310–11; *TSN* (5/31/50), 14; (8/8/51), 5, 6, 10. *US News* (4/18/50), 94–7. A third major league was apparently proposed by Ford Frick, commissioner of baseball, in a letter of November 1953, and by William Harridge, president of the American League, in 1959; *TSN* (1/1/59), 11, (1/14/59), 10. See also Miller, *Baseball Business*, 6, 83–5.

2 Average costs of new franchises were $2.1 million in 1961 and $1.9 in 1962; $5.6 million for the AL and $12.5 for the NL in 1969; $6.25 million for Seattle and $7 for Toronto in 1977; and $95 million in 1993. *USA Baseball* (3/17/92).

3 Interview: Campbell.

4 *TSN* (12/28/60), 1.

5 See chapter 1, note 131, concerning the pool of talent.

6 In millions it was $200 in 1950, $400 in 1960, $1200 in 1970, and $1400 in 1974. Celler (1952), 963; *TSN* (12/17/77), 4; *SI* (7/31/78), 37.

7 In millions, 21.2 for baseball, 6 for football, 4.7 for basketball, and 2.8 for

hockey in 1964. In 1974 it was 30 million for baseball, 10.9 for basketball, 10.2 for football, and 3.6 for hockey; Voigt, *American Baseball*, 110. Average attendance at pro games in 1967 was 53,281 for the NFL; 17,187 for baseball; 6859 for the NBA; and 11,225 for the NHL; *SI* (7/31/78), 37. More teams and a 162-game season (as opposed to 154 games) meant that average team attendance rose 8 per cent and game attendance rose 5 per cent in the decade.

8 In New York in 1970 Broadway shows cost $15 for the best seats, the Knicks and Rangers charged $8.50, and the Yankees $4.00; Zimbalist, *Baseball and Billions*, 53.

9 Scully, *Business of Baseball*, 104. He gives Detroit's average for those years as 1.588 million; it was 1.590. Boston was second. Detroit was third 1953–64 at 1.15 annually. New York drew 1.5 million and Chicago 1.2 in those years. United States, 'Professional Sports Antitrust Bill' (1965), 212.

10 Multiple regression analysis of Detroit's attendance with average league attendance and Detroit's won-lost percentage for each year over the entire period 1945–93 produces an F of 39.7 and significance to .0000. Current winning was a better predictor than won-lost percentage of the previous year, although that also produced a high significance level (F = 11.3, significance .0016). By decade, F and significance levels for won-lost percentage are as follows: 1945–54: 25.13, .0015; 1950–9: 8.32, .0235; 1960–9: 30.12, .0009; 1970–9: 38.58, .0004; 1980–9: 9.62, .0173; 1985–93: 3.50, .1106. By decade, won-lost percentages of the previous year are not significant. By the mid-1980s, success on the field was not enough to guarantee success at the gate. We will consider that further in chapter 9.

11 *DN* (9/27/63). The article mentions that Detroit needed 1.2 million fans at home to break even, but expenses could be reduced and radio-television income was rising. *Newsweek* (4/26/69) wrongly attributed losses in 1963–4 as Fetzer's motivation for a national television contract.

12 Records kept by Campbell. 'I always tried to make money. I was proud of making money.'

13 *Tiger Yearbooks*.

14 *TSN* (1/24/62), 20; *DN* (8/8/66), (5/29/67), (4/15/58).

15 Interview: Fred Smith. He always went to bars in the morning so he would not have to buy drinks for 'the house.' He also commented on the receptivity of nurses and other women in putting groups together.

16 *NYT* (8/16/64).

17 'The Big Sellout' (8/24/64), 12–17; 'A Sad Day for Baseball' (9/21/64), 26–7, 102–4. See also 'TV Kidnaps Sports,' *Nation* (29 May 1965), 336–8.
18 Quoted in *TSN* (4/25/66), 98. Similarly, see Rader, *American Sports*, 245.
19 They were about half of football's ratings in the 1970s; Rader, *In Its Own Image*, 53. Markham and Teplitz estimate that football passed baseball in total broadcast revenues in about 1970; *Baseball Economics*, 64.
20 The brewing, tobacco, and petroleum companies remained the principal local sponsors through the 1960s, when banking and insurance gradually become more important. Helyar, *Lords of the Realm*, 366–9; Horowitz, 'Sports Broadcasting,' 311–13. Judge Landis forbade beer advertising of the World Series on radio. *Broadcasting* heralded the new contract: 'Majors Get $25 million for 1965 Rights,' (3/1/65); *Television Age* called 1965 'The Wildest Season,' (2/15/65). *TSN* estimated that breweries were spending $20 million on baseball in 1962: (4/4/62), 1. That exceeds Horowitz's figures for total broadcast revenues, but it might have included other forms of advertising. As late as 1980, Miller was spending 85 per cent of its advertising budget on sports; Roberts and Olson, *Winning Is the Only Thing*, 129.
21 Interviews: Lee, Kitzer.
22 Horowitz, 'Sports Broadcasting,' 304; *SI* (7/31/78), 37. Average audiences for games on national network were (in millions): 11.4, NFL; 9.5, baseball; 7.2, NBA; 3.7, NHL. See also United States, 'Professional Sports Antitrust Bill' (1965), 38–190.
23 *DN* (1/16/65), (1/22/65). The *News* expected television rights to bring in another $500,000 annually, but television income proved to be much more.
24 The latter point was mentioned by Kitzer. Jim Long described WJR's role. Interviews.
25 Interview: Fenkell.
26 *FP* (1/30/65).
27 *Tiger Scorebook*, 1969.
28 *SI* (12/1/69), 92.
29 *FP* (2/19/65).
30 Table 10; *FP* (4/17/74).
31 Horowitz found that the metropolitan population base, the size of the network, and fan enthusiasm, not gate attendance, won-lost record, or income, were the key factors in determining local broadcast income throughout the majors; 'Sports Broadcasting,' 285–90. Kitzer emphasized the stability of Tiger baseball within the volatility of ratings, quite divorced from atten-

dance. He was speaking primarily of the period after 1975, during which he was responsible for marketing the Tigers for WWJ and WDIV, but the same applies to the earlier period. Interview.

32 *DN* (6/5, 6/9/61).

33 *FP* (4/28/72). Such a charity game was played annually.

34 *TSN* (2/8/61), 12; *FP* (4/1/61).

35 *FP* (8/17/62).

36 Chafets, *Devils' Night*, 19–20; Greenberg, *Middle Class Dreams*. Greenberg uses Macomb County as a case study in the rightward shift of American politics.

37 Widick, *Detroit*, 163.

38 Darden et al., *Detroit, Race, and Development*, 71–2, 167–9.

39 Chafets, *Devils' Night*, 135; Widick, *Detroit*, 211–12.

40 *DN* (10/27/72).

41 Three-part portrait of Fetzer. *FP* (1/30–2/1/79).

42 Interview: Horton.

43 Locke, *Detroit Riot*, 22ff; Darden et al., *Detroit, Race and Development*, 72–4; Conot, *American Odyssey*, 530–43; Lincoln, *Anatomy of a Riot*; Widick, *Detroit*, 166–85. Darden says 3800 were arrested, Lincoln's figures show total arrests over the period to have been 6670, Widick mentions 7200 on p. 184 but 3800 on p. 166. Lincoln's breakdown indicates that most were aged 16–20 rather than 'teenagers,' as Darden describes them. Darden (71) states that 33 were killed, but that is the figure of African Americans killed.

44 Retrospective in *FP* (11/25/84).

45 Freidel and Brinkley, *America in Twentieth Century*, 459–65.

46 *NYT* (7/24/67).

47 The words of Bill McGraw, a sports writer, later at the city desk of the *FP*; interview.

48 *Hard Stuff*, 173–9. Young would be elected mayor in 1973. He had run for council in 1961, but lost 'badly in the primary' (155). William Patrick, a graduate of Harvard, was the first African American councilman in Detroit, elected in 1957. Reverend Hill had unsuccessfully run for council earlier. Charles Diggs Jr was elected to Congress in 1954. Widick states that it 'was not a race riot ... [It was] a new sort of disorder: a social riot' (167).

49 Conot, *American Odyssey*, 530.

50 Interview.

51 Darden et al., *Detroit, Race, and Development*, 4–5, 46–51.

52 Young accused Michael McCormick, *News* editor, of distributing an internal memo calling for sensational stories about violence for suburbanites' consumption, but the *News* denied it; *Hard Stuff*, 203.

53 Conot, *American Odyssey*, 518–19, 609, 625–6; Widick, *Detroit*, 189–90, 201–5; *FP* (5/5/74); Young, *Hard Stuff*, 203; interview: George Cantor.

54 Moss, *Tiger Stadium*, 4.

55 *TSN* (8/20/58), 14; *FP* (5/20/69); McLain, *Strikeout*, 2; Jennings, *Balls and Strikes*, 131.

56 Interview: Ralph Snyder, who supervised the park.

57 *DN* (5/5, 9/4/55).

58 *TSN* (5/29/60), 14; *DN* and *FP* (7/18, 19/60); *DN* (8/26, 29/60). Mantle had a firecracker thrown at him in Chicago in 1957.

59 *TSN* (7/27/60), 11.

60 *TSN* (5/24/61); *FP* (6/9/61), (4/15/62).

61 *FP* (10/2/92) (retrospective account).

62 Snyder said that beer drinking was recognized as a problem, but it was the most profitable concession.

63 Falls and Astor, *Detroit Tigers: Illustrated*, 127; *Baseball Magazine* called Falls one of the ten most influential sports writers in America; Voigt, *American Baseball*, 328.

64 *DN* (9/4, 6, 18/68); Green, *Year of the Tiger*, 121.

65 *FP* (10/11–12/68). Police Commissioner Johannes Spreen called the damage 'regrettable but minimal.'

66 *FP* (6/11/72); *DN*, *FP* (10/4/72). See later accounts in *FP* (5/8/88), (7/6/94).

67 Interview: Falls.

68 *Post* (8/12/61), 19, 52–3; *Newsweek* (6/17/94), 93–4; Voigt, 'Counting, Courting, and Controlling,' 123; *American Baseball*, 288. *DN* observed that Yankee Stadium 'resembled a battlefield in 1976.' Yet *Harper's* remarked on the decline of rowdiness in the stands (7/66), 49–53; (7/67), 69–71. The horrified reaction of Kell and Kaline, who were broadcasting the Tigers–White Sox game in Chicago in 1979, is described in Wilber, *Love of the Game*, 239. For other incidents at away games for Detroit, see *FP* (4/21/69), (9/5/76); *DN* (5/17/70), (5/23–26/74). For incidents in other cities not involving the Tigers but covered in Detroit newspapers in the 1960s, see, e.g., *FP* (8/22/69), (4/26/73); *DN* (5/13/64), (6/3, 5, 6, 30/74). Commissioner Bowie Kuhn ordered a study of problems in the stands after a 10¢ beer night in Cleveland; *DN* (6/8/74).

69 Reprinted in *FP* (5/30/62).
70 *DN* (7/6/69); *FP* (4/28/70).
71 Veeck, *Veeck*, 177–8. Miller, *Baseball Business*, 66.
72 Quoted in *FP* (9/21/86).
73 Flood, *The Way It Is*, 34–43; Dolson, *Beating the Bushes*, 99–107; Roseboro quoted in *Los Angeles Times*, reprinted in *DN* (4/1/67). Olson, 'The Black Athlete.'
74 Interview: Freehan. Gary Ignasiak reported similar incidents in Georgia and North Carolina, where both restaurants and washrooms were restricted.
75 Interview: Bertoia.
76 *TSN* (8/3/55), 3; Murray, *Autobiography*, 235.
77 *DN* (3/29/88).
78 Interview: Green. Jackie Robinson also observed that southerners were often more embarrassed by mistreatment than were players from the north; *TSN* (6/6/56), 9.
79 *DN* (2/5/61); AP report in *DN* (11/16/61); *Ebony* (6/62), 35–42; Halberstam, *October 1964*, 59; Smith, *To Absent Friends*, 15–20.
80 Flood, *The Way It Is*, 79.
81 Related to Bill Nunn Jr in *Pittsburgh Courier*, reported in *TSN* (6/6/56), 9.
82 *Ebony*, 'Money Has Not Ended Spring Training Bias,' (6/62), 83.
83 UPI in *DN* (2/3/61).
84 Interview: Green.
85 Letters to T.H. Pool (2/9/94), Charles Cherry (2/24, 4/11/94); conversations (3/22–24/94).
86 Interviews: Brown, Horton. Campbell remembers Bruton as a 'real gentleman.' When the Tigers had Northrup and Stanley ready and had no room for Bruton after the 1964 season, Campbell tried to arrange a place for Bruton at Baltimore, but Bruton retired, noting that he would be forty, not thirty-seven, as records at that time indicated. Interview: Campbell.
87 Interview: Campbell. He remembers moving after Maury Wills could not find accommodation and stayed with Campbell, but it was five years later that the Tigers moved. *Detroit Tiger Media Guides*, 1961–3. Falls later praised Campbell, who 'tried to create an air of equality.' He had earlier established a separate dining room for black players, but they 'all went their own way'; *TSN* (2/28/83), 11. Perhaps they 'went their own way' because they resented segregated facilities.
88 *Ebony* (6/62), 83; *FP* (3/15/62); *DN* (5/5/62).

89 Interviews: Horton (the last two lines are from an interview in Audio-visual Collection, National Baseball Library), Brown, Keith.

90 *FP* (3/19/69); *DN* (3/21/69).

91 *FP* (3/19/69).

92 *FP* (3/13/69).

93 *FP* (4/24, 8/27/67).

94 Frank Angelo (managing editor) and George Cantor, *FP* (5/18, 19/69). Joe Falls criticized Horton for being supersensitive and wrote that there was no excuse for walking off the job; (5/20/69). Freehan also mentions his sensitivity; *Behind the Mask*, 62, 70.

95 *FP* (5/20/69). He admitted the booing 'stunned' him.

96 Interviews: Horton, Campbell, Brown.

97 *DN* (4/23/70).

98 Interviews: Brown, Horton. Horton says Earl Wilson also boycotted the dinner, but his name is not mentioned in the newspaper reports.

99 Interview: Campbell. See also *DN* (9/28/60); *FP* (10/26/60), (11/13/60); *TSN* (11/9/60), 24; (11/30/60), 26; (7/19/61), 3. Scheffing is quoted in *TSN* (11/30).

100 *TSN* (4/12/61), 5; *SI* (5/22/61), 27.

101 1960–1 comparisons: runs, 633 (7th), 841 (1st); home runs, 150 (2nd), 180 (1st); batting average, .239 (8th), .266 (1st); opponent runs, 644 (4th), 671 (3rd); ERA, 3.64 (4th), 3.55 (3rd). Average runs per team in the AL, 677, 734.

102 These categories are the creation of Bill James and Tom Boswell to measure total offensive production; Thorn and Palmer, *Total Baseball* (1990), 2644ff. The ratings are somewhat different in the 1994 edition.

103 *SI* (4/13/81), 95, 98; *DN* (4/6/73). His drop in batting average in 1962 to .243 was the biggest drop by a batting champion in a single year.

104 *All Sports* (1962), 22, 52–6; *Baseball Digest* (1957), 19–23. See also features in *Sport* (6/61), 48–51, 76–7; (11/64), 65–9. *SI* (7/20/64), 32.

105 *DN, FP* (6/25/62). It may have been 6 hours, 59 minutes, but the official scorer recorded it as 7 hours.

106 *FP* (7/23/62), (6/22/63); *TSN* (8/4/62), 4.

107 Interview: Bruton. Audio-visual Collection, National Baseball Library; Falls, Green, *FP* (4/5/79); see also (6/20/63) for criticisms of Dressen's 'wandering conversations that confused players.' He told Campbell his

biggest task was to keep players who didn't like him away from those who did; interview: Campbell.

108 Green, *Year of the Tiger*, 14. Falls called him a 'nobody,' fitting Campbell's image of the 'elderly, experienced, devoted' type of manager; *FP* (10/4/66).

109 *FP* (4/5/79).

110 Freehan, *Behind the Mark*, 8. Jim Hawkins said 'he left his players alone'; *TSN* (8/25/79), 22. Similarly, see *Bengal Tales* (2/94), 15.

111 McLain was purchased from the White Sox after the 1962 season and was in the Tiger farm system in 1963 and part of 1964. On seeing him warm up in 1964, Dressen told Campbell: 'We've caught lightning in a jar'; interview: Campbell. The Tigers had been prepared to draft whichever of three promising pitchers the White Sox left unprotected. They protected Dave De Busschere, former Detroit Austin Catholic basketball star and later an NBA star with Detroit and New York. Don Lund, then farm director, said they had heard that McLain could be a problem, but sought quality; interview: Lund.

112 *SI* (4/17/67), 70. On 5 June *SI* put Kaline on the cover and referred to the 'Year of the Tiger.' *SI* later thought the Tigers should have been ten games in front and had underperformed (8/28/67), 20.

113 Miller, *Down to the Wire*, 87.

114 *NYT* called his injury 'mysterious' (2/20/70); McLain, *Nobody's Perfect*, 5; McLain, *Strikeout*, 60; *SI* (cover story, 'Denny McLain and the Mob'); (2/23/70), 20. Interview: Campbell. McLain said in February 1994 that he would agree to an interview with me, but did not return five phone calls over the next two weeks.

115 For day-to-day coverage, see Miller, *Down to the Wire*; both *SI* and *TSN* weekly during September and *DN* and *FP*. For 1968 diary accounts, see Freehan, *Behind the Mark*, and Green, *Year of the Tiger*.

116 *SI* (4/15/68), 72; (4/29/68), 18–19.

117 Interview: Harwell.

118 1967–8 comparisons: runs, 683 (2nd), 671 (1st); home runs, 152 (2nd), 185 (1st); batting average, .243 (2nd), .235 (4th); ERA, 3.32 (7th), 2.71 (3rd); opponent runs, 587 (2nd, tie), 492 (1st). Average runs per AL team, 599, 533. The Tigers set still-standing team records for fewest runs allowed, fewest hits (1180), and most strikeouts (1115). For the 1969 season the strike zone was redefined as being from the armpit to the top of the knees and the mound was lowered from fifteen to ten inches above home

plate. In 1963 the strike zone had been defined as being from the top of the shoulder to the knees; the intent had been to speed up games by reducing walks, but the effect was to reduce hitting.

119 Hill refers to Brown as 'one of the best pinch hitters baseball has ever seen'; *I Don't Care*, 24. But 1968 was a career year. Brown was signed by the Tigers in the warden's office in Crestline, Ohio. He had been sentenced to 10 to 25 years for robbery at age 17. Prison director Chuck Harmon pushed the Tigers because they had few black players, a matter that Brown recognized as well. Brown admits his guilt in the robbery, but notes 'they cut the white guys loose.' He had a reputation of being great with youngsters. Miller, *Down to the Wire*, 32. Interviews: Brown, Fred Smith.

120 *TSN* (11/9/68), 4. Horton led the team in game-winning RBIs in 1966, 1968, and 1969 and in total 1965–72 with 83; Kaline was second with 68 in those years.

121 Larry Amman of SABR calculated early 'put-aways' vs. late-inning wins for Tiger pennant contenders as: 36, 26 for 1950; 37, 22 for 1961; 29, 12 for 1967; 31, 30 for 1967.

122 Regarding parties, see *DN* (7/1/86), (4/26/88); Freehan, *Behind the Mask*, 39–41. Occasionally, things got out of hand. Some were nearly barred from a favorite haunt, the Hummer Bar; interview: William Reedy, its owner. McLain is critical of his team-mates (*Nobody's Perfect*, 7), but his was an exceptional viewpoint. While his talent was admired by his team-mates, his persona was not.

123 'J.P. McCarthy Show,' *WJR* (8/26/94).

124 Interviews: Campbell, Stanley. Butler calls it a 'highly questionable tactic' and says Kaline offered to sit out the World Series, for which the Cards were 8–5 favorites; *Al Kaline* (205–8). Oyler had hit .135 for the season and had been 0 for September. Kaline hit .379 in the Series, Stanley .214 with two meaningless errors. Oyler played late-inning defense in four games but never batted.

125 Quoted in Smith, *To Absent Friends*, 240; Falls in *FP* (10/7/68); sports writers from other towns are also quoted that day in *SI* (10/14/68), 33. The Cards were made 8–1 favorites. There was a 1-hour, 14-minute rain delay in Game 4 in the fourth inning. Seven hundred writers attended the World Series; *TSN* (11/9/68), 4.

126 Harwell, *Tuned to Baseball*, 73. Interview: Harwell. To give Campbell credit, he made no criticism after advising 'to sing it straight.'

127 *FP* (4/26/88). When asked about pressure, Gibson said: 'I face more pressure every day just because of being a Negro'; *SI* (7/22/68), 28, 34.

128 *FP* (10/11/68). Later, he excused himself: 'During the 1968 World Series, I attracted unfavorable attention by missing a catch that might have been easy for me if I had not been completely bushed'; Flood, *The Way It Is*, 72. Both Eckhouse in 'Detroit *Tigers*' (169) and Voigt, *American Baseball* (177) wrongly refer to Flood's 'error.' *Tiger Yearbook* (1969) says he 'misjudged' it.

129 Interview: Campbell. In his career, Lolich won 217 games, 207 with the Tigers. He had 2832 strikeouts, 308 in 1971 when he was 25-14 in a still-standing Tiger record 45 starts and 376 innings (the latter for a left-hander; right-hander George Mullin pitched 382 innings in 1904); his 308 season strikeouts remain a record, as does his ten straight losses in 1967. Touted as Detroit's top prospect in 1962, he had become a left-hander after a motorcycle fell on him as a toddler in Portland, Oregon. He signed out of Lincoln High in Portland for $30,000 in 1958. *TSN* (4/11/62), 7; Green, *Year of the Tiger*, 13; *Bengal Tales* (1/94).

130 *DN*, *FP* (10/11/68).

131 *TSN* (10/26/68), 2. There is no mention of people discussing newspaper accounts because the Detroit papers were on strike. Freehan believed their absence helped the team by removing pressure; *Behind the Mask*, 93.

132 *DN* (10/9/68).

133 Interview: Jerry Green.

134 Eckhouse, 'Detroit Tigers,' 169.

135 *DN* (7/15/77).

136 Betzold, 'Tiger Stadium,' unpaginated.

137 Falls, *Detroit Tigers*, 9. Interviews: Falls, Harwell, Puscas. *MC* (10/13/84). In February 1993, in an AP release, Harry Atkins wrote: 'It was a magical time in the Motor City. Maybe the best the town has ever felt. And it came just when Detroit needed something to feel good about.'

CHAPTER 5 The Players

1 Duane Ward of the Toronto Blue Jays complained that players no longer talked baseball in the clubhouse because of these distractions; *Kitchener-Waterloo Record* (6/24/94).

2 Seven of the nine starters at Catholic Central signed major-league contracts and the team did not lose a game during Ray Herbert's four years

there. Reno Bertoia, Bob Bruce, Jerry Davie, and Arnold Earley all advanced from Trumbull's Class D National Championship team of 1951 to the majors. A bat signed by his team-mates of that year is one of Bertoia's mementos.

3 Education of Tiger players is consistent with samples for the majors as a whole. Reiss, 'Social Profile,' 233; Charnovsky, 'Major League Players,' 48.

4 Reiss, 'Professional Sports,' 106–10. Black players were generally sons of manual workers, however.

5 *TSN* (10/20/54), 10. Voigt, *American Baseball* (58–60), states that there were only 32 bachelors in the majors in 1953.

6 Gorman and Calhoun, *Name of the Game*, 6–7.

7 Except where otherwise noted, all of the following are extracted from interviews with the players mentioned, who were kind enough to share their experiences with me and, ultimately, with you.

8 Scully, 'Discrimination,' 238. Based on records in the *Flood v. Kuhn* suit.

9 Turner, *Heroes, Bums and Ordinary Men*, 133–40.

10 Clipping. Harwell Collection, Detroit Public Library.

11 *DN* (7/14/87).

12 Leflore, *Breakout*, 92ff. The story there is accurate, confirmed in interviews with Hawkins, Lew Matlin (who was with the entourage), and Jimmy Butsicaris. Katalinas, who had signed Kaline, called Leflore the 'biggest chunk of raw talent I have ever seen' (101). He never described Kaline as a 'chunk of raw talent.'

13 Dolson, *Beating the Bushes*, 59.

14 The quotation from Bunning is in Ryan, *Wait Till I Make the Show*, 101; Jordan, *False Spring*, 55ff.

15 *DN* (8/11/85).

16 Jordan gives a good account of the problem of finding transient housing; *False Spring*, 78, 271.

17 Brosnan, *Long Season*, 127. See also Feinstein, *Play Ball*, 73; Dolson, *Beating the Bushes*, 182; Bouton, *Ball Four*, 113.

18 Quoted in Wilber, *Love of the Game*, 206.

19 For careers lost as a result of the Second World War, see Van Blair, *Dugout to Foxhole*.

20 Newspaper references from clippings kept by Lerchen. Even Greenberg felt a threat from the minors; Berkow, *Hank Greenberg*, 64.

21 *FP* (2/17/61), on his retirement.

22 Turner, *Heroes, Bums and Ordinary Men*, 139.

23 Jordan, *False Spring*, 71–3.

24 Bak, *Cobb Would Have Caught It*, 325.

25 See *FP*, 'Fate Twists Career' (3/12/49); *TSN* (6/28/50), 5. Woody Fryman's doctor reportedly showed X-rays of Fryman's arm as an example of someone who should *not* be able to pitch; Turner, *Heroes, Bums and Ordinary Men*, 77–83. Regarding rotator cuffs, see *TSN* (5/3/81), 12–14.

26 *TSN* (11/25/51), 8; (1/24/52), 12; (1/5/55), 10. *TSN* applauded Gehringer's decision.

27 Interview, Audio-visual Collection, National Baseball Library. See also *TSN* (10/18/45), 3. *Baseball Digest* listed some off-season jobs, noting that 'only the high-salaried' did nothing; (2/57), 93–4.

28 DN (6/25/83); *TSN* (7/11/81), 28. Reprinted in *People* magazine and *Toronto Star* in March 1995.

29 Freehan, *Behind the Mask*, 6. See reviews in *DN*, Tuesday series in 1986, and *FP* (9/14/92) regarding alumni.

30 For the 1950s, see Celler (1957), 1413; (1952), 965. We lack precise figures for years between 1957 and 1967, between the second Celler Commission and Marvin Miller's appointment as lawyer for the players' organization. Estimates for those years are based on extrapolation and the fact that the median was always less than the mean salary.

31 *FP* (3/5/62).

32 Helyar, *Lords of the Realm*, 89. Confirmed in interview with Campbell.

33 Butler too states that Kaline was offered $100,000 but took $95,000; *Al Kaline*, 24ff.

34 Bak, *Cobb Would Have Caught It* (329), recounts a similar remark by Billy Evans.

35 In 1949 William Sawyer, manager of the Phils, forbade wives to travel with players or players to sign hotel checks: 'The honeymooning for the players is over, the plush days of high living and plush travelling are over'; *TSN* (8/24/49), 2; (7/6/49). Similarly, see *Saturday Evening Post* (3/25/50), 28–9.

36 Wilber, *Love of the Game*, 198. McAuliffe too mentioned stress on the family as the reason for his retirement; *TSN* (8/25/73), 11.

37 Wilber, *Love of the Game*, 55–62.

38 *DN*, Spring 1975. The only account of experiences from wives' perspective that I have discovered is Parr, *Superwives*, which deals only with stars' wives.

39 All taken from interviews at the Tiger Alumni charity game in Toledo, Ohio, July 1993 and verified by the individuals by phone and letter.

40 *DN* (3/29/88).

41 *FP* (7/9/51). It was probably the English-language McGill University in Montreal.

42 Interview: Northrup.

43 *Esquire* (6/53), 35ff. Veeck, *Hustler's Handbook*, 52–73. *Baseball Digest* (9/86), 50–1. See also numerous clippings in the Harwell Collection, Detroit Public Library. *TSN* did applaud Don Black's recovery from alcoholism; (7/23/47), 12.

44 In 1995 Walt Sweeney of the San Diego Chargers (football) won a million-dollar lawsuit against the NFL retirement plan because teams pushed drugs on him. 'Every team passed out drugs'; *Chicago Tribune* (8/6/95).

45 *SI* (7/1/68), 29.

46 *Play Ball*, 51.

47 *TSN* (6/22/48), 2; (5/3/50), 3.

48 Berkow, *Hank Greenberg*, 133; Jordan, *False Spring*, 187.

49 Feinstein, *Play Ball*, 24.

50 Fidrych and Clark, *No Big Deal*, 70, 188, 193; McLain, *Strikeout*, 86–93; *Nobody's Perfect*, 7; *DN* (4/16/73). Leflore, *Breakout*, 113–17. For general accounts, see Jennings, *Balls and Strikes*, 143–5; *Sport* (7/79), 30–4; *SI* (4/9/79), 90–104; *Playboy* (1/76); *Toronto Life* (5/17/79), 25. In the last, Ken Becker exhibited disgust with players' misbehavior, which included entering a bar with the invitation 'Who wants to screw a ballplayer' and sexual harassment of female flight attendants. As the dates indicate, 'sex and the ballplayer' received increasing attention in the late 1970s, following upon the sexual revolution within the United States earlier in the decade.

51 Brosnan, *Long Season*, 160.

52 Flood, *The Way It Is*, 50.

53 Hiller was quoted in *TSN* (1/1/77), 36, and (5/17/80), 19.

54 Ryan, *Wait Till I Make the Show*, 200–1.

55 *FP* (9/14/92).

56 Newspaper reports and other books give some examples. See *FP* (8/14/92); Tuesday series in *DN*, 1986. There is no need to mention names here.

57 Hearle, 'Career Patterns'; Reiss, 'Baseball and Social Mobility,' and 'Professional Sports'; Bookbinder, 'Work Histories.'

58 For discussion of the bias of alumni records, see Day, *Education for the Industrial World*, 177–212.

59 *FP* (12/16/76).

60 Jennings, *Balls and Strikes*, 176–8; Scully, 'Discrimination,' 180, 242; *Ebony* (6/62), 81–2; (6/69), 114–35. Articles include Loy and Elvogue, 'Racial Segregation'; Medoff, 'Positional Segregation'; Curtis and Loy, 'Positional Segregation'; and Phillips, 'Race and Career Opportunities.'

61 *FP* (9/21/86).

62 *FP* (9/21/86). The same article, however, includes testimony by a number of black players that they did not encounter prejudice once they were a member of the team. Leflore, who claimed unfair treatment by society at large, admitted: 'There are few athletes where you can notice prejudice face-to-face'; quoted in Golenbock, *Wild, High and Tight*, 69.

63 The following is based primarily on interviews with Ray Herbert and Reno Bertoia.

CHAPTER 6 The Era of Personalities, 1969–1977

1 Figures are estimates because records were not public and they differ slightly among different sources. Scully, *Business of Baseball*, 117; Markham and Teplitz, *Baseball Economics*, 88; *SI* (7/17/78), 75.

2 *TSN* (6/3/72), 4. He was responding to Commissioner Bowie Kuhn. See United States, 'Labor Relations in Professional Sport.' Owners regularly complained about soaring costs; e.g., AP in *DN* (4/4/71).

3 See note 1 above and Horowitz, 'Sports Broadcasting,' 290; *Forbes* (1/21/71).

4 *SI* (7/23/78), 42; *TSN* (11/18/78), 25.

5 It followed performance on the field at a statistical significance level of .0014. See chapter 4, note 10, concerning the statistical test.

6 *FP* (6/13/83).

7 Honig, *American League*, 247; Falls, *Detroit Tigers*, 84.

8 Interviews: Campbell, Warden.

9 *SI* (4/29/68), 18.

10 Freehan, *Behind the Mask*, 13, 170–83, 197; McLain and Diles, *Nobody's Perfect*, 8–9, 193; *SI* (7/29/68), 42–5. 'Gullible, irresponsible, arrogant, financially naive' was the judgment of *TSN* after his later conviction in criminal courts; (4/2/84), 18.

11 McLain, *Nobody's Perfect*, 156–7, 176; *SI* (7/19/93).
12 Harwell and Smith, *Tuned to Baseball*, 203.
13 Interviews: Cantor, Campbell, Falls, Green, Puscas.
14 Sports pages as good news was suggested to me by Michael Betzold.
15 *SI* (9/1/69), 58.
16 Kuhn, *Hardball*, 69–70; McLain, *Nobody's Perfect*, 18, 24–5; *Strikeout*, 12. Major stories appeared in *SI* (2/23/70), 16–21 (at the newsstands on 2/17); *NYT* (2/14/70); *FP* (2/15/70); and *DN* (2/20/70). Between 2/16 and 2/20, there was little press coverage, as no one would comment because of the legal implications. McLain had taken an advance on his 1970 salary, tipping Campbell to his financial problems.
17 Falls, *Detroit Tigers*, 37; Freehan, *Behind the Mask*, 223; *DN* (2/20/70); *DN* (5/20/86), after his sentencing to prison.
18 *FP* (2/15/70); *NYT* (2/20/70); McLain, *Strikeout*, 12; *Newsweek* (4/13/70), 48.
19 *DN* (7/2/70).
20 Interview: Hawkins. Campbell said Spoelstra was 'always pissed off about something but Denny went too far.'
21 *NYT* (9/10, 13/70).
22 *TSN* (6/26/76), 81.
23 *TSN, Index*, 266; see also (e.g.) *FP* (5/14, 8/26, 9/16/71); (7/5/72); (4/29/73).
24 *FP* (9/13/70).
25 Interview: Campbell.
26 Kuhn, *Hardball*, 72.
27 *FP* (10/11/70).
28 *FP* (2/24/70).
29 Interviews: Campbell, Cantor, Hawkins; Campbell's remarks are consistent with those quoted by Falkner, *Last Yankee*, 155–7.
30 Scheinin includes portraits of both McLain and Martin in his *Field of Screams: The Dark Underside of America's National Pastime*.
31 *FP* (9/25, 10/2/70); (4/4/71); (8/9/72); *DN* (10/21/72).
32 Falls, *Detroit Tigers*, 94, 133.
33 Falkner, *Last Yankee*, 36.
34 *FP* (7/7/72); Falkner, *Last Yankee*, 158.
35 Campbell was consistent. He used nearly identical words in *FP* (9/3/73), *Bengal Tales* (2/94), 16, and with me.

36 Interviews: Brown, Hawkins, and other players preferring anonymity. Falkner, *Last Yankee*, 170, 175; Golenbock, *Wild, High and Tight*, 178–80, 188. On national television, Tony Kubek defended Campaneris and criticized Tiger pitchers; Smith, *Voices of the Game*, 433.

37 *FP* (4/30, 5/2, 5/13/71); (4/20, 21, 8/16/72).

38 Martin and Golenbock, *Number 1*, 206–11.

39 Falkner, *Last Yankee*, 336. Hawkins said, 'Billy never lost a game.' Falls described Martin as 'a terrible loser'; *FP* (4/20/72).

40 *FP* (4/1, 3, 8/73); *TSN* (4/15/73), 26. On 1 April, Hawkins queried how much more the Tigers could take.

41 Interviews with players, one of whom worked as a bartender at the lounge. Falkner refers to the Blessitt incident 'which possibly involved a woman.' It was a second player and second incident that involved a player's wife.

42 Golenbock, *Wild, High and Tight*, 195. Writers guessed that he was visiting a woman but could not report it because of libel. Interview: Puscas.

43 Interviews: Campbell, Hawkins.

44 Interviews: Cantor, Carey, Hawkins; Golenbock, *Wild, High and Tight*, 191–200.

45 Interview: Campbell.

46 Martin and Golenbock, *Number 1*, 211; interviews in *Sport* (6/82), 20; Golenbock, *Wild, High and Tight*, 191–3.

47 *FP* (4/8, 9/1/73). Yet Art Fowler, Martin's pitching coach and bar companion, taught pitchers the spitter; Falkner, *Last Yankee*, 335.

48 Quoted in Falkner, *Last Yankee*, 334. For other positive assessments, see *TSN* (2/76); *SI* (2/88), 46; *Sport* (7/82), 24–31. *SI* (9/9/85), 10, concluded, however, that mistakes overshadowed his genius.

49 For a critique of the popular misapplication of statistical procedures to everyday information, see Paulos, *Mathematician*.

50 *DN* (9/5/71); *FP* (9/14/73); *Sport* (8/80), 62.

51 Interviews: Butsicaris, Reedy.

52 Falkner, *Last Yankee*, 336.

53 Interviews. Horton's interview in the Audio Visual Collection, National Baseball Library, is also positive. Lolich called him a 'very, very good manager. His off-field antics caused some problems'; *Bengal Tales* (1/94).

54 *TSN* (9/9/85), 10.

55 Interview: Campbell.

56 Miller, *Different Ball Game*, 39, 59; interviews with me and Audio-visual Collection, National Baseball Library.
57 For general discussion of 1966–9, see Berry, Gould, and Staudohar, *Labor Relations*, 59ff; Jennings, *Balls and Strikes*, 23ff; Roberts and Olson, *Winning Is the Only Thing*, 136; Zimbalist, *Baseball and Billions*, 18; Miller, *Different Ball Game*, 67–97; Korr, 'Marvin Miller,' 120–9.
58 *Time* (2/28/69), 79.
59 Jennings, *Balls and Strikes*, 29–32.
60 Interview: Miller.
61 Cf. Miller, *Different Ball Game*, 109, 184; Kuhn, *Hardball*, 77, 336.
62 Miller, *Different Ball Game*, 109.
63 *TSN* (12/30/72), 6. *TSN*'s editorial position blamed the players (10/12/72), 18. Miller admits that both the press and fans' polls were more favorable to management; *Different Ball Game*, 181–6. In 1962, when the minimum salary was $6000 and the median no more than $15,000, *NYT Magazine* was highly critical of players' benefits and of their distance from fans; (8/5/62), 12.
64 Interviews: Chass, Koppett, and Miller.
65 *FP* (12/5, 9/68); interviews: Campbell, Stanley.
66 *FP* (3/15, 23, 4/1/72); for similar disbelief in 1969, see *FP* (2/23/69).
67 Helyar, *Lords of the Realm*, 118. Confirmed by Hawkins.
68 Interviews: Hawkins, Freehan.
69 *FP* (4/1/72).
70 Interview: Falls.
71 *FP* (4/5, 6/72). Similarly, see Judd Arnett, *FP* (4/4/72); interview: Hawkins.
72 *FP* (4/2/72).
73 *TSN* (3/17/73), 8.
74 Interviews: Puscas, Cantor, Green, Lapointe. Bledsoe quoted in the *Kitchener-Waterloo Record* (3/4/94).
75 Anderson, *Contemporary Sports Reporting*, 7–15; Fountain, *Sportswriter*, 247–55; Kahn, *1947–1957*, 164–5; Mandell, 'Modern Criticism of Sport,' 119.
76 Interviews: Betzold, Falls, Hawkins, Puscas. In their memoirs, both Bouton and Flood recognized writers' closeness to teams and their tendency 'to be promoters' of the game. *Ball Four*, 410–11; *The Way It Is*, 91.
77 *TSN* (6/5/57); (6/12/57), 9.
78 The description of Spoelstra is by Hawkins. Interviews: Green, Hawkins, Spoelstra.
79 *DN* (4/5, 8/79); *Metropolitan Detroit* (1/80), 62.

80 *MD* (4/78), 70–1; interviews: Lapointe, McGraw.
81 Interview: Falls.
82 *Monthly Detroit* (3/82), 14–15. Interviews: Beer, Green. Two other present-day writers, offended by the loan, mentioned it in interviews.
83 *FP* (9/5/73).
84 *FP* (6/28/77).
85 *SI* (9/9/74), 63.
86 See accounts in Fidrych and Clark, *No Big Deal*; Benagh and Hawkins, *Go Bird Go*; *SI* (4/7/86), 45–66. He was tagged 'Bird' by a minor-league coach, Jeff Hogan, because Fidrych's arm-waving reminded him of 'Big Bird' on *Sesame Street*.
87 Interview: Carey.
88 *FP* (5/16/76); *TSN* (6/5/76), 8.
89 *SI* (7/12), 39–40; (4/24/77), 44–51; (10/30/77), 3.
90 Interviews: Holdsworth, Haase, Harwell, Hawkins, Vincent.
91 *DN*, *FP* (4/6/77).
92 *DN* (5/27, 28/77); *SI* (6/6/77), 20.
93 *FP* (8/8/74).
94 *TSN* (1/10, 4/24/74), 7.
95 Interview: Campbell.
96 Statistically, that Tiger draft was ranked second only to the Dodger draft of 1968 (fifteen future major leaguers, including Steve Garvey, Ron Cey, Bill Buckner, and Davey Lopes). In the rankings for the decade, Detroit placed sixth (of 24). For the 1980s, it would place dead last (of 26) – thus the problems of the nineties. Thomas, 'Baseball's Amateur Draft.'
97 Anderson, *Detroit Tigers*, 170–5; Halberstam, *October 1964*, 12; *TSN* (2/28/62), 15.
98 Interviews: Brown, Holdsworth, Horton, Ignasiak. For another critical view, see Hill, *I Don't Care*, 184–6.

CHAPTER 7 Free Agency and Big Money, 1977–1983

1 Interview in *Sport* (9/83), 17–20.
2 For baseball as a business in its early years, see Burk, *Never Just a Game*. Falls complained in 1983 that baseball had been a game for seventy-five years and a business for eight; *TSN* (5/2/83), 10. That is a nostalgic vision.
3 Quirk and Fort, *Paydirt* (221–2), list yearly figures, adjusted for inflation, by team.

4 The Gini coefficient of inequality increased from .354 (1965–74) to .415 (1976–7) to .510 (1986–91). Ibid., 237.

5 Quoted in Miller, *Different Ball Game*, 190–1. The letter is quoted in somewhat different words but with the same sense in Zimbalist, *Baseball and Billions*, 18, and Lowenfish and Lupien, *Imperfect Diamond*, 209.

6 Flood, *The Way It Is*, 15.

7 Cf. Kuhn, *Hardball*, 82; his letter is quoted in Miller, *Different Ball Game*, 191.

8 *NYT* (6/23/72). See also *Newsweek* (1/12/70); *Ebony* (6/6/70).

9 Quoted in Chass, 'Diamond Business,' 69. This is the best summary of the Flood case and Seitz's decisions although it is not easily accessible.

10 Miller, *Different Ball Game*, 214.

11 Carl Lee, Fetzer's advisor, warned that arbitration would increase salaries. Bill Haase, later in charge of Tiger finances, thought arbitration was more important than free agency per se in raising mean salaries. Interviews.

12 *NYT* (12/15, 16/74). Interview: Koppett.

13 Roone Arledge of ABC TV described owners as 'a loose confederation of operators and robber barons.' Roberts and Olson, *Winning Is the Only Thing*, 108.

14 Quoted in Chass, 'Diamond Business,' 70.

15 *USA Baseball* (2/17/95).

16 Miller, *Different Ball Game*, 243.

17 Quoted in Chass, 'Diamond Business,' 72.

18 Seitz decision as quoted in both Chass, ibid., 72–6, and Miller, *Different Ball Game*, 234–5. See also Berry, Gould, and Staudohar, *Labor Relations*, 54ff.

19 *NYT* (12/24/75).

20 Freedman, *Professional Sports*, 16.

21 Interview: Campbell.

22 *NYT* (12/25/75); *Esquire* (7/76), 20–2; *Newsweek* (1/5/76), 51; (3/8/76), 89; *Time* (3/29/76), 66. During the lock-out, however, *Time* called the reserve clause 'notorious' (3/15/76), 77. See also *TSN* (6/26/76), 18, (4/24/76), 12 (3/17/76), 18; and many articles throughout spring and summer. Regarding the relative honesty of the players' and owners' representatives, Chass and Koppett used nearly identical words. Interviews.

23 Chass, 'Diamond Business,' 76.

24 Frick, *Games, Asterisks, and People*, 193.

25 See statistical analysis in Scully, *Business of Baseball*, 90–1; Zimbalist, *Baseball and Billions*, 95–6; Quirk and Fort, *Paydirt*, 247; Gibson, 'Competitive Imbalance,' 153–6.

26 Kuhn, *Hardball*, 90; Steinbrenner quoted in *TSN* (5/17/81), 18.

27 Kuhn, *Hardball*, 77, 331, 334; *TSN* (3/3/81), 52; Miller, *Different Ball Game*, 1979; Miller: interview (4/12/80), Audio-visual Collection, National Baseball Library; *TSN* (9/12/81), 2–3.

28 *TSN* (9/12/81), 2, 3, 40.

29 Berry, Gould, and Staudohar, *Labor Relations*, 75.

30 *Sport* (6/85), 19. See also Miller: interview (4/12/80), Audio-visual Collection, National Baseball Library; fan poll in *TSN* (7/18/81), 24. Koppett estimated that 90 per cent of sports writers were still pro-management; interview.

31 *SI* (6/22/81), 17–21; *Time* (6/22, 29/81); *NYT* (6/16/81).

32 *DN* (5/19, 6/6, 8/1/81); *FP* (6/13, 15, 16/81).

33 *TSN* (4/10/76), 32; *FP* (5/14/76). Interviews: Holdsworth, Underwood.

34 *TSN* (7/28/81), 9. For concerns see *TSN* (8/15/81), 1–6 ('the worst crisis since the Black Sox'); *Time* (6/22/81); 'Money. The Monster Threatening Sports,' *SI* (7/17/78), 30–84; *SI* (7/19/80), 19ff; (11/5/81), 35–7.

35 *Washington Post* (2/18/84). Gutman claims that 80 major leaguers were using illegal drugs; *Baseball Babylon*.

36 See Miller, *Baseball Business*, 203, 263–5; Sands and Gammons, *Coming Apart of the Seams*, 6, 53; Chass and Godwin, 'Drug Abuse in Baseball'; Kuhn, *Hardball*, 303; *TSN* (11/28/81), 13, 16; (4/23/85), 1, 8; (10/7/85), 8; (10/14/85), 12; (10/7/86), 6; *Sport* (8/86), 39–40.

37 Interview: Falls. For recent problems, see *SI* (2/27/95), 18–21; *NYT* (2/26/95).

38 *Toronto Star* (1/8/95).

39 *TSN* (11/14/51), 2; *NYT* (5/17/57); Falls, *Detroit Tigers*; Falls and Astor, *Detroit Tigers: Illustrated*, 76. Al Aber used them to relieve muscle tension in his legs.

40 *SI* (4/9/62), 116; *TSN* (5/23/62), 36; Bouton, *Ball Four*, 171.

41 Interviews: Herbert, Green, Warden.

42 Interview with a companion who wishes to remain anonymous. Anderson claims Leflore was 'too high-priced.' *Detroit Tigers*, 187. That is wrong. *TSN* reported his problems in Montreal some years later: (10/7/86), 6.

43 Interview: Campbell.

44 *DN* (4/20/86).

45 Falls has 'never been exposed to anyone who was taking drugs'; Hawkins 'never saw but was aware of drugs ... We were never allowed in the trainers' room, which was physically set apart.' Vincent was reluctant to 'report marijuana use because lots of people used it.' Interviews: Falls, Hawkins, Vincent.

46 Interview: Brown.

47 *NYT* (12/26/89).

48 *TSN* (10/5/77), 27, and cf. its concern (3/19/77), 4, 14; *SI* (4/9/79), 34–7.

49 Interview: Chass.

50 *SI* (7/31), 37.

51 Berry, Gould, and Staudohar, *Labor Relations*, 75.

52 *SI* (4/28/80), 36; Anderson, *Contemporary Sports Reporting*, 4; Miller Beer was spending 95 per cent of its advertising dollar on sports in 1980.

53 Scully, *Business of Baseball*, 107; Zimbalist, *Baseball and Billions*, 48, 150.

54 *SI* (7/17/78), 58.

55 Baltimore's management personnel increased from 40 to 70 in a decade; Miller, *Baseball Business*, 269. Detroit was leaner than most.

56 Zimbalist, *Baseball and Billions*, 21, 67.

57 Ibid., 60; Scully, *Business of Baseball*, 118–20. Figures differ between them, especially for 1977.

58 Zimbalist, *Baseball and Billions*, 64–7; *USA Today* (11/28/90); *USA Baseball* (3/17/92).

59 Quirk and Fort, *Paydirt*, 11–16, 24–5, 52. Average ownership tenure was 11 years versus 6.5 years 1901–20.

60 Tiger drafting information based on the notes of Chass.

61 Interview: Campbell.

62 *Newsweek* (6/28/76), 62–6.

63 Interview: Campbell. See also Helyar, *Lords of the Realm*, 186.

64 *TSN* (7/10/76), 15; (10/15/77). A year later he repeated that free agency would be the 'ultimate ruination of baseball'; *DN* (5/21/78).

65 *FP* (4/2/83).

66 *TSN* (3/10/79), 36. Peter Kitzer of WWJ/WDIV-TV remembers that Fetzer thought that transfer of 'heroes' would create fan disloyalty. Interview.

67 *DN* (2/3/73); *FP* (9/18/78), (9/25/83); interview: Campbell.

68 Helyar, *Lords of the Realm*, 292–3. Confirmed in interview with Campbell.

69 *DN* (2/13/80); *TSN* (9/20/80), 9; (8/16/80), 15; (2/21/83), 39; *FP* (9/25/83); *DN* (8/26/84).

70 United States, 'Professional Sports Antitrust Immunity' (1982), 208.

71 *DN* (8/18/78); *Metropolitan Detroit* (4/78), 64–8.

72 *FP* (11/28/81); *TSN* (12/12/82), 44; interview: Campbell. Trades for Herndon and Lopez, mentioned below, were regarded as minor at the time.

73 Jennings, *Balls and Strikes*, 49; *SI* (5/9/89), 58. *Detroit Tigers Media Guide* lists first-round draft choices. Complete draft lists for all teams appear in Simpson, *Baseball Draft*.

74 *FP* (6/13/79).

75 Interview: Campbell.

76 *FP* (6/13, 14/79).

77 Hill, *I Don't Care*, 188, 230.

78 *TSN* (5/31/80), 9; (6/21/80), 9; (8/16/80), 15.

79 Cf. Hill, *I Don't Care*, 188; *TSN* (1/10/81), 35; (6/18/84), 7.

80 Interviews: Stanley, Young, Holdsworth, Underwood.

81 *TSN* (2/25/73), 2.

82 Interviews: Fenkell, Kitzer.

83 For an example of the frustration of television critics see *DN* (6/5/91).

84 1976 Yearbook; *TSN* (7/10/76), 15.

85 Interview: Campbell. In *Paydirt* (221–2), Quirk and Fort calculate Detroit's average prices as decreasing 1978–88 in 1991 dollars. Their calculations are different from mine for some years, based on prices listed in yearbooks, which imply some increase. In any event, increases were never significantly above inflation until the 1990s. They were as follows: $5.00, $4.00, $2.50, $1.50 in 1976; $7.50, $6.50, $3.50, $2.00 in 1981; $9.00, $7.50, $5.00, $3.50, 1983–5; $10.50, $8.50, $6.00, $4.00 in 1986; $15.00, $12.00, $8.00, $5.00 in 1994.

86 *FP* (9/6/76).

87 Darden et al., *Detroit, Race, and Development*, 99, 179; Rich, *Coleman Young*, 129, 175; Young, *Hard Stuff*, 218.

CHAPTER 8 The Golden Age of Detroit Baseball

1 Interviews in *Life* (3/17/52), 136–8; (3/24/52), 63–4.

2 The year before the 1972 strike, *Forbes* painted a dire picture of baseball's financial structure and declining television audience. 'The grand old game

has been groaning for some time but it really seemed to come apart at the seams last year' (4/1/71).

3　Noll, 'Economic Viability.'

4　Calculations in Zimbalist, *Baseball and Billions*, 58–9; *Toronto Star* (12/16/94); Noll, 'Baseball Economics.'

5　$715 million in total, or $625 million after deducting collusion penalties and adding franchise fees.

6　*USA Baseball* (4/26/95).

7　Zimbalist, *Baseball and Billions*, 48, 57, 150; Quirk and Noll, *Paydirt*, 11–16.

8　Estimates are as high as $500 million; *Toronto Star* (10/11/95).

9　*Broadcasting* (3/2/87), 47–8. *SI* warned the same year, however, that there was no real profit in sports broadcasting (10/12/87), 82–6.

10　Gorman and Calhoun, *Name of the Game*, 55; *Chicago Tribune* (11/27/95).

11　*TSN* (11/3/83), 1. Fetzer had gained the respect of his peers over the previous quarter-century. Bud Selig of the Milwaukee Brewers described him as 'prudent, philosophical, fair. He's all of those things in an industry that so desperately lacks those things'; *TSN* (3/10/79), 36. See also portrait by Kool, 'Enlightenment.'

12　Interviews: Lee, Campbell, Fetzer.

13　*DN* (6/6/84); Monaghan, *Pizza Tiger*, 310 and passim; the book is full of self-serving aphorisms and had to be given away to season-ticket holders, but it gives insights into Monaghan's psychology.

14　*DN* (10/10/84).

15　*DN* (5/6, 9/30, 10/16/84). Financing was at 12–13 per cent.

16　Interviews: Fenkell, Campbell, Haase.

17　*Crain's* (4/7/86), 1; *FP* (7/28/85). Based on Noll's report, 'Economic Viability.' When the owners in 1985 made outrageous claims of losses as a reason why the players could not continue to receive one-third of the $1.1 billion six-year television contract in 1984, the players' organization received the right to examine their books. Owners originally claimed that only 1978 had been a profitable year and that they had accrued losses of $92 million in 1982 and $66 million in 1983. Those figures kept being revised downward. For various claims, see TSN, *Baseball Guide* (1986), 9.

18　*FP* (10/6/87). Profits were also accurately reported in *TSN* (6/3/85), 26; *DN* (10/16/84); and *FP* (7/28/85).

19　Noll pointed out in his 1985 report that the Detroit sale was 'structured' so that player depreciation was 'elsewhere'; 'Economic Viability.' In 1994 he cautioned: 'Accounting practices for measuring some items, especially the decpreciation of capital investments and the value of intangible assets, are fundamentally arbitrary'; 'Baseball Economics,' 6.

20 Noll, ibid., 16–17; *Financial World* reported a profit in 1992 but a loss of $5.4 million in 1993 (5/24/93; 5/10/94). Noll may have used 'cash-flow accounting.' There is a sizeable inconsistency between the two evaluations of 1993 finances.

21 Confirmed in interview with Campbell. Campbell's statements to the press about finances were honest ones. They have been verified in every case in which I have had access to records. During this time, he stressed the profitability of the Tigers when Mayor Young and Domino's management (see chapter 10) were pleading financial woes as an excuse to build a new stadium. For Campbell's statements, see *FP* (10/6/87), (7/23/89); and *DN* (6/28/89).

22 Players Association. *DN* and *FP* have published Tiger salaries for various years. *NYT* has published players' salaries for all teams.

23 Noll, 'Baseball Economics,' 19.

24 A common retort by Campbell to any complaints. Interview: Snyder.

25 Criticism in *DN* (6/28/89). Interviews: Irwin, Matlin, Snyder.

26 Interviews: Campbell, Fenkell.

27 Noll, 'Baseball Economics,' 24. Interviews: Campbell and Fenkell regarding control of expenses.

28 Thomas, 'Baseball's Amateur Draft.' *Baseball America* had rated Detroit's farm system the worst in the majors, but General Manager Bill LaJoie dismissed this rating; *FP* (4/3/89).

29 See statistical test discussed in chapter 4.

30 'Fans ... are disproportionately drawn from these counties in Detroit's affluent and popular suburban perimeter'; club report.

31 Detroit Club Prospectus (1992). It was $33,241, behind only Washington and Houston in 1983, and that was held down by the income of $21,556 in the city proper. Widick, *Detroit*, 238.

32 *Crain's* (4/14/86), 1.

33 *DN* (6/11/84). Joe Lapointe, who moved from *FP* to *NYT*, mentioned Detroit as a small town and thought it 'unique in its attention to sports.' Bob Rathbun was surprised at how dominant sports figures were. Interviews. Jerry Green wrote: 'Sports is a matter of life and death in Detroit'; *DN* (4/20/80).

34 Interviews: Lee, Fenkell, Schembechler, Bill Wischman (of PASS). Half of the ballclubs were owned in whole or part by broadcasting companies then; *FP* (7/28/85)

35 WDIV brochures, made available by Joe Martelle (of WDIV). Unless otherwise cited, the following is based on material from WDIV and an interview with Joe Martelle. In 1985, 46 Tiger games were shown on WDIV, 80 on PASS, and 7 on NBC. WJR's radio network increased from 39 to 45 stations.

36 *TSN* (5/14/84), 17. Even pre-season games brought a 17.4 rating.

37 *Broadcasting* (3/2/87), 49–51; United States, 'Sports Programming' (1989), 383, 409; *FP* (4/8/91).

38 1987 WDIV brochure.

39 *FP Magazine* (4/10/83), 8–11; *TSN* (9/24/84), 18; *SI* (3/26/79), 58; (8/17/93), 66. Interview: Carey.

40 *TSN* (5/31/82), 26; for some of Gibson's and Rozema's problems in those years, see *FP Magazine* (4/3/94).

41 Detroit newspapers sensed that the Tigers entered the free-agent market because they needed one more player to put them 'over the top.' Campbell later denied such foresight: 'Sometimes you just get lucky'; interview. Evans hit only .232 with 16 home runs in 1984. He had much better years 1985–7.

42 The play-offs were worked by replacement umpires when major-league arbiters demanded a slice of the gate, and the final game of the play-offs was moved to an afternoon start because the first of two nationally televised debates between incumbent Ronald Reagan and Democratic presidential candidate Walter Mondale was scheduled at 9:00 p.m. on 7 October.

43 *AP, DN, FP* (10/15/84); *TSN* (10/1/84), 29; DN, *1984 Detroit Tigers*, 62. That summer Bill James had put him in the 'second division' of managers. *Sport* (7/84), 54. *SI* (5/2/88), 46–8 ranked him number one in handling players and the media, lower in other categories. Campbell believed him a great manager 'because of how he handles men'; interview.

44 Craig, *Inside Pitch*, 33, 45.

45 Chafets, *Devil's Night*, 24; Widick, *Detroit*, 248ff.

46 *DN* (2/12, 4/2/95). Interview: William Reedy, aide to Councilman Jack Kelley.

47 *Metropolitan Detroit* (7/84), 58–64; Young, *Hard Stuff*, 255.

48 *FP, DN* (10/15/84). See also editorial the next year, *DN* (4/8/85).

49 *NYT* (5/13/84), (10/15/84); *Newsweek* (9/3/84), 59–60; *MC* (6/2/84).

50 *NYT* (10/15/84). For the hourly change in *AP Reports*, see *FP* (11/26/84); the final *AP* report and pictures appeared on the front page of local Canadian newspapers, e.g., *Kitchener–Waterloo Record* (10/15/84).

51 *DN* (10/18/84); see also *Crain's* (4/9/85), 9.

52 *FP* (11/25, 30/84).

53 *DN* (5/27/80).

54 *FP* (6/18/80). *TSN* ran an editorial on the incident, (7/5/80), 14.

55 *FP* (8/11/83); *DN* (8/14/83); *TSN* (8/22/83).

56 *TSN* (5/20/85), 7. *DN* ran an editorial on the problem, (5/12/85).

57 *Chicago Tribune* (6/27/85); *NYT* (6/15/85).

58 Judge Damon Keith, a moderate African American leader, in *FP* (8/9/85); *FP* (1/30/87).

59 *FP* (10/15/84).

60 *TSN* (8/26/85), 40; *SI* (8/26/85), 32.

61 *SI* featured both the series and the play-offs: (10/5/87), 23–7; (10/12/87), 22–5; (10/19/87), 40–7.

62 Fernandez excused Madlock: 'He was doing his job'; *Toronto Star* (9/26/87). The elbow broke on contact with the artificial turf.

63 *New Yorker* (12/7/87), 86.

64 *DN* (10/5/87); *SI* (10/12/87), 22.

CHAPTER 9 A Franchise in Decline

1 From $97 to $83 million, putting Detroit 22nd among 28 teams after historically having been above the median. See *Financial World's* estimates; the latest (5/9/95), 47.

2 *DN* (10/2/94).

3 'Black political power has replaced labor clout as the major force in this unionized town'; Widick, *Detroit*, 240.

4 Interviews: Turner, Walker. See also Turner interview in *FP* (3/7/89). Another African American community leader, who requested anonymity, described Tiger Stadium as 'an island within Detroit where African Americans feel unwelcome.'

5 *FP* (11/25/84); Darden et al., *Detroit, Race, and Development*, 99.

6 *NYT Magazine* (5/17/87), 27–34, 56. *DN's Michigan* synopsized the article four months later (9/27/87).

7 *MC* (6/17/84).

8 Interviews: Walker, Campbell.

9 Interviews: Cohen, Fenkell, Campbell; for Tobik, see *FP* (12/12/89).

10 *FP* (3/7/89), (9/4/92).

11 *MC* (10/13/84), (6/17/84), (11/24/84).

12 Interviews: Campbell, Brown.

13 *MC* (11/24/84).

14 *Crain's* (4/6/87), 1.

15 Interviews: Cohen, Matlin, Turner. *MC* (7/2/84). Bob Buchta, from the Stadium Fan Club, in a separate encounter with Matlin, described him as 'the rudest, gruffest man I ever met.' Matlin conceded: 'I won't deny that I am gruff.'

16 Correspondence made available to me by Turner.

17 *FP* (3/7/89).

18 *DN* (8/6/91).

19 *USA Baseball* (3/21/96).

20 Interviews: Season-ticket holder Gregg Berendt, LaPointe, McGraw, Jim Cressman (*London Free Press*), and sundry fans.

21 Interviews: Cohen, Matlin, Snyder.

22 *DN* (6/25/89); *FP* (8/3/91); interview: Carey. See also *Detroit Monthly* (9/86), 26.

23 Interviews: William Reedy, aide to Councilman Jack Kelley and long-time friend of Billy Martin; Reverend Holley; 'Coach' Gonzalez, with four decades in sandlot baseball; Gary Ignasiuk and the writers expressed similar sentiments.

24 Interview: Matlin.

25 *Metropolitan Detroit* (3/85).

26 *MC* (3/16/85); *DN* (4/11/85). Interviews: Bob Berge, assistant to Mayor Young, Walker.

27 Interviews: McGraw, LaPointe, Vincent.

28 *SI* (5/17/93), 44–9.

29 *TSN* (8/24/60), 12; *Sport* (6/68); *TSN* (8/22/70); *NYT* (8/9/70); *Ebony* (6/80), 104–9.

30 As quoted in *DN* (4/9/87).

31 *USA Today* (4/12/87).

32 *MC* (4/18/87).

33 Interview: Holley. See also *DN*, *FP* (4/24–25/87); *MC* (5/22/87).

34 *DN* (6/28/87), (7/22/94).

35 *SI* (4/5/93), 108; *TSN* (12/28/92–1/4/93), 1.

36 See *Newsday* (2/21/93) regarding Schott's history of racist slurs. A former

Tiger player said that Schott for years regularly but privately had made racist comments at high school athletic events in Cincinnati.

37 *USA Baseball* (7/23/94).

38 A 'family atmosphere' was mentioned by Campbell, Cohen, Matlin, and Snyder in separate interviews. For the old-boy network in baseball, see Murray, *Autobiography*, 237.

39 Interviews: Brown, Herbert (batting-practice pitcher for the Tigers for 25 years after his retirement), Underwood; Wilcox in *FP* (8/4/92); Gibson quoted in Anderson, *Detroit Tigers*, 192.

40 Interview: LaPointe. Cantor, Green, McGraw, and Vincent expressed similar views.

41 Interviews: Haase, Cohen. *DN* (8/22/93). 'Fan Appreciation Night' began in 1988, a decade or two later than for some clubs.

42 Interview: Campbell.

43 Interviews: Campbell, Cohen, Haase, Matlin, Snyder.

44 *SI* (5/9/86), 109.

45 Interviews: Campbell, Schembechler. The *Washington Post* praised Schembechler's innovations (4/14/91).

46 Smith, *Voices of the Game*, 229–30. See also praise in *DN* (4/8/86), (4/4/88), (8/24/90).

47 Interview: Carey.

48 *FP* (12/20/90).

49 *DN*, *FP* (12/19–21/90), (12/29/90). Mitch Albom was quoted in Smith, *Voices of the Game*, 550, and in the *Washington Post*. For the national press, see *Chicago Tribune* (12/20/90); *TSN* (12/31/90). *Esquire* (7/91); *Washington Post* (9/30/91); (10/4/91); Smith, *Voices of the Game*, 550–1. Letters of protest appeared in *TSN* through February.

50 *Crain's* (12/24/90), 21; *FP* (1/9/91); *DN* (10/12/91).

51 *DN* (1/6, 7/91).

52 Interviews: Campbell, Fenkell, Harwell, Long, Schembechler. Cohen, Fenkell, Matlin, and Snyder all thought the instigator of Harwell's dismissal was Odenwald. If so, he had no opposition from Fenkell or Long.

53 Schembechler and Harwell agree about conversations about Harwell's possible duties one or two years hence.

54 Interviews: Carey, Harwell, Schembechler.

55 *DN* (1/6/91). Campbell said that he 'gave Falls the story in the basement of my condo'; interview: Campbell.

56 Interviews: Green, Vincent.

57 *FP* (1/17/92); *DN* (4/7/92); interview: Green.
58 Interview: Rathbun; opening quoted in Feinstein, *Play Ball*, 59.
59 Interview: Harwell, Rathbun; Feinstein, *Play Ball*, 313–16. The accounts are consistent.
60 *DN* (8/30/92).
61 *FP* (7/7/94). Interview: Rathbun. The threat not to talk to Harwell was in a press release concerning Feinstein's book. Harwell showed the press release to me. The quotation never appeared in the book.
62 Interview: Fenkell.
63 Interview: Long.
64 *FP* (4/15/94), (7/7/94); *DN* (7/3,8/94), (12/2/94).
65 Interview: Rathbun.
66 *DN* (3/5/95).
67 Ibid., (4/2/95).
68 Young, *Hard Stuff*, 286; 400 houses burned on the Hallowe'en weekend in 1986. The *Toronto Star* published a feature on Detroit, claiming it was 'past the point of no return,' the metropolitan area being one of 'apartheid' (7/11/93).
69 Rich, *Coleman Young*, 25.
70 Interview: Berendt.
71 *FP* (9/25, 27, 10/5/91); retrospective accounts in *DN* (2/16/94), *MT* (2/23/94).
72 Interviews: Cantor, McGraw.
73 When asked about collusion, Campbell laughed and said: 'I won't admit it, but I won't deny it either.'
74 Thorn and Palmer, *Total Baseball* (639) has a concise summary of the events. *TSN* ran a cover story with a picture of Gibson on the front page (12/9/85). Miller had accused the owners of boycotting free agents a decade earlier; *TSN* (10/15/77), 34. See also *FP* (8/8/85), (1/23/88); Helyar, *Lords of the Realm*, 349–50; *SI* (9/12/88), 60, regarding Detroit.
75 *FP* (2/19/94).
76 Interviews: Campbell, Schembechler. Schembechler said: 'He drained everything.' Haase, Matlin, and Snyder observed the cash-flow problem by the late 1980s; interviews.
77 *Forbes* (10/21/91). *FP* (2/11/85) had noted his spendthrift habits years earlier. Carl Lee said Monaghan approached ownership as if it 'were another toy'; interview.
78 *FP* (6/13/92); *Crain's* (10/14/91), 1; (8/3/92), 1, 31; (7/26/93), 1, 30. The

last was based on depositions filed in Schembechler's court suit against Monaghan. Campbell confirms a loan but not the amount.

79 Tiger press release (8/25/92).
80 *FP* (3/4/92). Carl Lee says, 'There is always a bigger fool available'; interview.
81 *DN* (3/27/96); *Financial World* (5/9/95), 47; (5/20/96), 56.
82 *DN* (8/4/92). *Bengal Tales* (2/94), 14–18. Interviews: Campbell, Schembechler.
83 Interviews: Campbell, Haase, Schembechler, Snyder.
84 *FP* (7/12/93), *DN* (8/22/93), *Crain's* (3/28/94), 10.
85 Zimbalist, *Baseball and Billions*, 51, 213; *Toronto Star* (6/25/95).
86 Salaries supplied by Players Association. They have been printed for various years in newspapers as well.
87 *Chicago Tribune* (8/6/95).
88 *SI* (7/10/95), 18.
89 *DN* (4/11/95).
90 WJR (10/2/95); for tributes, see *FP* (10/3/95).
91 Koppett, *Man in the Dugout*, 333; *FP* (4/9/90); *USA Baseball* (4/26/95). Interviews: Campbell, Underwood, Young.
92 Despite a 20-10 exhibition record, the Tigers' best since 1981, *USA Baseball* rated the 1996 team the worst in the majors as the season began. As it turned out, *USA Baseball* was right. They were doomed by a 5-39 stretch that left them 13-46 on 6 June. They then played nearly .500 ball until Labor Day before suffering a twelve-game losing streak and setting a major-league record for strikeouts (1268). They won only four games in September – none at home – and set league records (unofficial) for highest ERA (6.42), most home runs allowed (241), and most grand-slam home runs allowed (14). On 31 July, when their record was 34-72, they dispatched Fielder to the Yankees, Curtis to the Dodgers, and Greg Gohr to the Angels.
93 *FP* (10/31/95).
94 *DN*, *FP* (5/3/95); *Chicago Tribune* (5/7/95).
95 *Newsweek* (9/4/95), 26.
96 WJR (3/1/95).
97 *DN* (4/2/95), (10/29/95), (1/7/96).
98 *USA Baseball* (5/22/95); *NYT* (1/28/96).

CHAPTER 10 The Stadium as Symbol

1 The last privately built stadium exclusively for baseball was Dodger Sta-

dium, opened in 1962; Joe Robbie Stadium, now used by the Florida Marlins, was privately financed but built for football in 1987. For funding see note 3 below and CNN Special Report (10/25/95).

2 *TSN* headlined its issue of 7/15/53: 'Stadium Costs Beyond Reach of Owners.' Two years later, it declared Ebbets Field 'no longer suitable for profitable operation'; (5/24/55), 12. Thorn and Palmer, *Total Baseball*, declared the costs of 50,000 seaters 'virtually prohibitive' by the 1960s (269).

3 See Baade and Dye, 'Sports Stadiums'; Baim, *Sports Stadium*; Bess, *City Ballpark Magic*; Quirk and Fort, *Paydirt* (145–71) for investments. For historical perspective on other cities, see Markham and Teplitz, *Baseball Economics*, 48ff; Miller, *Baseball Business*, 71, 296–8; Richmond, *Ballpark*, 91–101; Zimbalist, *Baseball and Billions*, 136–8. The Toronto SkyDome cost $578 million, four times the original estimate, cost Ontario taxpayers an additional $23 million annually, and needed debt restructuring; *Toronto Star*.

4 Smith, *To Absent Friends*, 84.

5 Quoted in *DN* (4/1/52).

6 Smith, *Voices of the Game*, 221.

7 *SI* (9/9/74), 88–9; *TSN* acknowledged: 'Briggs Stadium is the best maintained baseball plant in the country'; (7/11/51), 7–8, It deemed it the 'most serviceable park in the majors' a dozen years later; (4/6/63), 14. In 1976, Richard Moss rated the ball field 'A' and the atmosphere 'A+' but the seating 'D' and the facilities 'D–'; *Tiger Stadium*, 206. Wood rated Tiger Stadium 'average' in the late 1980s; *Dodger Dogs*.

8 Interview: Jim Campbell.

9 Quoted in Betzold and Casey, *Queen of Diamonds*, 89.

10 *DN* (4/11, 12, 13/56), (5/13/56).

11 *TSN* contrasted parking in Detroit and at Milwaukee's County Stadium; (1/22/58), 8.

12 Interviews: Lew Matlin, Ralph Snyder, George Puscas. The last, a columnist for the *FP*, accompanied the city's Olympic Committee. The former two were Tiger executives.

13 Betzold and Casey, *Queen of Diamonds*, 89. The club then was spending only $100,000 annually for upkeep and $200,000 in repairs – no more than a decade earlier; *DN* (4/4/63).

14 *DN* (7/11/67).

15 Darden et al., *Detroit, Race, and Development*, 4–5, 46–51.

16 *DN* (11/30/71), (1/13/72); *Tiger Yearbook*, 1972; see also review in *FP* (8/24/91); Betzold and Casey, *Queen of Diamonds*, 91–100.

17 *DN* (1/13/72).

18 *FP* (6/6/72); *DN* (6/20/73); *TSN* (11/13/72), 14; *DN* (4/23/91).

19 Two hundred thousand people emigrated from Detroit and the number of requested guns within Detroit tripled in the two years following the 1967 riot. Murders in 1971–2 totalled 1109, exceeding the 988 for the entire decade of the 1950s. Conot, *American Odyssey*, 518–19, 530; Young, *Hard Stuff*, 173–9; Widick, *Detroit*, 189–90, 201–5.

20 *FP* (6/30/72). See also *TSN* (2/6/71); *DN* (2/3/73), (10/20/75), (1/20/77). In 1974 Fetzer called the stadium a 'noose around our neck' *DN* (10/19/74). The Mayor's Committee concurred that there were 'so many structural problems,' but Young later admitted that the conclusion was based entirely on information given by Fetzer.

21 *DN, FP* (9/30, 10/1/76). *DN* noted that the city had no money to take over the stadium.

22 *TSN* (3/26/77), 13 (regarding New York); (12/17/77), 16 (quoting *Parade*); *SI* (7/17/78), 43. Owners in established cities were slow to seek subsidies, but later ones 'show a mind-boggling greediness. Urban politicians later came to respond with alacrity to the most outrageous demands of sports entrepreneurs'; Kuklick, *To Every Thing a Season*, 135.

23 *DN, FP* (10/20, 21/76). *DN* reported that Rogell was the contact man (10/26/76), confirmed in interview with Rogell. *TSN* reported that Fetzer Enterprises would receive a $3.5 million tax break, against the stadium's appraised value of $8 million; see also *DN* (7/14/77), *TSN* (8/6/77) regarding taxes.

24 *DN* (3/21/79).

25 Interviews: Campbell, Henderson, Rogell, Young. Campbell said that only Fetzer would know for sure. Henderson said that returns from the 1978 investment were disappointing.

26 *Detroit Monthly* (5/88), 81–2 (hereafter *DM*).

27 Chafetz, *Devil's Night*, 294.

28 Detroit Baseball Club 'Prospectus,' 1992.

29 *DM* (5/88), 82; Snyder, in charge of stadium operations, confirmed the plans and that they were 'scrapped for lack of money.' The Mexican Hat Dance was never played on bat day because of fear of the vibrations. Matlin says the scoreboard was state-of-the-art in 1980. Interviews.

30 *FP* (5/12/91); Club Prospectus (1992). Mayor's press release (7/24/91). *FP* (5/25/83) reported that an average of $225,000 had been paid during the first five years. Quirk and Fort, *Paydirt*, estimated rent as $150–400,000 and

maintenance at more than $700,000 annually (147). The Tigers paid no rent after 1989.

31 Interview: Campbell; see also *DM* (5/88), 82.

32 *DN* (7/19/83), (3/7/88); *FP* (4/11/84). Campbell confirms Monaghan's original intention was to renovate, 'but we convinced him otherwise'; interview: Campbell. Monaghan had his private box redesigned in 1985 by John Davids, a young architecture student of Leonard Eaton at the University of Michigan. Monaghan and William Haase praised the park to him. No mention was made of a new stadium. Interview: John Davids. Davids became the principal architect for the Cochrane Plan.

33 Falls, *Die Hard Tiger Fan*, 134.

34 *Chicago Tribune* (6/27/85). Asked by me about this article, Campbell said, 'The town was riding high after the World Series. I wouldn't badmouth the stadium.'

35 *FP* (6/30/85); *DM* (5/88), 82.

36 Interviews: Campbell and Haase. Quotation is from Haase. Haase concluded that management had committed itself to a new stadium in 1985 when the report was being drafted, but Monaghan did not give approval until 'early 1986.' Haase was put in charge of planning; Snyder took charge of all Tiger Stadium maintenance.

37 Interview: Young. Haase confirms discussions with the mayor's office during these years. They are also mentioned in a mayor's press release of 4 October 1991 that refers to four meetings plus one with Governor John Blanchard.

38 Interview: Lapointe. Haase and Lapointe agree that Lapointe wrote the column with no urging from the Tigers; *DN* (7/28–8/5/87).

39 *FP* (8/23/87); (9/13/87). Betzold and LaPointe debated renovation versus new construction in 'Sunday Soundoff' in *FP* (2/7/88). Betzold did not mention in the second or later columns that he was a co-founder of the Stadium Fan Club. He was later 'taken off' the story.

40 Interviews: Betzold, Buchta, and Frank Rashid for this and following paragraph. Buchta regretted their choice of the name 'fan club' because it opened them to criticism as being mere nostalgia buffs. For a sympathetic account of the founders, see Amy Wilson's lengthy article in *FP* (4/3/94).

41 Kuklick, *To Every Thing a Season*, 190–1; *NYT* (4/20/88); *Inland Architect* (2/10/91).

42 *SI* (3/24, 31/78), 36. Miller, *Baseball Business*, 71, 272, 296–8. Markham and Teplitz, *Baseball Economics*, 48; Baade, 'Economic Rationale'; Baade

and Dye, 'Sports Stadium'; *Business Week* (5 December 1983), 110–12; *Newsweek* (12/28/87); Hines, 'Housing, Baseball and Creeping Socialism.'

43 *Tiger Stadium Fan Club Newsletter* (1/88), which recounts the club's formation; *FP* (11/12/87).

44 Tiger management was not about to encourage nostalgia; Lew Matlin stated that Dan Odenwald, who was in charge of public relations, was also afraid that organizers 'would blast management from the field.' Interviews.

45 *DN* (4/12/88).

46 Interview: Haase. Campbell had wanted to keep publicity away from the Tigers, but communications between the Tigers and Domino's were breaking down then as Monaghan's financial empire started to suffer from financial overreach. Letter to Rashid quoted in *TSFCN* (1/88). Campbell was 'correct' in his dealings with McDevitt but told Monaghan: 'I'll never like the son of a bitch'; interview: Campbell.

47 *FP* (1/6/88), (1/17/88), (1/22/88); *DN* (1/19/88), (2/3, 4, 5/88), (3/7, 9/88); clips from the press conference were carried on the local television shows. Young repeated in an interview to me in 1994 (six years after his original statement) that it could 'fall down in five years.' On 19 May 1989 he also said that it was 'about to fall down.' It has not yet.

48 Interviews: Buchta, Rashid.

49 *Unobstructed Views*, newsletter of the Fan Club (hereafter *UV*) (2/88).

50 *UV* (3/88) lists many; *Crain's Detroit Business* (1/19/88) was one of the first to support the Fan Club publicly and oppose a new stadium.

51 *DM* (5/88), 82–4; *DN* (4/12/88); *FP* (4/17/88).

52 *DN* (7/31/88), (8/11/88). Earlier *FP* had challenged the need for extensive structural repairs (4/17/88).

53 Interview: Snyder.

54 *FP* (8/22/88); Young had said to WDIV-TV on 20 April that Zetlin did not 'know what the hell he's talking about.' Monaghan admitted that the $45–100 million was merely 'an informal conversational affair'; *DN* (8/11/88).

55 *DM* (5/88), 157.

56 *FP* (7/19/92).

57 Mayor's press release, 24 July 1991.

58 *Crain's* (3/27/89); *DN, FP* (4/22/89).

59 Interviews: Campbell, Schembechler. See also chapter 9.

60 Interview: Haase.

61 Interview: Young.

62 *DN* (4/30/90). Campbell and Haase remain convinced that they were right

to ignore the Fan Club. Snyder calls that stance 'the Tigers' biggest mistake.'

63 *FP* (3/7/88).

64 Interviews: Campbell, Schembechler, Snyder.

65 Interview: Snyder. He noted, however, that 'there were good ideas in that report.' *BEI*, the architectural firm hired by Wayne County to evaluate the Cochrane Plan, claimed that the renovations would cost twice as much as estimated. They did not find any unrepairable defects, however. *UV* (6/91); *Crain's* (3/25/91).

66 Press conference of 22 January 1990. *DN* (1/20/90); *FP* (4/22/90); radio interview of 5/31 on WCSX (tape supplied by Tiger Stadium Fan Club).

67 *Crain's* (1/29/90); see also George Cantor, *DN* (1/20/90) and (4/30/90); Cantor later supported a new stadium when the county promised to provide funds; *DN* (5/9/90); see also *FP* (5/9/90), *Chicago Tribune* (5/10/90). *DN* (12/23/90) report on Dean Baim's research about economic returns from public subsidies challenged the hypothesis that the city would receive an economic boost. Baim's book (*The Sports Stadium as Municipal Investment*) appeared in 1994. See also Gershman, *Evolution of the Ballpark*, 230–8; Zimbalist, *Baseball and Billions*, 36–8.

68 McNamara warned that the Tigers might move to Miami; *DN* (4/23/91). Where he got that idea is a mystery. The idea that Detroit might qualify to move as a 'distressed franchise' appeared in *DN* (8/4/91). *UV* responded (9/91) with the official criteria – under which the Tigers did not qualify.

69 *UV* (10/1/90). A copy of the lease was obtained on 13 September; for varying opinion see *Detroit Legal News* (6/18/91), (7/2/91). The 1992 club's prospectus makes no mention of the possibility of nullifying the lease.

70 Interviews: Haase, Schembechler.

71 Interview: Cantor.

72 *FP* (2/27/91). Council president Maryann Mahaffey also criticized Monaghan for racism.

73 *MT* (4/3/91), 10; the *Los Angeles Times* referred to 'Monaghan's public relations gaffes,' criticized management generally and noted that 'public sentiment is running overwhelmingly to keeping the stadium within city limits' (4/7/91). *NYT* said that 'Tigers' management doesn't seem to care much for public opinion' (4/8/91).

74 Interviews: Haase, Schembechler. *DN*, *FP* (4/23/91); *DN* (5/9/91).

75 *DN*, *FP* (4/23/91); *DN* (5/9/91). Charlie Vincent, *Free Press* sports colum-

nist, remarked, 'I was at the Economic Club and saw the speech as very con-
frontational' (interview). Having listened to a tape of the address, I would
agree. Two years later, Vincent challenged Schembechler's credibility
because of his own deposition in a lawsuit against Monaghan: 'Since this is
what Schembechler said in a sworn deposition, I assume what he says here is
the truth, or the truth as he knows it: that the Tigers were a financially
sound organization on their own and that their money problems were the
result of deficits in the rest of Monaghan's empire. What then, was the truth
on April 22, 1991 when Schembechler made his infamous 'rusty girder'
speech to the Economic Club of Detroit?' *FP* (7/29/93).

76 *UV* (6/91).
77 Cantor said, 'I have never seen a man's reputation turn with such a sudden
jolt.' Young complained that the Tigers had not been returning his calls for
two years; interview.
78 *Crain's* (3/25/91). Congress, however, had forbade the selling of tax-exempt
bonds to finance construction of stadiums in 1986; *DN* (4/23/91).
79 *FP* (4/20/91). Schembechler endorsed the project, promising to pay rent
and put a surcharge on tickets – that meant fans would pay; *DN* (4/23/91).
80 *FP* (4/27/91), (5/2/91), (5/31/91); mayor's press release (7/24/91). Young
said there 'has always been a conflict between the county and the city. I
always intended the stadium to be in Detroit'; interview.
81 A series of published polls showed taxpayers, especially outstate ones, generally opposed to using public funds for a stadium. Even in the tri-county
area, three to one were opposed. *DN* (8/4/91), (8/7/92), (7/17/94); *UV* (6/
94); *FP* (4/27/91), (10/14/92), (9/28/95).
82 Interview: Haase.
83 *FP* (5/9/89); *DN* (4/24/91).
84 The coalition included Louis Beer, Walter Briggs IV, Rev. Ervin Brown of
Christ Church of Detroit, Father Larry Carney of St Anne's, Karl Greimel,
Bishop Thomas Gumbleton, State Senator John Kelly, Bruno Leon, Ron
Malis of Porter Street Station, Father John Meyer of St Peter's Episcopal
Church, Charles Moon, the National Trust for Historic Preservation, Rev.
William Quick, Sister Carol Quigley of Core City Neighborhoods, Sasha
Roberts of F.O.C.U.S. Inc., Jean Shapero, John Stroh III, Ed Strong of the
Briggs Community, Kim Stroud of Cityscape, the Tiger Stadium Fan Club,
Brian Tremain of the Corktown Preservation Society, Elliot Trumbull, and
Dr Edward Turner. Source: *UV* (9/91).

85 *UV* (9/92).

86 *FP* (1/16/93), (6/16/93). *DN* (Ilitch interview, 8/22/93).

87 *FP* (7/16/93). He is more wary in (10/9/93).

88 *FP* (3/24/94).

89 *DN, FP* (3/23–26/94). 'Themed entertainment' districts were popular among planners across the country; *Newsweek* (9/11/95).

90 *FP* (3/20, 3/24/94), *DN* (5/13/94). *Crain's* (3/28/94) warned that it would not assure Detroit's revival and many retailers expressed disinterest in locating within the development.

91 (5/1/94). The next day an *FP* editorial called for more public discussion of funding. See also McGraw, *FP* (6/6/94).

92 *DN* (6/19/94); *DN/FP* (1/22/95). His promise never to move in *DN* (8/27/92).

93 Ibid. (2/19/95).

94 *FP* (2/26/96).

95 *DN, FP* (9/21/95); *DN* (10/29/95), (10/28/95); *UV* (11/95). Suggestions to bypass the legislature to obtain funding had been suggested in *DN* (3/29, 8/20/95). The tentative plan was announced on 24 August. Originally it was to be east of Woodward on an eighty-acre tract, but was moved west when speculators pushed land prices there too high. It was then moved back east when the Lions joined the venture. *FP* (10/9/95), (8/21/96).

96 *MC* (3/19/96), *FP* (3/12, 17/96). They supported casino gambling as well after years of opposition.

97 *DN* (3/20, 23, 24).

98 *Newsweek* (9/12/94), 46. Interview: Berendt. Similarly, see *LA Times*, quoted in *DN* (12/12/95), commending 'a kinder, gentler sermon' and noting the mayor's outreach to the suburbs.

99 Maryland's secretary of state had ruled appropriation bills not subject to referendum in order to bypass popular opposition to public funding of Baltimore's stadium. Richmond, *Ballpark*, 101.

100 Zimbalist, *Baseball and Billions*, 136; Quirk and Fort, *Paydirt*, 129. The latter described Tiger Stadium as 'scheduled for replacement' (125).

101 Feinstein, *Play Ball*. The State of Maryland avoided a referendum when the Secretary of State ruled that appropriation bills were not subject to referendum and the courts upheld him. Richmond, *Ballpark*, 91–101; he concurs that Williams 'blackmailed' the city.

102 United States, 'Sports Programming and Cable Television' (1989), 273.

103 Baim, *Sports Stadium*, 169, 175, 190–1; see also Baade and Dye, 'Sports Stadiums'; Quirk and Fort, *Paydirt*, 145–71; *Chicago Tribune* (9/2/95); *Barron's* (8/19/96), 23–6.
104 Noll, 'Baseball Economics,' 28.
105 Interviews: Cantor, Rev. James Holley, Vincent; *DN* (2/13/94). Johnson on 'Spotlight on the News' (WXYZ-TV, 3/1/92).
106 *FP* (10/9/95).

EPILOGUE

1 Roger Angell described the season eloquently; *New Yorker* (10/17/94), 68–76.
2 *Metropolitan Detroit* (4/81), 138.
3 Chass, 'Diamond Business,' 78.
4 Quoted retrospectively in *Atlanta Constitution* (3/26/95).
5 A chronology exists in *DN* (4/2/95) and in TSN, *Baseball Guide*, 180–1.
6 *FP* (9/5/94). *USA Today Baseball Weekly* was more prescient than Fehr, warning that the owners were adamant; (6/15/94), 4.
7 Will in *DN* (3/16/90); *Newsweek* (9/14/92), 72–3; *Time* (4/12/93), 55–9.
8 *DN* (8/12/95); *Lansing State Journal* (8/14/95); *DN* (8/11/95).
9 *USA Baseball* (8/30/95); *Time* (8/22/94), 36; *Newsweek* (8/22/94), 46–52. See also *SI* editorial 'I don't care if you never come back' (9/12/94), 86. 'In Memoriam,' *NYT* (9/5/94). *Maclean's* (Canada's national magazine) (9/19/94), 13.
10 *FP* (8/29, 9/5/94; 4/3, 4/10/95). *DN* (3/28/95).
11 *FP* (8/31/94).
12 The agreement had not been approved by the players' association at this writing. See *NYT* (3/17/96) and *USA Baseball* (3/22/96).
13 *USA Baseball* (2/17/95).
14 *DN, FP* (10/4/94); *USA Baseball* (4/11/95),6.
15 *Newsday* (2/5/95); quoted in *Toronto Star* (2/6/95).
16 *Chicago Tribune* (10/1/95); *NYT* (3/31/96).
17 *Financial World* (5/9/95), 46–7.
18 Ibid., (1/8, 8/13/95). *USA Baseball* (4/1/95), 6.
19 *USA Baseball* (4/5/96). Fielder's salary of $9.2 million was the highest in baseball.

20 Reuter poll on 27 April before the season began. September poll in *Chicago Tribune* (4/16/95). For the 1960s and 1970s, see Noverr and Ziewacz, *The Games They Played*, 339.

21 *DN*, *AP* (2/19/95).

22 *Tampa Tribune* (3/17/95); *USA Baseball* (3/15/95), 14; *New York Daily News* (3/18/95).

23 *SI* (7/10/95), 18.

24 Quoted in *Toronto Star* (4/17/95).

25 *Chicago Tribune* (11/27/95).

26 Ibid. (6/25/95).

27 At the 1996 All-Star Game break, major-league attendance was up 5.4 per cent from its level at the 1995 break, but down 17 per cent from July 1994. Ten million ballots were cast for All-Star selections in 1996, up 73 per cent from 1995.

28 *Newsweek* (9/16/96), 78–9; *SI* (9/30/96), 31–40; *NYT Magazine* (10/6/96), 60–1.

29 Quoted in Zimbalist, *Baseball and Billions*, xiii.

Bibliography

A NOTE ON SOURCES

Printed Sources

1. Government publications: For baseball and sport generally, a number of U.S. congressional inquiries provide both statistical information and testimony. The most important of these are the two Celler Commissions (1952 and 1957), which include unique financial statements for all teams and hundreds of pages of testimony from owners, executives, players, and writers concerning their perceptions of the state of the game. Other reports include data concerning broadcasting and labor relations. Those that I cited are listed in the second section of this bibliography (under 'United States'). James Miller (*Baseball Business*) prints a more complete list.

2. Newspapers: The *Detroit News* and *Detroit Free Press* are important for editorial positions and for the information that zealous sportswriters reported. Both newspapers generously allowed me to use their clippings files and (for the last decade) computer searches of topics.

   I also availed myself of microfilm copies of those two newspapers, available at the Detroit Public Library and Wayne State University. From those libraries I also used microfilm copy of the African American weekly publication, the *Michigan Chronicle*. African American newspapers have been neglected in most studies of American sport. *Unobstructed View*, the Tiger Stadium Fan Club newsletter presents its views.

   For national publications, I used the *New York Times Index*, the *International*

Index to Periodical Literature, and *Readers' Guide to Periodical Literature* to ferret out relevant articles. For recent years there are a host of on-line services available; I used Lexis-Nexis. The Fulton County Library (Atlanta) has a good collection of southern newspapers. *The Sporting News* also printed excerpts of opinion from other national newspapers. Players and friends supplied some clippings.

   TSN is an invaluable source for the first thirty years of this study. Its conservative editorial policy reflected the baseball establishment, but individual reporters began to depart from the party line, especially after the death of J. Taylor Spink. Leonard Koppett and Murray Chass, both of whom also wrote for the *New York Times*, were among the first to sympathize with players in their confrontations with owners. *TSN* also published lengthy excerpts from congressional committees and court decisions. *USA Today Baseball Weekly* is better for financial information in recent years.

3. Statistics: Fred Smith's *S.T.A.T.S.* reproduces Tiger players' records, 1934–90 and lists important trades. *TSN*'s annual [*Official*] *Guide* (the title varies) and *Official Baseball Register* give complete player and team records for each year. *TSN*'s *Complete Baseball Record Book* catalogues all individual, club, and league records. John Thorn and Peter Palmer (eds) in *Total Baseball* (1989 and 1995) list career and annual records for all players as well as attendance figures and results of post-season play. It also includes excellent summary articles on a variety of topics; the articles in the earlier edition are better. *The Baseball Encyclopedia* provides similar information. *Tiger Yearbooks* and *Media Guides* supply biographical data on players, which I used to build a prosopography. They also are a source for advertisers, ticket prices, starting times, and special events.

4. Memoirs concerning players' experiences are listed in the main section of this bibliography.

Manuscript Collections

The Library of Congress Manuscript Room has papers of Emmanuel Celler, Branch Rickey, and Arthur Mann, Rickey's assistant. The last two collections are disappointing, but the Celler papers reveal how he moved from sympathy for to criticism of the baseball establishment during the course of hearings. The University of Kentucky has the papers of Happy Chandler, but I did not consult them.

The Harwell Collection in the Burton Historical Collection within the Detroit Public Library contains eight boxes of clippings, photo albums (1941–55) and media guides (1955–68), scrapbooks, and about 200 books and pamphlets. The collection includes material for both Detroit and other teams. Much of it concerns the period before Harwell joined the Tigers.

The Hall of Fame Library at Cooperstown, New York, has team press guides, yearbooks, and press releases, rather uneven players and officials clippings files by name, interviews within the audio-visual section, an extensive collection of secondary literature, including periodicals, and *TSN*'s record books.

Finances

Although there are gaps, the Tigers' available records are among the most complete for any team. The Celler Commission and records published at the time of the sale of the Tigers in 1956 (published in *TSN* but not used in any other book) allow examination of the Briggs years. Jim Campbell provided records for his three-decade tenure. Detroit newspapers published information filed with the State of Michigan during the 1980s. The club's own report of 1992, prepared for buyers, is extensive.

Interviews

The unique source in this book is the more than 100 interviews that I conducted with former players and, executives, grandsons of Walter Briggs, and with sports writers, community leaders, and Marvin Miller. These were supplemented with audio-visual material from the Hall of Fame Library and tapes of television interviews, provided by the Tiger Stadium Fan Club.

Other

The Society for American Baseball Research (P.O. Box 93183, Cleveland, Ohio 44104) has an extensive collection of unpublished papers and tapes; they are uneven in quality but should be perused. The Major League Baseball Players Association (12 East 49th Street, New York, New York 10017) is very generous in providing materials for researchers; my thanks to Arthur Schack. The National Association of Minor Leagues (201 Bayshore Drive S.E., St Petersburg, Florida 33701) will also send materials. The offices of Major League Baseball will not.

WORKS CITED

Anderson, Douglas. *Contemporary Sports Reporting* (1985)
Anderson, William. *The Detroit Tigers: A Pictorial Celebration* (1992)
Angell, Roger. *Five Seasons: A Baseball Companion* (1977)
Baade, Robert. 'Is There an Economic Rationale for Subsidizing Sports Stadiums?' Heartland Institute Study no. 13 (1987)
Baade, Robert, and Richard Dye. 'Sports Stadiums and Area Development: A Critical Review,' *Economic Development Review* 2 (August 1988), 265–75
Baim, Dean. *The Sports Stadium as Municipal Investment* (1994)
Bak, Richard. *Cobb Would Have Caught It: The Golden Age of Baseball in Detroit* (1991)
Ball, Donald, and John Loy. *Sport and Social Class* (1975)
Becker, Ken. 'Your Toronto Blue Jays: The Brats of Summer.' *Toronto Life* (May 1979), 18–25
Benagh, Jim, and Jim Hawkins. *Go Bird Go* (1976)
Berkow, Ira. *Hank Greenberg: The Story of My Life* (1989)
Berry, Robert, William Gould, and Paul Staudohar. *Labor Relations in Professional Sports* (1986)
Bess, Philip. *City Ballpark Magic* (1989)
Betzold, Michael, and Ethan Casey. *Queen of Diamonds: The Tiger Stadium Story* (1991)
Bianculli, David. *Teleliteracy: Taking Television Seriously* (1994)
Bluthardt, Robert. 'Fenway Park and the Golden Age of the Baseball Park.' *Journal of Popular Culture* 21 (Summer 1987), 43–52
Bookbinder, Harold. 'A Study of the Work Histories of Men Leaving a Short Life Span Occupation.' *Personnel and Guidance Journal* 34 (1955), 164–7
Bouton, James. *Ball Four and Ball Five: An Update* (1981)
Brosnan, James. *The Long Season* (1961)
Buchta, Robert. 'Baseball's Anti-Trust Exemption: Its History and Current Function.' Unpublished (1992)
Burk, Robert. *Never Just a Game: Players, Owners, and American Baseball to 1920* (1994)
Butler, Hal. *Al Kaline and the Detroit Tigers* (1953–73) (1973)
Chafets, Ze'ev. *Devil's Night and Other True Tales of Detroit* (1990)
– 'The Tragedy of Detroit.' *New York Times Magazine* (7/29/90), 20–6 and passim

Charnovsky, Harold. 'The Major League Professional Baseball Players: Self-Conception Versus the Popular Image.' *International Review of Sport Sociology* 3 (1968), 39–55

Chass, Murray. 'Diamond Business.' *Athlon Baseball 1995*, 68–78

Chass, Murray, and Hal Godwin. 'Drug Abuse in Baseball.' In R.E. Lapchick, ed., *Fractured Focus: Sport as a Reflection of Society* (1986), 277–309

Child, Malcolm. *How to Play Big League Baseball* (1951)

Cobb, Ty, with Al Stump. *My Life in Baseball: The True Record* (1960)

Conot, Robert. *American Odyssey* (1974)

Craig, Roger. *Inside Pitch* (1984)

Curtis, James E., and John W. Loy. 'Positional Segregation in Professional Baseball: Replications, Trend Data and Critical Observation.' *International Review of Sport Sociology* 13:4 (1978), 5–23

Danzig, Allison, and Joe Reichler. *The History of Baseball: Its Great Players, Teams, and Managers* (1959)

Darden, Joe, et al. *Detroit, Race, and Uneven Development* (1987)

Day, C.R. *Education for the Industrial World* (1987)

Detroit News. *1984 Detroit Tigers: The Magic Season* (1984)

DiMaggio, Joseph. *Lucky to Be a Yankee* (1946)

Dolson, Frank. *Beating the Bushes* (1982)

Dworkin, James. *Owners versus Players: Baseball and Collective Bargaining* (1981)

Eckhouse, M. 'Detroit Tigers: The Connection of Detroit Baseball and Stability.' In *Encyclopedia of Major League Baseball Team Histories: The American League* (1991), 140–82

Eitzen, D. Stanley, and George Sage. *The Sociology of American Sport* (1982)

Falkner, David. *A Great Time Coming: The Life of Jackie Robinson* (1995)

– *The Last Yankee* (1992)

– *The Short Season* (1986)

Falls, Joe. *The Detroit Tigers: Its Greatest Teams* (1975)

– *So You Think You're a Die Hard Tiger Fan* (1986)

Falls, Joe, and Gerald Astor. *The Detroit Tigers: An Illustrated History* (1989)

Feinstein, John. *Play Ball: The Life and Troubled Times of Major League Baseball* (1993)

Fidrych, Mark, and Tom Clark. *No Big Deal* (1977)

Flood, Curt, with Richard Carter. *The Way It Is* (1971)

Fountain, Charles. *Sportswriter: The Life and Times of Grantland Rice* (1993)

Freedman, Warren. *Professional Sports and Antitrust* (1987)

Freehan, Bill. *Behind the Mask: An Inside Diary* (1969)

Freidel, Frank, and Alan Brinkley. *America in the Twentieth Century*. 5th ed. (1982)

Frick, Ford. *Games, Asterisks and People: Memoirs of a Lucky Fan* (1973)

Gentry, Curt. *J. Edgar Hoover: The Man and His Secrets* (1991)

Gerlach, Larry. *The Men in Blue: Conversations with Umpires* (1981)

Gershman, Mike. *The Evolution of the Ballpark* (1993)

Gibson, Campbell. 'Competitive Imbalance.' *Baseball Research Journal* 24 (1995) 153–6

Goldstein, Warren. *Spartan Seasons: How Baseball Survived the Second World War* (1980)

Golenbock, Peter. *Wild, High and Tight: The Life and Death of Billy Martin* (1994)

Gorman, Jerry, and Kirk Calhoun. *The Name of the Game* (1994)

Green, Jerry. *Year of the Tiger* (diary, 1968) (1969)

Grier, William H., and Price M. Cobbs. *Black Rage* (1968)

Greenberg, Stanley. *Middle Class Dreams: The Politics and Power of the New American Majority* (1995)

Guschov, Stephen. 'The Exemption of Baseball from Federal Antitrust Laws.' *Baseball Research Journal* 23 (1994), 69–74

Gutman, Dan. *Baseball Babylon* (1992)

Guttmann, Allen. *Sports Spectators* (1986)

– *A Whole New Ball Game: An Interpretation of American Sports* (1988)

Halberstam, David. *October 1964* (1994)

– *Summer of '49* (1989)

Harwell, Ernie. *The Babe Shined My Shoes* (1994)

Harwell, Ernie, and Fred Smith. *Tuned to Baseball* (1985)

Hearle, Rudolf. 'Career Patterns and Career Contingencies of Professional Baseball Players, and an Occupation Analysis.' In Donald Ball and John Loy, *Sport and the Social Order* (1975), 457–520

Helyar, John. *Lords of the Realm* (1994)

Hill, Art. *I Don't Care If I Never Come Back* (1980)

Hines, Thomas. 'Housing, Baseball and Creeping Socialism: The Battle of Chavez Ravine, Los Angeles.' *Journal of Urban History* 8 (Spring 1982), 123–43

Honig, David. *The American League* (1983, 1987)

Horowitz, Ira. 'Sports Broadcasting.' In Roger Noll, ed., *Government and the Sports Business* (1974), 275–323

Irwin, Richard. 'A Historical Review of Litigation in Baseball.' *Marquette Sports Law Journal* 1 (Spring 1991), 283–300

James, Bill. *The Bill James Historical Baseball Abstract* (1988)

Jennings, Kenneth. *Balls and Strikes: The Money Game in Professional Baseball* (1990)

Jordan, Pat. *A False Spring* (1975)

Kahn, Roger. *The Era 1947–1957* (1993)

Karst, Gene, and Martin Jones. *Who's Who in Professional Baseball* (1973)

Kiehr, Harvey, J.E. Haynes, and F.I. Firsov. *The Secret World of American Communism* (1995)

Kool, Nancy. 'Enlightenment and the Oldest Tiger.' *Monthly Detroit* (April 1981), 32–41

Koppett, Leonard. *The Man in the Dugout* (1993)

Korr, Charles. 'Marvin Miller and the New Unionism in Baseball.' In Paul Staudohar and James Mangan, eds, *The Business of Professional Sports* (1991), 115–34

Kramer, Gerry. *Instant Replay* (1966)

Kuhn, Bowie. *Hardball: The Education of a Baseball Commissioner* (1987)

Kuklick, Bruce. *To Every Thing a Season: Shibe Park and Urban Philadelphia 1909-1976* (1991)

Leflore, Ron, with Jim Hawkins. *Breakout: From Prison to the Major Leagues* (1978)

Lieb, Frederick. *The Detroit Tigers* (1946)

Lincoln, James. *The Anatomy of a Riot* (1968)

Locke, Hubert. *The Detroit Riot of 1967* (1969)

Lowenfish, Lee, and Tony Lupien. *The Imperfect Diamond: The Story of Baseball's Reserve System and the Men Who Fought to Change It* (1980)

Loy, John W., and Joseph F. Elvogue. 'Racial Segregation in American Sport.' *International Review of Sport Sociology* 5 (1970), 5–24

McLain, Denny, and Dave Diles. *Nobody's Perfect* (1975)

McLain, Denny, with Mike Nahrstept. *Strikeout: The Story of Denny McLain* (1988)

Manchester, William. *American Caesar: Douglas MacArthur, 1880–1964* (1978)

Mandell, Richard. 'Modern Criticism of Sport.' In Donald Kyle and Gary Stark, eds, *Essays on Sport History and Sport Mythology* (1990), 119–36

Marazzi, Rick, and Len Fiorito. *Aaron to Zipfel* (1985)
– *Aaron to Zuverink: A Nostalgic Look at the Baseball Players of the Fifties* (1982)
Markham, Jesse, and Paul Teplitz. *Baseball Economics and Public Policy* (1981)
Martin, Alfred Manuel, and Peter Golenbock. *Number 1* (1980)
Mead, William. *Even the Browns ... The Early Forties* (1978)
Medoff, Marshall H. 'Positional Segregation and Professional Baseball.' *International Review of Sport Sociology* 12:1 (1977), 49–56
Miller, James. *The Baseball Business: Pursuing Pennants and Profits in Baltimore* (1990)
Miller, Jeff. *Down to the Wire* (1992)
Miller, Marvin. *A Whole Different Ball Game: The Sport and Business of Baseball* (1991)
Monaghan, Tom, with Robert Anderson. *Pizza Tiger* (1986)
Moss, Richard. *Tiger Stadium* (1976)
Murray, Jim. *Autobiography: Jim Murray* (1993)
Neithercut, Mark. *Detroit Twenty Years After: A Statistical Profile of the Detroit Area Since 1967* (1987)
Noll, Roger. 'Baseball Economics in the 1990s.' Report (1994)
– 'The Economic Viability of Professional Baseball.' Report (1985)
Noverr, Douglas, and Lawrence Ziewacz. *The Games They Played: Sports in American History 1865–1980* (1983)
Obojski, Robert. *Bush League: A History of Minor League Baseball* (1975)
Olson, Jack. 'The Black Athlete – A Shameful Story.' 5 parts. *Sports Illustrated*, July 1 (pp. 72–7), 8 (18–32), 15 (28–43), 22 (28–41), 29 (20–35), 1968
Parr, Jeanne. *The Superwives* (1976)
Paulos, John. *A Mathematician Reads the Newspaper* (1995)
Phillips, John. 'Race and Career Opportunities in Major League Baseball: 1960–1980.' *Journal of Sport and Social Issues* 7 (1983), 1–17
Plimpton, George. *Paper Lion* (1966)
Pluto, Terry. *The Curse of Rocky Colavito* (1994)
Quirk, James, and Rodney Fort. *Paydirt: The Business of Professional Team Sports* (1992)
Rader, Benjamin. *American Sports: From the Age of Folk Games to the Age of Spectators* (1983)
– *In Its Own Image: How Television Transformed Sports* (1984)
Reiss, Steven. 'Baseball and Social Mobility.' *Journal of Interdisciplinary History* 10 (Fall 1980), 245–60

- 'Professional Sports as an Avenue of Social Mobility in America: Some Myths and Realities.' In Donald Kyle and Gary Stark, eds, *Essays on Sport History and Sport Mythology* (1990)
- 'A Social Profile of the Professional Football Player 1920–82.' In Paul Staudohar and James Mangan, eds, *The Business of Professional Sports* (1991), 222–46

Reston, James. *Collision at Home Plate: Lives of Pete Rose and A. Bartlett Giametti* (1991)

Rich, Wilbur. *Coleman Young and Detroit Politics* (1989)

Richmond, Peter. *Ballpark: Camden Yards and the Building of an American Dream* (1993)

Ritter, Laurence. *The Glory of Their Times* (1984)

Roberts, Randy, and James Olson. *Winning Is the Only Thing: Sports in America Since 1945* (1989)

Robinson, John Roosevelt, and Charles Dexter, eds. *Baseball Has Done It* (1964)

Rogosin, Donn. *Invisible Men: Life in Baseball's Negro Leagues* (1983)

Ryan, Bob. *Wait Till I Make the Show: Baseball in the Minor Leagues* (1974)

Sands, Jack, and Peter Gammons. *Coming Apart at the Seams* (1993)

Scheinin, Richard. *Field of Screams: The Dark Underside of America's National Pastime* (1994)

Scully, Gerald. *The Business of Major League Baseball* (1989)

- 'Discrimination: The Case of Baseball.' in Roger Noll, ed, *Government and the Sports Business* (1974), 221–73

Seymour, Harold. *Baseball: The Golden Age* (1971)

Simons, William. 'Jackie Robinson and the American Mind: Journalistic Perceptions of the Reintegration of Baseball.' *Journal of Sport History* 12 (Spring 1985), 39–64

Simpson, Alan. *The Baseball Draft: The First Twenty-Five Years* (1990)

Sinclair, Robert, and Bryan Thompson. *Metropolitan Detroit: An Anatomy of Social Change* (1977)

Smith, Curt. *Voices of the Game ... Baseball Broadcasting 1921 to the Present* (1987)

Smith, Fred. *Tiger S.T.A.T.S.* (1991)

- *Tiger Tales and Trivia* (1988)

Smith, Leverett. *The American Dream and the National Game* (1975)

Smith, Red. *To Absent Friends* (1982)

Sommers, Paul, ed. *Diamonds Are Forever: The Business of Baseball* (1992)

Spalding, Albert G. *America's National Game* (1911)

Spigel, Lynn. *Make Room for TV* (1992)

Sporting News, The. *Complete Baseball Record Book*

– *Complete Baseball Guide* (1942–1996)

– *Index to The Sporting News, 1975–1990* (1992)

Stump, Al. *Cobb: A Biography* (1994)

Sullivan, Neil. *The Minors* (1990)

Thomas, David. 'Baseball's Amateur Draft.' *Baseball Research Journal* 23 (1994), 92–6

Thorn, John, and Pete Palmer, eds. *Total Baseball* (1989)

Turner, Dan. *Heroes, Bums and Ordinary Men: Profiles in Canadian Baseball* (1988)

Tygiel, Jules. *Baseball's Great Experiment* (1983)

United States. 'Broadcasting and Televising Baseball Games.' Senate Committee on Interstate and Foreign Commerce. 83rd Congress, Session 1, 1953

– House Committee on the Judiciary. Study of Monopoly Power. Pt. 6: Organized Baseball.

– 82nd Congress, Session 2, 1952. Report no. 2002 [First Celler Commission]

– House Committee on the Judiciary. Subcommittee on Antitrust. Pt. 3: Organized Professional Team Sports. 85th Congress, Session 1, 1957 [Second Celler Commission]

– 'Professional Sports Antitrust Bill.' Senate Committee on the Judiciary. Subcommittee on Antitrust Monopolies, 89th Congress, Session 1, 1965

– 'Labor Relations in Professional Sport.' 92nd Congress, Session 2. 1972

– 'Professional Sports Antitrust Immunity.' Hearings Before the Judiciary Committee, 97th Congress, Session 2, 1982, and 99th Congress, Session 1, 1985

– 'Sports Programming and Cable Television.' House Committee on the Judiciary. Subcommittee on Antitrust Monopolies, 101st Congress, Session 1, 14 November 1989

Van Blair, Rick. *Dugout to Foxhole – Interviews with Baseball Players Whose Careers Were Affected by World War II* (1994)

Veeck, Bill, with Ed Linn. *The Hustler's Handbook* (1965)

– *Veeck – as in Wreck: The Autobiography of Bill Veeck* (1962)

Voigt, David. *American Baseball*. Vol. 3 (1987)

– 'Counting, Courting, and Controlling Ball Park Fans.' In Peter Levine, ed., *Baseball History* (1992), 3: 92–129

Weinberg, Gerhard. *A World at Arms: A Global History of World War II* (1994)

Westcott, Richard. *Diamond Greats: Profiles and Interviews* (1988)

White, G. Edward. *Creating the National Pastime, 1903–1953* (1996)

Who's Who in Baseball (1916–)

Widick, B.J. *Detroit: City of Race and Class Violence* (1989)

Wiggins, David. 'Wendell Smith, the *Pittsburg-Courier-Journal* and the Campaign to Include Blacks in Organized Baseball, 1933–1945.' *Journal of Sports History* 10 (Summer 1983), 5–29

Wilber, Cynthia. *For the Love of the Game* (1992)

Wood, Bob. *Dodger Dogs to Fenway Franks – and the wieners in between* (c. 1988)

Young, Coleman. *Hard Stuff: The Autobiography of Coleman Young* (1994)

Zimbalist, Andrew. *Baseball and Billions* (1992)

Index

Note: Only substantive mentions of people appear in the index. For individual players' roles in pennant races and World Series, see those sections. Tables and appendices are indexed topically. References in the notes should be followed from the textual index.

Ackerman, Al, 213
Adams, (Dr) Charles, 228
African American community, 5, 75, 83–4, 124, 202, 225–9, 231, 269–70, 277
Agee, Charlie, 58
Albom, Mitch, 49, 239
Anderson, Sparky, 192, 198–200, 217–18, 220–2, 228, 231, 236, 248, 251–2, 283
Angelos, Peter, 282
anti-trust exemption, 30–3, 279
arbitration, 183, 185, 197–8, 246, 280
Archer, Dennis, 253, 273–4
attendance: Detroit, 15, 49, 57, 62–3, 78, 81, 94–5, 116, 156, 164, 178–9, 197, 210–12, 215, 225, 250, 284, 290–1; league, 13–14, 16–17, 49, 93–4, 155–6, 182, 192–3, 204, 225, 277, 282–4, 287–8, 296

auto industry, 5, 44–5, 47–8, 74
awards and titles, 10, 12, 28, 67, 80, 119, 163

Beckman, Frank, 244
Beddoes, Dick, 173–4
Bell, Buddy, 252
Berendt, Gregg, 245, 275
Bergman, Dave, 129, 216
Bertoia, Reno, 72, 80, 107–8, 128, 139, 143–7, 151, 153
Betzold, Michael, 59, 174, 262
Blanchard, (Gov.) James, 267

Blessit, Ike, 167
Blue, Vida, 195
Boone, Ray, 67, 70
Boston Red Sox, 58, 69
Bouton, Jim, 145, 147, 191
Briggs, Spike, 57, 69, 73, 75–7, 79, 83

Briggs, Walter O., 5, 15, 42–3, 45, 50–4, 57, 59, 69, 73, 136, 256
Brinkman, Ed, 162–3
Brookens, Tom, 198–9
Brooklyn Dodgers, 3, 20, 34, 195
Browalski, Ed, 232
Brown, Gates, 61, 107, 110–13, 130, 145, 152, 165, 169, 192, 227–8
Brown, Ike, 113, 133
Bruton, Bill, 71, 110, 152
Buchta, Robert, 262, 265, 275
Bunning, Jim, 79, 115–16, 128, 131, 170
Busch, Gussie, 171

Cain, Bob, 128, 134, 138, 147
Calvert, Paul, 144
Campaneris, Bert, 165
Campanis, Al, 233–4
Campbell, James, 5–7, 56, 71, 78, 86–92, 104, 110, 112–14, 117, 134, 136–8, 152–3, 158–64, 170–3, 175–6, 179–80, 186, 191, 195, 197, 199, 201–2, 207–10, 221, 227–8, 234–6, 246, 252, 258, 260–1, 264, 268–9
Cantor, George, 158, 173, 267–8
Carey, Paul, 177, 230, 236, 239, 241, 243
Cash, Norm, 70–1, 103, 115–16, 145, 179
Cavanagh, Jerome, 99, 257
Celler Commission, 6–7, 18, 31–4
Chandler, Happy, 23, 27
charity activities, 50, 57, 99, 113, 153–4, 230–1
Chass, Murray, 171–2, 187, 192

Chicago Cubs, 12, 42
Chicago White Sox, 109
Cicotte, Al, 153
Cincinnati Reds, 43, 86, 217
commissioners of baseball. *See* under specific names
Cleague, (Rev.) Albert, 102
Cleveland Indians, 16–17, 34, 70–1, 201–2, 275–6, 284
Clinton, Bill, 281
Cobb, Ty, 41–3, 203
Cobo, Albert, 75, 256
Cochrane, Mickey, 42–3
Cohen, Irwin, 227, 230
Colavito, Rocky, 70–1, 115–16, 136
Coleman, Joe Jr, 162–3, 168
Coleman, Joe Sr, 128, 134, 143, 147
Conner, Ed, 256
court decisions, 27, 30–3, 183–4, 258, 274
Craig, Roger, 72, 218
Crockett, (Judge) George, 102
Cronin, Joe, 168

Daniel, Dan, 52, 174
D'Annuzio, Louis, 129
Davids, John and Judy, 268
Davie, Jerry, 128, 133–4, 138, 143, 147–8, 150
Delsing, Jim, 146
Detroit: crime, 44–5, 102, 198, 218, 220, 253, 258, 269–71; economy and population before 1945, 44–7, 295; economy and population after 1945, 5–6, 47–8, 99–100, 156, 197–8, 202, 211, 218–20, 226, 253, 257, 271, 295, 326; suburbs, 5–6,

46, 48, 100, 211, 213, 226, 245,
    258–9, 266, 269–71, 275
Detroit baseball before 1945, 4–5,
    40–4
Detroit Lions, 6, 49, 75, 94, 156, 176,
    211, 232, 244, 256, 258–60, 269
Detroit Pistons, 6, 156, 176, 201, 211,
    214, 227, 232, 244, 258–9, 269,
    273
Detroit Red Wings, 156, 176, 201,
    211, 214, 239, 244, 247, 258–9,
    273
DeWitt, Bill, 71, 78, 81, 99
Dietz, Mike, 243, 249
Dobson, Pat, 145
Doby, Larry, 23, 27, 60–1, 83, 85, 110
Dressen, Charlie, 116, 134
Dropo, Walt, 67, 69
Duggan, Michael, 269–71
Dykes, Jimmy, 71–3

Egan, Wish, 54
Evans, Billy, 53, 55–6
Evans, Darrell, 197, 216
Evers, Hoot, 54, 69, 133–4, 236

Falls, Joe, 3, 5, 72, 93, 102, 104–5,
    123, 158, 173–5, 177, 190, 217–21,
    232, 240–1, 243
fans: composition of, 5, 98, 212–13,
    227, 230; reactions of, 49, 122–3,
    173, 192–3, 239, 280–4; violence
    of, 42, 103–6, 166, 219–21, 252;
    women, 16, 81, 193, 213–14
Faul, Bill, 147
Fehr, Donald, 189, 279
Feliciano, José, 121

Fenkell, 'Doc,' 57, 77–8, 97, 200, 210,
    227, 240
Ferrell, Rick, 236
Fetzer, John, 5–6, 75–8, 91, 95–6,
    100, 113, 163, 194, 196, 201, 206,
    215, 248, 257–9
Fidrych, Mark, 105, 146, 176–9
Fielder, Cecil, 226, 231, 249
Finley, Charlie, 171, 187, 195
Flood, Curt, 106, 109, 122, 147,
    183–4
Ford, Henry II, 74, 102
Foytack, Paul, 149
franchises: expansion, 92–3; finances
    (see revenues and profits: Detroit,
    other franchises); moves, 19–20
free agency, 55, 97, 155, 182–7, 192,
    195–6, 200, 204, 216, 245–6, 278,
    282
Freehan, Bill, 107, 129, 137, 143–4,
    151, 153, 172
Frick, Ford, 14, 32, 93, 187

Gaherin, John, 186
Garver, Ned, 32, 69, 141
Gehringer, Charlie, 42–3, 54, 69, 74,
    135, 138, 190
Gentry, Rufus, 52, 185
Giamatti, A. Bartlett, 4, 189
Gibson, Bob, 120, 122
Gibson, Kirk, 197–8, 214–15,
    246
Ginsberg, Joe, 128, 131, 137–9, 143,
    149, 153
Gordon, Joe, 71, 113
Gordon, Lou, 258
Green, Jerry, 72, 174–5, 219, 241–2

Green, Lenny, 86, 107–10, 140, 143, 169, 191
Greenberg, Hank, 10–12, 42, 51–3, 62, 80, 136, 146
Grich, Bobby, 195
Griffith, Clark, 3, 10–11, 22, 92, 106
Gromek, Steve, 61, 70, 139, 148

Haase, Bill, 207, 230, 235–6, 267–71
Hansen, Harvey, 75–9, 84–5
Harris, Bucky, 72
Hart, (Sen.) George, 274
Harwell, Ernie, 5, 64, 82–3, 97, 119, 121, 201, 226, 236, 238–44, 268
Hawkins, Jim, 160, 172–5, 178
Hearst, John, 228
Hebner, Richie, 135
Heilmann, Harry, 43–4, 50, 64, 82–3, 243
Henderson, Tom, 231–2
Herbert, Ray, 128, 138–9, 143, 148, 153, 191
Hernandez, Willie, 216
Heydler, John, 21
Hill, (Rev.) Charles, 83
Hill, (Rev.) George, 84
Hiller, John, 43, 103, 128, 133, 148
Hoeft, Bill, 137–8, 143, 146
Holdsworth, Fred, 130, 133, 148–9, 200
Holley, (Rev.) James, 61, 229, 234
Holtgrave, Vern, 128–9, 134
Horton, Willie, 100, 103, 110–13, 129, 134, 137–8, 148, 152, 167, 169, 180, 226
Houk, Ralph, 176, 180

House, Frank, 56
Houtteman, Art, 54, 70, 134
Howard, Elston, 24, 108
Hubbard, Orville, 100
Hunter, Catfish, 185
Hutchinson, Fred, 32, 62, 72

Ignasiak, Gary, 133, 145, 148
Ilitch, Michael, 206, 209, 225–6, 242, 247–8, 255, 272–4

Jackson, Reggie, 187–8
Johnson, Art, 269, 277
Jordan, Pat, 131

Kalifatis, George, 196–7
Kaline, Al, 43, 67–8, 73, 80, 89, 103, 105, 116, 117, 120, 128, 133, 136–7, 139, 153, 172, 179, 201
Kansas City Athletics, 216–17
Katalinas, George, 89–90, 128
Keith, (Judge) Damon, 111–13
Kell, George, 5, 54, 63, 69, 82, 97, 132, 134, 144, 199, 201
Kelly, (Sen.) John, 266, 270
Kemp, Steve, 180, 197–8
Kennedy, John F., 86, 99
King, Martin Luther, 99, 101
Kitzer, Peter, 200–1
Klein, Joe, 248, 251
Knorr, Fred, 75–8
Koppel, Ted, 233
Koppett, Leonard, 171–2, 185, 187, 252
Kretlow, Lou, 56
Kryhoski, Dick, 128, 131, 134, 137, 142, 149

Kuenn, Harvey, 67–8, 70, 79–80, 145
Kuhn, Bowie, 159, 162, 171, 183–5, 194, 206

LaGrow, Lerrin, 165
Lajoie, Bill, 236
Landis, Kenesaw Mountain, 3, 10, 22, 42, 55
Landswirth, Henry, 110
Lane, Frank, 70–1, 136
LaPointe, Joe, 175, 220, 232–3, 235, 261–2
Lary, Frank, 68, 115
Lee, Carl, 75, 78, 96, 206
Leflore, Ron, 130, 147, 191, 199, 228
leisure and recreation, 18; amateur baseball, 3, 14, 50, 57, 99; other sports, 3, 14, 49, 75, 93, 95–6, 193, 205, 211, 213–14, 227, 232, 238, 244, 247, 256, 258–60, 273, 282 (see also Detroit Lions, Pistons, Red Wings)
Lerchen, George, 56, 59, 128, 131–4, 138, 140–1, 143, 150
Lobsinger, Donald, 102
Lolich, Mickey, 121–2, 143, 157, 180, 231
Long, Jim, 240, 243
Lund, Don, 89–91

McAuliffe, Dick, 112, 118, 172, 179
McCarthy, J.P., 5, 170
McCosky, Barney, 54
McDevitt, John, 264–7
McGraw, Bill, 175, 233, 245, 263, 273
McHale, John, 71, 73, 84, 138, 186

McHale, John Jr, 229, 252, 273
McLain, Denny, 43, 103, 117–21, 143, 147, 157–63, 172, 174–5, 190
McNally, Dave, 182, 186
McNamara, Ed, 269–71
MacPhail, Lee, 23, 136
MacPhail, Leland Jr, 188
management: Detroit Baseball Club (see also specific names): 66, 71–2, 89, 114, 138, 152, 163, 168, 171, 176, 198–9, 207, 209, 226–30, 232, 234–8, 247–8, 252, 267–70, 317–18
Mantle, Mickey, 127, 145, 158
Marentette, Leo, 129, 145
Martin, Billy, 70, 130, 133, 144–5, 163–70
Matlin, Lew, 201, 228–9
Matthaei, Fred, 256
Maxwell, Charlie, 68
Medwick, Joe, 42, 103
Messersmith, Andy, 182, 185–6
Mexican League, 21–2, 31, 90
Middlesworth, Hal, 174, 202
Mierkowicz, Ed, 133
Miller, Marvin, 30, 170–1, 184, 188–9
Milliken, (Gov.) William, 218
Minnesota Twins, 224
minor leagues: Detroit farm clubs, 54–6, 70, 86–91, 127, 132–3, 180–1, 210, 236–8, 292, 307; general, 14, 34, 36–7, 90, 131–3, 288
Monaghan, Thomas, 6, 64, 153, 206–8, 215, 225–6, 237–8, 246–8, 255, 261, 264–5, 267–70
Morris, Jack, 180, 197–9, 216, 246

Moss, Les, 198–9
Moss, Richard, 185–6
Murphy, Robert, 29–30, 79

NAACP, 110, 231, 234, 269, 277
Navin, Frank, 41–3
Negro Leagues, 10, 21, 229, 314
Newhouser, Hal, 11–12, 43, 51, 54,
    57, 62, 69, 80, 135–6, 190
New York Giants, 20, 24
New York Yankees, 24, 26, 53, 86,
    98, 109, 114–15, 204, 214, 234
night baseball, 5, 14–15, 57, 81
Nixon, Richard, 171
Norman, Bill, 68, 72–3
Northrup, Jim, 118, 120, 122, 129,
    132, 138, 140, 143, 150, 169,
    179–80

Oakland Athletics, 165–7, 185
Odenwald, Jeff, 229, 236, 240
O'Donnell, Doris, 174
O'Malley, Walter, 20, 36, 195
O'Neill, Steve, 10, 72
Oyler, Ray, 120, 145

Parrish, Lance, 180, 197–9
Patrick, Van, 75, 82–3, 243
Peek, Lonnie Jr, 228
pennant races, 11–12, 16, 62–5, 114–
    19, 161–2, 164–7, 176, 214–17,
    221–4, 249–51, 294–5
Petry, Dan, 180, 197–8
Philadelphia Athletics, 14, 17, 19, 23,
    42, 54
Philadelphia Phillies, 23, 26, 183
Phillips, Jack, 138, 148
Pierce, Billy, 54, 71

Pinson, Vada, 228
Pittsburgh Pirates, 26, 29, 204, 284
players: alcohol and drugs, 70, 144–5,
    157, 161, 163, 167, 169, 189–91;
    camaraderie, 120, 142–4; career
    satisfaction, 147–50; education,
    129, 144, 149–50; housing, 109–
    13, 132, 139–42; injuries, 116–17,
    133, 157, 179; later careers and
    other jobs, 43, 135–6, 148–53,
    302–3; salaries and bonuses, 28, 34,
    50–2, 79, 127–31, 135–8, 183, 187,
    194–5, 197–8, 204–5, 208–10, 225,
    249, 251, 279–82, 289, 293, 301,
    305, 309; sexual activities, 141–2,
    146–7, 167–8, 178; signings and
    releases, 127–32; social origins,
    87, 125–6, 130, 299; wives and
    families, 126–7, 132, 139–42,
    300
players' associations and unions:
    American Baseball Guild, 28–30;
    Major League Baseball Players'
    Association (MLBPA), 30, 170,
    184–9; other, 30, 79
press: local, 29, 32, 50, 53, 60, 84–6,
    93, 158, 160, 163–4, 172–8, 189,
    220–1, 231, 239, 241–3, 261–2,
    265–6, 268–9, 272–3, 277, 280;
    national, 17, 21–2, 25, 30–3, 48–9,
    93, 144–5, 159–61, 171–8, 184–7,
    189, 219–21, 233–4, 239, 253, 256,
    279–81
Price, Jim, 172
promotions and marketing: 57, 81,
    94–5, 201–2, 210–11, 228–30,
    235–6, 248, 327–8
Puscas, George, 124, 173, 189

race relations: baseball, 20–8, 58–62, 83–7, 106–13, 151–2, 169, 225–9, 233–4, 304, 313–16; Detroit (city), 3, 5, 46–8, 99–100, 123–4, 213, 218–19, 245, 258–9, 266, 269–70

Rashid, Frank, 262, 264–5

Rathbun, Bob, 242–5

Ravitz, Mel, 266

Reagan, Ronald, 189, 213

Reinsdorf, Jerry, 247, 279

reserve clause, 29–33, 127, 182–7

revenues and profits: Detroit Baseball Club, 6, 34, 51, 78–9, 88, 93, 94, 182, 196, 207–10, 225, 244, 245–7, 259–60, 267, 273, 276–7, 291–2, 306–7, 309, 326–9; other franchises, 20, 34, 155, 182, 194–5, 203–4, 247, 277, 282, 309, 326

Rickey, Branch, 20–3, 27, 54

riot of 1967, 3, 6, 100–2, 123–4, 204

Ripken, Cal Jr, 283

Rizzs, Rick, 242–5

Robinson, Aaron, 54

Robinson, Jackie, 20–7, 61, 109

Rodriguez, Aurelio, 162–3, 199

Rogell, Billy, 43, 57, 257

Rolfe, Red, 71, 132

Roosevelt, Franklin D., 10, 14

Roth, (Judge) Stephen, 102

Rozema, Dave, 180, 198–9, 215

Ryan, Bob, 131

St Louis Browns, 11, 17, 19, 34, 36, 69

St Louis Cardinals, 11, 26, 36, 42, 54, 120–2, 183, 194, 284

sales of Detroit Baseball Club, 73–8, 206, 225

Salsinger, H.G., 5, 29, 44, 55–6, 60–1, 76, 79, 174, 203

San Diego Padres, 217

Scheffing, Bob, 71, 114, 116

Schembechler, Bo, 208, 236–41, 247–8, 267, 269–70

Schott, Marg, 234

scouting, 80, 87–90, 125–9, 168, 177, 198, 210, 238, 320–5

Second World War, 9–10

Seitz, Peter, 182, 185–6

Selig, Bud, 278–9, 281

Short, Bob, 162, 171

Sisson, Harry, 43, 73–4, 78, 88

Smith, Lyall, 15, 60, 64, 85, 93, 256

Smith, Mayo, 116, 120, 122, 163

Smith, Randy, 252

Smith, Wendell, 21

Snyder, Ralph, 59, 90, 229–30, 266, 268

Sorenson, Lary, 244

Sparma, Joe, 157

Spicer, Gary, 240–2

Spink, J.G. Taylor, 23, 32–3

Spoelstra, Watson, 160, 175

spring training, 10, 87, 106–12, 132, 158, 167, 177, 283

stadiums
– Detroit: Bennett, 40–1; Briggs/ Tiger, 5, 43, 48, 50, 75, 208–9, 254–77, 292, 309; Navin, 5, 41; Cochrane Plan, 268; controversy over, 6, 330–2; funding, 255, 257–9, 260, 263–8, 270–6; maintenance and renovations, 260–1, 264–8, 270
– other cities: 18–19, 41, 255, 261–3, 275–6

Stanley, Mickey, 120, 139, 147, 172, 200

Staub, Rusty, 180, 197

Steinbrenner, George, 51, 187–8

Stengel, Casey, 103, 113–14

Stoneham, Horace, 20

Stroud, Joe, 272

strikes, 170–3, 185, 188–9, 246, 278–80, 282–3

Talbert, Bob, 243

Taubman, Alfred, 271

Tebbetts, Birdie, 54, 139

television and radio, local: announcers 5, 43, 64, 82–3, 97, 168, 170, 200–1, 226, 238–44, 308, 319 (see also specific names); audiences/ratings, 6, 58, 82, 156, 204, 212–14, 239, 243–4, 308; cable, 212–14, 327–8; revenues, 97–8, 211, 239, 292, 297, 307, 309, 327–9; rights, 75, 82, 97–8, 156, 200–1, 212–14; sponsors, 82, 200–1, 213–14

television and radio, national: announcers, 24, 30, 36; audiences/ratings, 15, 17–18, 36–7, 97, 193, 205, 283–4; cable, 193, 205, 284; revenues, 20, 30, 156, 193, 280, 282, 284, 289, 309, 327–8; rights, 15, 35–7, 95–7, 156, 205

Thompson, Jason, 180, 198–9

ticket prices and concessions: Detroit, 58, 80–1, 94, 156, 178, 211–12, 249, 260, 283; league, 14, 155–6, 281, 298

Tiger Alumni Organization, 153–4

Tiger Stadium Fan Club, 262–2, 274–5, 277

Tighe, Jack, 72

Timmerman, Tom, 129, 137, 148, 151

Toronto Blue Jays, 194, 216, 222–3, 282

trades, 53–4, 69–71, 85, 162–3, 179–80, 183, 191, 198, 216, 223, 251

Trammell, Alan, 43, 143, 180, 197–9, 251

Trout, 'Dizzy,' 11, 55, 69

Trucks, Virgil, 12, 51, 67, 69, 128, 143, 150

Turner, (Dr) Edward, 61, 226, 228–9

Tyson, Ty, 43

Ueberroth, Peter, 246

Underwood, Pat, 129, 135, 198, 200

Veeck, Bill, 19, 23, 27, 36, 60, 75–7, 94, 106

Veryzer, Tom, 180, 198

Vincent, Charlie, 227, 229, 233, 242, 272

Vincent, Francis (Fay), 246, 279, 284

Virgil, Ozzie, 84–5

Vitto, Gary, 243, 252

Wakefield, Dick, 52, 56

Waldmeir, Pete, 123, 176, 219, 240, 273

Walker, Tom, 226–7, 231–2, 241

Warden, Jon, 129, 135, 142–3, 148–9, 191

Was, Joanne, 245, 271

Wertz, Vic, 69
Whitaker, Lou, 143, 180, 197–8, 251, 281
White, Bill, 234
White, Hal, 128, 134, 139, 143, 148
Wilcox, Milt, 133, 197
Wills, Maury, 38, 86
Wilson, Red, 138, 143, 148
Woods, Ron, 113
World Series: 1934, 42; 1935, 42; 1940, 43; 1945, 12; 1947, 17; 1949, 35; 1968, 120–2; 1978, 156; 1984, 207, 217–18; 1995, 284

Young, Coleman, 60–1, 83–4, 101, 218, 245, 258–62, 266–7, 271, 274
Young, Kip, 130, 135, 140, 145, 148, 200

Zeller, Jack, 53, 55
Zepp, Bill, 129, 135, 141–2, 144
Zetlin, Lev, 265